D0982833

Athalya Brenner is professor emerita of Hebrew Bible/Old Testament at the University of Amsterdam, The Netherlands, and Professor in Biblical Studies at the Department of Hebrew Culture Studies at Tel Aviv University, Israel. She holds an honorary PhD from the University of Bonn, Germany. She is general editor of the Feminist Companion to the Bible, co-editor of *Genesis, Exodus and Deuteronomy,* and *Leviticus and Numbers* in the Texts @ Contexts series (Fortress Press, 2008, 2012, 2013), and author of *I Am: Biblical Women Tell Their Own Stories* (Fortress Press, 2004).

Gale A. Yee is Nancy W. King Professor of Biblical Studies at Episcopal Divinity School, Cambridge, Mass., and General Editor of Semeia Studies. Her books include *Poor Banished Children of Eve: Women as Evil in the Hebrew Bible* (Fortress, 2003); she edited *Judges and Method: New Approaches in Biblical Studies,* 2nd ed. (Fortress Press, 2003), and co-edited *Genesis* and *Exodus and Deuteronomy* in the Texts@Contexts series (Fortress Press, 2008 and 2012).

JOSHUA AND JUDGES

JOSHUA AND JUDGES

ATHALYA BRENNER AND GALE A. YEE, EDITORS

Fortress Press
Minneapolis

JFM Library
[illegible] Street
Minneapolis

JOSHUA AND JUDGES

Texts @ Contexts Series

Copyright © 2013 Fortress Press. All rights reserved. Except for brief quotations in critical articles or reviews, no part of this book may be reproduced in any manner without prior written permission from the publisher. Visit http://www.augsburgfortress.org/copyrights/contact.asp or write to Permissions, Augsburg Fortress, Box 1209, Minneapolis, MN 55440.

Cover image: Cover Image: Christian Hugo Martin, *Composition on prussian blue*, Burn paper work, 103, 5×153, 5 cm. 2007/10

Cover design: Laurie Ingram
Library of Congress Cataloging-in-Publication Data

Joshua and Judges / Athalya Brenner and Gale A. Yee, Editors.
pages cm. – (Texts @ contexts)
Includes bibliographical references and index.
ISBN 978-0-8006-9937-6 (print : alk. paper) — ISBN 978-1-4514-2632-8 (ebook)
1. Bible. O.T. Joshua–Criticism, interpretation, etc. 2. Bible. O.T. Judges–Criticism, interpretation, etc. I. Brenner, Athalya, editor of compilation. II. Yee, Gale A., 1949- editor of compilation.
BS1295.52 .J67
222'.206–dc23
2012044781

The paper used in this publication meets the minimum requirements of American National Standard for Information Sciences—Permanence of Paper for Printed Library Materials, ANSI Z329.48-1984. Manufactured in the U.S.A.

This book was produced using PressBooks.com, and PDF rendering was done by PrinceXML.

JKM Library
1100 East 55th Street
Chicago, IL 60615

CONTENTS

Part II. Case Studies in Judges

Other Books in the Series

texts ⊕ contexts

Athalya Brenner and Nicole Wilkinson Duran
Series Editors
Editorial Committee
Hebrew Bible
Athalya Brenner, Cheryl Kirk-Duggan, Kari Latvus,
Archie Chi-Chung Lee, Gale A. Yee
New Testament
Nicole Wilkinson Duran, James P. Grimshaw, Yung Suk Kim,
Teresa Okure, Daniel Patte
Volumes
Hebrew Bible

Genesis
Exodus and Deuteronomy
Leviticus and Numbers
Joshua and Judges
New Testament
Matthew
Mark
John
First and Second Corinthians

SERIES PREFACE, UPDATED: TEXTS IN/ AT LIFE CONTEXTS

The Editors

Myth cannot be defined but as an empty screen, a structure. . . . A myth is but an empty screen for transference.[1]

שבעים פנים לתורה ("The Torah has seventy faces")[2]

The discipline of biblical studies emerges from a particular cultural context; it is profoundly influenced by the assumptions and values of the Western European and North Atlantic, male-dominated, and largely Protestant environment in which it was born. Yet like the religions with which it is involved, the critical study of the Bible has traveled beyond its original context. Its presence in a diversity of academic settings around the globe has been experienced as both liberative and imperialist, sometimes simultaneously. Like many travelers, biblical scholars become aware of their own cultural rootedness only in contact with, and through the eyes of, people in other cultures.

The way any one of us closes a door seems in Philadelphia nothing at all remarkable, but in Chiang Mai, it seems overly loud and emphatic—so very typically American. In the same way, Western biblical interpretation did not seem tied to any specific context when only Westerners were reading and writing it. Since so much economic, military, and consequently cultural power has been vested in the West, the West has had the privilege of maintaining this cultural closure for two centuries. Those who engaged in biblical studies—even when they were women or men from Africa, Asia, and Latin America—nevertheless had to take on the Western context along with the discipline.

But much of recent Bible scholarship has moved toward the recognition that considerations not only of the contexts of assumed, or implied, biblical authors but also the contexts of the interpreters are valid and legitimate in an inquiry into biblical literature. We use *contexts* here as an umbrella term covering a wide range of issues: on the one hand, social factors (such as location, economic situation, gender, age, class, ethnicity, color, and things pertaining to personal biography) and, on the other hand, ideological factors (such as faith, beliefs, practiced norms, and personal politics).

Contextual readings of the Bible are an attempt to redress the previous longstanding and grave imbalance that says that there is a kind of "plain," unaligned biblical criticism that is somehow "normative," and that there is another, distinct kind of biblical criticism aligned with some social location: the writing of Latina/o scholars advocating liberation, the writing of feminist scholars emphasizing gender as a cultural factor, the writings of African scholars pointing out the text's and the readers' imperialism, the writing of Jews and Muslims, and so on. The project of recognizing and emphasizing the role of context in reading freely admits that we all come from somewhere: no one is native to the biblical text; no one reads only in the interests of the text itself. North Atlantic and Western European scholarship has focused on the Bible's characters as individuals, has read past its miracles and stories of spiritual manifestations, or "translated" them into other categories. These results of Euro-American contextual reading would be no problem if they were seen as such; but they have become a chain to be broken when they have been held up as the one and only "objective," plain truth of the text itself.

The biblical text, as we have come to understand in the postmodern world and as pre-Enlightenment interpreters perhaps understood more clearly, does not speak in its own voice. It cannot read itself. *We* must read it, and in reading it, we must acknowledge that our own voice's particular pitch and timbre and inflection affect the meaning that emerges. Biblical scholars usually read the text in the voice of a Western Protestant male. When interpreters in the Southern Hemisphere and in Asia have assumed ownership of the Bible, it has meant a recognition that this Euro-American male voice is not the voice of the text itself; it is only one reader's voice, or rather, the voice of one context—however familiar and authoritative it may seem to all who have been affected by Western political and economic power. Needless to say, it is not a voice suited to bring out the best meaning for every reading community. Indeed, as biblical studies tended for so long to speak in this one particular voice, it may be the case that that voice has outlived its meaning-producing usefulness: we may have heard all that this voice has to say, at least for now. Nevertheless, we have included that voice in this series, in part in an effort to hear it as emerging from its specific context, in order to put that previously authoritative voice quite literally in its place.

The trend of acknowledging readers' contexts as meaningful is already, inter alia, recognizable in the pioneering volumes of *Reading from This Place* (Segovia and Tolbert 1995; 2000; 2004), which indeed move from the center to the margins and back and from the United States to the rest of the world. More recent publications along this line also include *Her Master's Tools?* (Vander Stichele and Penner 2005), *From Every People and Nation: The Book of Revelation in Intercultural Perspective* (Rhoads 2005), *From Every People and Nation: A Biblical Theology of Race* (Hays and Carson 2003), and the *Global Bible Commentary* (*GBC*; Patte et al. 2004).

The editors of the *GBC* have gone a long way toward this shift by soliciting and admitting contributions from so-called third-, fourth-, and fifth-world scholars alongside first- and second-world scholars, thus attempting to usher the former and their perspectives into the *center* of biblical discussion. Contributors to the *GBC* were asked to begin by clearly stating their context before proceeding. The result was a collection of short introductions to the books of the Bible (Hebrew Bible/Old Testament and New Testament), each introduction from one specific context and, perforce, limited in scope. At the Society of Biblical Literature's (SBL) annual meeting in Philadelphia in 2005, during the two *GBC* sessions and especially in the session devoted to pedagogical implications, it became clear that this project should be continued, albeit articulated further and redirected.

On methodological grounds, the paradox of a deliberately inclusive policy that foregrounds differences in the interpretation of the Bible could not be addressed in a single- or double-volume format because in most instances those formats would allow for only one viewpoint for each biblical issue or passage (as in previous publications) or biblical book (as in the *GBC*) to be articulated. The acceptance of such a limit may indeed lead to a decentering of traditional scholarship, but it would definitely not usher in multivocality on any single topic. It is true that, for pedagogical reasons, a teacher might achieve multivocality of scholarship by using various specialized scholarship types together; for instance, the *GBC* has been used side-by-side in a course with historical introductions to the Bible and other focused introductions, such as the *Women's Bible Commentary* (Newsom and Ringe, 2012). But research and classes focused on a single biblical book or biblical corpus need another kind of resource: volumes exemplifying a broad multivocality in themselves, varied enough in contexts from various shades of the confessional to various degrees of the secular, especially since in most previous publications the contexts of communities of faith overrode all other contexts.

On the practical level, then, we found that we could address some of these methodological, pedagogical, and representational limitations evident in previous projects in contextual interpretation through a book series in which each volume introduces multiple contextual readings of the same biblical texts. This is what the SBL's Contextual Biblical Interpretation Consultation has already been promoting since 2005 during the American annual meeting; and since 2011 also at the annual international SBL conference. The consultation serves as a testing ground for a multiplicity of readings of the same biblical texts by scholars from different contexts.

These considerations led us to believe that a book series focusing specifically on contextual multiple readings for specific topics, of specific biblical books, would be timely. We decided to construct a series, including at least eight to ten volumes, divided between the Hebrew Bible (HB/OT) and the New Testament (NT). Each of the planned volumes would focus on one or two biblical books: Genesis, Exodus and Deuteronomy, Leviticus and Numbers, Joshua and Judges, and later books for the HB/OT; Mark, Luke-Acts, John, and Paul's letters for the NT.[3] The general HB/OT editor is Athalya Brenner, with Archie Lee and Gale Yee as associate editors. The general NT editor is Nicole Duran, with Daniel Patte and Teresa Okure as associate editors. Other colleagues have joined as editors for specific volumes.

Each volume focuses on clusters of contexts and of issues or themes, as determined by the editors in consultation with potential contributors. A combination of topics or themes, texts, and interpretive contexts seems better for our purpose than a text-only focus. In this way, more viewpoints on specific issues will be presented, with the hope of gaining a grid of interests and understanding. The interpreters' contexts will be allowed to play a central role in choosing a theme: we do not want to impose our choice of themes upon others, but as the contributions emerge, we will collect themes for each volume under several headings.

While we were soliciting articles for the first volumes (and continue to solicit contributions for future volumes), contributors were asked to foreground their own multiple "contexts" while presenting their interpretation of a given issue pertaining to the relevant biblical book(s). We asked that the interpretation be firmly grounded in those contexts and sharply focused on the specific theme, as well as in dialogue with "classical" informed biblical scholarship. Finally, we asked for a concluding assessment of the significance of this interpretation for the contributor's contexts (whether secular or in the framework of a faith community).

Our main interest in this series is to examine how formulating the content-specific, ideological, and thematic questions from life contexts will focus the reading of the biblical texts. The result is a two-way process of reading that (1) considers the contemporary life context from the perspective of the chosen themes in the given biblical book as corrective lenses, pointing out specific problems and issues in that context as highlighted by the themes in the biblical book; and (2) conversely, considers the given biblical book and the chosen theme from the perspective of the life context.

The word *contexts*, like *identity*, is a blanket term with many components. For some, their geographical context is uppermost; for others, the dominant factor may be gender, faith, membership in a certain community, class, and so forth. The balance is personal and not always conscious; it does, however, dictate choices of interpretation. One of our interests as editors is to present the personal beyond the autobiographical as pertinent to the wider scholarly endeavor, especially but not only when *grids of consent* emerge that supersede divergence. Consent is no guarantee of Truthspeak; neither does it necessarily point at a sure recognition of the biblical authors' elusive contexts and intentions. It does, however, have cultural and political implications.

Globalization promotes uniformity but also diversity by shortening distances, enabling dissemination of information, and exchanging resources. This is an opportunity for modifying traditional power hierarchies and reallocating knowledge, for upsetting hegemonies, and for combining the old with the new, the familiar with the unknown—in short, for a fresh mutuality. This series, then, consciously promotes the revision of biblical myths into new reread and rewritten versions that hang on many threads of welcome transference. Our contributors were asked, decidedly, to be responsibly nonobjective and to represent only themselves on the biblical screen. Paradoxically, we hope, the readings here offered will form a new tapestry or, changing the metaphor, new metaphorical screens on which contemporary life contexts and the life of biblical texts in those contexts may be reflected and refracted.

Notes

1. Mieke Bal 1993: 347, 360.

2. This saying indicates, through its usage of the stereotypic number seventy, that the Torah—and, by extension, the whole Bible—intrinsically has many meanings. It is therefore often used to indicate the multivalence and variability of biblical interpretation, and does not appear in this formulation in traditional Jewish biblical interpretation before the Middle Ages. Its earliest appearances are in the medieval commentator Ibn Ezra's introduction to his commentary on the Torah, toward the introduction's end (as in printed versions), in Midrash *Numbers Rabbah* (13:15-16), and in later Jewish mystical literature.

3. At this time, no volume on Revelation is planned, since Rhoads's volume *From Every People and Nation: The Book of Revelation in Intercultural Perspective* (2005) is readily available, with a concept similar to ours.

Abbreviations

AB   Anchor Bible

ABD   *Anchor Bible Dictionary*. Edited by David Noel Freedman. 6 vols. New York: Doubleday, 1992.

AJSL   *American Journal of Semitic Languages and Literatures*

AOAT   Alter Orient und Altes Testament

ARM   *Archives Royales de Mari,* ed. A. Parrot and G. Dossin. Paris: Imprimerie National, 1940–

BA   *Biblical Archaeologist*

BDB   Brown, Driver, and Briggs, *A Hebrew and English Lexicon of the Old Testament*

Bib   *Biblica*

BibInt   *Biblical Interpretation*

BT   Babylonian Talmud

BTB   *Biblical Theology Bulletin*

CAT   M. Dietrich, O. Loretz, and J. Sanmartin, *The Cuneiform Alphabetic Texts from Ugarit, Ras ibn Hani and Other Places*. Munster: Ugarit-Verlag, 1995

CBQ   *Catholic Biblical Quarterly*

CTA   A. Herdner, *Corpus des tablettes en cunéiformes alphabétiques*. Paris, Imprimerie National, 1963

CTH   *Catalogue des texts Hittites.* Laroche 1971

Gen. Rab.   Genesis Rabbah

HALOT   Koehler, Ludwig, Walter Baumgartner, and J. J. Stamm, *The Hebrew and Aramaic Lexicon of the Old Testament.* Translated and edited under the supervision of M. E. J. Richardson. 4 vols. Leiden: Brill, 1994–1999.

HTR   *Harvard Theological Review*

IBC   Interpretation: A Bible Commentary for Teaching and Preaching

Int   *Interpretation*

JAAR   *Journal of the American Academy of Religion*

JANES   *Journal of the Ancient Near Eastern Society*

JANESCU   *Journal of the Ancient Near Eastern Society of Columbia University*

JAOS   *Journal of the American Oriental Society*

JBL   *Journal of Biblical Literature*

JES   *Journal of Ecumenical Studies*

JFSR   *Journal of Feminist Studies in Religion*

JHS   *Journal of Hebrew Scriptures*

JNES   *Journal of Near Eastern Studies*

JQR   *Jewish Quarterly Review*

JSOT   *Journal for the Study of the Old Testament*

JSOTSup   Journal for the Study of the Old Testament: Supplement Series

JT   Jerusalem (Eretz Israel) Talmud

KBo   *Keilschrifttexte aus Boghazköi.* Wissenschaftliche Veröffentlichungen der deutschen Orientgesellschaft 30, 36, 68–70, 72–73, 77–80, 82–86, 89–90. Leipzig, 1916–.

KUB   *Keilschrifturkunden aus Boghazköi*

LXX   Septuagint

MT   Masoretic Text

NCB   New Century Bible

NIB   *New Interpreter's Bible*

NovTSup   Supplements to Novum Testamentum

OBT   Overtures to Biblical Theology

OTL   Old Testament Library

OTS   *Oudtestamentische Studiën*

RSO   *Rivista degli studi orientali*

SBL   Society of Biblical Literature

SBLABS   Society of Biblical Literature Archaeology and Biblical Studies

SJOT   *Scandinavian Journal of the Old Testament*

SThZ   *Schweizerische Theologische Zeitschrift*

TAik   *Teologinen Aikakauskirja*

TDOT   G. J. Botterweck and H. Ringgren, eds. *Theological Dictionary of the Old Testament.* Translated by J. T. Willis, G. W. Bromiley, and D. E. Green. 15 vols. Grand Rapids, 1974–.

TH   Prefix of excavation numbers from the French excavations at Mari (Tell Hariri)

ThTo   *Theology Today*

TWOT   *Theological Wordbook of the Old Testament*

UF   *Ugarit Forschungen*

VT   *Vetus Testamentum*
WBC   Word Biblical Commentary
ZAW   *Zeitschrift für die alttestamentliche Wissenschaft*

The editors worked to make this volume accessible both to scholars and to interested readers who have no knowledge of Hebrew. Throughout the volume, Hebrew words are presented mostly in Hebrew letters. A transliteration of those words often follows in italics, in popular rather than academic transliteration, for the *sound of the original language.*

Acknowledgments

The editors would like to express their thanks to the Episcopal Divinity School, Cambridge, Massachusetts, for providing funds for an indexer for this volume and the *Exodus and Deuteronomy* volume (2012). For this we are most grateful!

List of Contributors

Meir Bar Mymon is a Ph.D. candidate at the school of philosophy, Tel Aviv University. He earned a master's degree in biblical studies from Tel Aviv University in 2007. His main field of interest is reading the Hebrew Bible via poststructuralist methods, especially of Derrida, Foucault, and Barthes; and the examination of ways of readings, identity processes, reader response criticism, and the construction of mythologies that shape our political/cultural reality. He is currently in a student exchange program in Science Po Paris, focusing on political science aspects of the Hebrew Bible.

Ryan P. Bonfiglio is a Ph.D. candidate in Hebrew Bible at Emory University. He earned a bachelor's degree at Princeton University and a master of divinity at Princeton Theological Seminary. His primary research interests include hermeneutical theory, biblical iconography, and the reception history of the Bible. He is an instructor at Candler School of Theology and serves as a lay leader in the Presbyterian Church (USA).

Athalya Brenner is professor emerita of Hebrew Bible/Old Testament at the University of Amsterdam, the Netherlands, and professor in biblical studies at the Department of Hebrew Culture Studies at Tel Aviv University, Israel. She holds an honorary Ph.D. from the University of Bonn, Germany. She edited the first and second series of *A Feminist Companion to the Bible* (1993–2000). Among her other publications is *I Am: Biblical Women Tell Their Own Stories* (Fortress Press, 2005) and *Performing Memory in Biblical Narrative and Beyond*, edited with Frank Polak (2009).

Ora Brison is a Ph.D. candidate at the Department of Hebrew Culture Studies at Tel Aviv University, Israel. She earned a master's degree in ancient Near Eastern cultures at the Department of Archaeology at Tel Aviv University. Her main field of interest focuses on female heroines in the Hebrew Bible and the mythological texts of the ancient Near East. Among her publications are "Aggressive Goddesses, Abusive Men: Gender Role Change in Near Eastern mythology," in *VI Congresso Internazionale di Ittitologia Roma, 5–9 settembre*

2005, Studi Micenei ed Egeo-Anatoloci 49, ed. Archi Alonso and Francia Rita (2007), part 1, 67–74 (Rome); and "Nudity and Music—Seduction Scenes in Anatolian Myths," in *Sounds from the Past: Music in the Ancient Near East and Mediterranean Worlds*, Bible Lands Museum (Jerusalem [forthcoming]).

Walter Brueggemann is William Marcellus McPheeters Professor Emeritus of Old Testament at Columbia Theological Seminary. He is a past president of the Society of Biblical Literature and an ordained minister in the United Church of Christ. He has recently written *Disruptive Grace* (Fortress Press), *David and His Theologian*, and *The Practice of Prophetic Imagination* (Fortress Press).

Trent C. Butler is a freelance author and editor and has served as editorial director at Holman Bible Publishers and Chalice Press, and as assistant professor of Old Testament at the International Baptist Theological Seminary in Rüschlikon, Switzerland. He has published Word Biblical Commentary volumes on Joshua and on Judges, Holman Old Testament commentaries on Isaiah and on Hosea, Joel, Amos, Obadiah, Jonah, and Micah, and the Holman New Testament commentary on Luke. He edited the Holman Bible Dictionary and the Holman Bible Atlas. A totally revised second edition of the Word commentary on Joshua is forthcoming, and his volume, *Exploring the Unexplained: A Practical Guide to the Peculiar People, Places, and Things in the Bible* was published in 2012.

Naomi De-Malach has taught literature from primary school to university level in Israel and the United States. Her major interests are critical pedagogy and the social and political aspects of the teaching of literature. Her book, *Lo al Ha-Yofi Levado* (Beyond Aesthetics; in Hebrew), appeared in 2008, and was awarded the Israeli Yizhar Prize for 2009. She teaches literature and education at Oranim Academic College of Education, Qiryat Tiv'on, Israel.

Yonina Dor was chair of the Bible Department at Oranim Academic College of Education, Qiryat Tiv'on, Israel. Her Ph.D. (Hebrew University, Jerusalem) is about the expulsion of foreign women in Ezra-Nehemiah. Her research interests are Ezra-Nehemiah, marriages of Israelites with foreign wives, biblical ethics, and biblical myths. Another area of interest is the didactics of Bible teaching in contemporary Israeli state education and the teaching of the Bible within a humanistic framework.

Bradley Embry is assistant professor at Northwest University in Kirkland, Washington. His primary area of research is in literary and narrative readings of the Hebrew Bible, in particular within the Pentateuch, Judges, and Ruth. His recent publications include "The 'Naked Narrative' from Noah to Leviticus: Reassessing Voyeurism in the Account of Noah's Nakedness in Genesis 9.22-24" in the *JSOT*, and "The Endangerment of Moses: Towards a New Reading of Exodus 4:24-26" in *VT*. He is currently coeditor of a project titled *Early Jewish Literature: Introduction and Reader* (forthcoming).

L. Daniel Hawk is professor of Old Testament and Hebrew at Ashland Theological Seminary and an ordained minister in the United Methodist Church. His work explores the ways narratives construct and contest group identities, the problem of violence in biblical texts, and the mythic aspects of biblical narrative. Among his recent publications is *Joshua in 3-D: A Commentary on Biblical Conquest and Manifest Destiny* (2010).

The Rev. Cheryl A. Kirk-Duggan is professor of religion, Shaw University Divinity School, Raleigh, North Carolina, and an ordained elder in the Christian Methodist Episcopal church. She has written and edited over twenty books, including as coeditor for *The Africana Bible: Reading Israel's Scriptures From Africa and the African Diaspora* (Fortress Press, 2009), and coauthored *Wake-Up! Hip-Hop, Christianity, and the Black Church* (2011). A former Semeia Studies editor, Kirk-Duggan was the 2009 recipient of the Excellence in Academic Research Award, Shaw University. With degrees in music and religious studies, Kirk-Duggan conducts interdisciplinary research spanning religious and women's studies, Bible, culture, pedagogy, spirituality and health, justice, violence, and sexuality.

Kari Latvus is a docent (Old Testament exegesis) and university lecturer (2009–2012) at Helsinki University. Previously, he worked at the Diaconia University of Applied Sciences, Finland, and at Lutheran Theological Seminary in Hong Kong. His main fields of interests are Hebrew Bible poverty texts, study of *diaconia*, and postcolonial and contextual analysis. He is also a chair of the SBL consultation on Poverty in the Biblical World. Among his publications are *God, Anger and Ideology: The Anger of God in Joshua and Judges in Relation to Deuteronomy and the Priestly Writings* (1998); "Reading Hagar in Contexts: From Exegesis to Intercontextual Analysis" in *Texts@Contexts: Genesis* (Fortress Press, 2010); and several articles about the origin of *diaconia* and diaconal ministry.

Pamela J. Milne is a professor in the Faculty of Arts and Social Sciences at the University of Windsor in Ontario, Canada. Her research and publications are in the areas of secular feminist approaches to the Hebrew bible and in equity/diversity studies. Among her publications are "Doing Feminist Biblical Criticism in a Women's Studies Context" in *Atlantis* 35/2 (2011), "Voicing Embodied Evil: Gynophobic Images of Women in Post-Exilic Biblical and Intertestamental Texts" in *Feminist Theology* 30 (2002), "Labouring with Abusive Biblical Texts: Tracing Trajectories of Misogyny" in *The Labour of Reading: Desire and Alientation in Biblical Interpretation* (1999), and "Administrative Pimping for Fame and Profit," in *Women's Education des femmes* 11/3 (1995).

Janelle Stanley holds master's degrees from Union Theological Seminary and Columbia University's School of Social Work, and has specialized in the study of trauma from both the clinical and religious perspectives. Janelle won the Muilenburg Prize for Excellence in Biblical Scholarship in 2012, and has published on religion and psychology in the *Journal of Religion and Health*. Janelle's clinical work focuses on children who have been victims of violence, trauma, and abuse; she currently works as a social worker with at-risk adolescents at a public high school in East Harlem.

Royce M. Victor is professor of Old Testament and Hebrew language at the Kerala United Theological Seminary, Thiruvananthapuram, Kerala, India, and ordained minister of the Church of South India. He earned his Ph.D. in biblical interpretation (Hebrew Bible) from the Brite Divinity School of Texas Christian University, Fort Worth, Texas. His main field of interest is postcolonial and contextual interpretation of the Bible. His recent publications include *Colonial Education and Class Formation in Early Judaism—A Postcolonial Reading* (2010).

Gale A. Yee is Nancy W. King Professor of Biblical Studies at Episcopal Divinity School, Cambridge, Massachusetts. She is the author of *Poor Banished Children of Eve: Woman as Evil in the Hebrew Bible* (Fortress Press, 2003), *Jewish Feasts and the Gospel of John* (2007 [1989]), *Composition and Tradition in the Book of Hosea* (1987); editor of *Judges and Method: New Approaches in Biblical Studies* (Fortress Press, 2007); former general editor of Semeia Studies; and one of the coeditors of *The Fortress Commentary on the Old Testament* (forthcoming).

Introduction

Gale A. Yee and Athalya Brenner

This land is your land, this land is my land . . .

I roamed and I rambled and I followed my footsteps
To the sparkling sands of her diamond deserts
While all around me a voice was sounding
This land was made for you and me.

This land is your land, this land is my land . . .[1]

Land is central in Joshua and in Judges. It is defined as a pledged land, promised by the Hebrew God to his very own people. Much as the link between the God and his people is described as exclusive, later also as monogamist and monotheistic, so is the land. Other gods there might be; local inhabitants are acknowledged as such. But the link god-people-land excludes those inhabitants from legitimate ownership of their own land, although their actual existence is never denied. The foreignness of the Israelites, their original identity as newcomers from Mesopotamia and Egypt, is proudly stated as a token of positive Otherness.

Thus the land is viewed as Israelite property as well as, paradoxically, an object of collective desire; attaining tangible rather than conceptual, wishful ownership of it is reflected in the biblical text as "just" but at the same time difficult, risky, fraught with tension, and elusive. This is the story of Joshua and Judges: How the land was acquired; how groups that came to be known as Hebrews or Israelites or Judahites joined the land's indigenous and invader inhabitants and saw it as their very own.

Thus the motto for this Introduction, from the title and repeated lyrics of Woody Guthrie's song, "This land is your land, this land is my land," is used here ironically. Its usage here suggests exclusivity, not inclusivity. These books, like other biblical writings (mainly assigned by scholars to the various deuteronomic and deuteronomistic traditions preserved in the Bible), contain an awareness of a previous claim by Other inhabitants but reject its validity, citing divine promise to the claimants as justification, and human non-compliance with the divine demand for exclusivity as a reason for the difficulties in realizing the promise.

Land can be acquired by war and hostile invasion and by more peaceful means, such as slow infiltration, social integration, acculturation, and shared economic interests. Evidence from the new biblical archaeology points to the more sedentary and longer process of settlement by the newcomers in the land that even they called the land of Canaan; the biblical text too bears enough traces of that, in reports of economic transactions and intermarriage, for instance, not to mention the much-touted intermingling of religious beliefs and cultural norms. Had it not been like that, the biblical conflict of nativeness and Otherness, of transcending boundaries while also establishing them and working to acquire a distinct group identity, would not have been that pronounced. Nevertheless, the literary medium chosen to express the realization of land-bound identity is that of warfare stories, *pace* the reality. In their recorded collective memory, those groups of "Israelites" became a nation around one land and one God through conquest, in the spirit of the times.

This largely or partly and also self-contradictory (between Joshua and Judges at the very least) fictive story of successful and at times "necessarily" cruel colonialism has since become internalized justification, on many fronts, for making "your land" into "my land," with "God on our side." It is perhaps less important whether the ban to Yhwh[2] and the destruction of enemies in his name is historical or is culturally borrowed from other contemporaneous people, than the knowledge that it has been adopted by later cultures and is still practiced today, with divine justification of course. This is our legacy, and this is what our contributors struggle with, knowing full well that the process described in Joshua and Judges has wielded, and still does, enormous influence in the Western world: in this volume, the ideological rather than the historical implications are discussed. Like in the case of the biblical exodus traditions, the question must be asked, together with the textual Joshua: "Are you with us, or with our foes?" (Josh. 5:13); in your context, are you for the Canaanites and their later metaphorical equivalents, or for the Israelites and their metaphorical existence in your own life? In other words, "Which side are you on?"[3]

PART 1: WHAT DO WE, WHAT CAN WE DO, ABOUT JOSHUA AND JUDGES?

In the opening essay of this volume, "The God of Joshua: An Ambivalent Field of Negotiation," Walter Brueggemann tackles the hermeneutical dilemma in

Joshua that describes God legitimating violence so that Israel can occupy a land already inhabited by other peoples. Brueggemann examines this theological difficulty first from the perspective of Israel's covenantal chosenness by God that bound the two parties in an exclusive relationship. The violent seizure of the land is the function of this chosenness. The consequence of this violence on the chosen's behalf is, for Brueggemann, the negation of the "Other"—the book of Joshua's main story line. This violent exclusion of the Other also underscores the fact that the book of Joshua exhibits no voices of dissent, divine or human, that stop short of violence, even though such voices of protest appear in other parts of the biblical tradition. Brueggemann appeals to Robert Polzin's insight that the traditions of Deuteronomy and the deuteronomistic history participate in a dialogue between "authoritarian dogmatism" and "critical traditionalism." Although the book of Joshua primarily exhibits the former, Brueggemann observes that critical traditionalism opens a space to continue a dissenting critique of the ideology of chosenness and violence that is espoused in Joshua.

Having written commentaries on Joshua and Judges in the evangelical Word Biblical Commentary series, Trent C. Butler approaches these books as a fledgling in postcolonial studies for this volume. He argues in "Joshua-Judges and Postcolonial Criticism" that the binaries of the West and the Rest and colonizer/colonized, which he sees in many postcolonial studies, cannot be easily applied to Israel as the colonizer of Canaan and the non-Israelites as colonized in Joshua and Judges, or vice versa. Each narrative and each character in these books stands somewhere on the continuum between colonizer and colonized at different parts of the narrative, and we must examine them as such.

In "Teaching Bible Stories Critically: 'They did not spare a soul'—The Book of Joshua in an Israeli Secular Education Environment," Yonina Dor and Naomi De-Malach approach Joshua from the context of the Bible curriculum in Israel's secular state school system. They pose a difficult question: How do instructors teach the biblical texts that are included in this curriculum, but whose explicit message offends their ethical values? Using Joshua as a test case, Dor and De-Malach first examine the wide range of Jewish attitudes toward Joshua from the talmudic period to present-day intellectuals, leaders, and educators. The book of Joshua provided ideological support for Zionism, the conquest of the land, and the expulsion of its residents, while others fear that the book will legitimate further violence in present-day Israel. The authors then investigate the history of approaches in teaching Joshua in Israel's state school system, which has increasingly excised chapters of the book in its curriculum. Particularly omitted are those references to the extermination of the inhabitants of the land, thus bypassing the moral questions that the book raises. In the major part of their essay, they offer another way of critically reading and teaching Joshua, one that transmits the Bible as the basis of Jewish and Israeli identity, while stimulating criticism and challenging several of the traditional truths that form the basis of the national ethos.

Cheryl Kirk-Duggan, in her contribution, "Inside, Outside, or in Between: Feminist/Womanist Hermeneutical Challenges for Joshua and Judges," comments at length about the violent nature of these biblical books and their continued influence on unethical behavior toward the Other within and outside communities. She lists atrocities committed against Others in contemporary Western cultures, especially American ones (both North and South) that are similar to those narrated in Joshua and Judges, and the analogy makes her even more uncomfortable. These texts, for her, are not empowering or comforting texts. Finding faith, love, and consolation in them is not easy, especially while looking at many stories there where female figures play a prominent role. And yet this must be done; and a cautious approach to these texts of violence must be exercised.

Kari Latvus, himself from Finland, examines "The Finns' Holy War against the Soviet Union: The Use of War Rhetoric in Finnish History during the Second World War." Specifically, he studies the latter part of 1941, when the Finns seemed for a while to be successful in their military endeavor, named the Continuation War, and the data analyzed is the newspaper *Kotimaa* and the *Teologinen Aikakauskirja* (*Finnish Journal of Theology*). The Lutheran church supported the war. Latvus shows how the influence of biblical literature in that context was not dependent only on direct quotations from biblical sources. While there were not many direct appeals in theological rhetoric to Joshua and Judges, to Latvus's own surprise, the spirit of these same biblical books—emphasis on divine chosenness dependent on righteous individual and collective behavior, a feeling of divine support, and promise for land, translated as it were into the Karelia Isthmus and beyond—was apparent in the materials examined. This is an important lesson for all of us: the Bible is everywhere in our lives, in our contexts, even if specific quotations are seldom or even never made. The impact, use, and abuse are there.[4]

The springboard of L. Daniel Hawk's essay, "Indigenous Helpers and Invader Homelands," is his reflection on a bronze statue of the Indian Maid of Fort Ball, near Tiffin, Ohio, where he grew up. This nameless woman evidently assisted American soldiers during the War of 1812, becoming one of a number of indigenous helpers in the master narrative of American expansionism. Hawk sees parallels in the ways biblical Israel and America both construct national identity through stories of conquest. Both portray the natives as misusing or afflicting the land. They thus need to be subdued and vanquished, so that the invaders may impose order and cleanse the land of any natives who remain. Throughout this violent process stands the indigenous helper, who welcomes and supports the conquerors. In the book of Joshua, this mythic figure is Rahab.

PART 2: CASE STUDIES IN JUDGES

Although the book of Judges seems to be about male heroes, Athalya Brenner notes that women abound in the book, and stories about daughters begin and end it. Thus her title, "Women Frame the Book of Judges—How and Why?" For Brenner, this is not accidental. She uses the work of Yairah Amit on the editing of Judges and Ingeborg Löwisch on the genealogies in 1 Chronicles 1–9 to argue that the editing of Judges incorporated women by design. Editing usually occurs during times of crisis, and crisis brings women to the forefront in the work of memory. The closing frame, Judges 17–21, usually regarded as added later to an earlier core, is essential to the extant structure of the book, where women appear throughout. To remove these chapters would detract from the book's structure, in the same way that removing chapters 30–31 and the important female figures in these would upset the structure of the book of Proverbs.

Ora Brison's experience in an abused women's shelter alerted her to the violence against women in Israel and influenced her choice of dissertation topic. To offset the experience of abused and humiliated women, she chose to write her thesis on strong, independent, and aggressive women: biblical heroines and heroic goddesses. In "Jael, *'eshet heber* the Kenite: A Diviner?" Brison argues that Jael's encounter with Sisera was not sexual or maternal, as many scholars believe, but religious and cultic. She finds parallels between Jael and Sisera with the medium of Endor and Saul in 1 Samuel 28. Just as Saul seeks a diviner for military counsel, so does Sisera flee to the tent of Jael to consult her and the gods in the face of his humiliating defeat.

In "Choosing Sides in Judges 4–5: Rethinking Representations of Jael," Ryan P. Bonfiglio observes that the difficulties his Italian immigrant grandparents faced as they settled in the United States give him insight into the dilemma that Jael may have faced as a non-Israelite, non-Canaanite outsider who had to choose sides. Bonfiglio takes up certain postcolonial observations about marginal groups in a dominant culture. They might be forced to imitate the culture, language, and values of the dominant group. Or they might assimilate and behave in ways that earn them rewards and affirmations from the dominant group, like those labeled "model minorities" in the United States. Bonfiglio sees two different biblical portrayals of Jael's heroism. Judges 4 depicts her as a model minority, a heroine for Israel as a faithful outsider. She faces a choice in siding with the Israelites or with the Canaanites, and by choosing the former, she becomes a heroine for Israel. Judges 5, however, eliminates the outsider language in describing Jael. She does not choose sides in Judges 5. Her defeat of Sisera is an act of self-defense against a potential rapist, presenting her as a model of agency and resistance for women.

Gale A. Yee's "The Woman Warrior Revisited: Jael, Fa Mulan, and American Orientalism" is the third essay in this volume to focus on Jael, reading Jael from Yee's Chinese American context. What inspired Yee's previous articles on Jael was her fascination with the Chinese woman warrior Fa Mulan. In this essay, she is able to explore the history and mythology surrounding Mulan more deeply. Yee argues that both Jael and Mulan share intercontextual features in their warriorhood, their slippery ethnicities, their (trans)gendering, and their long reception history that chronicles their oftentimes contradictory portrayals through the centuries. Yee highlights the American Orientalism of Disney's depiction of Mulan, arguing that it has been significant in the racial and gender formation of young Asian American females.

According to Meir Bar Mymon in "This Season You'll be Wearing God: On the Manning of Gideon and the Undressing of the Israelites (Judges 6:1–8:32)," Gideon puts on his masculinity the way he (Bar Mymon) had put on his Israeli military uniform and became the *Man*. The military forces young men to undergo a severe process of gender deconstruction and reconstruction, so that they are completely assimilated into the hegemonic masculinity of warriors. Not only do they become the *Man* in this process, but the process also confirms the military as an all-hegemonic male establishment. The *Man* and the military need and reinforce each other in this ongoing symbiotic relationship. In the same way, not only does Gideon undergo a long process of masculinization, but so does Yhwh himself. Yhwh needs Gideon to manifest his own male dominance, just as Gideon needs Yhwh to become a warrior. However, just as Gideon undressed himself of Yhwh, creates an ephod, and reenters civilian life, Bar Mymon took off and returned his uniform, and left the Israeli army to break free from the bloody games of war. Gideon showed him the possibilities of being a different kind of *Man*.

Institutional marginalization directly influences Pamela J. Milne's study, "From the Margins to the Margins: Jephthah's Daughter and Her Father." After her religious studies department was dissolved, Milne was moved to women's studies, but had to learn qualitative research methods and how to interview human subjects in order to teach their core course in feminist research. To hone her qualitative research and interviewing skills, Milne devised a project to discover whether or not feminist scholarship, biblical and other, is reaching beyond the academic feminist community. Her article presents the results that she derived from having a small group of undergraduate and graduate volunteers interpret the story of Jephthah and his daughter from their different gendered and religious or a-religious perspectives.

Royce M. Victor grew up in India, where the finest literary works on Indian culture and life are revered: the *Ramayana* and the *Mahabharata*. His essay, "Delilah—A Forgotten Hero (Judges 16:4-21): A Cross-Cultural Narrative Reading," interprets Delilah in light of a nameless courtesan in these works who sacrifices her life for the good of the country. Her story has been immortalized by writers, artists, and more recently in film. Victor argues that Delilah is a Philistine who works on behalf of her country to rid it of a violent social bandit whose only virtue was his superhuman strength. She is often depicted as a prostitute working solely for money. But for Victor, Delilah risks her life in entering into a relationship with a fearsome threat to the community, and is successful in subduing him. She is a forgotten hero, like the nameless courtesan in Indian legends who is able to bring rain to her country at great danger to herself.

In "Narrative Loss, the (Important) Role of Women, and Community in Judges 19," Brad Embry reads the story of the Levite concubine's rape from his specific religious context, teaching at a Christian liberal arts university in the Pentecostal-Holiness Assemblies of God tradition. Having heard no sermons on Judges 19 or Bible studies discussing it, Embry saw how *unimportant* Judges 19 was in his denomination, which believes that the Bible provides parameters for its communal identity. He therefore explores the ramifications of omitting Judges 19 from the biblical narrative, especially for his community of faith. Pivotal in his essay is the importance of the female figure in Judges 19. Her rape, dismemberment, and death are potentially that of the whole nation. Her terrible fate provides the only critique powerful enough to awaken the community to its degenerate state. Her story is a vital reminder of a community's capacity for horrendous evil and must not be elided from the large biblical story.

Janelle Stanley's essay, "Judges 19: Text of Trauma," is informed by her backgrounds in both clinical social work and biblical scholarship. She reads Judges 19 as a text displaying the classic symptoms of trauma: dissociation, repetition compulsion, and fragmentation. Dissociation is the desire to psychologically deny, flee from, or eliminate the trauma. Dissociation is evident in the characters' lack of names in Judges 19 and the very truncated description of the concubine's rape in verse 25. Repetition compulsion is the attempt by the psyche to enable a different outcome of the traumatic event. In Judges

19, this is evident in the double speeches of the old man and the repetition of the old man's speech by the Levite (19:17b, 20), and by duplication with the parallel story in Genesis 19. Fragmentation occurs when the psyche cuts off memories of the unbearable experience, distributing it to different parts of the self. Stanley sees this most clearly in the Levite's dismemberment of his concubine. The whole story reveals the psyche's attempt to "construct the narrative," the most important aspect of trauma therapy. In the retelling of the story, healing emerges.

> So now as I'm leavin'
> I'm weary as Hell
> The confusion I'm feelin'
> Ain't no tongue can tell
> The words fill my head
> And fall to the floor
> If God's on our side
> He'll stop the next war.[5]

We end this introduction with a quotation from Bob Dylan, as relevant today as when it was first composed, for the past and the present and for the future, if we wish to have a future. It is not easy to take sides for or against Joshua and Judges, the texts or their continued influence or the symbols they have become. So many factors are at stake. Each critical essay here collected proves the point in its on way. These essays also show how grappling with the questions raised is relevant in cultures, confessional and secularist alike, in which the Hebrew Bible functions as cultural heritage. When things have been said and analyses done, we all share Dylan's plea: whatever our side is, let there be peace; if God is on our side, whatever that side is, let him stop the next war. Let Us stop the next war.

Notes

1. From "This land is your land, this land is my land," by Woody Guthrie, lyrics 1940, first recording 1944.

2. In this volume, as in other volumes of this series on the Hebrew Bible, contributors use Bible/bible, God/god, and various spellings of the god of the Hebrew bible (such as YHWH, Yhwh, Yahweh) as befits their views and beliefs.

3. For extensive bibliographies on religion and violence, including violence in the Hebrew bible and scholarship thereon, see for instance Charles Bellinger's bibliographies on the Wabash

Center website (http://www.wabashcenter.wabash.edu/resources/result-browse.aspx?topic=549&pid=427 and http://www.wabashcenter.wabash.edu/resources/article2.aspx?id=10516).

4. For a recent collection about war literature in the Hebrew Bible and its influence on contemporary contexts, see the articles in Kelle and Ames 2008.

5. Last stanza, Bob Dylan, "With God on Our Side," recorded 1963 on the album *The Times They Are a-Changin'* (some say inspired by Rom. 8:28-39).

PART I

What Do We Do, What Can We Do, about Joshua and Judges?

1

The God of Joshua

An Ambivalent Field of Negotiation

Walter Brueggemann

The contours of critical issues in the book of Joshua are relatively clear, even though these issues have not been settled in any consensus. For that reason, I do not need to engage further those critical questions, but can move to a post-critical probe of theological-interpretive matters concerning the text of Joshua. What follows is a theological probe in the manner of a "second naïveté" that may strike one as rather fanciful. Or it may be regarded as a theological fantasy informed by what I have been reading lately. At any rate, let me consider what must be an important interpretive question in the book of Joshua, namely, the matter of legitimated violence and, beyond that, the indispensible commitment of YHWH to that violence on behalf of Israel at the expense of the prior inhabitants of the land.

I

The interface of YHWH and violence is, in the end, an acute theological embarrassment. Commentators have been remarkably agile in overcoming that embarrassment by a variety of interpretive strategies:

- An evolutionary hypothesis that does not need to take early "primitive" texts seriously, as they have been better superseded and displaced by better, subsequent texts.
- A distinction between ancient text and reutilization in the Persian ("canonical") period, when ancient memory has been purged of its literal toxic quality and now functions in a more credible way as a conviction of faith, but without any literal intention.

- A variety of approaches, as with Douglas Earl, to read mythologically or symbolically, past the unmistakable substance of the text, this way in particular in the service of Christian interpretation (Earl 2010).

Each of these approaches no doubt has merit, and I have no wish to denigrate them or the interpreters who practice them. Nonetheless, they all smack, in one way or another, of a Marcionite temptation to select and cherry-pick the text for what is most palatable, and to dismiss or deny what is most objectionable in it. These are, in the end, various strategies to explain away the text. I have no doubt that the harshness of the text, including its violence, requires some such reading agility.

Given that, however, it remains to admit that the statement of the text persists and continues to wound and to authorize systemic wounding. The land is still described as violently seized; and the God of Israel is still narrated as the legitimator of that violent seizure. As a result, for all of our hermeneutical imagination, we still have before us texts that wound. These texts offer a God willing to enact, and capable of enacting, summary violence against the enemies of the chosen people and in the service of the divine promise.

II

In what follows, I will articulate three probes in an attempt to understand more fully, and in an effort to consider the responsibility of ongoing theological interpretation in the light of the witness of the text. I do so in the context of our own acutely violent society in a violent world, in an awareness that theological ideologies, interpretations, and institutions regularly collude in supporting violence as a proper and moral undertaking, sometimes in local authoritarian and patriarchal ways and sometimes in colonizing military actions. It is of course an enormous stretch from ancient text to contemporary legitimation, but the texts remain available precisely for such legitimation, a stretch often undertaken with an untroubled conscience.

PROBE 1

The violent seizure of the land is the function of the chosenness of Israel by YHWH to be YHWH's "treasured possession" (Exod. 19:5; Deut. 7:6; 14:2; 26:18). It is impossible to follow the narrative account of the book of Joshua except with an assumption of chosenness that binds Israel to radical Torah obedience (1:7-8; 8:30-35; 23:6) and to covenant fidelity of an exclusionary kind (23:7, 12-13). Conversely, the chosenness of Israel binds YHWH to a singular commitment to and passion for the well-being of Israel that comes to mean safe settlement in the land (see Deut. 26:16-19).

I have learned the most in recent times about chosenness from the critical reflections of Todd Gitlin and Liel Leibovitz in their book, *The Chosen Peoples* (2010). They accent that the chosenness of Israel, in the tradition of Israel, is integrally and intrinsically linked to the chosenness of the land. Thus the initial promise to Abraham concerns the land (Gen. 12:1-3), and the declaration to Moses at the burning bush concerns guidance to the land (Exod. 3:8). In the founding traditions, the commitment of YHWH to Israel is all about land that is promised and that must be taken.

The counter side of chosenness, as Gitlin and Leibovitz show, is that others must be "unchosen" and that the "unchosenness" must, perforce, face land loss and land defeat. The unchosen, as adversaries of the promise of God, will not and cannot hold the land. In their extrapolation from this conviction of people and land, they observe that as God chooses this people, so this chosen people becomes the chooser. Thus in the Song of Deborah, "New gods were chosen," clearly the God who will defeat Sisera and the Canaanites for the sake of the land (Judg. 5:8). That the chosen can choose a God gives the initiative in the relationship to the chosen and suggests an act of ideological self-promotion. The connection to the land and its seizure, clearly enough, means that violence is intrinsic to the status of chosenness, for the land to be *given* is the land to be *taken*, as is required.

Two extrapolations are offered by Gitlin and Leibovitz that may be taken, mutatis mutandis, as claims from the book of Joshua that have continuing contemporary force. The authors trace, in summary fashion, the way in which that ancient chosenness has eventuated in contemporary Zionism that practices a messianic passion for the land that exempts the land and all of its questions from any ordinary political reasoning. They dare to suggest a straight line from Joshua to the contemporary linkage of land and people.

Second and of more immediate interest to me, Gitlin and Leibovitz trace the same chosenness in American self-understanding from the earliest Europeans in America through the Puritans to the imperial expansion of the United States. They observe that the most expansionist of U.S. presidents—Jefferson, Jackson, Polk, and Theodore Roosevelt—traded on chosenness (cast in evangelical language) as warrant for imperial expansion. They draw a line, moreover, from the earlier expansionists through Roosevelt directly to George W. Bush and his elective wars. Most recently, that same expansionism has been pursued in the decision of Barack Obama to launch a new U.S. military base in Australia. Of course, the book of Joshua cannot directly receive credit or blame for such a contemporary practice. But with equal clarity, the texts persist in ways that make chosenness a warrant for legitimate violence that is a living out of a distinct God-given destiny. Regina Schwartz has judged that *monotheism* is intrinsically violent, and now we may see that the status of *being chosen*—in ancient election or as contemporary exceptionalism—draws palpably from such an ideology for the practice of violence (Schwartz 1997).

Gitlin and Leibovitz are not sanguine of any remedy for such claims of chosenness: "When a people declares themselves chosen, or act as if they are, or were, there is no rolling back the history that ensues. The clock cannot be reset to zero. We cannot choose to be unchosen. We cannot end the ordeal. The cycles of race hatred, revenge, and war cannot be rescinded, erased from memory. History is unsparing" (Gitlin and Leibovitz 2010: 191). They hope that the chosen may choose differently in time to come: "The chosen people must choose" (Gitlin and Leibovitz 2010: 192). More radical is the project of Mark Braverman (2010) and the authors he cites, that chosenness must be renounced if violence is to be curbed. It is astonishing that the biblical tradition, so grounded in the neighborly Torah, could narrate the violence without objection or even without notice. It is surely even more astonishing, in my judgment, that critical scholars, religiously committed, could for a very long time pass over the issue without notice, so contained has been our reading in grip of the ideology of chosenness. It is chosenness that propels the chosen, chosen God and chosen people together, to perpetrate violence.

PROBE 2

The violence perpetrated for the sake of chosenness consists in the negation of the "Other" (Brueggemann 2009). The covenant that provided the basis for "chosenness" in the deuteronomic History (and so in the book of Joshua) is an exclusionary enterprise with no room for the Other. In the book of Joshua, the Other consists of all the previous inhabitants of the land of promise (the land promised in the act of chosenness), inhabitants given in the text in various forms that are highly stylized and summarized in the list in 12:1-24. All of them are to be rejected and eliminated in order that YHWH can keep the land promise made to the chosen covenant partner, Israel.

There are in the tradition of Israel, to be sure, early signs that YHWH had room for "the Other." The initial promise to Abraham, variously reiterated, has the "families of the earth" in purview as recipients of divine blessing (Gen. 12:3;

18:18; 22:18; 26:4; 28:14). But there is none of that here. The dismissal of the Other for the sake of the chosen is, inevitably, a prescription for violence.

I have come at this issue of the Other through the remarkable book by Martha Nussbaum, *The Clash Within*, her critical exploration of the clash between Hindus and Muslims in India (Nussbaum 2007). Her book, as indicated by its title, is deliberately and forcibly a response to Samuel Huntington, who in his book *The Clash of Civilizations* (1996) anticipates a future inescapable conflict between Islam and Western civilization. Given Huntington's premise, one could judge that conflict narrated in the book of Joshua between Israelites and Canaanites is a harbinger of what Huntington anticipates, an anticipation on his part that has, in important ways, become a self-fulfilling prophecy that has shaped ideology and consequently policy. Nussbaum, to the contrary, denies that the conflict in India is between Hindus and Muslims. She finds that the "clash," among both the Hindu and Muslim persons she interviewed, is not between those two "sides" in that conflict. It is rather a "clash" between two types of people within the society itself.

> The clash between proponents of ethnoreligious homogeneity and proponents of a more inclusive and pluralistic type of citizenship is a clash between two types of people within a single society. At the same time, this clash expresses tendencies that are present, at some level, within most human beings: the tendency to seek domination as a form of self-protection, versus the ability to respect others who are different, and to see in difference a nation's richness rather than a threatto its purity" (Nussbaum 2007: 15).

That is, the propelling conflict is between those who need to exclude the Other and those who can welcome (or at least tolerate) the Other in an ordered society. By the end of her book, Nussbaum has moved her argument even further. She proposes:

> The real "clash of civilizations" is not "out there," between admirable Westerners and Muslim zealots. It is here, within each person, as we oscillate uneasily between self-protective aggression and the ability to live in the world with others (Nussbaum 2007: 337).

The clash is between self-protective aggression and the ability to live with the Other!

Now it is of course a huge leap from contemporary India and Nussbaum back to the book of Joshua. It is, however, a leap I propose to make in order to consider afresh the force of violence narrated in the book. In the book of Joshua, the main story line is the elimination of the Other for the sake of the promise of the chosen.

There are, to be sure, side notes to the contrary in the book of Joshua. In his close study of the ban authorized by Deuteronomy, Robert Polzin (1980: 123) observes that there is a narrative indication of "a relaxation of application of the ban," so that exceptions are made for Rahab, for the Gibeonites, and for the booty and cattle of northern cities (11:11-14). Polzin judges that what is being "mocked" is the sweeping authoritarian dogmatism of total destruction commanded by Deuteronomy (Polzin 1980: 127). Polzin sees the text making room for the processing of outsiders and so can find a "clash" within between the total rejection of Others and a more-restrained or humane treatment of the others. While Polzin's point is well taken as an important hermeneutical insight, I judge, nonetheless, that hostility toward the Other that issues in legitimated violence against the Other is the main story line.

And if we can more fully consider the ideological struggle that Polzin discusses—an ideological struggle that may have been ancient in the memory of Israel and is "contemporary" in the exilic or postexilic contestation of Israel—we may ask a theological question about the character of YHWH and how YHWH is disclosed and portrayed in this ideology-laden narrative. As a theological possibility, I dare to suggest that the text witnesses to a "clash" within the character of YHWH, a clash that is endlessly adjudicated in the witness of Israel. On the one hand, YHWH has concern for the other peoples who are entitled to life and to land. Patrick Miller has found evidence of this allowance in Deuteronomy 2, where the text concerns the land of Israel's "kin." Thus Miller judges, "The Lord's stories with other peoples are made a part of Israel's story" (Miller 2000: 599). The extreme articulation of this trajectory is the promissory oracle of Isaiah 19, in which it is assured that a peaceable Fertile Crescent will include many peoples blessed by YHWH:

> On that day there will be a highway from Egypt to Assyria, and the Assyrian will come into Egypt, and the Egyptian into Assyria, and the Egyptians will worship with the Assyrians.
>
> On that day Israel will be the third with Egypt and Assyria, a blessing in the midst of the earth, whom the Lord of hosts has blessed saying, "Blessed be Egypt my people, and Assyria the work of my hands, and Israel my heritage. (Isa. 19:23-25).

Indeed, the text goes so far as to distribute YHWH's pet names for chosen Israel to other peoples, so that in anticipation YHWH has many chosen peoples. The prophetic oracle goes well beyond the narrative of Deuteronomy 2, but that entire trajectory is against exclusionary chosenness.

However, it is clear that in the book of Joshua the exceptions of Rahab, the Gibeonites, and the northern cattle are only that—exceptions—to the general resolve of YHWH. The several traditions attest distinctly and differently and do not, on their own, perform the "clash." When the traditions are taken in sum, however, there is clearly an unresolved clash in the tradition that is given to us as an unresolved clash in the character of YHWH. Nussbaum proposes that what counts is that pervasive "oscillation" in how one handles the options toward the Other in particular circumstance. Clearly the traditionists are not of a single mind concerning the Other, and one may dare to see that YHWH is not single-minded either. Given that, insofar as chosenness propels the book of Joshua, the "clash" is resolved in an exclusionary direction, with consequent violence. I judge that the noted exceptions only call attention to the wholesale enactment of covenantal violence to which YHWH is here committed. The struggle for the legitimacy of the Other is an ongoing project in the Bible, and the clash runs on in the text and, not surprisingly, in our long tradition of interpretation. That unsettled question, however, is rooted in the clash within YHWH, who occupies the text.

PROBE 3

The practice of chosenness that violently excludes the Other is exacerbated by the absence of dissent that one might expect in a lively, dialogical, covenantal tradition. But, of course, a tradition that is deeply set in an exclusionary ideology is not a welcoming matrix for dissent. Now it may be unreasonable and inappropriate to expect that there should be dissent to the program of chosenness that issues in violence, because revolutionary movements will not tolerate such "weakening of the hands" of their force.

I have had two thoughts about this question. First, YHWH, in YHWH's wholesale command to destroy the Other, indicates no misgiving or second thought or reservation, no large dissent from violence in a way of mercy. That is because YHWH is here totally committed to the enterprise, passionate for the exclusiveness of the chosen, and zealous to deliver on the land promise that goes with chosenness. Perhaps that is all we might have expected.

But I am also thinking, to the contrary, for example, of YHWH's reflective, self-critical soliloquy in Hosea 11:8-9:

> How can I give you up, Ephraim?
>> How can I hand you over, O Israel?
> How can I make you like Admah?
>> How can I treat you like Zeboiim?
> My heart recoils within me;
>> my compassion grows warm and tender.
> I will not execute my fierce anger;
>> I will not again destroy Ephraim;
> for I am God and no mortal,
>> the Holy One in your midst,
>> and I will not come in wrath.

Gerald Janzen has made the case that these questions are not rhetorical but are serious questions posed by YHWH about YHWH's knee-jerk reaction to Israel's disobedience (Janzen 1982). YHWH is caught up short at the edge of violent destructiveness. YHWH reverses field and makes a new resolve out of compassion, a deeply moved emotive reversal. That astonishing fresh resolve is echoed with an infinitive absolute in Jer. 31:20:

> Is Ephraim my dear son?
>> Is he the child I delight in?
> As often as I speak against him
>> I still remember him.
> Therefore I am deeply moved for him;
>> I will surely have mercy on him, says the Lord.

Both statements are about divine compassion that radically undercuts more ferocious resolve to enact a violent response to disobedience. Admittedly, a divine response to covenantal disobedience on the part of Israel is not the same as divine violence against an outsider to covenantal chosenness; but the parallel is enough to notice that, in these two cases in the Latter Prophets, YHWH has enough individuated freedom, so that YHWH need not react to disobedience according to the harsh sanctions of the Torah. As I have followed Gitlin and Leibovitz concerning chosenness and Nussbaum about Otherness, now I suggest following D. W. Winnicott (1965), that YHWH in the book of Joshua is an agent of unqualified exclusionary violence; YHWH has not enough of an individuated self to have freedom to step outside of the reaction mandated by covenantal symmetry. In the prophetic poetry I have cited, YHWH does exhibit that individuated freedom. By contrast, in the book of Joshua, YHWH has no freedom beyond the mandates of chosenness. Without this self-critical freedom that introspection requires, YHWH must, perforce, be completely defined by, and summoned to act by, the uncompromising ideological force of the land promise. Thus there is not in the book of Joshua any hint of self-critical capacity on the part of YHWH that might cause an interruption of violence on behalf of the chosen against the Other.

But second and more important, there is no dissent against violence voiced by Israel. I came to this awareness by appeal to the way in which Moses is narrated as a dissenting voice to the destructive resolve of YHWH against Israel. In Exod. 32:11-13, Moses vigorously protests against YHWH's resolve to consume Israel in the wake of the incident of the golden calf. Moses appeals to YHWH's self-interest and self-regard and to the tradition of the ancestors in order to motivate YHWH to an alternative decision. At the center of his intervention, in v. 12, is the triple imperative of petition:

> Turn . . .
> Change . . .
> Do not bring evil.

The dissent of Moses interrupts YHWH's resolve, which seems to have been an emotive reaction rather than a considered decision. The dissent of Moses creates space for YHWH that YHWH could not, from YHWH's self, entertain. Thus Moses acts in a daring way to summon, for an instant, YHWH's best self.

That same transaction is narrated in Numbers 14. Again YHWH has resolved to disinherit Israel (v. 12). And again, Moses dissents from the divine resolve and persuades YHWH otherwise. Moses reminds YHWH of what is at stake for YHWH's own reputation (vv. 13-16). In an appeal to YHWH's power (vanity?), he quotes back YHWH's self-announcement from Exod. 34:6-7:

> The Lord is slow to anger,
> and abounding in steadfast love,
> Forgiving iniquity and transgression
> but by no means clearing the guilty,
> visiting the iniquity of the parents on the children
> to the third and the fourth generation. (Num. 14:18)

Finally, after the quote comes the big imperative (v. 19): "forgive," with an appeal to the memory of Exodus 32. In both narrative instances, Moses boldly pushes into a divine resolve of destructive punishment and mitigates that resolve. In Num. 11:11-15, the matter is somewhat different, but Moses' boldness against divine anger is the same.

What strikes me is that there is no such protest or dissent in the book of Joshua against the divine resolve to destroy the inhabitants of the land. To be sure, as I recognize, it would be a very different matter to protest divine resolve against the Canaanites rather than against Israel, as Moses has done. But the analogue is close enough to note. Thus Joshua is narrated and the characters in it are fully ensconced in the ideology of chosenness, with its implications for land seizure. The difference is that Moses was not so fully ensconced in the ideology of obedience, so that he could protest the divine violence. Here there is no such restraint against the divine violence that is an enactment of the ideology of chosenness. To paraphrase Senator Lloyd Bentsen against candidate Dan Quayle, "Joshua, you are no Moses." Such a dissent might have not worked. But it is nonetheless striking that such a note is absent in the narrative. And in the ideology of chosenness, such a dissent will remain mostly absent for a very long time to come. Perhaps in our belated retrospect on this text, it becomes the task of interpretation to issue a dissent against YHWH's evident proclivity to partisan violence, a dissent that Joshua could not and did not undertake.

III

I suggest that these three propositions on divine violence are at the center of the interpretive work that may yet be undertaken in the book of Joshua:

> 1. Following Gitlin and Leibovitz (2010) on chosenness: The violent seizure of the land is a function of chosenness.
> 2. Following Nussbaum (2007) on Otherness: The violence perpetrated for the sake of chosenness consists in the negation of the Other.
> 3. Following Winnicott (1965) on individuation: The practice of chosenness that violently excludes the Other is exacerbated by the absence of dissent that one might have expected in a largely dialogical tradition. Neither YHWH nor Joshua is differentiated enough to stake out any freedom in the face of the totalizing ideology of chosenness.

I finish with an appreciative reflection on the distinction made by Robert Polzin, plus a couple of concluding observations. In his programmatic appeal to V. N. Voloshinov (aka Mikhail Bakhtin) Polzin, in his three important books, posits a dialogic quality for the narrative books of ancient Israel, including of course the book of Joshua.[1] He sets up that dialogical transaction as an interpretive tension between what he terms "authoritarian dogmatism" and "critical traditionalism." By the former, he means the hard-nosed, nonnegotiable command for absolute obedience voiced in the tradition of Deuteronomy.[2] By "critical traditionalism," Polzin means the evidence of the text itself that exercises interpretive freedom and imagination in order to soften or break the absoluteness of Deuteronomy. It is the intent and burden of Polzin's argument to show that critical traditionalism is an enterprise of immense importance that precludes taking the tradition as flat and one-dimensional. It is the case that I happen to think that the evidence for critical traditionalism in the book of Joshua is much less substantial than Polzin does, but that is not at all my point here.

Rather, I want to take up Polzin's analysis in an appreciative way, and connect his categories to the force of violence that is evident in so much of the narrative of Joshua. Polzin makes his case around the flat command of the ban (herem), and then shows that critical traditionalism relaxes that divine insistence. I wish to transpose Polzin's "authoritarian dogmatism" into the absoluteness of chosenness that is intrinsically violent and that brooks no dissent, and to take his "critical traditionalism" as a softening of radical chosenness that interrupts the commanded violence. In this way, Polzin's critical traditionalism amounts to a mode of dissent, the very dissent of which I find no evidence in the book of Joshua. Polzin keeps his argument at a more formal level, and I wish to bring his formal argument down to the actual reality of divinely legitimated violence.

Given that transposition that I believe is faithful to and congruent with Polzin's argument, the critical traditionalism finds such divinely authorized violence to be unacceptable and unbearable and begins to enact loopholes in that radical ideology. I suggest, moreover, that one cannot soften or relax the command to violence without—at the same time—softening the claim of chosenness so that the outcome, in a particular circumstance, may be an exemption from the systemic violence that otherwise pertains to all of the unchosen. Thus I judge that Polzin's categories constitute a modest dissent, a first step against the ideology of chosenness and consequently a first mitigation of divine violence. No character in the book of Joshua gives voice to this mitigation. But the traditionalists who hide in the text set in motion a trajectory, in modest and cautious ways, that can indeed become a place from which to interpret outside the ideology of chosenness, with its indispensible complement of violence.

From that extrapolation from Polzin's work, I draw two conclusions. First, the critical traditionalism concerning the book of Joshua has made a beginning, but did not go very far in its critique of the ideology of chosenness and violence championed by authoritarian dogmatism. It did not go very far, perhaps, because that ideology of chosenness was and is so powerful. Or perhaps it did not go very far because the exilic or postexilic reprise on chosenness, and its reclamation of the land, was so compelling in that circumstance. Or at a theological level, it did not go very far because YHWH is a recalcitrant character who has not yet reached an individuated capacity for free action, beyond the reactive possibilities permitted by the inherited dogmatism.

Second, in the face of not having yet gone very far, it follows, I suggest, that the ongoing work of interpretation must extend Polzin's critical traditionalism much further against the authoritarian dogmatism that still occupies the text. That is, interpretive work might be to imagine how the stay in the land might be enacted differently. If the chosen were less vigorously chosen, if the violent counterpoint of chosenness were rejected, and if dissent were more energetically voiced to YHWH, a different tale might be told. YHWH, with accompanying chosenness and violence, is to some extent a product and construct of Israel's testimony; and so to bear alternative testimony may be to permit YHWH to become a different, more credible character with a more individuated sense of free agency that is not captivated by authoritarian dogmatism.

The outcome of such work will be to continue the dissent: not only to expose ideology that overrides the facts on the ground but also to bear witness to God, who may yet occupy the textual tradition (and, therefore, occupy the land) differently. If that is a continuing possibility, then "criticism" in our society is not simply a rational project of conforming the Bible to Enlightenment categories; it is to participate in the theological, dialogical exchange already evident in the text, a process whereby the past and the future may be reimagined short of self-serving, violence-generating ideology.

I do not need to tell you that this enterprise (already evident in the daring work of critical traditionalism) is of huge urgency among us now. It is urgent because every chosen people—Israel and the United States among them—imagines God as singularly committed to the reassuring violence that serves the maintenance of privilege, entitlement, and preeminence in the world. The God who may be sketched differently in critical traditionalism may be a God who continues to make more room for the unchosen, who keeps free from overcommitted violence, and who takes dissent seriously as the offer of a credible alternative in touch with the facts on the ground.

The dialogic transaction of interpretation that Polzin has located in the text indicates that our interpretation, like that of the antecedent authoritarian dogmatism, remains always under negotiation and well short of finality. To remain short of finality is urgent both for the character of God and for the life of the world. We know very well that final readings lead to final solutions. The authoritarian dogmatism voiced in the book of Joshua offers a final solution to the "Canaanite problem" (see Levenson 1985). If we are unthinking, as easily happens among chosen people, we can be taken in by the continual attractiveness of such finality. The insistence of critical traditionalism is that it need not be so, and it continues to need not be so.

Notes

1. In addition to *Moses and the Deuteronomist*, already cited (1980), see also Polzin's *Samuel and the Deuteronomist* (1989), and *David and the Deuteronomist* (1993).

2. Polzin regards the commands of Deuteronomy so absolute as to constitute "authoritarian dogmatism." Note should be taken, however, of Bernard Levinson in *Legal Revision and Religious Renewal in Ancient Israel* (2008), who proposes that Deuteronomy represents an imaginative interpretive move beyond Sinai. If one considers the arguments of both Polzin and Levinson, we may see a recurring dynamism between old established tradition and new interpretation. In the long run, the new interpretation becomes part of the settled authoritative tradition.

2

Joshua-Judges and Postcolonial Criticism

Trent C. Butler

With this essay, a Joshua/Judges veteran becomes a neophyte in postcolonial studies. Joshua grabbed my attention over forty years ago during an M.Div. seminar with Dr. Don Williams. An assigned paper on the Song of Deborah led me into new depths of critical study and new amazement with the accomplishments of women in the "patriarchal" Hebrew Bible. Dr. Paul Redditt and I gleefully reconstructed a cult history of the major Israelite cultus on Mount Tabor and its relationship to that of Ebal and Gerizim.

A doctoral dissertation on the "Song of the Sea" under Dr. Phillip Hyatt at Vanderbilt brought me into the forest of dating criteria in relation to Hebrew poetry and Hebrew narrative. The Deuteronomist greeted me, and that mysterious sister of Moses—Miriam—lurked in the background without serious personal contact.

Just a bit over thirty years ago, Dr. John D. W. Watts invited me to write the Joshua volume for the Word Biblical Commentary (WBC) series. The volume received some strong reviews, but the author remained dissatisfied. Joshua stood incomplete without Judges. Then just over ten years ago, the WBC Judges volume fell in my lap. Here I could not avoid questions I had skirted earlier, namely, the unheroic presentation of biblical main characters and the multiple perspectives under which the same data could be presented.

In 2011, Dr. Ralph Hawkins forced me to deliver a paper at the SBL Joshua/Judges group, a group I had started and passed off to him. He assigned me the subject of postcolonial approaches to Joshua and Judges. A revamped edition of that paper appears here as a result of the editors' kind invitation.

Here, then, a newcomer reports on a not-quite-so-new philosophical methodology in biblical studies—Postcolonialism. I will try to summarize for you this philosophy and critical reading method and its possible application to the study of Joshua and Judges

In reviewing just a bit of literature on this field, I have become fascinated with its relevance and with the passion its devotees bring to a text. Still, I must stand with those outsiders Uriah Kim describes: "It is difficult for those who have never experienced being treated or represented as an 'Other' in relation to the Western subject to understand all the fuss Postcolonialism has stirred. Why can't the Rest of the world just follow the program outlined by the well-meaning folks from the West?" (Kim 2007: 161).

A few volumes in the Chalice Press offerings and Uriah Kim's contribution to Gale Yee's *Judges and Method* (2007b) forced me to take the postcolonial approach to texts seriously, without totally selling out to a method that brought terrific insights and yet appeared to have encompassed so much material within its territory that it lacked clear definition.

Postcolonialism attempts to offer a way of reading the Bible as shorn of Western assumptions and accretions. The heart of Postcolonialism, as far as I can see, is this philosophical view of humans as either colonizers or colonized with its invitation to read literature through the eyes of the colonized.

Stephen D. Moore finds that postcolonial criticism is "not a method of interpretation . . . so much as a critical sensibility acutely attuned to a specific range of interrelated historical and textual phenomena" (Moore 2006: 7). And Kim calls us to employ analytic tools and insights from Postcolonialism to interpret the Bible against the grain of Western interpretations of the text, beginning with the plight of the Rest rather than the situation of the central participants in the text (Kim 2007: 165).

ASKING POSTCOLONIAL QUESTIONS

Since biblical exegesis is basically the skill of asking the right question at the right time, it is appropriate to see the questions that postcolonial biblical criticism asks. Kim divides these questions into three levels: text, scholars, and interpreters. Here then are some possible questions related to the study of Joshua and Judges on those three levels.

TEXTUAL STUDY

- Who were the Israelites? Who were included in and excluded from this group identity? How are Israelites portrayed in the text?
- Who were the non-Israelites? What assumptions about them lie behind the text? How are they depicted in the text? Does the text reflect stereotypes about them?

- Do the non-Israelites speak? Who speaks for them? Are we given access to their point of view?
- How does the text construct difference among people? Is the difference real, ideological, or imaginary?
- Who commissioned the text? Does an empire stand behind the text? Does this text have a clear stance for or against the political imperialism of its time? What unequal power relations are evident in the text?
- Are there suppressed and neglected voices in the text?
- Who are the marginalized or the Other in the text?

MODERN BIBLICAL SCHOLARSHIP

- What questions and concerns does the scholar bring to the text?
- Whose history, experience, and interests are being inscribed in the scholarship? From whose perspective or context is the text being interpreted?
- Does the accepted scholarship on the biblical text advance the interests of the West at the expense of the Rest?
- Does biblical scholarship appeal to nationalism, Orientalism, and other ideological discourses to express the superiority of the West over the Rest?
- How do biblical scholars portray the non-Israelites and the Israelites? Do they speak for the Israelites or the Other?

CONTEMPORARY INTERPRETERS

- Who sees themselves as the Israelites in our time? Why? Who are designated as non-Israelites in our time? Why?
- How can the contemporary interpreter read the Bible without perpetuating the "us and them" paradigm that constructs one group as superior to another?
- How is the text unsafe (oppressive) as well as safe (liberative) for the interpreter's context?
- What questions and concerns arise from one's context when interpreting the text?
- What ethical responsibility does the contemporary reader have in light of the fact that the Bible and its interpreters had a role in forming unequal relations between the West and the Rest in the past

that are still sustained by contemporary readers today? (Kim 2007: 167–69).

These postcolonial questions must be modified a bit prior to utilizing them in biblical study. The following lines will attempt to show that the scholar cannot begin to study with an understanding of Israel as the colonizer and non-Israelites as the colonized, or vice versa. We will show that the situation is much more complex than that. Similarly, we must ask if the colonizing question can be prejudged as West against the Rest in every instance. Is the West always seeking to colonize or to maintain the results of colonization? Does the wide-ranging Rest never participate as the colonizer rather than as the colonized? Does the postcolonial scholar always identify with some colonized Other and never with the West?

Postcolonialism Reads Joshua and Judges

Textual Study

Postcolonial investigation is particularly appropriate for discussing the book of Joshua and the book of Judges, since one of the major issues in Joshua and Judges is the identification of Israel as distinct among kindred nations.

What are the differentiating marks and characteristics qualifying one as an Israelite over against Canaanites, Jebusites, Girgasites, Ammonites, Philistines, Moabites, and all the Other "ites"? Must an interpreter identify with either north or south? Does one find loyalty and self-identity at the level of clan, tribe, or all Israel? What institution, if any, lies behind the "all Israel" nomenclature? How are the troops with Joshua related to the troops with Gilead or Jephthah? Who is "all Israel" before the Davidic monarchy?

Such questions thrust us squarely in the minefield of perspective. The final author/editor of Judges casts the entire Joshua/Judges narrative under the flagship of "all Israel" (Josh. 3:7, 17; 4:14; 7:24-25; 8:15, 21, 24, 33; 10:15, 29, 31, 34, 36, 38, 43; 23:2; Judg. 8:27; 20:34). Yet, as is obvious, the individual narratives reflect a much narrower clan or tribal perspective. The text as oral narrative depicts national heroes overcoming national enemies. The text as a written national leadership inventory asks probing questions concerning the leadership style and faithfulness of Israel's "heroic" leaders. The final text stands on Israel's side but yet fails to find an Israel that meets God's criteria as people of God. This portrayal leaves Israel as an ambivalent people seeking true identity.

As for non-Israelites, Joshua and Judges present a field day for scholars. Non-Israelites are Canaanites and all the Other "ites" in Judges. The text creates an Us/Them relationship between Canaanites and Israelites, a cultural distinction that archaeologists find hard to affirm. Specialists in the history of religion face similar problems as Gideon slips from Baal worshiper to Yahweh worshiper, and the people of Yahweh's covenant face the people of El-Berith and of Baal-Berith in Shechem, a central sanctuary for the people of Yahweh (Joshua 8 and 24; Judges 9).

Stereotypes appear in most folk narratives. Joshua and Judges prove no different. Joshua is the perfect leader against whom all others are judged. Caleb is the valiant patriarch setting the example for the next generation. Othniel, the exemplar for all successors, is painted in broad strokes with few definable actions. Deborah is the valiant lady who delivers her country from enemies in a totally unexpected manner. Not just the enemy but Israel also finds its leaders stereotyped yet distinctive.

In which camp do we place Rahab, Achan, Jael, Meroz, and the tribes who do not answer Deborah's call to battle, the Gibeonites, Abimelech, Micah and his mother, Jebusites, and Benjaminites? Are they presented realistically or ideologically? No straightforward answer appears. Certainly, folk ideology and narrative hides behind the crusty, bread-eating Gibeonites and the huge anti-Israelite coalitions. Much can be said about Samson as a folk hero. Still, one must ask, are Israel's enemies portrayed as the Rest with whom the reader is supposed to react sympathetically?

The writer does not mute the non-Israelites. Many of them speak, for the Israelite stories appear in dialogue format. We hear voices from Rahab, the Gibeonites, Achan, Micah's mother, and Sisera's mother, each from a different perspective—Rahab's confession of faith; Achan's confession of sin; the Gibeonites' words of deception; the unfulfilled daydreams of Sisera's mother about her son's victorious acts; and Micah's mother lying about her money. These varied "Israelite statements" do not represent political or religious points of view. They represent reaction statements in view of the actions and intentions of the other party—Israelite or Canaanite. They prepare for war, not for philosophical exchange.

Differences among people find expression mainly on the religious plane. Gibeonite deception leads to temple service. Rahab's confession leads to religious protection. Micah and his mother's arguments over an idol lead to the loss of the local high place. Coalition attack results in divine victory. Over and over again, the distinguishing point of view is religious, not political or even ethnic. Former enemies join against an invader representing a new God.

Must we lay down a line moving from pure Israelite to absolute non-Israelite? Or can we allow certain characters to be at different places on the line in different narratives or contexts? In what way do we incorporate the insight Katherine Doob Sakenfeld eloquently expressed in her SBL presidential address? She says we may identify with the Canaanites in Joshua but with the Israelites as the Other in Judges (Sakenfeld 2008: 13).

Obviously, Israel commissioned the text to testify to God's great power in establishing them in the new land. Again, we face the question of the nature and perspective on Israel. The people of Israel grow into nationhood size as the Others, colonized by the Egyptians. They wander in the wilderness as a free nomadic people, neither colonizers nor colonized, except by God. They cross the Jordan under divine mandate not only to colonize but more drastically—to exterminate. Israel's history then becomes complex, as they both colonize some "Canaanites," whatever that term embraces, share the land with Others, and find themselves at times colonized by Philistines, Syrians, Phoenicians, and so on. They extend their role of colonizers under David and Solomon, but finally end up as colonized and deported people under Assyria and Babylonia.

At which part of their journey did Israel commission the text? Folk lore and hero stories rise out of an emerging people. An all-Israel perspective paints the text as the individual clans and tribes gain new identity as one people among others. The growing all-Israel, national perspective represents a nation exercising control over—that is, "colonizing"—other similar emerging peoples. This final perspective governs an Israel pictured as conquering the land, distributing it, and joining as a united covenant people. At this time, Israel fights the imperialistic tendencies of Philistine, Syrian, Egyptian, and Assyrian powers.

Israel, then, knows both sides of the coin. They have lived as colonized, equal land sharers, and colonizers. The interpreter of an extensive collection of literature such as the Bible cannot classify a group as colonizers or colonized as a static category, for the same group may well fit different categories at different places in the literature, and at different times and contexts.

What does such postcolonial categorization mean for the study of Joshua and Judges? In discussing Judges 4–5 with Korean women church leaders, Sakenfeld "expressed the discomfort that I and many women peers in North America experience with Jael's murder of Sisera, to which the response came swiftly: 'your place as a U.S. woman is with Sisera's mother, waiting to count the spoils. In retrospect this was surely a Postcolonial (or neocolonial economic) reading and challenge, although none of us marked it as such at the time" (Sakenfeld 2008: 12–13).

The student of Joshua and Judges cannot simply identify with Israel and its manifest destiny. The student should look at the text from many angles and perspectives. Each narrative and each character stands somewhere on the axis running from colonizer to colonized. A close examination of the text may bring you to identify with and read the text as a very unexpected party-in-the-text.

Take a few quick examples. Israelite spies (Joshua 2) reconnoiter the promised land, or at least one town in it. In their minds, these Israelites are colonizers, though they have yet to colonize any part of the promised land. In the view of the Canaanites of Jericho, these Israelite spies and the army they represent are threatening invaders, plotting on taking the Canaanites' land and destroying them and their culture. Rahab, the central character of the story, stands somewhere in the middle of the axis. As a madam, running a house of prostitution (if indeed that is what she is doing), she in a sense is a colonizer over the women who work for her, since Rahab determines their daily culture and occupation. Culturally, Rahab is a Canaanite observing most of the cultural rules, regulations, and habits of her native culture. Religiously, Rahab has crossed the cultural wall from apparent cultural Baal worshiper to Yahweh fearer. She admits the spies as members of an enemy culture whose religion she is adopting and from whose armies she desires protection. She is willing to move from being part of the Canaanite, colonizer group to being the colonized by the Yahweh, invading group.

Rahab thus demonstrates a person perilously walking the axis plank somewhere between colonizer and colonized in various areas of her life. Reading the Jericho narrative from the Rahab perspective becomes much more complex and problematic when one adopts a standard postcolonial approach. How does a postcolonialist read a story leading to colonializing but not yet there, with characters having feet on both ends of the axis? Canaanites see the end coming before a single battle has been waged. Are the "colonized" those to whom the land is promised or those who momentarily control the land? Is colonization a fact within the narrative or an attitude imparted by the narrator? Can a people be a Rest prior to the annihilating battle?

The Gibeonites force yet another vantage point on us. They are insiders who choose to appear as outsiders. They are colonizers who seek to become colonized. They are the enemy who becomes part of the inside group. They are part of the inside Israel group but only as a Rest or Other among the Israelites, becoming slaves, not citizens.

What status would Rahab or a Gibeonite or Jabin claim to have? How would this relate to the status Israel accorded them? What does the introduction of southern and northern campaigns lend to the story? Having won the battles and conquered the kings of the central and southern portions of the land, what role does Israel play as it faces the northern coalition? Is Israel the central figure, the colonizer, or still the colonized? How do you describe the role of the northern opponents who control the majority of the northern portion of the land but who are about to be colonized by Israel?

WESTERN BIBLICAL SCHOLARSHIP

The central issue for Western biblical scholarship appears to be the exercise of power. Who controls or exercises power over another group? This creates the categories and vocabulary used—colonizer, colonized, Other, Rest, East, West. Power echoes forth from the Others' self-identity as the afflicted, the colonized, the powerless, the defeated, the Rest. So Sakenfeld learns from Korea, and Kim looks to the period after World War II while seeing himself as part of the Asian American community in the United States. Much of the work is related to feminist and liberation theology. All these launching pads for postcolonial theology see themselves gradually emerging from a place of weakness to one of comparative power. Such interpretation insists on finding an author taking sides in a text. Only two sides appear as options: The Rest or the whole? The East or the West? The powerful or the weak? Such a portrayal of options appears to limit the artistic ability and creative interpretation of the world. Putting out such limited options forces the theory into reality. Does South Korea become part of the West in its explanation of the situation with North Korea? Is Sudan East or West? Does one automatically support Iran or Iraq since they are Eastern powers? Surely we must grant modern readers and writers much more freedom and interpretative creativity than to press then into one of two categories.

The book of Joshua leads us to see that people groups, armies, city-states, nations are more than labels for the controlling power, the insider, the Other, the Rest. Each group is individual, with individual traits, and might well be colonized and colonizer at the same moment. Or a group may define itself with one label, while we would read their narrative and place them in a totally different grouping with another distinct label. Of course, Israel had their own labeling mechanism. They simply devoted a chapter to listing everyone they had defeated, placing each in the one category—dead. That is, I suppose, the ultimate Otherness.

Let us now look afresh at the land-distribution narratives. The Transjordanians have the right ethnicity, the right patriarchal lineage, but they receive their inheritance outside the symbolic boundary of purity, the Jordan—right ethnicity (qualified for insider status), but wrong geographical location (outsider). They make an interesting case when compared with another group, the Gibeonites, who are exactly the obverse: wrong ethnicity, but inside the boundary of the "pure" geographical location. In both marginal cases, the standard of demarcation turns out to be voluntary submission to the authority structure represented by Joshua and his military men; the alternative is the standard punishment for Otherness: death.

John Mansford Prior insists: "For both agriculturalists and pastoralists the key socio-economic right is the right to use land as a source of livelihood. And indeed the conquest is undertaken in order to obtain land for the Israelite tribes. The Israelites as a nation-in-the-making, freed from slavery in Egypt, needed land on which to construct a nation. Joshua 1–12 depicts the mass displacement of seven peoples (3:10; 24:11) and 31 kings (petty city lords) (12:9-24) from the 'land of Canaan' to make way for the People of God" (Prior 2006: 30).

Among the allotments, Israel pauses in Judges 1 to admit that certain groups of Israelites could not gain control of their assigned property. Thus Prior notes: "The Book of Judges reflects an 'Israelite' nation that is both complex and hybrid in composition. It may have been the case that the 'Israelites' consisted largely of 'natives' of Canaan who either moved to the freedom of the hillsides from the slavery of the lowland cities, or who revolted against their masters. Thus 'Israelites' are those who accepted the Lord and rejected the hegemony of the Canaanite cities. At the end of Judges (Judges 20), we read of intertribal war, a tragic travesty of the unity proclaimed throughout *Joshua*" (Prior 2006: 31).

Some Israelites live in the territory Israel conquered abutting the territory of other tribes. These tribes may have loose control of their land, may be serving the native Canaanites as subjects, may even live in land that is ostensibly controlled by Egyptians but occupied by Canaanites who have made Israel into forced laborers. The combinations become ever more complex.

Is colonializing an actual fact of history, or is it a spirit of mind of the people? Can I, having decided to engage a piece of literature from a postcolonial perspective, simply divide the characters into the domineering and the Rest, colonizers and colonized, Western and non-Western?

Sakenfeld explains:

> The story can still be read as a story of a weak Israel rejecting the temptation to participate in the Canaanites' religious-cultural hegemony, to which they have thus far succumbed, and trying to stake out their own sociocultural as well as physical space. On the other hand, we know enough of modern colonial history to see how

readily the story of Judges 4–5 can be read from the perspective of Israel's dominance, all the more so as the theological framing ties the themes of Judges back to Joshua. The image in Judges is still one of recent arrivals, now pictured as a weaker/small group, trying to establish themselves in the midst of powerful but despised native inhabitants, inhabitants who have temporarily, but only temporarily, overrun the intruding outsiders. In such a reading, the colonized are again the Canaanites. Parallels are legion to modern stories of "settlers" who described themselves as "beleaguered," and to original inhabitants who have resented and resisted their presence. (Sakenfeld 2008: 14)

Uriah Kim, in the subtitle to his article (2007), asks the important question: "Who Is the Other in the Book of Judges?" He begins by stating that Western scholarship sees Judges as developing the national identity of Israel. "Other cultures have their own methods of narrating history and their own assumptions about the past" (170). Modern scholars thus do violence by the very act of constructing the Other. Judges shows competition among several nations for the land. These nations wanted to live in the land as much as did Israel. Kim exclaims: "The habit of equating the Rest with Israel's opposition and thereby vindicating the taking and exploiting of the land and its resources and the acts of hostility against the Rest needs to be stopped" (173).

Looking at identity, Kim sees the understanding of Israel as a matter of blood relationships and therefore "natural," as a complete blockage to incorporating the Other into Israel. The Israelite identity with the land was a major roadblock, since they had no natural ties to the land. They were admittedly outsiders. They had to build a theological tie in the absence of a natural one. Israel's separate tribes or groups united by seeing the Other as negative, as wanting to destroy Israel (175).

Judges sees the ongoing quest for identity but never gives a final answer. Too many individuals or groups are liminal or hybrid—tribes of Machir and Meroz; Jael, the murderer whose husband is treaty-bound to Jabin; Delilah; the Benjaminites; the Midianite soldier whose dream encourages Gideon; the Jebusites in Jerusalem.

One clear identifying boundary for Israel appears to be marriage inside the twelve tribes, but Samson quickly oversteps that rule, to be followed by David and Solomon. Kim concludes that Israel's identity is tied to maleness, women being a danger to neuter the sons of Israel (Kim 2007: 177–78).

In the Joshua narrative, landmarks and inscriptions also play their part; for each victory a monument of stones is erected (for Jericho, Josh. 7:26; for Ai, 8:29). These stones represent the narrative identity of Israel, an Israel that stands united in the narrative that the stones urge parents to relay to children. Such stones praise the God of victory and the fulfiller of promises. Yet such stones likewise reveal the hardship and violence Israel endured to take the land. Stones call Israel to unity in politics as well as in narrative. Israel fails to answer the call, being preoccupied with internal fighting and external defense. Israel faces many "Others." But who can, with surety, distinguish between colonizer and colonized in the narratives of the stones, and in the political reality of the hero narratives in Judges? Postcolonial criticism appears to invite scholars to a free-for-all slugfest in which traditional, Western theories and actions become wrong by definition while Eastern philosophy and method assuredly point the way out of the wilderness and into justice.

CONTEMPORARY INTERPRETERS

Taking all these complexities into consideration, we must conclude that Judges knows neither the identity of Israel nor the identity of the Other. Following the focus of Postcolonialism, Kim concludes with a current note: "Unless we see ourselves in the Other and see the Other in ourselves, we are in danger of repeating the habit of making enemies of our neighbors, representing the Other negatively in order to sanction our use of violence against them" (2007: 180).

And Prior adds: "Confrontation is thus legitimized by the group's authorities through creed and cult. This official sanction is ideological, drawing from violent models of the past, newly imagined as integral to their social representation in the present. Heroes and violent incidents of the past are recalled; epics recounted and martial songs sung to arouse primordial emotions. In such ways violence becomes ingrained in recurring patterns" (Prior 2006: 32).

This newcomer to postcolonial biblical study must, still, listen carefully to Musa Dube: "We cannot be neutral. Wherever we are located, we need to reexamine how our biblical and theological discourse works within the Postcolonial framework. Whatever methods we use in our studies, we need to ask how they address or how they do not address and why they remain silent toward Postcolonial realities of our world" (Dube 2004: 293). And we can conclude with Sakenfeld:

3

Teaching Bible Stories Critically

"They Did Not Spare a Soul"—The Book of Joshua in an Israeli Secular Education Environment

Yonina Dor and Naomi De-Malach

They cut down their populations with the sword until they exterminated them; they did not spare a soul. (Josh. 11:14)[1]

INTRODUCTION

The mind rebels against the cruel impression left by the story of Joshua's conquest of Canaan.[2] We cannot accept with equanimity the description of the Israelites' passage like a storm from town to town, slaughtering the residents, men and women, young and old, setting fire to their cities, sometimes hanging their kings, and then going on to the next stop in their march of victory (Joshua 1–12). And they do so with God's blessing and assistance and in fulfillment of the divine promise: "Every spot on which your foot treads I give to you" (Josh. 1:3). Those for whom respect of human rights is a supreme value find it extremely difficult to identify with this legacy. The worldview grounded on the chauvinistic axiom that the native population is monolithic, and that none of the original inhabitants should be allowed to survive, poses a moral problem that must be addressed. Should we teach the chapters of the book of Joshua that deal with the conquest in our schools? This question illustrates the dilemma that Bible teachers face when teaching chapters that are included in the standard curriculum but whose overt message offends their own worldview. A similar problem is posed by various other issues: the status of women postulated by

Gen. 3:16 ("and he shall rule over you"); the "double portion" allotted to the firstborn son (Deut. 21:17); the acceptance of slavery as part of the natural order; and so on. The problem is intensified when we are training teachers to teach these topics.

Among the primary goals of the Bible curriculum in Israel's state (secular) school system is the providing of pupils with knowledge of the Bible's content and an understanding of its heterogeneity, presenting diverse beliefs and opinions, and cultivating their ability to deal with the changes of opinions and values in it (Bible Curriculum 2003: 8, 10). In this essay we focus on the *ethical* dimension: not merely noting that values have changed but also positioning beliefs and views at the center of study, with their discussion being an educational opportunity for clarifying moral values and the meaning of justice. The approach presented in this essay can serve as a point of departure for dealing with questions of ethics and morality in the training of future Bible teachers and, after that, in the schools where they will teach.

In her study of the Bible's place in Israeli identity, Anita Shapira points out the back-and-forth movement in the perception of the Bible: originally a national and religious asset, Zionism turned it into a secular and cultural text with historical, literary, humanistic, and national dimensions. But after the (political) religious movements had begun to appropriate it to suit their own views, its status in Israeli society declined (Shapira 2006: 33). The archaeological digs at biblical sites, which used to be at the center of young people's search for their roots, have been replaced by trips to Poland.[3] In light of this analysis, Shapira asks in her conclusion whether it is possible to restore the Bible to the center of Hebrew culture.

We believe that the picture is more complex. Even though the status of the Bible in the schools has declined, it remains central to adult culture; there is a new vogue among the public at large of looking for links between the Bible and daily issues. Every weekend, the national newspapers offer their readers original homilies on the weekly Torah portion in the context of current events; every discussion of topics on the public agenda is spiced with insights and comparisons to biblical stories and characters. Many secular Israelis who are interested in the "Jewish bookshelf" participate in study groups; there are various programs involving Reform Judaism, and mixed religious and secular groups.[4] Works of literature and drama, and in the plastic arts too, are based on biblical stories and characters and turned into new confections on a regular basis. Moreover, various social-change movements in Israel and in the world draw on biblical passages when they formulate their worldviews.[5]

Is it conceivable that the schools—the main channel for the transmission of culture in Israel—will continue to teach biblical material as history, with an eye that is free of criticism, and ignore the unavoidable contexts of the present? The education of future teachers could play a key role in modifying the current situation, and serve as a lively public discourse about the Bible, current events, and Bible teaching in the schools.

The book of Joshua is a conspicuous case of a constitutive narrative that was once perceived as relevant to the fulfillment of Zionism, but whose plain meaning is now hard to accept. We will use it as a test case for problems related to teaching the Bible. We propose to present the concept of חרם (pronounced *cherem*, "proscription") and the account of its implementation as a lead-in to a reading of the narrative that is critical and subversive,[6] but nevertheless anchored in respect for the biblical texts in the context of their own age, with the goal of investigating their moral validity vis-à-vis the standards of our own day. The challenge is to construct—and deal boldly—a painful link between the most acute problems of our contemporary society and our problematic traditions. Without such a link, the Bible will remain remote and fossilized. With it, there can be an insightful discussion that shakes the dust off chapters of the Bible and restores them to the center of our culture.

In the first part of this essay, we will briefly survey the successive stages of attitudes toward the book of Joshua over the generations, starting with the talmudic sages and ending with contemporary thinkers, leaders, and educators. In the second section, we will examine the history of approaches to teaching the book of Joshua in state schools in Israel, looking at the curriculum and analyzing several items from the relevant textbooks. The core of our proposal, to be offered in the third part of the essay, is to conduct a *critical reading* of the book. On the one hand, we will express our fundamental opposition to the whole approach of the "Book of the Conquest" (Joshua 1–12); on the other hand, we will show that it is not monolithic and in fact harbors multiple voices. Finally, we will address the problems associated with teaching Joshua today and suggest a way to train teachers to do so through engaging in a critical and complex reading of the book and dealing head-on with the moral problems it raises.

THE SUCCESSIVE STAGES OF ATTITUDES TOWARD THE BOOK OF JOSHUA

Until the nineteenth century, the status of the book of Joshua as a historical document was unchallenged. Nowhere in the Bible do we find a direct expression of moral qualms about the fate of the original inhabitants of the land. The book of Joshua does not beat its breast over the extermination of the seven nations, but understands it as a means to guard the Israelites against the nations' corrupt mores and as the realization of divine injunction. Another implicit assumption of the book is that conquest by the sword conveys title to the land. Although this idea is not stated directly, the details of the various incidents during the conquest, the lists of the cities captured, and the sequence of events express it indirectly. This notion seems to have been axiomatic in the ancient world. But already among the talmudic sages there were voices that did not accept the conquest as a matter of course and felt a need to justify it, whether by means of a midrash stating that Joshua tried to persuade the Canaanites to accept his conditions—submit or emigrate peacefully—but they turned him down,[7] or by means of other ideas.[8] Contemporary commentators who demur at the idea of the proscription base themselves on these voices (Ben-Artzi 1986: 22–27; Greenberg 1986: 14–27; Simon 2002: 40–44; Ravitzky 1999: 145–48, 156–57). But the prevalent attitude justifies the violence wreaked on non-Jews then as now as required by the situation, despite the expressions of moral sensitivity about this point.[9] In our eyes, the common reliance on the homiletic solutions proposed by the talmudic sages and their heirs is inadequate. It is true that in some cases they offer inspiring alternatives; in many others, however, their explanations seem to be forced and unpersuasive. In any event, without denigrating the value of the oral law, we are working within the context of the Bible curriculum of the Israeli secular school system, in which the direct bond with the ancient and authentic text is the core of the pedagogic experience and the role of the exegetical tradition only secondary.[10]

In the pre-state era and the first years after independence, biblical narratives were the longed-for estate of Zionism. Intellectuals and educators such as Shaul Tchernichowsky and Ben-Zion Mossinson saw Joshua son of Nun as the hero of a people fighting for its land.[11] A possible explanation for this is the apparent simplicity of the book of Joshua, which provided emotional and ideological backing for Zionism, the conquest of the land, and the expulsion of its residents. David Ben-Gurion placed the book of Joshua at the very center of the Zionist ethos: "Moses was great, very great, but the true founder of the Jewish nation, the Israeli nation, was Joshua son of Nun" (Gvaryahu 1989: 71). And again, "No biblical commentator, Jewish or Gentile, in the Middle Ages or today, could have interpreted the chapters of Joshua as well as the valiant deeds of the Israel Defense Forces during the past year" (Meisler 1950: 123; Keren 1983: 67). This attitude fit in perfectly with the idea that "the Bible plays a decisive role of the first importance in creating the collective and individual inner language of our consciousness and unconsciousness" (Rosenberg 2003: 294). Leah Mazor has collected instructive examples from the Hebrew prose of the pre-state, and poetry and remarks by leaders and educators, that reflect the admiration for Joshua and his project of conquering the land that prevailed during that period and the first years after independence (Mazor 2003: 21–46). In those days, people ignored aspects such as whether there was justification for burning all the cities of the ancient inhabitants of the land, as described in the Bible; the killings and expulsions carried out during the War of Independence (1948–49) drew their inspiration from the book of Joshua.

Over the years, however, cracks began to appear in the myth of Joshua who set out to fulfill the prescription of Deuteronomy: "In the towns of the latter peoples . . . you shall not let a soul remain alive" (Deut. 20:16). The process began with intellectuals and educators. Martin Buber called not to accept what is found in the Bible if it runs counter to God's voice that resides in the human conscience.[12] Samuel Hugo Bergman (1970) stated unequivocally: "What shall a modern Jew do when confronted with a scriptural text that conflicts with his moral sense? . . . We have nothing better with which to defend man's most precious possession—his freedom and his responsibility—even if it is seems to be against God himself."[13] George Tamarin (1973) presented Jewish pupils with two conquest stories, one drawn from the book of Joshua and the other from a closely parallel account of his own invention about a fictional Chinese commander named Lin who supposedly lived three thousand years ago. He asked the pupils whether they believed that the conduct of the two military leaders was justified. He found that 60 percent of the pupils who received the biblical text fully justified Joshua's actions, but only 7 percent of those who received the "Chinese" text justified Lin's conduct (Tamarin 1973: 187). In the Israeli situation, identification with Joshua led to identification with his actions and lulled the pupils' exercise of their critical faculties. Drawing the lesson of his study, Tamarin warned against the danger inherent in reading the story of Joshua's conquests in its plain sense (183–90). Although he was interested in more general questions about the form of national education in Israel, his article insisted that the question of our relationship to the Bible in general and to the book of Joshua in particular should not be taken for granted.

After the Six Day War (June 1967), a vigorous debate erupted in Israel about the issue of the occupation of, and settlement in, inhabited areas. On one side were those who saw the Jewish settlements in Judea and Samaria as fulfilling the religious precept of settling the land and found support for that in the book of Joshua, with its ethos of taking possession of the land and eliminating its inhabitants. One exponent of this view was Rabbi Shlomo Aviner: "I thank you, Joshua, the conqueror of our land, for not getting involved in demography, but taking possession of our inheritance. . . . You were not afraid and you did not make excuses, and insisted on not conceding a single inch of our land. And you too, King David, the conqueror of our land, who completed all of our conquests" (Aviner 1982: 30).[14]

The other side was appalled by such moral depravity and continual assaults on the residents of the occupied territories. Here voices called attention to the fact that the concept of "proscription," which meant the extermination of the entire autochthonous population of the country, is violent and totally incompatible with the principles of a contemporary society that inscribes on its banner the values of pluralism, respect for others, and equal worth for all human beings.[15] Directly related to this, the attitude of the section of Joshua that recounts the conquest of the land, with its generalization, demonization of the Canaanites, and indifference to their humanity, was strongly censured. Teachers and public figures began expressing the fear that Joshua might serve as a crude spiritual guide to corroborate ideologies of violence. Moshe Greenberg put it very well:

> The most serious problem with teaching the book of Joshua in the schools is the danger that pupils may apply the message of the conquest narrative to our situation today: the Canaanite enemy equals the Arab enemy and the appropriate way to deal with it is by expulsion and extermination. This danger is so great that there is room for asking whether we are truly allowed to teach this book in our country today. . . . The evil in making the message of the book of Joshua contemporary is that if our pupils compare today's enemy with the Canaanites, the former will be viewed as the embodiment of absolute evil, with whom negotiations and peace are inconceivable. Such an attitude denies the divine image to an entire population, encourages and justifies an inhuman attitude towards it, and permits any cruel act towards it (in parallel to the biblical decree of proscription). In today's circumstances, it is only a short step from here to turning into beasts (Greenberg 1986: 15–16).

S. Yizhar was even more furious:

> The horrifying description in the book of Joshua, of how one inherits, dispossesses, and annihilates a people, and calls it "settlement." How can one people have the right to dispossess

another people and inherit its land? And why is there an obligation to exterminate a people living on the soil of its homeland?

This is the extreme of radical fanaticism that has been known throughout history. And not only among us. At one time it was the Catholic Inquisition, while at some other time it is radical Islam that is gaining strength. On the other hand, borders are being opened today throughout Western Europe and the boundaries that used to exist between countries that massacred millions in this very century are being abolished: it is happening and it is possible. . . . This is why, with all my might, I rise up in revolt against Joshua!

. . . The Holocaust did not put an end to Jewish fanaticism and the ability to invade the village of Silwan, to throw Arab residents out of their homes into the streets . . . and to dance there with a Torah scroll . . . with the book of Joshua. . . . And the book of Joshua flutters above these Jews. . . . There are no goals that justify killing people or taking their property only because I am stronger (Yizhar 1993: 149–51).[16]

The line that Yizhar drew between several cases of enslavement and genocide in various cultures and the influence of the account of Joshua's extermination of the Canaanites comes up from time to time in these and similar contexts. Horrendous historical examples of the influence of the biblical ideology can teach us about its inherent dangers because of either its problematic nature, or the abusive use of biblical ideas in various times and spaces.[17] The Open University of Israel, too, addresses the topic. The syllabus for its course on genocide includes units on the genocide in Rwanda, by Nazi Germany, against the Armenians, and others. The first chapter is titled "Genocide in the Bible."[18] In addition, the linkage between the problems raised by the stories of the Joshua conquest and proscription and their relevance in the stormy situation of Israel today, as noted by Greenberg and Yizhar, requires us to deal with the narrative about the career of Joshua son of Nun.[19]

Since the 1980's, there has been a growing interest in the morality of the Bible in international academic studies, various Catholic circles, and among intellectuals.[20] Kasher (2006) suggests several explanations for this phenomenon.[21] To these we would add the political situation in the Middle East, especially after the Six Day War. Despite the rise of interest in moral issues among biblical scholars in Israel and abroad, the topic remains far from the center of Bible studies. Most scholars prefer to focus on the interpretation of the biblical text, its sources, and its editorial history, rather than on its moral validity

(Clines 1997: 23). It may be assumed that this influences how teachers approach the Bible in their classrooms, as we shall discuss below.

The awakening of general interest in problems of morality and the Bible has amplified the need to explain the concept of proscription in Joshua. Although some contemporary Bible scholars have viewed the conquest narrative as historical fact (Malamat 1969: 1:51–64 [Hebrew] = 1976: 1:47–66 [English]; Kaufmann 1970: 61–62), most scholars try to explain away the apparent genocide in various ways. Some take it as self-evident that there has been a change in ideologies and values over the generations, and try to understand proscription in the context of the ideology of that period (Niditch 1993: 58–61). Others explain that the biblical precept of proscription was rooted in concepts of the ancient world that were found among many peoples.[22] In historical and archaeological scholarship, the current consensus is that the account of the storming and conquest of Canaan, as found in Joshua, is without factual basis.[23] It is generally accepted that the description of the total conquest of the land in a single campaign is based on the reworking of fragmentary ancient traditions and fictional additions, in light of the national-religious ideology of the deuteronomistic editor, who presents any contact with foreign nations as a source of assimilation and idolatry. A battle was being waged for national identity; the most extreme manifestation of this view was the fanatical idea that it would have been better to exterminate the Canaanites once and for all.[24] However, even though the mentality of the deuteronomistic editor left its strong imprint on the Bible, including on Joshua 1–12, his is not the only attitude. Other biblical sources (such as Joshua 13–19 and Judges 1–3) tell a different story and attest to the gradual infiltration of Canaan by the Israelite tribes.

A plausible explanation of the origins of the ideology of proscription is the Israelites' weakness in the period when Deuteronomy and then Joshua were composed. The aspiration to rule over and destroy the enemy was realized by an imaginary story of the conquest of the land in a single campaign (Amit 1986: 21). This gave retrospective expression to the belief that had their ancestors acted as they should have in the distant past and exterminated all of the previous inhabitants, those foreign nations would not have been able to lead Israel into sin and there would have been no grounds for its later punishment and suffering. This idealization of an imaginary past constitutes a sort of acceptance of the justice of the Israelite nation's suffering at the time the story was composed. Moreover, the texts were intended chiefly as a strict warning against any contact with foreign ways.[25] But, in contrast to the radical notion that the Canaanites must be destroyed, the weight of humanistic values in the Bible far exceeds that of the precept of proscription. The manifestations of biblical humanism associated with our topic include the law that mandates equality for foreigners and even love for the stranger (e.g., Deut. 10:19 and 25:17) and the call to absorb foreigners into Israel and admit them to its society (e.g., Isa. 2:2-3, 56:6-7).[26] Nevertheless, none of these explanations diminishes the significance of the problem. On the contrary, they actually amplify it: if the precept of genocide was never realized or applied, and if it was intended merely to serve other ideas, why then did proscription acquire canonical status? And, seeing that it did, how are we to relate to it?

HOW THE BOOK OF JOSHUA IS TAUGHT IN THE ISRAELI STATE SYSTEM

The place of Joshua in the Israeli mind is largely determined by the state education system. The extensive selections from the book that were included in the curriculum in bygone decades have been trimmed back over the years. The fourth-grade Bible syllabus for 1922–1923 included Joshua 1–11, 14, 18:1-10, 20, and 22-24 (Yonai 1997: 35). The curricula of 1949–1950, 1955–1957, and later years specifies that the book be studied in three grades—fourth, eighth, and tenth (68–70). Later, the number of chapters studied was reduced further. The curriculum introduced in 2003 (and updated in August 2005) assigns limited space to the book, which continues to receive substantial attention only in elementary school (up to and including the sixth grade). In the fourth grade, twenty-two class sessions are allotted to the book, covering most of chapters 1–11, as well as chapters 14 and 24 (Bible Curriculum 2003: 39). The selection of verses reveals an intentional evasion of the blunt descriptions about the inhabitants of Canaan's annihilation. For example, Joshua 11:14 (cited as the epigram to this article) was not included in the syllabus. In junior high school, the curriculum required intensive classroom teaching only of Joshua 1. Chapters 2, 6, and 9 were to be studied in the form of directed reading, with the pupils learning on their own, followed by a general classroom summary in one or two sessions (58 and 64). Yairah Amit, who headed the team that devised this Bible curriculum, was not happy with this drastic reduction. She explains that it was a compromise between the book's necessary inclusion as a chapter in biblical history and the cutback in the number of class sessions imposed on the curriculum authors.[27]

Thus the curriculum emphasizes the conquest narratives that end in compromise (Jericho and Gibeon). Except for the fall of Jericho, it ignores the extermination that dominates the conquest chapters.[28] The book is totally absent from the required subject curriculum for senior high school. The elective unit called "Battle for a Moral Society" ignores it; in "Law and Society in the Bible: Characteristics, Values, and Dilemmas," the law of proscription is mentioned, but the heading "additional biblical sources" does not include any references to its implementation in Joshua. By contrast, the Bible curriculum focuses on the link between the text and its near and more remote contexts in the Bible (9)—and surely there is a link between the law and its implementation. The suggestions of what pupils can do to earn a fifth credit in Bible (the highest credit for any matriculation subject), an interdisciplinary project of some sort, do not mention Joshua. It seems, however, that the embarrassment occasioned by the book's messages was a factor in the reduction, and that the elimination of the proscription stories is an attempt to get around the moral problem. The curricula, workbooks, and textbooks we looked at can give us a feel for how the book is taught today.

The first attempt to survey the place of Joshua in elementary school textbooks was by Galia Zalmanson, who examined three textbooks.[29] In her article, she shows how the books ignore the moral issues associated with the brutality of the conquest and deal almost exclusively with its military aspects. In addition, they blur the difference between the boundaries of the land of Israel in the past and the current boundaries of the state of Israel, and employ the phrase "The Promise Land" as if its meaning is obvious, both then and now. Zalmanson criticizes the way the books develop an analogy between the behavior of Joshua's army and the modern Israeli Defense Forces, without recognition of the moral danger inherent in such an analogy. After looking at these books and several others,[30] we found corroboration for her arguments and identified some more tendencies in the current crop of textbooks:

1. It is clear that the textbooks' authors made a great effort to interest pupils in the biblical world and to stimulate their identification with it by means of diverse appeals to the pupils' imagination, inviting them to picture life in ancient times. For most authors, however, the world of the past is exclusively that of the Israelites. For example, Parida and Sela's textbook (2004: 9, 78, 93) has a recurrent feature titled "Chen imagines" (this heading rhymes in Hebrew: *Chen Me'damyen*). Chen (a Hebrew personal name) imagines that he sees Joshua mourning Moses' death, that Joshua's will has been found in an archaeological excavation, and that he is a military correspondent embedded in the Israelite forces and reporting on the battle of Gibeon ("we didn't have time to kill all of them," he writes). Chen never imagines that he is a Canaanite, a Gibeonite, or a citizen of Jericho. We found a similar attitude in other books that we looked at, although to a slightly lesser extent.[31] As a rule, so far as the textbook authors are concerned, it seems to be enough for the pupils to identify with the ancient

Israelites and with the hegemonic voice in Joshua; there is no need to listen to the other voices that might rise from the book and to try to understand them as well. Moreover, when books do mention non-Israelite characters, no mercy is shown to them. Eliah Shahor's book (1996) highlights the cruel sequence of abuse that Joshua wreaks on the captive kings, beginning with treading on their necks and ending with killing them, hanging their corpses from a tree, and, finally, tossing their bodies into a cave and sealing its entrance. Shahor asks why Joshua was not content with merely throwing their bodies into the cave, and answers:

> Yes, Joshua could have done that. Had he killed them and tossed aside their bodies, it would have been an act of humiliation. But this was not enough for Joshua, who wanted to humiliate these kings even more. We may assume that Joshua wanted to demonstrate the power and glory of the Israelites to other kings in Canaan. He wanted the killing and humiliation of the kings to show the other rulers of Canaan what they could expect if they attempted to fight against Joshua and the Israelites. (Shahor 1996: 211)

Shahor's sangfroid when analyzing these events is troubling. He explains that killing the kings was not enough to terrify the others. Hence it was appropriate to torture and humiliate them while they were still alive and then to put their corpses on public display.

2. As Zalmanson notes, the textbooks direct pupils' attention to linguistic phenomena, geographic details, and military strategy, but evade the moral questions raised by the text.[32] For example, Keren (2002: 50, 60, 92) offers questions for discussion that deal with the advantages and disadvantages of besieging the town, the punishment meted out to Achan, and the southern Canaanite kings' decision to attack Gibeon but not Gilgal. She takes the right to dispossess and annihilate the residents for granted. A similar attitude can be found in the book by Yehudit and Oded Lipschits (2000). At the climax of the story about the conquest of Jericho—"then they utterly destroyed all in the city, both men and women, young and old, oxen, sheep, and asses, with the edge [lit., the mouth] of the sword" (Josh. 6:21 [RSV])—the point Lipschits and Lipschits choose to focus on is the meaning of the term לפי חרב (*lephi cherev*, "with the mouth of the sword"; 2000: 61). The authors engage in a fine and interesting discussion of whether a sword has a mouth, but do not propose a classroom discussion of the actual meaning of the verse. So too with the battle of Ai: they make interesting points about tactics and about the story's ahistorical

nature and propose a creative project—publishing a class newspaper. But there is not a single word about the crux of the story—the slaughter of all the city residents (74–78).

3. When, nevertheless, the textbooks do get into moral issues, the focus is apologetics rather than on a discussion of the story. An example is how they deal with the issue of proscription. Rivka Hagag makes do with a general note about the pupils' assignment: "Talk about the topic of proscription" (Hagag 2004: 97). The other books that take up the issue attempt to justify it; most of them rely on the argument that it was common practice at the time (Parida and Sela 2004: 67; Korach-Segev and Silberman 1994: 42; Tirosh and Geller-Talitman 2000: 51); the implication is that this suffices to justify the proscription. Lipschits and Lipschits delve deeper into the subject and add an explanation: "The main purpose of the law of proscription is to keep the Israelites from intermarrying with the residents of Canaan, to keep them from learning their customs and religion, and to keep them from mixing with them." And again, "It is important to know that the law of proscription was never implemented in full and that diverse groups continued to live in various parts of the Land of Israel" (Lipschits and Lipschits 2000: 59). The presentation of the proscription issue as it relates to Jericho focuses from the outset on resolving the problem. The learned explanation neutralizes any authentic encounter with the topic.[33]

In general, we found that the textbooks are aware only of the hegemonic voice in Joshua, and are quick to offer apologetics for the moral problems raised by the story. They all share the belief that experiential teaching can cover up their evasion of value clarification and discussion of moral issues. A precondition for augmenting the focus on moral issues is for those who train teachers to prepare future teachers for a critical reading of the textbooks they will be using in their classes. Education students must be provided with tools for selecting what they consider appropriate supplementary texts for dealing with moral content, or to bolster this aspect of their teaching when the textbooks are deficient. The curriculum and the textbooks' evasion, as well as the diminished attention to Joshua in schools and the removal of sections that we find unpleasant today, runs strongly counter to the interest that the book continues to arouse in educational research. It is essential that we augment consideration of this question in light of the trend, dominant today, of promoting the teaching of leading texts using a dynamic and critical approach that spurs a pluralistic ethical discussion, with human beings at its center (Alpert 2002: 21–25). Intellectuals, scholars, educators, and teachers who care are looking for a relevant way to deal with the narratives of the conquest of Canaan in Joshua. It behooves the education system, too, to participate.

Another Way of Reading of the Book of Joshua

We would like to offer an example of dealing with controversial texts. To do so, we will propose two related readings of Joshua that can be included in training teachers. On the one hand, ours is a critical reading that presents the violent conquest as immoral, while explaining its reasons and background; on the other hand, it is a subversive reading, one that seeks to lay bare the conflicting forces at work within the book itself and to present the text as complex rather than one-dimensional. By "critical reading," we mean a reading that goes against the grain:[34] a reading that does not stick to its guns but actually points out the errors in its own path, does not accept its own values (or at least not all of them), and sometimes even opposes them. This method of critically reading values, characters, and actions described in various texts and the way the text presents them is well known. We can always find critics who choose to read against the text, not only with it. Feminists read against masculine texts; Marxists and neo-Marxists read against writings that support the class structure; postcolonialists read against the image of the East; and so on.[35] The Bible invites a critical reading;[36] the classical commentators did not hesitate to express negative judgments of exemplary figures and their values, seeing such criticism as an expression of humanity that did not undermine the love of Israel.[37] When we join these critical voices, we want to expose the bias with which Joshua presents the Other as subhuman, inferior beings unworthy of living on the soil destined for Israel. The outdated values that lie beneath the text may have represented our ancestors, but they no longer speak to us. We are bound to come out against them when we see them as expressions of arrogance and oppression. There is nothing new in a critical reading of this sort, including of Joshua. As S. Yizhar wrote in this context: "This is why, with all my might, I rise up in revolt against Joshua!"[38]

We must recognize, however, that it would be wrong and unfair to expect to find correspondence between our contemporary values and texts that were written thousands of years ago. When we read a text composed more than two millennia in the past, we must accept that its values cannot coincide with our own. Over time, many other texts have been devised and written, worldviews have changed, and reciprocal influence between Jewish culture and world cultures has evolved, leading to vast philosophical changes. Another problem arises from the fact that, for Jewish pupils in the state of Israel, the Bible is not just a book like any other. The Bible is the cradle of our civilization; its story is understood as constitutive of our history, and Joshua son of Nun is one of our ancient leaders. Some see this link as direct and substantial; others view it symbolically. But both groups see the Bible as the constitutive ethos of the Jewish people.

So we cannot shrug off this issue and approach the text as if we were going to read some foreign literature, as many have proposed, including Zakovitch, who writes seemingly innocently, and with perhaps a certain willful naïveté: "I am unable to know or understand the barrier that faces teachers when they teach the book of Joshua. Do we teach only literature with which, and with its values, we feel total identity? Do we hide our faces from great literature that expresses a different outlook than our own?" (Zakovitch 2003: 13–14). When it comes to dealing with this dilemma, we prefer Daniel Boyarin's approach in his study on sexuality in the Talmud. Boyarin describes the tension between his criticism, as a modern feminist, of the talmudic concepts of the body and sexuality, on the one hand, and his identification with Judaism and its texts as a rabbinic Jew, on the other. He proposes resolving this tension by means of the term "generous critique." Instead of apologetics, we need to exercise criticism of the Other "from the perspective of the desires and needs of the here and now, without reifying that Other or placing myself in judgment over him or her in his or her there and then" (Boyarin 1995: 21). Following Boyarin, we propose to employ the method of "generous critique" in our reading of Joshua: as part of our culture, but a part that requires demurring at some of its implications. We will avoid apologetics, but will go beyond criticism and try to understand the reasons that led the Bible's authors to write what they did in the way they did. In our eyes, both *critique* and *generous* are expressions of familiarity: it is precisely our sense of participation in the Jewish tradition that rouses our need to criticize, but the criticism is mixed with sympathy and generosity because it comes from the inside.

Still, it is not enough to oppose the text, even generously, because doing so ignores its complexities. Commentators and scholars have dealt with the polyphony of opinions in the Bible and proposed ways to resolve their contradictions. The talmudic sages and the classical commentators resolved contradictions by means of their learned homiletic method. Although the dominant voice in textual studies today explains Bible contradictions as the result of the fusion of multiple sources and levels of editing, we still hear the idea that the text must be taken as a single work that, by the nature of its creation, incorporates different voices (Cohen 1999: 66). In contrast to Jones (1999: 188), who defines the narrator of Joshua as "neutral," we see him rather as a complex author, vacillating and conflicted with himself. This author cannot hide that he is presenting a text that has gone through a process of revision—with material inserted, deleted, and reworked—and that includes contradictory elements that pull in different directions, some reinforcing the book's dominant voice while others working against it. Critics who start from different viewpoints note that a text is not only the herald of hegemony, but also part of the battles between competing forces; it is not only a "conduit of power," but also "a site of struggle and contestation" (Ryan 1989: 202). Commentators have applied different names to this phenomenon. Gershon Galil and Yair Zakovitch (1994: 12–13, 124) define it as direct or indirect criticism of Joshua. Menachem Peri speaks of the counter story latent in biblical narratives as participating in conflicts between ideologies: "The biblical story is an arena of dialogism . . . of conflicting human agendas" (Peri 2005: 193). Yairah Amit (2000: 45–91) finds "hidden polemics" that can be exploited for the analysis of biblical stories. In order to deal with the different voices, Elaine Showalter (1986: 266) proposes a double reading of every text: to absorb the dominant tale, but also to look for the story that has been stifled. A counter-reading exposes the power mechanisms and opposes them, whereas a subversive reading joins with the forces of opposition latent in the text itself and amplifies their voices.

One way of dealing with the tension between our values and past values is to listen closely to the text and consider whether, beneath its uniform surface, there might be voices of protest that undermine the hegemonic outlook it proclaims. We attempt to reconstruct the power struggles reflected by the patchwork text in front of us, to widen the cracks that appear in its uniform facade, and to extract through them the statement that has been silenced. Although we will not go so far as to assert that the polyphony makes it impossible to identify the dominant voice, we will try to hear and amplify the voices that the text "tries" to stifle or erase, to reinforce the voices of criticism and the challenges to the text that emerge from the text itself.

It may be difficult to combine critical, subversive teaching with the goal of inspiring love for and identification with the people of ancient Israel as depicted in the Bible. In fact, a complex attitude exists at the foundation of every authentic intimacy, since love must always include recognition of the loved one's flaws. Despite the difficulty, we believe that an ethical approach to the ancient source contributes to its vitality. By contrast, ignoring the dilemma and flattening the story to leave only remote and irrelevant information distances it from the heart. In what follows, we will provide an example of another reading of several cruxes in Joshua, outlining a way of teaching texts that stimulates perplexity and disagreement.

1. "THEY CUT DOWN THEIR POPULATIONS WITH THE SWORD UNTIL THEY EXTERMINATED THEM" (JOSH. 11:14): DID THEY REALLY?

Joshua 1–12 describes the conquest of Canaan as cruel and absolute, in accordance with the divine ordinance: "They cut down their populations with the sword until they exterminated them; they did not spare a soul" (Josh. 11:14). This implies utter proscription and slaughter of every human being—man and woman, young and old: extermination, burning, hanging, and destruction.[39] These cruel descriptions are embedded in a picture of a swift and total conquest carried out by the Israelites as a united force. The entire country is taken by storm, following a clear geographical order: starting in the center, moving to the southern hills, then turning to the cities of the north: "Joshua took all that land: the hill country [of Judah], the Negeb, the whole land of Goshen, the Shephelah, the Arabah, and the hill country and coastal plain of Israel. . . . Apart from the Hivvites who dwelt in Gibeon, not a single city made terms with the Israelites; all were taken in battle" (Josh. 11:16, 19 [NJPS modified]). Although this maximalist picture hardly seems to be realistic, it has been firmly planted in the national imagination for generations, because a people's worldview is determined not only by historical facts but also by picturesque scenes and dramatic stories that speak directly to the heart. That the picture of Joshua burning down the cities on top of their inhabitants, one after another, was included in the Bible gives it the status of a classic tale. Against this background, questions such as how nomadic tribes could overcome an organized and settled population, or what interest they could have had in burning everything, if their goal was to settle down in the land, fade into the background.

The incident of the Gibeonites (the Hivvites) provides evidence of an alternative tradition that challenges the picture of total conquest found in Joshua 1–12. We read that the people of Gibeon deceive Joshua and the elders (Joshua 9). Their ambassadors say that they have come on a long journey and explain their interest in concluding an alliance with Israel by the remoteness of their country. Joshua and the elders believe their story and make a pact with them. Soon, however, they discover that these people actually live nearby and have lied to extort the oath not to attack them. Now Joshua is bound by his oath not to harm them. Gibeon is the supreme example of how the land's ancient inhabitants adapted themselves to the new situation of Israelite control. Its residents were enslaved and continued to live in Israel for generations; they were even among those who returned from the Babylonian exile (Neh. 7:25). The picturesque details of the Gibeonites' ploy are a means to explain their survival among the Israelites for generations at the lowest rung of the temple servitors, as "hewers of wood and drawers of water" (Josh. 9:27). The legendary nature of this etiological tale explaining the Hivvites' survival undermines its historical credibility. It is quite impossible to ignore the disproportion between the piety and righteousness of Joshua and the elders, who did not dare go back on their oath to the Gibeonites, and the ease with which they burn down cities on top of their inhabitants, with no signs of hesitation. Gibeon is presented as exceptional among the towns of Canaan; the text notes explicitly that, of all the Canaanites, the Gibeonites alone survived among the Israelites (11:19). But the exception proves the rule: even though the Gibeonites were saved from extermination, the presentation of their case as a one-time deviation reinforces the dominance of the proscription model.

Similar ambivalence, but in the opposite direction, is provided by Rahab's fate against the background of the destruction of Jericho. Although Jericho was torched and its residents massacred, thereby fully realizing the proscription, the fate of Rahab and her family interferes with this picture and reveals a different reality: the acceptance, for many generations to come, of a Canaanite family living in Israel. Elsewhere in Joshua, in Judges 1–3, and throughout the rest of the Bible, we encounter a picture of close and troubled proximity between Israelites and Canaanites: independent confrontations by each tribe with its enemies, local wars, and the subjugation of towns and tribal units beside a two-way cultural influence and intermarriages, condemned by the prophets. This complex picture supports an understanding of gradual Israelite settlement in the county. It indicates that the land was not conquered in a single war under Joshua's leadership; nor was all of it even conquered by Israel. Many Canaanites were defeated and killed, but others survived alongside the Israelites, became serfs, and continued to live in their towns. As time went by, Israelite units consolidated in the country, forged by the continual warfare against the peoples of Canaan (Ahituv 1996: 40–41; Galil and Zakovitch 1994: 22–31; Na'aman 2006: 8–19; Finkelstein and Silberman 2001: 105–18). As these new groups, later to be known as "Israel," coalesced, they experienced processes of assimilation into the local environment. The campaign for isolation from the surrounding cultures led to the formation of a separate and distinct Israelite society. The dominant position in Bible studies and historical and archaeological scholarship is that the model of gradual occupation is factual, whereas the picture of an almost instant conquest and proscription is a retrospective ideology imposed by the new ideas of Deuteronomy, which ordains the destruction of all the ancient peoples of Canaan. This can be explained as a reaction, accepting the justice of one's fate: because they failed to exterminate the autochthonous peoples, Israel was punished by a perpetual and existential religious conflict with them. This actually strengthens the view that there is a solid basis for interpolations that subvert the hegemonic text (with its account of conquest and proscription), such as the stories of the Gibeonites and of Rahab.

On balance, weighing the extermination model of entire native populations against that of their enslavement by and assimilation into Israel, the second seems to be less cruel. But one can also raise for critical consideration the question of whether assimilation of minorities into a majority or dominant culture is something we deem appropriate today. The contrast with the multicultural ideal of our age affords us another opportunity to shed light on the gulf between past and present values. We may lessen the contradiction between the idea of proscription for all towns on the one hand and that of gradual settlement on the other, and see the ghastly description of the proscription and total extermination as a radical and excessive overstatement of a normal conquest mode, a view already mentioned with regard to the successive stages of modern attitudes toward Joshua. This, too, is unsatisfactory, but at least is not as cruel and radical as the descriptions of Joshua 6–12. Both stories—the destruction of Jericho (chapters 2 and 6) and the enslavement of the Gibeonites (chapter 9)—represent one of the two models of the Israelites' gaining control of the country. Although each of the two sections of Joshua is marked by a uniform stand—proscription in the Book of Conquest (chapters 1–12), gradual settlement in the Book of Inheritance (chapters 13–19)—these stories of Rahab and the Gibeonites offer two contradictory but synchronous elements: destruction and enslavement. In Jericho, the precept of proscription is realized, but the door is left open to the admission of Rahab and her descendants into the people of Israel. In Gibeon, the people are enslaved rather than proscribed, but the sense of the missed opportunity to kill them resounds through the chapter. These two stories raise the fierce dilemma between the obligation to exterminate the peoples of Canaan without exception and fidelity to other commitments to human beings and to God. The fact that two stories of compromise with the ancient inhabitants of the land are included in the Book of Conquest, which emphasizes proscription, reflects the fierce tension about the treatment of the ancient inhabitants of the land.

2. A MANTLE OF RIGHTEOUSNESS

Any manifestation of violence that causes human suffering and the loss of human life stirs our opposition and can be accepted only if related to the protection of human life. The tendency to obscure and suppress any discussion of the legitimacy of violence is dangerous. The first chapter of Joshua presents the vision of the ancient Israelites' seizure of the land from its ancient inhabitants in a very "pure" and elegant fashion. The phrase "every spot on which your foot treads I give to you, as I promised Moses" (Josh. 1:3) represents the miracle of the occupation of the land as a gift of divine grace. The verb נתן (n-t-n Qal, "give") is repeated eight times in this chapter (vv. 2, 3, 6, 11, 13, 14, 15´2); but the phrases "armed" (חמשים, chamushim) and "fighting men" (גבורי החיל, gibborey hachayil; v. 14) hint at a tradition of warfare. Why should there be any need for weapons and warriors if one only has to set foot in a place in order to acquire it? The notion of the land as gift serves as a gentle introduction to the brutal continuation, which describes the seizure of the land by force and the extermination of its inhabitants. This dynamic is also found in the war with the kings of the South (ch. 10). The verse that we all learned by heart in childhood—"Stand still, O sun, at Gibeon, O moon, in the Valley of Aijalon!" (10:12)—is grand and vivid. Our attention is focused on the extraordinary miracle and the poetry. But we must not ignore the fact of what the miracle is intended to leave time for—"Joshua captured Makkedah on that day and put it and its king to the sword, proscribing it and every person in it and leaving none that escaped" (10:28 [NJPS modified])—and that the same fate is meted out to all the other cities of the South. Even if the biblical narrator was not disturbed by the contrast between the sublime rhetoric and the brutal slaughter, we are. The picture of the land of Israel as gift, set against the background of the lofty and elevating atmosphere of the miraculous opening, as if rivers of blood are not shed in the process, is an illusion. It is merely a mantle of righteousness intended to cover up the cruel core of the story in order to make it palatable.

3. THE CHARACTERIZATION OF JOSHUA

The presentation of Joshua, too, shatters the perfect façade that chapter 1 pastes on the conquest of Canaan. Joshua, as depicted in chapter 1, is a man endowed with every virtue: a warrior, bold and courageous, Moses' heir and counterpart, a Torah scholar, enjoying the support of God and the support of the people, and obeyed by all. Later, too, he resembles Moses by working miracles and winning victories: the crossing of the Jordan (3:9–14); his encounter with the captain of the divine host (5:13–15); the zenith—when the sun and moon obey his command; and, summing up, "Joshua took all that land" (11:16–20 [NJPS modified]). But a critical voice that undercuts Joshua and highlights his failings creeps into the stories about Jericho and Gibeon. What, after all, is the justification for the detailed account of the spies and their adventure with Rahab? Was there any point to their espionage? After all, Jericho fell by a miracle; the intelligence-gathering operation initiated by Joshua was superfluous. The only significant point is the heavy price exacted by the commitment to allow a Canaanite family to survive, in violation of the divine injunction. And Joshua is the father of that failure.[40]

So too with the episode of the Gibeonites. The pact with them is presented as a searing, one-time failure: the Israelites do not proscribe the four Gibeonite cities. Why do they fail to verify the Gibeonites' story? Why are they so quick to eat of their provisions and not to ask the Lord for guidance? How can someone who has no problem burning down city after Canaanite city be so easily deterred from breaching a verbal commitment to an enemy that deceives him so shamelessly? The story blames these failures on the leaders. Joshua has what may be called ministerial responsibility for the debacle; or, worse yet, he is unable to impose his authority on the elders and tribal chiefs. One can see this implied criticism as the mark of an author who wanted to undermine Joshua's unblemished image[41] (and see also Zakovitch 2003: 17).

4. RAHAB

Another crack in the conventional view of the conquest results from the presentation of Rahab. The dominant pattern in Joshua never individualizes Canaanites. To a man and woman, they are all passive pieces on the chessboard, intended only to serve as extras in the epic of the Lord's victories on behalf of Israel. Rahab, though, is portrayed as an individual, with abundant details about her behavior, dialogue, and advice to the spies. With the exception of the kings of the city-states, she is the only minor character in the Book of Conquest who is given a name. On the one hand, she speaks for the local population and reveals their frame of mind in light of the Israelite invasion; on the other hand, her first concern is to save her family and father's house. The author even assigns the high praise for the God of Israel (2:9-11) to a harlot, of all people, as another indication of her quality and to widen the crack in the otherwise unchallenged negative depiction of non-Israelites. That someone so impressive is a citizen of Jericho undermines the book's trivial and undifferentiated stereotype of the Canaanites. Rahab's indirect characterization also challenges the conventional notion of the harlot. *Targum Jonathan*, which renders the Hebrew word *zonah* as a "vendor of food," may have been accepted by the medieval commentators; but we hold to the standard meaning of the word, "harlot or prostitute."[42] At first sight, her presentation as a harlot is degrading; but despite this profession, which the Bible always deems contemptible, Rahab is depicted as a woman of power and responsibility. She is a vivid character, intelligent and respected. She overshadows the spies, who are pallid, weak, and lacking in initiative, and who accept all of her ideas and conditions. Not only is she a Canaanite and harlot, but Rahab is also a woman. Thus she also departs from the common biblical model of the passive woman who figures only in her familial and sexual role.

5. THE TREATMENT OF THE GIBEONITES

The guile of the Gibeonites, who manage to preserve themselves against the Israelite onslaught, is held to their discredit by readers predisposed to pass harsh judgment on the autochthonous residents of the land. Such readers will be favorably impressed by the fidelity to their word exhibited by Joshua and the elders and accept it as a sign of respect for the name of the Lord they invoke in their oath. The imposition of perpetual servitude on the Gibeonites is viewed as appropriate punishment for their deceit. It is possible, however, to subvert the ostensibly self-understood and to extract from chapter 9 admiration for the Gibeonites as the only Canaanite group not exterminated by the Israelites and who manage to survive in their four cities. Shechem was also a Hivvite town, and that important city, too, had a special destiny, in that it was never conquered and Joshua convened the Israelites there to institute a covenant (ch. 24).

It is true that the tasks imposed on the Gibeonites in the temple—drawing water and hewing wood—were among the lowliest. Nevertheless, temple servitors, of whatever level, were always viewed with respect in Israel. One proof of this is the explicit references to them in the Priestly writings and in the literature of the Second Temple period.[43] Surely the message conveyed by the Gibeonites' survival among the Israelites "to this very day" undermines the strong consensus that there is no place in Israel for the Hivvites and other locals. This point could lead into a discussion of the status of minorities in biblical Israel and in every human society.

To sum up, what can we infer from unraveling the traditional concepts strongly anchored in the national consciousness, from the challenge to the conventional notions, and from the exposure of other possibilities? We think that the advantage of a subversive reading is, first of all, that it highlights the fact that every text may say more than one thing. The goal is to extract the text's multiple aspects and full complexity. By this we do not mean arriving at a bottom line or unambiguous truth, but listening to the inner dialogue beneath the text and leaving room for submerged voices that do not represent the norm or the dominant view. A subversive reading is compatible with the Jewish mode of study, impressively represented in the Talmud, and practiced in the *yeshivot* and *batei midrash*. The method is based on sharpening disagreements, contradictions, and arguments, with the goal of clarifying issues and not necessarily reaching a conclusion (see, for example, Ta-Shma 2006: 80–84). One must not deny the coarse and unpleasant nature of the dominant ethos in Joshua; but the foregoing examples demonstrate that there are other and subversive voices speaking between the lines of the story about the annihilation of the Canaanites.

ANOTHER WAY OF TEACHING THE BOOK OF JOSHUA

The training of future Bible teachers for Israeli secular schools is based on the secular-scientific worldview prevalent in academic institutions. Sometimes the students are comfortable with this outlook; sometimes they are torn between it and the traditional values on which they were raised and which are accepted by their pupils or upheld by their superiors in the school. Sometimes teachers set aside criticism because of their respect for the unifying cultural value of constitutive traditions, sensitivity toward pupils from traditional families, or the wish to stay out of trouble (Dor and Yaniv 2004: 17–56). The fear of getting entangled in disagreements is not unique to teachers of the Bible. In her study of education for peace, Devorah Kalkin-Fishman found that the discourse of Israeli teachers is close to that of the hegemonic ideology and that they make maximum effort to steer clear of conflict (Kalkin-Fishman 2002: 108–10). It may be assumed that teachers find it easier to survive in the system if they avoid sensitive issues, including political ones, given that it may be risky to express an opinion in areas where there are political disagreements such as the treatment of Arabs. But the system must not preserve a consensus of silence on controversial issues, because the real challenge is posed precisely by a discussion of what is not self-understood. In the training of teachers, it is important to examine the coherence and unity of the message of each text, to subject the narrative to criticism, and, when necessary, to be bold enough to reject a message that seems to be outmoded.

Only a few chapters of Joshua are included in the post-primary curriculum: this is a given factor. Some schools choose not to teach any part of Joshua; many teachers devote only one or two class sessions to the book in order to fulfill the minimum requirement.[44] The question of whether it is appropriate to teach the book, given its messages, continues to trouble the public at large.[45] This issue needs to be discussed when teachers are learning how to teach the Bible; Joshua can serve as an instructive example of the constant vacillation about selecting chapters that are appropriate for pupils to study. Our position is that despite the strong temptation to eliminate from curriculum and teaching these ancient stories that collide with our worldview, leaving in only beautiful and lofty chapters written in sublime language, we also have an obligation to deal with messages that are hard to digest. We need to restore to the curriculum of primary and post-primary education the appalling descriptions in Joshua 10–11 and to highlight the stories of Rahab's family and the Gibeonites as reflections of the ethical debate about the attitude toward gentiles that took place in ancient Israel. Joshua's cruel proscription needs to be incorporated into the senior high-school elective units on law and society, in the chapter that deals with the topic of proscription. In contrast to those who would like to write embarrassing stories out of our culture, we propose addressing them head-on. In the name of educational credibility, one cannot merely extract a message of acceptance and reconciliation from the text and paper over the "you shall not let a soul remain alive" that reveals our shame.

As we have shown, the current generation of elementary and junior-high textbooks obfuscates the severity of the conquest and proscription problems. This phenomenon is an integral part of the evolving attitude toward Joshua. The explanation we propose—namely, that this expresses an evasion of contemporary political contexts in Israel—is also part of the attitude evolvement. We propose training teachers so that they will know how to enhance the teaching of Joshua, how to read and teach it in new ways, in the spirit of our approach. It is not enough to note that ethical values have changed since biblical times; rather, the book must be read critically. It is not enough to listen exclusively to the dominant voice in it; rather, it must be read subversively. Joshua should be used today as the basis for critical reading by teachers, as the basis for teaching critical reading to pupils and for recognizing the legitimacy of multiple aspects in the Bible. In this way, the book can serve as the underpinning for self-criticism and for a multifaceted view of the past and the present and of the links and differences between then and now. Because the ultimate goal of education is to develop an ethical approach to life, and not merely to convey information, the material studied will be felt as relevant only if there is immediate interaction between the information acquired in the classroom and the living space outside the book and the classroom. The link between the account of the Canaanite extermination in Joshua and the relations between Jews and Arabs in Israel today is reason enough for looking the subject straight in the eye. Exposure to an ideology of exterminating the other offers an opportunity to deal with both the general human aspect and the Jewish aspect of this question. Teaching the story of the conquest of Canaan in this way can be combined with a humanistic ethos of the relations between Israel and

Other peoples, as is done today in other countries that must deal with difficult chapters of their history. In South Africa and Ireland today, the schools work indefatigably to present the narrative about the problematic past in a way that offers an opportunity for self-criticism, for deriving lessons, and for humanistic education.[46]

Prospective teachers have to be made aware that conducting this kind of reading is like entering a minefield. Great care and sensitivity are required when making the connection between the conquest of Canaan and extermination of its inhabitants, as recounted in the Bible, and the Zionist settlement of the land of Israel in the twentieth century. The contention that political issues are out of bounds in the schools must be rejected. But dealing with such a topic certainly does require adhering to the standards of loyal debate: relevant discussion, a commitment to employing valid arguments, avoidance of one-sided preaching for the teacher's own position, and consensual codes of moderation and mutual respect.

In a study of the teaching of the Bible in schools, teachers mentioned problems they encountered when discussing this controversial issue in their classrooms, as well as themes such as the visiting of the parents' sins on their children, the expulsion of Hagar, God's hardening of Pharaoh's heart, and so on. For example, one junior high school teacher said:

> It is clear to pupils that here the term "herem" means genocide . . . They explain that all the Arabs, too, must be killed, that it is not a matter of choice, that the land belongs to us, and if the Arabs stubbornly insist on being here then one has to kill them. I make a very clear statement in reaction to such remarks. First of all that it is impossible, it is impossible to kill. One cannot exterminate a people. A fierce debate develops in the classroom. At their age they are very extreme on every issue. When there were terrorist attacks recently, my pupils wanted to go to Nazareth to kill Arabs, "because that's what you've got to do." . . . Here I had an opportunity to say that proscription is an immoral idea. These are very difficult moral dilemmas. I don't know myself how to give them an unequivocal answer. The relevance of the law of proscription reveals the complexity of life. And this is in eighth grade. (Dor and Yaniv 2004: 23)

Furthermore, this teacher thought that it also made excellent sense to link the topic of the Gibeonites as hewers of wood and drawers of water (Josh. 9:21) to the status of Palestinians working in low-paying jobs in Israel. It is very difficult to conduct a lesson that deviates from the dry mode of instruction, which sums up issues in a hands-off fashion, in a way that all can live with and that does not lead to complications. This teacher's courageous decision to bring the biblical dilemma into contact with daily life today and her pupils' feelings did indeed let the genie out of the bottle. The class period ended with more questions hanging in the air than at the start of the discussion. But her approach produced a special and vital form of learning.

Victoria Gross, another teacher who is apprehensive about the moral sensitivity of her junior high-school pupils, wrote about another, more complex effort to teach in this spirit (Gross 1978: 176–80). She turned her classroom into a parliament—one day, a Gibeonite parliament, another day an Israelite parliament—in an attempt to force her pupils to put themselves in the shoes of both ancient peoples and become aware of their existential considerations—moral, military, and practical. Gross encouraged them to make the obvious comparison to the relationship between Israelis and Palestinians. "It isn't healthy to think that the enemy is necessarily a coward or a fool"—she taught them (179). Gross rejected the simplistic reading of the conquest narratives and turned them into an educational opportunity for multidimensional thinking. This produced a twofold benefit: on the one hand, making the story come alive brought it closer to the teenagers and made it part of their cultural world; on the other hand, their education was enriched by the experience of putting themselves in the other's place.

These examples highlight the paradoxical position of Bible teachers who are trying to achieve two contradictory goals at one and the same time: to pass on the Bible as the basis of Jewish and Israeli identity, but also to stimulate criticism and to challenge several of the traditional truths that are the foundation of the national ethos. Some would argue that this approach poses a risk to the status of the Bible for the younger generation. In our opinion, even if there is such a risk, it is accompanied by great hopes for turning a Bible story into an educational lever precisely because it touches a sensitive nerve in our lives. We should make it plain to prospective teachers that this complexity requires slow but steady progress in teaching critical reading. The first seeds for discussion can already be sown in elementary school. For teenagers, we suggest amplifying a critical and subversive discussion in the spirit presented here. The approach to reading Joshua proposed here is only one path, out of many, for training education students in this type of reading, so that they are able to adopt the method when they deal with other texts as well, making it possible to criticize a text with neither totally rejecting it nor postulating a dichotomous opposition of good guys and bad guys; and to know that the line of demarcation between moral behavior and immoral behavior does not always coincide with the borders between nations or religions. Critical reading is a tool that can serve them in the future and to enhance their clear-headed and complex vision even when dealing with constitutive texts.

Obviously, our proposals should not be seen as offering unequivocal solutions to the problems presented here. Nor have we gone into the details of a complete didactic plan. We wanted to emphasize one of the goals of critical learning—education for tolerating uncertainty, recognizing the limitations of our ability to find a solution, and accepting that there is more than one answer to a single question. We have already noted the deep roots in the Jewish tradition of the system of academic debate that produces no clear conclusion. Here we share the outlook of Gerald Graff (1992), who argues in favor of teaching conflicts. Graff was writing about the teaching of literature, but we believe his remarks are relevant for teaching the Bible as well, and certainly for other fields. According to Graff, most curricula rest on the assumption that one has to resolve a disagreement before introducing it to pupils—an assumption that reflects teachers' distaste for tackling controversies and disagreements. According to him, consensus is not a prerequisite for coherent teaching; we must not be afraid that exposing pupils to conflicts will confuse or deter them. On the contrary, he holds, teachers must present the controversy and anchor it in issues of conflict, without being afraid of political implications (Graff 1994: 10). In the spirit of his ideas, and without fear or favoritism, we must present pupils with conflicts related to the questions raised by Joshua, against the background of both that age and our own, and encourage them to express their own positions.

Placing the conflicts at the center and steering a candid discussion of the biblical narrative's implications build naturally on the long Jewish tradition. The Bible is the constitutive book of the people of Israel, because in every generation Jews have mined it for the texts relevant to them, evaluating and interpreting the texts afresh as best suits their needs. It is appropriate for prospective teachers who are about to join the ranks of Bible teachers to learn to continue this tradition and to engage in ethical criticism of every story and every idea in the treasured possessions that are planted so deeply in our hearts, while providing a stage for diverse opinions to the point of disagreement. We believe that when Bible classes become an arena for casting light on relevant questions of contemporary life, the thirst "to know the fountain" will return to our provinces.

Notes

1. Biblical passages are presented in the NJPS translation unless otherwise indicated.

2. This essay was originally published in Hebrew in the periodical *Dapim* 47 (2009). It is here published by permission and also modified. The Hebrew original can also be read at http://www.mofet.macam.ac.il/ktiva/dapim/Documents/dapim47.pdf. Translated by Lenn Schramm.

3. Simon (2002: 34–35) explains the shift from identification with the Bible to identification with the Holocaust as an expression of pragmatic Zionism (preventing a second Holocaust), in contrast to ideological Zionism, whose time has passed, and also perhaps as an expression of the yearning for a national myth that is beyond challenge.

4. These include organized programs such as *Bina*, *Alma*, the Midrasha at Oranim Training College, Beit Berl College, *Shittim*-the Holiday Institute, the Leo Baeck Institute, and others, as well as larger and smaller groups of senior citizens and private voluntary groups.

5. These issues include feminism, the campaign for the ethical treatment of animals, the campaign for human rights, the war on poverty, the war on racism, and many more. For details, see Kasher 2006: 12n76.

6. By "critical reading" we mean a reading that criticizes ideas and attitudes presented in the text, not a philological and literary Bible criticism that aims at uncovering the diverse textual sources in the Bible, their authors, purposes, and the circumstances of their composition.

7. Joshua dispatched three proclamations to the Canaanites before the Israelites entered the land: "Whosoever desires to go, let him go; and whosoever desires to make peace, let him make peace; and whosoever desires to make war, let him do so. The Girgashites departed, and so were given a land as good as their own . . . Africa. The Gibeonites made peace. The thirty-one kings waged war and were defeated" (*JT Shebi'it* 6:1 [16b]).

8. Such as *Gen. Rab.* 1:2, which holds that the conquest of Canaan was the realization of the divine plan for dividing up the earth among the various nations; *Sifre Deut.* §202, according to which they were not killed if they repented of their idolatrous ways.

9. Bin-Nun (2001: 36–45) goes to extremes to minimize and justify the violence of Joshua's campaigns, and then applies the same justification to the violence that was unavoidable for Zionism as well. See also Bin-Nun and Medan, in Medan 2000 (esp. 29, 35, 38); Rosenberg 2000.

10. The question of the combination of Bible study and the study of talmudic literature in the state school system deserves serious discussion in its own right.

11. See Tchernichowsky (1937: 194) in his poem "I Have a Melody" (Hebrew: *Mangina li*):

> Who are you, O blood, that boils inside me? The blood of the generation of the
> wilderness? Yes! / The blood of the conquerors of Canaan is my blood, streaming and
> never resting. / Once again there calls to me the fierce song, the melody of blood and
> fire: / Climb the mountain and smash the pastureland. Whatever you see—possess!

Ben-Artzi (1986: 20) writes: "In the Bible, the Zionist movement found an expression of its aspirations and longings. . . . Figures such as Joshua, Gideon, Saul, David, and others became major sources of inspiration for the education of Hebrew youth." For additional remarks in this vein about the role of the Bible in Hebrew education, see Mossinson 2005: 39–40.

12. Buber (2002: 62–64) exemplifies this position with the argument that Samuel simply did not understand what God was saying if he thought that he demanded that Saul cut Agag to pieces.

13. Bergman 1970: 37–40. See also Amihai 1971: 95. A report on Mordechai Segal's criticism of Joshua's approach can be found in Kafkafi 1988: 199. For details and further examples, see Mazor 2003: 37–46.

14. So, too, Rabbi Zvi Yehuda Kook: "The conquest of the Land of Israel in order to establish our rule in it is a divinely ordained war. It is a Torah precept and cannot be otherwise . . . Joshua made it plain to the inhabitants of the land: this land is ours. It is under our sovereignty"

(1982: 18–19). Something similar can be found in Eldad 1972: 5–6. The most explicit remarks were those by Rabbi Hess (who later showed sympathy for Baruch Goldstein's 1994 massacre of Muslim worshipers in Hebron): "Thus Purim is not over, and the day will come yet when we will be summoned to this holy war of the extermination of Amalek." Rabbi Hess's remarks, in which he identifies the Palestinians with Amalek, were published in *Bat Kol*, the student newspaper at Bar-Ilan University, in 1986. No copy of this issue is available today at Bar-Ilan University or at the Israeli National Library (See Elitzur 2004: 140–41).

15. In biblical Hebrew and other Semitic languages (as made clear by the Moabite Stone), *cherem* refers to a ban on coming into contact with some person or object or to its consecration to the deity. The normal use of this noun in the Bible, as well as of the verb derived from it (c*h-r-m* Hif.), attaches religious significance to the precept to exterminate, dispossess, and destroy the residents of Canaan (Weinfeld 1988: esp. 141–45; Sister 1955: 115–57; Lohfink 1986: 181–85; BDB 355–56). But the Bible also refers to the notion of total punishment for transgressions by the Israelites themselves or by some of them, notably Achan's family (Joshua 7), Korah (Numbers 16), and others.

16. See also Bergman's comment (1970: 38) on "in the towns of the latter peoples, however, which the Lord your God is giving you as a heritage, you shall not let a soul remain alive" (Deut. 20:16): "We cannot help but ask ourselves whether there is any connection, God forbid, between these words and our deeds in various Kafr Kassems. . . . Can it be true even that God commanded such genocides?" (On Oct. 29, 1956, during the Sinai Campaign, Israeli border policemen killed forty-eight Kafr Kassem civilian residents who violated a curfew they did not know about.)

17. Prior (1997), followed by Jones (1999), discusses the exploitation of the Bible to support colonialist objectives in Latin America, South Africa, and Israel.

18. See the series of Israel's Open University booklets on genocide, and especially the introductory volume (Oron 2006: 27n14, and 110 and 160), and the list of topics in this series. The back cover of the book refers to "genocide in the Bible." For a definition of the term "genocide," see Oron 2006: 21–27.

19. Educational researchers who advocate critical learning emphasize the importance of having students analyze what they study in light of their own lives. See, e.g., Harpaz 2005: 286–89; Zohar 1996: 48–50.

20. Kasher (2006: 2–18) describes these critical trends at length. For a long list of references on the topic, see especially n76.

21. Among Kasher's explanations: the renaissance in attention to biblical morality in the Catholic Church in the wake of the Second Vatican Council, 1962–1965; the influence of scholars such as Childs and Rogerson on enlisting attention for questions of biblical morality; social movements such as feminism, which have promoted discussion of moral issues in the Bible. See the references in Kasher 2006: 2–3.

22. Amit 1986: 18; Loewenstamm 1965: 290. But some challenge this argument, which was formerly the general consensus, and assert that it is groundless. Studies of how the Egyptians, Mesopotamians, Romans, Gauls, Germans, and Celts treated nations they conquered have found reports of terrible atrocities, but nothing like an ideology of total extermination. See Jones 1999: 190–91. Other than ancient Israel, the only written testimony to the annihilation of an enemy people is that of the Moabite Stone; see Rabin 1970: 928.

23. Ahituv 1995: 45–53; Herzog 2001: 56–58; Na'aman 2006: 14; Finkelstein and Silberman 2001: 72–94; Nelson 1997: 2–5. Those who hold to traditional opinions, by contrast, still see Joshua and the Bible in general as reliable evidence of past events. See Bin-Nun 2001: 4–16; Simon 2001: 37–40.

24. In addition to the autochthonous Canaanite peoples (for instance Deut. 7:1-5), the Torah prescribes the extermination of Amalek (e.g., Deut. 25:19) and describes less extreme massacres of Moabites (2 Sam. 8:2-3), Edomites (1 Kgs. 11:15-16), Midianites (Num. 31:1-12), and others. See Gilender and Friedman (forthcoming): 2–12, 19–26; Sister 1955: 117–20.

25. Nelson (1997: 5) suggests another explanation: at the time when the story coalesced (early in the history of the united monarchy), there was a need for a founding national narrative.

The idea of a systematic and successful conquest, leading to gaining control over the previous inhabitants, was intended to justify the Israelites' presence and their right to the land in which they had settled.

26. On the pluralistic attitude toward strangers and members of foreign peoples in the Bible, see Dor 2006: 231–35.

27. Conversation with Yairah Amit, March 1, 2007.

28. This article was published in 2009. In 2010, the curriculum was updated, and the number of chapters from Joshua was increased. The more problematic chapters (10–12), which describe the proscription in all its cruelty, are still omitted.

29. Zalmanson (Zalmanson-Levy 2005: 131–145) looked at an early edition of Parida and Sela, as well as at Korah-Segev and Silberman 1994 and Tirosh and Geller-Talitman 2000. Zalmanson goes no further than criticism of the textbooks, and avoids criticizing the stand of the book of Joshua itself.

30. We also looked at Hagag 2004; Lipschits and Lipschits 2000 and its teachers' guide (it is true that this textbook is defined as intended for the upper elementary grades in the state system, but according to the new curriculum Joshua is not studied in these grades, so that the textbook becomes relevant for junior high school); Parida and Sela 2004; Keren 2002; Shahor 1996; and the teacher's guide for Tirosh and Geller-Talitman 2000.

31. In Korach-Segev and Silberman (1994: 41), we found a lone note that invites pupils to imagine how the people of Jericho felt when they saw the Israelites marching around their walls. By contrast, pupils are frequently invited to write an imaginary story from Joshua's point of view: an account by a soldier who crossed the Jordan with Joshua (35), a page from Joshua's diary (55), a congratulatory note from Joshua to his forces (62), and so on. We found a more complex picture in Tirosh and Geller-Talitman 2000. Alongside the diary of Joshua's grandson (14) and a newspaper issue marking the thirtieth day after Joshua's death (89), there is also a survey of a family in Jericho (21), the speech by the king of Ai (46), and similar ideas.

32. We also encountered evidence of the tendency to evade moral questions at a conference on "Teaching Bible Today" (Oranim College, March 25, 2005). In a lecture on teaching Joshua, the speaker said that when she addressed the concept of *cherem* she referred to the ostracism of children by their classmates. This might have happened because of the modern meaning of the word *cherem*, which in Biblical Hebrew meant extermination, and in modern Hebrew means also confiscation, boycott, or ostracism. This lexical change has enabled teachers to divert classroom discussion away from the moral issues in Joshua.

33. This fully corresponds with the procedure employed by Bible scholars who avoid any judgment of the human values presented in the Bible: see Clines 1997: 28–29.

34. Our approach derives from the method followed by the greatest educators, going back to the talmudic sages. See Greenberg 1986; Kafkafi 1988: 199 on the views of Mordecai Segal; Simon 1991: 13–30; Sister 1955: 98–157.

35. We could never have enough room to list all the ways of reading against the text and must make do with three examples of books that were pioneers in their field: with regard to feminist literature, Fetterley 1978; with regard to Marxism, Lukács 1938/1969; and for postcolonialism, Said 1978.

36. See above, n4, on the distinction between critical reading in the classical sense and critical reading of the Bible.

37. For example, Nahmanides on Gen. 16:6, about the expulsion of Hagar: "Our mother sinned by abusing her, and so did Abraham by letting her do it."

38. Yizhar 1993: 149, quoted more fully on 44–45 above.

39. Extermination: e.g., Josh. 6:21; 10:10; destruction: 11:14; wiping out: 11:21; capture and burning of cities: e.g., 10:28, 32; 8:28; 11:11; and hanging: 11:29.

40. The idea that the spies episode is a fiasco for Joshua was proposed by Zakovitch (Galil and Zakovitch 1994: 18–19).

41. Another detail that may give rise to a critical question in ch. 1 is the relevance of the condition, "Let not this Book of the Teaching cease from your lips, but recite it day and night, so

that you may observe faithfully all that is written in it. Only then will you prosper in your undertakings and only then will you be successful" (Josh. 1:8). For those who believe in divine providence, the link is clear; but nonbelievers who lack the mindset of the faith world require an explanation of the presentation of perpetual Torah study as a condition for victory in the forthcoming campaign. This is the place to draw students' attention to the religious notion of the reward for Torah study and to the author's deuteronomic educational bent, revolutionary in its time—placing the Torah at the center of Israelite existence and framing its study and observance of its precepts as a condition for the conquest and control of the land (see Weinfeld 1984: 115–22). Nelson (1981) points out the requirement that the king study the Torah, in the law of the king (Deut. 17:18-19) and Josiah's public reading of the Torah and renewal of the covenant (2 Kgs. 23:2, 23), as a deuteronomic convention employed to model Joshua on Josiah.

42. Considering that, outside Rahab's story, the word *zonah* in the singular or plural occurs another thirty-three times in the Bible in the standard sense, Jonathan's exegetical translation amounts to a *hapax* and is consequently weak. See also BDB 275–76 for זנה (*z-n-h*).

43. Such as their inclusion in the list of the returnees to Zion, Ezra 2:42-58.

44. Mazor (2003: 43n105) reports schools that do not teach Joshua.

45. According to Eli Eshed (2000), "The book of Joshua is the book of an imaginary fantasy that presents a false picture . . . myths of unparalleled power to inspire profound hatred." Goldreich (2006) asserts that Shulamit Aloni, when minister of education in the early 1990s, removed or tried to remove Joshua from the curriculum because it includes genocide. Another topical echo is reflected by the debate on the *Hofesh* ("Freedom") website: see, e.g., Orbach 2007, Tibbon 2006.

46. See "Where History Isn't Bunk" 2007, which reports that after the abolition of apartheid in South Africa the message of the old curriculum was replaced by a new message of acceptance and reconciliation. In Ireland, the nationalist outlook was replaced by an open perspective with broad horizons.

4

Inside, Outside, or in Between

Feminist/Womanist Hermeneutical Challenges for Joshua and Judges

Cheryl Kirk–Duggan

INTRODUCTION

When I think of biblical texts for empowering, inspiring, or comforting people, Joshua and Judges do not come to mind. Rarely have I heard sermons or lectures on these texts. I hear the occasional reference to Joshua and the battle of Jericho during African American history month, as it provides the language for one of the historical African American spirituals, "Joshua Fit the Battle of Jericho." I have heard sermons on or references to Josh. 24:18, "As for me and my house, we will serve the Lord." Characters from Judges, particularly Samson, are popular textual resources for Sunday school literature and vacation Bible school narratives. I have not heard any sermonic or philosophical critique of Jephthah regarding poor parenting or regarding the Levite as an abusing, homicidal maniac. Never have I heard any sermons or Christian education lessons of any sort on Jephthah's daughter (Judges 11) or the secondary wife of the Levite (Judges 19). These two females are rarely the subjects of conversation regarding women in the Bible. However, with the emergence of feminist and womanist biblical hermeneutics since the 1970s, these characters have increasingly become focus of scholarship and discussion. Rahab (Josh. 2:1-24; 6:22-23) sometimes gets a nod because she is in the lineage of Jesus (Matt. 1:5). Neither Joshua nor Judges receives heavy subscription in lectionaries. Invited to write a commentary on Joshua and Judges for preachers, I began to read these books carefully, chapter by chapter, to let the received texts tell me how to structure the commentary beyond the publishing houses' particular requirements. With page upon page of terror, blood and guts, theft and abuse,

I could not, reading from my twenty-first-century lens, find good news. I did not want to superimpose questions on these stories; rather, I wanted to let the texts tell me what I needed to do regarding hermeneutical strategies.

As I read these texts, questions focused on the story line, emerging themes and ideas, and what issues were problematic for me; that is, what was intriguing, confusing, or just seemed odd. As a womanist/feminist scholar, one who uses an interdisciplinary exegetical lens to expose any systems of oppression and misuse of power—including class, gender, sexual orientation, race, age, and ability—and who seeks justice remedies in community, I also had conversations with others, female and male, about these texts and new horizons where research and scholarship need to focus to provide meaningful and timely discourse. In the conversations, I heard sentiments that corroborated my discoveries, and some new thoughts that were in concert with my thinking. Conversation partners include scholars in Bible, sociology of religion, and theology: Wil Gafney, Kim Russaw, James Ashmore, Cheryl Townsend Gilkes, and Joellyn Stokes. My essay examines selected issues around women's experience in Joshua and Judges, taking seriously feminist/womanist epistemology, philosophy, exegesis, biblical commentary, and activism/praxis. After providing an overview of my own contextual space of reading and the particular lens I look through, this essay (1) explores challenges around violence in the text; (2) examines questions raised by the function and characterization of God, war, and humanity; (3) analyzes challenges for woman characters and woman readers; and (4) suggests areas of proposed new scholarship.

"My mama told me when I was young": Personal Context and Methodology

Godfather of soul, the late James Brown, popularized a classic R&B song, "It's a Man's Man's Man's World," that makes one wonder about the battles of the sexes: "This is a man's world / This is a man's world / But it wouldn't be nothing, nothing / Without a woman or a girl."[1] I grew up believing this was a world for women and men, equally. My awakening to sexism and gender disparities occurred during my graduate education in seminary and religious studies. Initially puzzled by the desire to create a women's group, I had an accelerated education about male bias, about women not being the sons their dads wanted, about verbal, mental, physical, emotional abuse at home, school, and work. While privilege based on dominant culture membership was a bygone conclusion due to racism, I had to heighten my awareness of gender and class oppression. Privilege in the classroom often translated into dominant-culture students brownnosing with faculty because of their sense of entitlement. "This is a man's world" then and now, in some sections within the academy, and in particular among faith communities. I have been in meetings of faith-based national meetings and professional guilds where a man received approval for relating a concept, when the thoughts of a woman who had stated the same thing earlier in the same meeting were dismissed or not taken seriously. Such mindfulness was personally jarring, because my immediate, precollege world did not affirm male or Anglo-Saxon superiority. I sang my first solo at age four, afraid of no one, and enjoyed the notoriety that placed me on a path of performance. That I received tons of love, support, and affirmation at home and in the community bolstered my confidence and made me believe the world was my oyster, despite obstacles like racism. As a graduate student, I began to see that the phrase "this is a man's world" identifies the seat of power yet indicates an emptiness of reality minus women, the poor, and the disenfranchised. Several life experiences make me keenly aware of the dance between disparity, injustice, and power.

I grew up in a house where my parents were friends and lovers, and they supported us, their three children. With a father who was the first African American deputy sheriff in the state of Louisiana, legal matters and justice issues existed at the forefront of our reality. Because my father was in that position, numerous people sought his counsel. He did what he could to help people be law-abiding citizens, and he provided support when they were in trouble. Such conscientization at home heightened my awareness about national and international current events, politics, and injustice.

I was a teenager during the 1960s, a time of change and turbulence across the world, in religion, and in society. Pope John XXIII called for *aggiornamento*: for a new wind blowing, for transformation within the church. He opened Vatican II with African drummers drumming and invited non-Catholic observers to the sessions (1962–1965). Subsequently, people would hear the Mass in the vernacular language instead of in Latin, many nuns would no longer wear a habit, and laypeople would become more active in church work. A move for more ecumenical and interfaith work also emerged, particularly in the United States; these events shaped my understanding of ecumenicity, ultimately toward interreligious dialogue.

In the world, countries across Africa began revolutionary action against colonialism, declaring their independence. In the United States, the 1960s civil rights movement shook the foundations of racist oppression, born of colonial rule that perpetuated forced enslavement of persons of African descent. Despite the fact that President Abraham Lincoln, amid the Civil War (1861–1865), rendered slaves free with the Emancipation Proclamation (1863), people who could not read or write due to laws of segregation were still at a disadvantage. Many in the rural South ended up as sharecroppers, another form of enslavement. To ensure that liberation of the enslaved was not successful, Jim Crow laws were instituted.[2] Many Christian theologians and clergy, using the so-called curse of Ham (Gen. 9:25-27), taught that whites were God's chosen people. Using bogus research and skewed science, social Darwinists, eugenicists, craniologists, and phrenologists claimed blacks were inferior to whites in every way. News media reinforced anti-Black stereotypes by using pejorative terms to name and describe African Americans.[3] The call in the 1960s for an end to legalized racism (being terrorized because you were black), segregated public facilities, limited access to legal rights, and disenfranchisement did not come without a cost.

What does this history have to do with my reading of Joshua and Judges? United States and world history reflect legalized oppression and violence. Such violence parallels violence in Israel's conquest, seeking to gain and occupy Canaanite land under divine sanction. Conquest robs others of their rights, land, and sometimes their lives. Several acts of violent contemporary historical events echo the bloodletting on Canaanite soil, both in the United States and globally.

In the United States, one of the galvanizing events for the 1960s civil rights movement was the brutal murder, in 1955, of Emmett Till, a fourteen-year-old African American teenager, in Money, Mississippi, by white men. They killed him for going into a store and allegedly speaking to a white woman. This heinous event and the subsequent trial became a catalyst for moral outrage and a move to work for social justice, as other brutal murders followed.[4] Such murder and genocide occur in Joshua and Judges. The destruction of Jericho (Joshua 4, 6) echoes the wars in Iran, Iraq, and Afghanistan in the twenty-first century. Issues of capital punishment resulting from Achan's misdeeds (Joshua 7) reflect conquering and bloodletting under the guise of empire building globally. The conquest of Ai, under Joshua's direction, in which twelve thousand die, reminds us of the destruction of the twin towers September 11, 2001. Joshua's triumph in Gibeon provides a lens for us to examine the connections many people make between their religious faith and patriotism as justification for war. The story of the Levite and his secondary wife (Judges 19–20) parallels the horrific global statistics regarding domestic violence. The saga of Jephthah and his daughter (Judges 11) can foreground the heinous assaults on women and children, from sati to sexual trafficking. The rhetorical formula recounting Israel's cycle of disobedience, punishment, crying out, and deliverance echoes the cyclical nature of wars in the twentieth and twenty-first centuries. Such events, historically and biblically, record how hatred kills and disregards human life, embodying evil and a pathological will to power.

My studies exploring the problem of evil as it relates to violence and justice reflect the greed that underlies conquest, access to power, and the ways one can justify violence when faith erroneously and zealously influences civic politics. Studying slave narratives and African American spirituals, I discovered expressions of enslaved persons' creativity, their experience of culture, religion, and their desire to survive and flourish amid terrorism and the heinous injustice of forced immigration. Another life-changing moment was participating in a fact-finding tour to Central America during seminary, where I saw violence, faith, and resilience amid systemic oppression in a different context.

Several moments on my seminarian fact-finding tour in Central America were life-changing, *kairos/chronos* moments. Leaving the international airport, a car backfired and we all hit the floor of our tour bus. We knew of the Sandinistas and the persecution in Nicaragua; also that in December of 1980, an El Salvadoran military death squad raped and murdered Jean Donovan, an American lay missionary, and three nuns—Dorothy Kazel, an American Ursuline nun and missionary to El Salvador, and two Maryknoll missionary sisters, Maura Clarke and Ita Ford (Lernoux et al. 1995). In Nicaragua, we met with *campesinos*, people of faith who met in their homes for worship and political action, to make sure people had water, electricity, and food. At a refugee camp nearby, I saw a baby running around without a diaper on because the mother was washing the only diaper they had. Coffee was the major export; yet refugees had to cut their coffee with corn to have enough to make a cup. On one stop, people offered us orange juice to drink. We knew that this was probably the only juice they had. We were to avoid drinking anything other than bottled water or soda, because the water probably had bacteria that our systems could not process. Yet, out of respect for this community, none of us refused the juice. To refuse would have been to dishonor their hospitality. Standing at the foot of Archbishop Oscar Romero's crypt was an incredibly moving experience. How could anyone assassinate a cleric while he was preparing the Eucharist?[5] I almost came undone when visiting with the Mothers of the Disappeared, who shared with us numerous picture albums with driver's-license-sized photos of people who had left for work, school, or an errand, never to be seen again. In El Salvador, I peered out of the hotel window and saw teenagers packing assault weapons and rifles. College students from that region spoke about standing on street corners to collect money to pay a professor's salary, as they bemoaned that their university library, which held the country's historical documents, lay in ruins from bombings. I felt the weight of the revolution for liberation of our Central American sisters and brothers, and knew that I somehow had to make justice and the exposure and transformation of violence a priority in my life.

Recent work on systemic oppression caused me to revisit the heinous practice of lynching. The volume *Without Sanctuary: Lynching Photography in America* (Allen 2000) contains picture postcards of people grinning while someone is either hanging from a tree or their bodies lay burning on a fire, often after someone had eviscerated their organs. Thus, long before trekking to the Super Bowl or to March Madness NCAA tournament games, people would take train rides to cities where lynchings were taking place as sport, reminiscent of Greco-Roman coliseum antics.

Along with these experiential events, career moves and academic pursuits in North Carolina and California moved me into women's studies, which placed issues of misogyny, patriarchy, classism, sexism, and heterosexism at the center of my radar. Finally, in North Carolina, I was approached by a social worker to create workshops designed to help clergy and social workers learn each other's language so that both groups could do a better job of preventing and intervening in situations of domestic violence. During this time, I saw how often perpetrators could use biblical texts to cause harm. I became aware of the challenges women face from larger society and the men in their lives, and learned how often women sabotage themselves and other women. Another critical factor that shapes how I read and hear texts concerns my philosophy of life.

My philosophy of life derives from the concept of *laughing and dancing with God*. All that I am, do, and engage—is God-centered. As performer and pedagogue, my goal is to facilitate people's capacities toward creative, analytical, critical thinking so they experience the freedom to be curious about everything, to ask the hard questions, to respect ambiguity, and have the chutzpah to challenge everything, the grace to laugh, and the gift to use these tools in building a balanced, holistic, healthy, spiritual life and ministry. As one who embraces womanist epistemologies, philosophies, and praxis, I have set out the principles of my womanist methodology in detail in the *Exodus and Deuteronomy* volume of this series (Kirk-Duggan 2012: 5). Therefore, here I limit myself to the observation that womanist biblical hermeneutics merges the study of exegesis, theology, ethics, culture, and other related disciplines to examine and learn from biblical texts and expose oppression/violence, with the hope of the transformation and empowerment of all people. Womanist biblical scholars exegete and explore Scriptures and other texts amid massive systemic oppression, calling for justice, new hermeneutics, accountability, and transformation.

What You See Is What You Get; Really?
Challenges when Mining Joshua and Judges

The books of Joshua and Judges open up an androcentric, patriarchal world rife with violence, conquest, incompetence, and perhaps irony. Blood cries out from the soil on page after page, blood from those conquered and slaughtered because they worshiped the wrong God, but no one ever seems to try to convert them or evangelize them toward worshiping the God of the progenitors of the text. Judge after judge, each a quasi-nomadic warlord, is generally incompetent. Granted, Deborah has strong command, yet the prowess of Jael, Deborah's female counterpart, offsets the cowardliness of Barak, Deborah's male assistant. Why Sisera leaves his failing men and his chariot remains a mystery. Jael's seemingly premeditated murder of Sisera does not emerge from the text as a moral issue. Jael mothers, perhaps seduces, Sisera, and she drives a peg through his mouth (often mistranslated as temple), violent seduction at its best (Judges 4–5). How to engage a twenty-first-century epistemic perspective regarding the roster of female characters in Joshua and Judges makes for interesting contemplation.

Two named women, Rahab (Joshua 2) and Achsah (Joshua 15), and five named sisters, the daughters of Zelophehad, Mahlah, Noah, Hoglah, Milcah, and Tirzah, (Joshua 17), appear in Joshua. Many more women, named and unnamed, appear in Judges: Achsah (Judges 1); Deborah and Jael (Judges 4–5); Sisera's unnamed mother (Judges 5); Gideon's unnamed concubine and many wives (Judges 8), Abimelech's unnamed mother (who is Gideon's concubine wife), and the unnamed woman who kills Abimelech (Judges 9); Jephthah's daughter, his unnamed prostitute mother, and wife (Judges 11); Ibzan's thirty daughters whom he gave in marriage and thirty daughter-in-laws for his thirty sons (Judges 12); Manoah's unnamed wife, Samson's mother (Judges 13); Samson's unnamed Philistine wife of Timnah (Judges 14); the Gazan whore and Delilah (Judges 16); Micah's unnamed mother (Judges 17); the Levite's raped secondary wife or concubine (Judges 19–20); and the four hundred young virgins of Jabesh-Gilead and the daughters of Shiloh (Judges 21). These texts press us to explore questions about women's function, their abuse, violence and the role of God, and contemporary parallels and applications of these texts. Subsequent sections of this essay on God, war, and humanity, and on female entrepreneurs, prophets, and warriors, address these concerns, particularly regarding the impact of gender and class, along with the overwhelming sense of ethnic cleansing or genocide. First, we explore why Joshua and Judges are inherently problematic.

Studying Joshua is problematic because it reeks with violence and reverberates with attempts at genocide. Reading, teaching, researching, and preaching from this text is extremely difficult through a post-Holocaust, post-9/11 lens and lived reality. Studying such contexts and their leaders, like a Hitler who convinced millions of the wisdom of his *Mein Kampf*, when he looked totally opposite of his Aryan norm, might help us better understand the plight of leaders in Joshua and Judges. We can learn about the risks of charismatic gifts and the complexities and differences that occur when one receives authority by virtue of birth and entitlement, versus power acquired through sanction of divine violence, particularly when an individual or group serves as scapegoat. A comparative analysis of a Hitler juxtaposed with the oppositional leaders Joshua fought, along with miscreant leadership in Judges, reflects the impact of personality, sociocultural context, and the role of faith-based or civil religion in the political success or failure of a particular nation state. That capacity to keep one's head stuck in the sand when reading stories of contemporary domestic abuse and genocide alongside the Nazi's heinous acts against Jews, gypsies, mentally challenged persons, and homosexuals who were mutilated and gassed, some after experiencing Mengele's horrific experiments, in concert with Joshua and Judges reveals the human potential to hate and destroy. Scriptural and Western history also invites the question of theodicy, of the goodness of God and the choices of humanity. One could read the successful conquest in Joshua and thwarted conquest as sagas, where the generally poor excuses for judges are merely puppets of YHWH, and represent classic cases of poor management and ego run amok. A review of current history shows that these texts are essential for our study if we are to face our own complicity in violence. Many of us, even now, live in countries where enslavement occurs in the guise of sweatshops, sexual trafficking, and being required to live in a particular geographic area without the luxury of relocation.

If we read the work of Robert Warrior (Warrior 1991, 2005) and spend time with our Native American and First Nations sisters and brothers—whose land was stolen, who were given blankets infested with smallpox, who today live in forced imprisonment, enslavement on reservations due to conquest and manifest-destiny mentalities—then Israel does not come out looking so good, and the ways of its God are frightening. Joshua magnifies the effects of many (black and other) literal Christian readings of the text that identify with the Israelites against the Canaanites. Some posit that violence in Joshua, a deuteronomistic theological matter, pertains to acts that defy God, where people are arrogant and self-focused, and that Israel's assaults are more like modern liberation campaigns that overthrow oppressive regimes (Creach 2003: 14–15). Such a position will not faze those who do not read Hebrew, who have not studied these texts with the tools and insights of higher education, but follow the literal meaning of the words. Some find Judges difficult and challenging because of the imbecilic leadership as evinced in Samson and Jephthah, and the repetitive rhetorical deliverance formula. The book of Judges repeatedly engages a cycle that moves from disobedience to deliverance and back again. While it seems ludicrous that Israel continuously makes the same mistakes, achieving the same results, we see the same behaviors modeled in contemporary dysfunctional settings: people continue to do the same thing and expect different results, and apparently fail to learn from history. In the twentieth and twenty-first centuries, major world powers fail to understand that empires do not last; most often, such governmental structural politics and their entire infrastructures collapse from within.

Joshua and Judges make for a fascinating study regarding leadership and empire building. Feminist biblical scholars have explored the lives of women in Joshua and Judges, reflecting on the deuteronomistic theological shaping, according to which sin results in a curse and goodness/obedience begets blessing. Such shaping not only reflects the reality of patriarchy but also depicts hierarchy among women—fertile mothers trumping sexually active unmarried women. In any case, women in both social locations are the property of their fathers or husbands. There are, nevertheless, rare occasions where equality exists between genders: situations where women and men become offerings to God, that is, are destroyed in holy war (Josh. 6:21), are victims of their father's sin (Josh. 7:24), are war victims (Josh. 8:25), and are to listen to reading of the law (Josh. 8:35). Within this patriarchal setting, however, some women, often outsiders, become leaders. Rahab, one outside of Israel's normative expectations, is a foreigner and a harlot, who is an entrepreneur who exists as a head of household. Deborah, an arbiter of covenant fidelity, leads as prophet, judge, and helps to deliver Israel. Jael, a foreigner like Rahab, receives the glory for the demise of Sisera, a character who speaks in chapter 4 but never in chapter 5. Usually, it is the woman who does not speak (Laffey 1988: 85–93). While most biblical women have little authority, power, or voice, and are marginalized in every respect, women who become visible, like Rahab, best understand YHWH and negotiate for the well-being of their people. Amid a group of unlikely leaders/judges, Deborah, as mother of Israel, and Jael, a guerilla fighter who seduces and then kills Sisera, are triumphant; they transcend normative biblical parameters, though their character development parallels the decline of Israel's relationship with YHWH (Fewell 1998a: 69–71; Fewell 1998b: 73–74). Thus, when comparing male and female leadership in Judges and in culture, we see disparities, biases, and exceptions. Gender plays a definite role in biblical leadership, regarding both access to power and expectations and assumptions. The text does elevate women, particularly Rahab and Deborah: They are named; they have power and are in relationship with YHWH. This divine connection allows them to access authority and power, and connects them with espionage of spies and war for the sake of Israel.

When engaging a comparative analysis of these texts with biblical warfare and twenty-first-century types of violence, one must factor in individual roles and authority. The functions of gender, class, race, ability, and age of the leader must come into play when doing assessment. These attributes affect people's perception of the text, notably when connecting the academy and faith communities. Because the world remains highly patriarchal, it becomes important to bring to the text questions that explore the varieties of difference. In a world where the presence of nuclear devices means we can destroy the planet, it becomes important to explore the dynamics of gender, class, race, familial history, and personal attributes in history and Scripture to help people wrestle with what happens when a leader embodies attributes of her or his mentor, who may be gracious and benevolent, or fascist and tyrannical. We cannot assume that biblical or historical female leaders will be more just or empathetic than male leaders; much depends on her socialization, empathy, leadership capacity, her understanding of leadership, the complexities of leadership within inclusive and exclusive communities, and divine activity and intention. Sometimes her choices bring about peace; other times, her choices engender violence.

The psychological, relational, and physical violence—sometimes instigated by, other times perpetrated against, women and girls—creates an intriguing juxtaposition of power over against victimhood. Today, we have women as heads of state and of military organizations, like Deborah; there are women who are madams and entrepreneurs running their own businesses, like Rahab. It is important to parse texts around military prowess, taking into consideration the myriad of differences when dealing with adjudication of power that causes destruction to people and property. We also have global and domestic laws that protect women from violence by others in most jurisdictions in the world. The heinous acts perpetrated against Jephthah's daughter and the secondary wife in Judges would today garner life jail sentences or the death penalty. Further, many questions are left unanswered in the text, questions we must ask.

Where is Jephthah's daughter's mother? Where is the community or extended family when the demise of Jephthah's daughter occurs? Jephthah already has God's favor (Judg. 11:29), so he does not need to privilege his ego, as if he needs a second guarantee for divine favor. One wonders about the nature of the relationship the daughter has with her parents that she is so willing to be a sacrifice. Since the Abraham/Isaac story (Genesis 22) seems to put an end to child sacrifice, why is there no ram in the bush in this case? Such realities reinforce the role of woman, daughter, or wife as property or possession. She is not fully human, as in the case of a man; thus she has no rights. The mother does not matter because she is property, and she did not produce a son. The daughter may have a form of Stockholm syndrome, where she shifts into the role of victim, for she has already bonded with her perpetrator, who is not holding her shackled as a captive but is making her captive as sacrifice. Jephthah may use his daughter in this manner because, as the son of a prostitute who was shamed and driven away by his half-brothers, he consciously or unconsciously feels rejected. He then finds his daughter repulsive because of his unresolved issues with his mother. His daughter may physically resemble his mother, which makes her an even more likely target, and as sacrifice to YHWH, her death becomes an acceptable mode of extermination. We would do well to engage Judges 11 in teaching, researching, and preaching, to help people understand the complexities of father/daughter relationships, and the various ways domestic violence can play out and damage lives.

Given how the Levite story of Judges 19 ends, one significant question is why the concubine or secondary wife left, given the precarious situation for ancient women. Was she aware that something ominous was about to occur? What does the function of women as property have to say to the frequency of domestic violence, notably domestic violence that ends in a ritual murder?

Within the text, hospitality and access to power determine who speaks and who gets relegated to the status of victim. A womanist reading signals the need to honor the complexities of the text. Thus Koala Jones-Warsaw posits that the old man tried to halt the horrific plan of the men of Gibeah of Benjamin who want to rape the Levite, for in their sociocultural context heterosexual rape was less offensive than homosexual rape (Judg. 19:23-24). Neither the secondary wife nor the Levite speaks during her gang rape; the text does not say why the virgin daughter was spared. Jones-Warsaw suggests that the Levite dismembers the secondary wife's body as a way to attain justice, in response to the Benjaminites' folly, which is an act punishable by death. Making a personal matter public, the Levite does not reveal his part in this heinous crime, nor is he punished for his acts. In this culture, women are victims, and men are victims because of their interconnectedness, at the levels of person, family, clan, and tribe. The extension or lack of hospitality is also interrelated: the secondary wife is not a guest in her father's home, and the kidnapping of the daughters of Shiloh was about regenerating the almost lost Benjaminites, since Israelites would not give their daughters in marriage to them. Jones-Warsaw reminds us that to limit our focus to one area of oppression or victimization fails to deal with the myriad levels of oppression within society (Jones-Warsaw 1993: 174–83). Globally, the expanse of military or governmentally endorsed genocide, rape as weapon, massacres in public spaces, and increased domestic violence and sexual assault supports Jones-Warsaw's argument that we problematize any readings of texts that reduce the analysis to one issue. The intersections of various differences reflect much more systemic interconnecting oppression and violence. Some find Judges more helpful because it helps us realize that the genocide did not succeed and that the conquest was not accomplished. Others find Judges a rich resource for metaphors and catalysts for raising significant questions. The use W. E. B. Du Bois (1994 [1903]) makes of *shibboleth* (Judges 12:1-6 about Jephthah killing Ephraimite fugitives whose word pronunciation gives them away) can lead to a discussion about the management of difference when we do not have visual cues to construct race. Gideon's question—"Where be all his miracles?" (Judg. 6:13)—helps one to talk about the relationship of the KJV to the African encounter with English in North America and its contribution to Ebonics.[6] Sociologist of Religion Cheryl Townsend Gilkes has heard helpful sermons from Judges that have criticized those stories quite adequately. She mentions that Walter Thomas has a great sermon on Jephthah, and the poet, novelist, and professor Maya Angelou and others redeem Judges when they sing the spiritual: "I opened my mouth to the lord, and I won't turn back; I will go, I shall go to see what the end's gonna be" (personal correspondence with Cheryl Townsend Gilkes, October 2011). Gilkes has a sermon on Samson, "Baaad as God Wants Me to Be!" using basketball player Dennis Rodman as the hook for mining that narrative. She posits that a key point in exegeting such texts is focusing on the use of power, for even when oppressed people are at the bottom of society, they still wield a cultural power that they do not use properly. They need to be self-conscious about using that power for good social transformation and not just blindly wanting to "tear that building down." As a former Army chaplain, Wil Gafney preached many sermons on Deborah and Jael, since their military exploits were much used in chapel sermons. She has preached on the violation of the Levite's spouse in connection with the sexual humiliation of Jesus prior to and during the crucifixion. When thinking historically about military pursuits, how do we problematize war, place, and significance of land and conquest in light of these texts and the history of war and its connections with colonialism and oppression, given that between 180 and 200 million people died due to war, massacre, or atrocity in the twentieth century (personal correspondence with Wil Gafney, October 2011)? Conversely, Joelynn T. Stokes has used Judg. 1:12-15, on Achsah, to posit that while life is not fair, when we seek God for forgiveness, compassion, and wisdom, we will realize the blessings God has for us (personal correspondence with Joelynn Stokes, October 2011). Others find the theme of call and command in Joshua powerful in that specific stories have lessons of overcoming difficult sociocultural locations.

Thus, for many readers from oppressed communities, Joshua and Judges may stand between a sense of triumph and the overwhelming amount of violence, particularly the heinous manner of it against women. When reading from a twenty-first-century lens, to make theological sense of texts that appear to suggest God condones and commands violence means that we may not find good news or anything liberative in the text. The text may indeed support and require violence. Some may even justify the violence when limiting the issues to covenantal relationship between YHWH and Israel with obedience as a prerequisite. Nevertheless, when the oppression and violence is real in the text, particularly when doing a close reading in the original languages, it becomes important to recognize that the text may indicate actions that are illegal, unethical, and immoral in the twenty-first century. To teach, research, preach, and write about these texts, one needs to appreciate the tension between the ancient experience and the contemporary application.

WEBS OF DECEIT OR WEBS OF GLORY: ABOUT GOD, WAR, AND HUMANITY

The messages about God, war, and humanity require a cautious approach. These texts need a great deal of reflection, particularly when engaging some Christian audiences where war is a metaphor, and when patriotism and faith become merged as one, their weapons not only carnal but also spiritual. Both Joshua and Judges sanction religious war and sanctify violence. Both reinforce ethnic hierarchies that are easily translatable into divinely commanded racial and religious categories.

Divine lessons of love and compassion seem remote from these texts, and failure is a cycle of evil that "just keeps on giving." Some argue, for example, that Judges 19 stands for the proposition that same-gender-loving people are riddled with sin. Such an interpretation completely ignores the myriad other sins that occur in that text: from the rape, devaluing, and disregard of human beings, to the lies told about the woman's death in order to initiate a war. In the United States, a few years ago we experienced a president (George W. Bush) who lied to start a war, making a personal vendetta a public, international battle. He spent billions maintaining the war, while at the same time claiming there was not enough money to support health care for the underprivileged. He pressed a law that made sure our children in public schools did get left behind educationally, and allowed the rich to get richer at the expense of others. Notably his vice president, who was actually running the country, became filthy rich through his connections with Halliburton.[7] And like the war-initiating Levite of Judges 19, no fault was found with the forty-third president of the United States. After all, he was a "good Christian" who promised to stop same-gender-loving people from getting married or obtaining familial rights, which, according to early interpreters of the Judges 19 text, is the only "sin" worthy of concern. Stokes sums it up as "Hate love and love war" (personal correspondence with Joelynn Stokes, October 2011).

In addition to personal and communal violence, many contemporary evangelicals and dispensationalists argue for the protection and expansion of the state of Israel as the only legitimate claimant to the lands of the Bible. When we examine history, we often see a sense of manifest destiny and conquest. From the earliest civilizations of 3000 BCE to 2000 CE, there have been empires where one person or a set of persons had power, authority and control over others. This control always involved conquest of land and genocide; yet ultimately, every historical empire of record has fallen. These scenarios invite the question as to what we can learn about allegiance, obedience, egomaniacal judgment, and faulty leadership in Joshua/Judges, and how one locates and understands the movements of God in the twenty-first century through these texts.

The word *lead* in the Bible usually refers to God's leadership, followed by poor human leadership and a few neutral situations. Prior to the installation of kingship, YHWH was *the* leader, the king. Societal leaders included elders of the city, town, or tribe who often served as administrators; experts who advise others (prophets, priests, healers); entrepreneurs who excel in war and prowess (warriors, workers); and entertainers who set the tone for reflection, play, and celebration (singers, psalmists, and instrumentalists). In Joshua and Judges, there is no playbook or standard operating procedure for prophets or judges. People became leaders through appointment (Joshua by Moses), election (David), divine call (Moses), and by birth (Solomon). Obedience to God or God's appointed leader is the primary criterion for evaluation of good leadership (Houston 2004: 227–28).

To comprehend the nature of this God and how to reconcile a God of war and violence in a canon with the God of beauty, creation, and love is to understand how some believers and scholars conflate their faith with their patriotism. A few decades ago, Robert Bellah coined the phrase "American civil religion" (Bellah 1984): we live out our civic lives in a religious manner as we share common religious characteristics expressed through beliefs, symbols, and rituals that provide a religious dimension to all aspects of life in these United States. For many Christians and other believers, their religious and civic commitments intersect and merge into one system with their study of Scripture. In the United States traditionally, major political figures place their hands on a Bible to be sworn in, and those who testify in court also place their hands on a Bible to swear to tell the truth, despite the so-called separation of church and state. (Such sentiments are not new; let us remember that John Calvin wanted Switzerland to be a theocracy.) A few judges continue the practice, but there is no legal requirement for such a custom. Those in the military also take oaths to serve and defend their country and are trained to kill. For military personnel, the violence in Joshua and Judges would resonate. Yet there may be a disconnect on or off the battlefield when thinking through whatever values ground their moral compass; it might be easy to lose perspective and all sense of reality. The amount of soldiers returning with PTSD (post-traumatic stress disorder) and the number of suicides following returns from combat indicate these texts provide an opportunity for interdisciplinary analysis, toward helping soldiers who are trained to kill, receive training as to how to decompress and not internalize their sensibilities of killing the enemy. When soldiers return home and the enemy is a family member who simply disagrees with them, domestic violence often occurs, because there is no filter for the "warrior" to disconnect the "kill or be killed" mentality from threat at home. Such analysis that deconstructs faith, war, valor, and manifest destiny mentalities that thrive on conquest in Joshua and Judges can inform our understanding of biblical theological anthropology, and provide a nuanced lens for exploring the place and function of biblical and historical wars, and the roles and function of women and men in patriarchal settings amid covenantal relationships.

These texts are complex, and while rife with violence, they require a reading that takes seriously the interconnectedness of women with other women and women with men. On the one hand, when women and girls are simply property of their fathers or husbands, it would seem that patriarchal texts would not bother to name any woman in stories that focus on divine action, human response, conquest, land, and tribal life. That a woman is named indicates she is named for a reason: because of her faithfulness, the impact she has on her family, that she gives birth to an important son, or that she is a savior figure for Israel. On the other hand, if these ancient women were afforded an opportunity to speak to the God who allows their abuse, their answers would probably parallel those of modern-day women: some think they are at fault; others are numb and will return to be the brunt of more abuse. Some would embrace opportunities for liberation. Some would confront the God of Israel and ask for reparations; some accustomed to being deemed inferior or submissive would not find problems with a God who allows, even requires, oppressive treatment of the other, particularly the foreigner who worships the wrong god.

Joshua and Judges can be meaningful for military personnel, police officers, others in seats of power/authority, and perpetrators along with victims of domestic violence and abuse in ways that do not glorify violence, and simultaneously honors people's vocations. They can learn about conflict resolution, shared governance, and the import of having power *with* others, rather than power *over* others. These texts are also critical for mental health professionals, pastoral theologians, and clergy as case studies for sessions on preventive strategies around familial and systemic violence. While many of the women in Joshua and Judges experience violence, there are also women who step into leadership roles with aplomb and assurance.

FEMALE ENTREPRENEURS, PROPHETS, AND WARRIORS: WOMEN IN/AND THESE TEXTS

Judges has the most atrocious ("extravagant" à la Phyllis Trible [1984]) violence against women in the canon. There are some scary episodes in these texts. Priestly hacking, dismemberment, and killing women are an abomination. These murders create tremendous theological risk, in the way that Renita Weems speaks of theological risks: when thinking about marriages amid excessive violence; when dealing with relational connectedness and intimacy with people; when grappling with the unresolved aspects of our experiences with God and God's beneficence and omnipotence (Weems 1995: 99). For women who hear God sanctioning violence against them or against all women or even against "Other" women, such violence reinforces these hierarchies rather than examining and dismantling them. We need to hear women's voices, and make sure that alternate perspectives that include women's views in the story are lifted from the text. In the global reality, systems and institutions have only recently begun to take violence against women seriously, understanding that rape is a crime of control where the victim is not to be scapegoated, and domestic violence needs to be prosecuted. We must not be cavalier in thinking that violent Scriptures do not have an impact in a hyper-masculine, misogynistic society. The work of Marie Fortune, scholar, author, and founder of the Faith Trust Institute is critical for dealing with Joshua and Judges.[8] The Faith Trust workers expose and offer training and insight into systemic abuse by clergy.

While scholars have done significant historical-critical work on violence in Joshua-Judges, taking women's experience and the appropriation of women's lives in the text seriously, it is vital to deal with divine presence amid violence in more creative ways, and to find where there may be some hope for and support of women. God sanctions violence in Joshua to allow the Israelites to overtake land that was already inhabited by Canaanites. In Judges, God allows a judge to use violence to overtake the enemy, only to be replaced by Israel repeatedly engaging in disobedience. The God who created the Israelites also created the Canaanites, but the texts fail to indicate why Canaanites are the scapegoats. There is other land that is not inhabited. Yet to honor the promise of Gen. 12:1-3, where God promises Abram to make his name great—and thus to have relations with Abram's people in perpetuity, to give him a son, and to give him and his people land—the price is Canaanite genocide and the conquests of the land in Joshua, and several failed attempts in Judges. God and Israel commit acts of violence for the sake of covenant promises. This price seems too high, in which the ends justify the means. Conversely, sometimes the ends of a story may take a systemically oppressive story and engage a reversal, and a triumph.

In Josh. 6:22-23, for example, when the spies come back and protect Rahab, there is no mention of a husband; and father, mother, and brothers all belong to her. The space Rahab occupies is usually held by the father. She seems to be of marriage age, is engaged outside the moral code, and saves everyone—very similar to Jephthah, who gets driven out and disinherited because of his mother, then gets recalled by the same half-brothers who booted him out when they need a hero (Judg. 11:1-11). In Joshua and Judges, many of the heroes are shady or suspicious characters. (Think for instance about Samson.) Rahab is not a typical female stereotype in that her story does not pertain to the right woman marrying the right man to have the right son to inherit the land; she is a foreigner, and her concern is for her own folk and family, and for Israel.

Were Rahab not introduced as the harlot, and we were to take away her profession and her gender, she would be considered a hero. She helps save the two Israelite spies. Rahab is the leader of her family with all the markings of male head of household. Here is a woman who has influence and power.

Often women have influence; but many times they have no power. With such disconnects, some women become passive-aggressive; others submit; some are shrewd and are able to get men to do what they want through suggestion and manipulation. Some women are clueless because they accept the status quo. Rahab as a case study provides opportunities to explore family systems, the exercise of power beyond traditional categories, the role of stereotypes in individual and communal perception, and how gender plays in societal expectation. Rahab strategizes and thinks of her family in her negotiations. Conversely, Samson (chs. 14–16) does not think of anyone other than himself, until he is blinded and seeks revenge.

Thus work needs to be done to take seriously that words and texts matter. When taken literally, many of these texts annihilate the invisible, the Other, notably women, both figuratively and actually. This is not to say that there are no redeeming virtues at all in these texts. Some suggest that Judges condemns the atrocities against women as evidence of what goes wrong when people are left to their own devices. Viewing the texts with fresh eyes allows us to see lessons for living today, often illustrated by the very one that is marginalized in that text.

An interdisciplinary reading of Joshua and Judges that takes multiple oppressions of class, gender, race, ability, age, and sexual orientation seriously can bring powerful insight, particularly when coupled with the reality that we have the technology to annihilate psychologically (cyber-bullying) and physically (weapons of mass destruction). Such a reading can help us see the women in the texts from a different perspective, particularly when we analyze the lives of the women, in connection with the men in their lives. In patriarchal societies, even when men are not present, they still have incredible influence on the lives of women. In the 1939 film adaptation of the Clare Boothe's play *The Women*, not one man appears on-screen the entire movie, but the women's conversations focus on the men in their lives. In various conversations about men, this oppressed group of women oppresses each other through spiteful conversation, tearing down each other's reputations at social gatherings. The stories of the many abused and battered women in Joshua and Judges reflect the experiences of women in society. They remind us of the import of teaching about justice and mutuality, and about the need to have respect for others and ourselves. In analyzing the functions these women perform, we can learn a great deal about the beauty of health relationships, the cost and cyclical nature of violence, and the intersection of systems in the lives of people, and the choices that lie before them. We become privy to a much richer conversation when our epistemic perspectives shift, as we privilege the voices of these women.

Still Waiting for the Revolution? Avenues for New Scholarship

From a feminist/womanist perspective, there are several questions we need to contemplate in addition to those already raised. For instance: How should we analyze and appropriate these texts given the global socioeconomics and political world in which we live? Perhaps these texts can help us wrestle with the other of racial ethnic identity and country of origins, of genocide, ethnic cleansing. Studies on genocide and the disdain for the Canaanites might help us grasp how violence related to racial ethnicity fuels acts of terror, particularly by those with anti-Semitic, anti-Islamic, and Aryan sensibilities. All of us in the United States are immigrants of some sort; and most persons from other countries have to relate to "foreigners." What can these texts teach in that regard?

From a womanist perspective, we need to take seriously the way enslaved Africans, stolen and forced to settle in the United States, used these texts, and we must ask what they say to us today in a post-Holocaust, post-Maafa[9] world. Analyzing Joshua and Judges using feminist/womanist biblical hermeneutics provides an opportunity to help pedagogical and religious readers do a critique that is not dependent on either a literal reading or on reading hierarchically through the Israelite perspective. While many feminist scholars have done work on Joshua and Judges, continued exploration—particularly around the intersections of oppression in a global society where class disparities are even more intense—can unveil new insights into connections around systems, power, and culture. Along with existing scholarship that focuses primarily on gender, there is room for further discussion around the complexities of class and privilege. In particular, faith traditions must reckon with the notion that the same God who created the Israelites created the Canaanites. Joshua and Judges can provide insight as we explore the ideology of the modern nation state. What effects did these texts have on issues such as "Manifest Destiny" in the United States,[10] on Western colonial power in the nineteenth and twentieth centuries, and on the U.S. self-image in the post–Cold War era? How do we read these texts around land and conquest when there is no land that is not owned by some country, as we continue to deal with wars caused when personal projects are made public; when some governmental regimes are intent on becoming empires; when companies speculate on the price of oil; and when gas becomes more expensive within slow economic situations, particularly when we are now connected globally?

Given that one in four persons in the United States is a victim of domestic violence and sexual assault, we must read these texts in a way that tells people how they should *not* act, in conversation with themes like Mic. 6:8 ("He has told you, O mortal, what is good; and what does the Lord require of you but to do justice, and to love kindness, and to walk humbly with your God." NRSV), and Gen. 1:26-31 ("Then God said, "Let us make humankind in our image, according to our likeness""). And how do we understand inheritance connected to land today? How do we use more technology and cultural artifacts like film, art, and music to flesh out what these texts say, as a way to offer critique about ways in which oppression occurs and how we need to be accountable?

Joshua and Judges are complicated texts that have a great deal to say about the human condition. Joshua and Judges require that we who believe in liberative pedagogical and exegetical analysis cannot rest until we mine deeper and further into "what mean these texts." Music and lyrics, particularly those focused on freedom, help expose oppression and violence, where some people begin to see the levels of turmoil that otherwise may remain oblivious. For example, the women's a capella group Sweet Honey in the Rock[11] sings about freedom from diverse perspectives, insisting on the import of transforming all types of violence such as found in Joshua and Judges. The group sings about freedom from diverse perspectives; particularly telling is their song, "We Who Believe in Freedom Cannot Rest until It Comes." In sum, my poem below speaks to my reading of characterizations and issues raised by Joshua and Judges; speaks to why we have only just begun to learn from these texts; speaks to why we must continue, with all deliberate speed to read, analyze, wrestle with the intersections of conquest, land acquisition, power, God, covenantal relations, politics, family, and the cost and injustice of violence—divine or human.

> They came, sometimes conquering, other times being a fool
> Sometimes a fool for God, other times a fool, an imbecile who inept, incorrigible—
> could not lead effectively; could not stand for righteousness; was dysfunctional;
> And then some were mighty warriors; others ingenious entrepreneurs, moving us to ask,
> what mean these things—a foreign woman turned hero; a Nazirite disgraced; land riddled with blood; bodies dismembered; a prostitute's son expelled then reclaimed—
> people hurting people, people misbehaving, people disbelieving, cycles of

violence and pain—what mean these things?

Israel now out of Egypt but in Canaan's land

Promised in Genesis, engaged in Joshua, conquest denied in Judges

what mean these things?

Such questions, we must ask, to do our work with integrity,

hopefully, toward liberation—for the texts, and for us.

Notes

1. http://www.metrolyrics.com/its-a-mans-mans-world-lyrics-james-brown.html.

2. Jim Crow (1877 to mid-1960s) was the label for the rigid legal, racial caste system and way of life operating mostly but not solely in southern and border states. This system viewed African Americans as inferior and as second-class citizens. Scholars and persons living through the era of Jim Crow use this term to describe segregation laws, rules, and customs that emerged after Reconstruction ended in 1877 and continued until the mid-1960s. Jim Crow reflects "Black Codes" that took away many of the rights that had been granted to African Americans through the Thirteenth, Fourteenth, and Fifteenth Amendments. Thomas Dartmouth "Daddy" Rice, a struggling white "actor," popularized the song "Jim Crow," modeled after the singing of either a young black boy or an old black man. Rice performed as "Jim Crow," beginning in 1828, as an extremely stereotypical black character. Depictions of blacks as dancing, singing, grinning fools found a market with many white audiences. Within a decade, the term "Jim Crow" was accepted parlance as a collective racial epithet for Blacks. Blacks used the term "Jim Crow" to describe the despicable "separate and not equal" plight they experienced due to socio-cultural, legal segregation. A failure to abide by these laws could cost a person her or his life. See "Who Was Jim Crow," Jim Crow Museum of Racist Memorabilia; http://www.ferris.edu/news/jimcrow/who.htm; Viewed December 2012.

3. See http://www.ferris.edu/jimcrow/what.htm.

4. On June 12, 1963, white supremacist Byron De La Beckwith assassinated African American civil rights leader Medgar Evers in Mississippi. On September 15, 1963, a bomb exploded at Sixteenth Street Baptist Church, Birmingham, Alabama, an African American congregation, killing Denise McNair (11), Addie Mae Collins (14), Carole Robertson (14), and Cynthia Wesley (14) while they were attending Sunday school. This church was a meeting place for civil rights leaders. Witnesses saw a white man place a box under the church steps; the blast hurt twenty-three others as well. On June 21, 1964, Ku Klux Klan members brutally murdered three men working in Mississippi, during Freedom Summer, who had gone to register black voters and to investigate the burning of a black church: a twenty-one-year-old black Mississippian, James Chaney, and two white New Yorkers, Andrew Goodman (20) and Michael Schwerner (24). Ku Klux Klan members also murdered Viola Liuzzo, a white Unitarian Universalist civil rights activist committed to educational and economic justice from Michigan, after the 1965 Selma to Montgomery marches in Alabama. Nationally, the November 1963 assassination of U.S. President John F. Kennedy; the June 1965 assassination of African American nationalist and religious leader Malcolm X; the April 1968 assassination of Nobel Prize winner, pastor, and civil rights leader Dr. Martin Luther King Jr.; and the June 1968 assassination of U.S. Senator Robert F. Kennedy reflect a tremendous amount of blood running unjust on U.S. soil—due to sociopolitical desire and a legacy of racist hate. Please see http://www.olemiss.edu/mwp/dir/evers_medgar/index.html; http://www.english.illinois.edu/maps/poets/m_r/randall/

birmingham.htm; http://www.infoplease.com/spot/bhmjustice4.html; http://www25.uua.org/uuhs/duub/articles/violaliuzzo.html.

5. Romero had begun to protest the brutal murders of at least 75,000–80,000 Salvadorans, as well as the 300,000 disappeared persons who were never seen again, noting that a million had fled, and there were a million homeless fugitives in a country of 5.5 million persons. He requested that international aid be stopped in acknowledgment of the social injustice. A paid assassin murdered the archbishop a day after he had asked soldiers and police to disobey orders contrary to God's will. He was killed as he officiated a funeral Mass in the Chapel of Divine Providence Hospital, March 1980, San Salvador, El Salvador (http://kellogg.nd.edu/romero/pdfs/Biography.pdf).

6. Psychologist Robert L. Williams and a group of African American scholars coined the term *Ebonics* at a conference, "Language and the Urban Children," St. Louis, Missouri, U.S.A., January 1973, from two terms, *ebony* (black) and *phonics* (sounds), which thus means "black sounds"; that is, all-encompassing language of West African, Caribbean, and U.S. enslaved descendants of Niger-Congo African origin (Williams 1975: 100; Smitherman 1997: 8).

7. Former U.S. Vice President (2001–2009) Dick Cheney received deferred compensation and retained stock options from Halliburton, an energy company, where he served as CEO (1995–2000), while in office. Halliburton's KBR (Kellogg Brown & Root) subsidiary that handles engineering, construction, and related services is the principal U.S. government contractor working to restore Iraq's oil industry in an open-ended contract awarded without competitive bidding (http://www.cbsnews.com/2100-250_162-575356.htm).

8. The Faith Trust is a U.S. national, multi-faith, multi-cultural training and education organization with global reach working to end sexual and domestic violence (http://www.cpsdv.org/).

9. "Maafa," also known as the African Holocaust or Holocaust of Enslavement, is a cluster of terms or sociopolitical neologisms that refer to the Atlantic slave trade and at times to the Arab slave trade.

10. "Manifest Destiny" is a nineteenth-century belief in expansionism in the United States, often related specifically to Anglo-Saxons, as manifest or self-evident, as if the U.S. were destined or ordained to expand across the continent. Though used earlier, in 1845 the American columnist and editor J. L. O'Sullivan coined the term "Manifest Destiny" to promote the annexation of Texas and the Oregon County to the United States (www.historytools.org/sources/manifest_destiny.pdf).

11. Sweet Honey in the Rock, a Grammy Award–winning African American female a cappella ensemble founded in 1975, sings a repertoire steeped in black sacred music of the church, "the clarion calls of the civil rights movement, and songs of the struggle for justice everywhere" (http://www.sweethoney.com/about/group.php).

5

The Finns' Holy War against the Soviet Union

The Use of War Rhetoric in Finnish History during the Second World War

Kari Latvus

INTRODUCTION

The Second World War was a traumatic experience for Finland. The nation had achieved national independence in 1917, after having been colonized by Sweden (from the twelfth century to the War of Finland, 1808–1809) and then part of the Russian Empire, although autonomous. The 1918 Civil War remained fresh in the Finns' memory. When the Soviet Union attacked Finland in 1939, its national independence was seriously threatened. Finland was poorly prepared and equipped, only a minor player compared to the imperial military power of its eastern neighbor. For Finns, the Soviet Union represented imperial power, imperialistic aims, and atheistic and Communistic ideologies, while Finns understood themselves as representatives of the western and Christian world (Lavery 2006: 106–9, 113).

The aim of this article is to analyze the reception of the Old Testament (OT)[1] in Finland during the Second World War. The specific period of this study is the latter part of 1941, and the data analyzed is the newspaper *Kotimaa* and the Finnish theological journal *Teologinen Aikakauskirja* (*Finnish Journal of Theology*). In 1941, *Kotimaa* was a church-oriented newspaper published twice a week, each issue having four pages. *Teologinen Aikakauskirja* contained altogether 513 pages in 1941, consisting of scholarly and professionally oriented articles, reviews, and short notices.

My research question is this: how were the Hebrew Bible texts about the land, conquest, and re-conquest used in the context of the Finnish war? The presupposition before the analysis was that there are similarities and connections between Finnish texts and the OT conquest stories in Joshua and Judges. These OT stories were part of my academic biography and part of my doctoral dissertation (Latvus 1993; English version Latvus 1998). The presumed common theme was God's guidance in the conquest of the land, with the land being taken from the enemies and given to the Israelites/Finns. This was a central theme in the Deuteronomistic History (DH) and a burning issue in the context of the Finnish war. A well-known metaphor used about the Winter War (1939–1940) between Finland and the Soviet Union was the fight between "white" David and "red" Goliath (1 Samuel 17).

The reception of biblical texts in Finland during the Second World War has not actually been analyzed earlier. Nevertheless, it is worth mentioning that Janne Helin (2006) studied the religious and ideological concepts used during the Winter War, and concludes that religious and mythological metaphors were widely used and an important element in national rhetoric.

METHOD

The primary method of this study is reception analysis. In the European context, this approach is based on the philosophy of Hans Georg Gadamer (*Truth and Method*, ET 1982). Gadamer discusses the history of effects (*Wirkungsgeschichte*) and emphasizes that events and texts have an affect on history. Interpreters are affected by earlier (and current) events; and when texts are read in a new situation, interaction between several elements always occurs. According to Gadamer, interpretation always leads to a fusion between past and present interpretive horizons. This approach acknowledges that texts have always been read and reinterpreted throughout history as connected to the readers' context. A well-known example of this hermeneutical approach is the commentary on Matthew written by Ulrich Luz (1989; 2007). Luz illustrates how the text of Matthew has been read and perceived in various ways throughout the centuries. Each reading creates a new dimension for the text and enhances its meaning. Sometimes the ensuing interpretations can even contradict the (probable) original intention. For instance, in Matt. 25:31-46, "Least brothers" was originally—most probably—a reference to other Christians; however, this expression was at times understood simply as a reference to unknown human beings.

Based on Gadamer, reception analysis not only considers the history of effects, *Wirkungsgeschichte*, but also points out that the reader and the reading context deserve special attention too. As an offshoot of reader response literary theory, reception analysis focuses on the role, meaning, and value of the reader. Texts have their meaning, but the understanding process always happens through someone and in a certain context (Rhoads 2005: 9–14). Reception analysis aims to find and confirm a connection between a biblical text and its usage in a later document. It then focuses on the contents, ideology, and motives of the reception. Thus the essential task of the study is to give sufficient attention to the context of the reception in order to understand why particular texts were used, in which connection they were used, and what the motives of the writers were.

The first part of the present analysis can also be called an "intertextual analysis" (Huttunen 2011: 148–53), in which the connection between the Bible and a later source is explored. Finding such a textual connection may be easy if, for example, a biblical passage is quoted in a later text. Not all relevant connections, however, are so explicit. Thus it is helpful to divide my observations into four categories:

> 1. Direct connection. The intertextual, later source has a direct and unambiguous connection to the OT: a text is quoted and/or mentioned with reference to a certain passage.
> 2. Verbal connection. The source has a verbal connection to the OT, but the specific reference is missing. The text may, however, include a quote or an allusion from the Bible.
> 3. Ideological connection. The source has an ideological connection to the OT. "Ideological connection" means that similar ideas and attitudes are used in both texts.
> 4. Ambiguous connection. The source has an ambiguous link to the OT, or the connection between the OT and the period studied is not articulated explicitly. Yet, even without an explicit connection, there are still grounds to assume that the later writer created an implicit connection.

SOURCES

The newspaper *Kotimaa* is well-known in Finland, especially in church-related circles. During the Second World War, it represented mainstream Lutheran views. The newspaper issues analyzed in this study are available in microfilms. Each issue contains news about the war and political and religious analyses of it, but the major part focuses on various aspects of the church: church administration, decisions made in the church, and stories about the situation on the front and in local parishes. An important role is also assigned to spiritual writings, which resemble short sermons (Murtorinne and Heikkilä 1980: 127–61).

Teologinen Aikakauskirja (*TAik*; *Finnish Journal of Theology*) represented the highest academic and professional theological study in Finland. The editor, A. F. Puukko, was a professor of OT exegetics at the University of Helsinki, a famous scholar, the author of *Das Deuteronomium. Eine literarkritische Untersuchung I-II* (1909/1910) and several Finnish academic textbooks. According to Juha Seppo, *TAik* had an important academic and political role in the Finnish media during the Second World War (1997: 526–55).

HISTORICAL CONTEXT

The Second World War in Finland was fought in two phases: The Finnish-Soviet Winter War (November 30, 1939–March 13, 1940) and the Continuation War (June 25, 1941–September 19, 1944). In the Winter War, the Soviet Union attacked Finland, following a secret agreement with Germany. In the secret protocol of the Molotov-Ribbentrop Pact, Finland belonged to the interest sphere of the Soviet Union. The Winter War lasted only four months and was followed by the Moscow Peace Treaty. As a result of the war, the Soviet Union occupied about one-tenth of Finland's territory: the eastern part of Finland (the Karelian Isthmus including Vyborg, the second-largest city in Finland). Some strategic areas in the coastal area (such as the Hanko Peninsula) were given to the Soviet Union and occupied by Soviet troops. Finland, however, remained independent. The outcome of the war was eloquently described as the heroic miracle of the Winter War (Lavery 2006: 118–23).

The Continuation War, again against the Soviet Union, started in practice on June 22, 1941, although it was officially declared on June 26, and lasted until September 19, 1944. Although Finland and Germany had the Soviet Union as a common enemy, and certain cooperation with the Germans existed, from Finland's point of view the Continuation War was perceived as a separate, Finnish war. During the early months of the war, both Finland and Germany were successful. The Soviet troops were pushed quickly eastward, and the Finnish army reached the country's earlier border in just a few weeks, at the end of August 1941. A politically ambiguous and widely debated act was the Finnish occupation of East Karelia. Although officially Finland did not support an ideology of a greater Finland, some right-wing political and religious groups wanted to unite all Finnish ethnic groups. These views were especially promoted in the Academic Karelia Society, but also by the commander in chief of the Finnish army, C. G. Mannerheim. Mannerheim made his political opinions widely known in the "Order of the Day" (*Ylipäällikön päiväkäsky*) (Murtorinne 1975: 101–2; Nilsson 2010: 111–14).

CONQUEST OF THE LAND IN JOSHUA AND RE-CONQUEST AMONG THE PROPHETS

In the book of Joshua, no other theme is as important as the occupation of the land of Canaan; the entire discussion about the land in the OT would not make sense without the book of Joshua. Land as promised, conquered, lost, and re-conquered is a fundamental historical, theological, ideological, and hermeneutical issue in it. These aspects are analyzed by Walter Brueggemann (2002), who argues that the land is an essential theological theme and that the texts are based on a fairly reliable historical reality (and see also Brueggemann's essay in this volume). As a critical corrective to Brueggemann, Keith Whitelam (1996) and Michael Prior (1997) point out that while the question about the land and its ownership is a highly complex theme in the OT, the questions become even more complicated when the texts are applied to the present world. Whitelam strongly argues that the stories of conquest that follow the national agenda unjustly define the Canaanites as Others (1996: 79–101, 119–21). As John J. Collins claims, usage of the violent conquest paradigm in order to legitimate war against other people is highly questionable (Collins 2005: 62–64; see also Scheffler 2009: 1–17).

At the beginning of Joshua, Yahweh orders Joshua and the people to cross the Jordan and go to the land (הָאָרֶץ, *ha'arets*). God will give (from נתן Qal, *n-t-n*) the land to them (Josh. 1:2), and no one will stand against them because Yahweh promises to be with Joshua (אהיה עמך). The following chapters describe the war against the Canaanite kings (chs. 2–11), after which the land is divided among the Israelite tribes (chs. 12–22). Two farewell speeches end the conquest in chapters 23–24. Among the key ideas in the book of Joshua is the trust that Yahweh fights on the side of the Israelites: "The Lord your God fights for you" (Josh. 23:3, 10: הנלחם לכם יהוה אלהיכם הוא).

The earliest version of the book (by the historical redactor, DtrH) describes the conquest as an unconditional promise and gift given by God. Later, deuteronomistic and post-deuteronomistic redactors add warnings and conditions to these promises in passages such as 1:8-9, 12-18; 7:1, 9-26; chs.

22 and 23 (Latvus 1998: 85–86). The promised land was ambiguous: it was promised to the fathers but lost in the imperial invasion by the Babylonians (2 Kings 24–25). Thus the given land would eventually be destroyed and ruined. The image of a devastated and ruined land is used especially in prophetic literature: for example, in Isa. 1:7-9; Jer. 4:5-10 (cf. Isa. 24:1-13). Prophetic literature also includes new promises about rehabilitation, re-conquest, and rebuilding in passages such as Isa. 49:14-20 and Ezek. 36:1-38.

Although the book of Joshua seems to be a central story about the conquest of Canaan and a junction of several ideological streams, the question of having the land and living in the land goes far beyond this book. First, the story of the conquest is needed in order to understand land ideology in the Hebrew Bible. Without the story in Joshua, the promises to the fathers in Genesis would not be fulfilled. In a similar way, the DH requires a beginning, and prophetic promises about the restoration of the ruined land and cities can be understood only in connection with the DH (Brueggemann 2002: xvii–xviii). It is important to remember this connection between Joshua stories and OT land ideologies in general when the texts about land, conquest, and re-conquest in the Finnish wartime context are studied. Thus this study cannot be limited to the book of Joshua and its direct reception but must also appeal to related texts that touch on the land issue, even if the connection to Joshua is only implicit.

ANALYSIS

After this introduction it is time to focus on the Finnish wartime reception of biblical promises about the land.

KOTIMAA

In *Kotimaa*, biblical passages are mentioned and also quoted frequently. Many of the texts are from the New Testament, but OT texts also appear. This study is limited to the reception of the OT texts. At least some, if not most, of the texts follow lectionaries of the church year.

I am limiting my analysis to the beginning of the Continuation War, the latter part of 1941, because during those months the Finnish army re-conquered the lost territory, as well as central parts of Great Karelia beyond the former border. Karelia is an area culturally connected to Finland—hence perceived as belonging to Finland—but through the centuries has been divided between Finland and Russia/the Soviet Union. It therefore seems very probable that the central evidence about how the OT was used can be found within this frame. As backup confirmation, I also surveyed the sources in 1942, but no new evidence appeared.

Kotimaa 44/27, June 1941, comments on the beginning of the war in the first-page headlines and texts. Relevant to this study is that, in the same issue, the military pastor E. Rinne wrote an article titled "Today," which follows the ideology of God's war and sees Finland, without any hesitation, as God's instrument:

> In the same way as Finnish men nearly two years ago, in the early part of our struggle, felt that they were soldiers for the free proclamation of the gospel, so are they now a weapon in the hand of the Lord, when God's judgment confronts the eastern movement of ungodliness in order to destroy it. . . . Forward in the name of God and in his power. The sign of the cross will win.[2]

In the following issue (*Kotimaa* 45/1, July 1941), several writings emphasize the same theme. Lutheran bishops give an "exhortation," stating: "The cruel enemy has attacked our country again and started annihilative acts. God has given us a task to defend, with all our might, our native country, the Christian faith, and the freedom granted to us by God, so that we could leave them as an inheritance for future generations." In conclusion, the bishops quote Isa. 54:7: "For a brief moment I forsook you, but with great compassion I will gather you."[3]

On the same front page, Pastor Hannes Anttila quotes Ezek. 36:33-35 in the section "Today" (the same title was used by several writers) as follows: "Thus says the Lord God: On the day that I cleanse you from all your iniquities, I will cause the cities to be inhabited, and the waste places shall be rebuilt. And the land that was desolate shall be tilled, instead of being the desolation that it was in the sight of all who passed by. And they will say, 'This land that was desolate has become like the garden of Eden; and the waste and desolate and ruined cities are now inhabited and fortified.'"

Anttila addressed the text to a specific target: to the personified Karelia ("you beautiful Karelia"), who has been desolate but will become like "the garden of Eden—at least for Finns." A strict connection between the text and context is explicit in the writing: "Your ruined cities we will rebuild, your desolate fields will be like golden waves, your lakes will glitter." Still, Anttila points out that both the outer and inner renewal of Finns was also needed: the promise of God's good gifts was conditional.

Further, Eino Kalpa, a military chaplain, wrote under the heading "Great Moment of Our Nation": "God guides nations and individuals like a great and wonderful God. . . . As Finns and Christian soldiers we are guardians and have a task to defend and destroy the biggest lie in world history. . . . A dream of a great and undivided Finland will become true." Kalpa does not refer to any specific biblical passages. He repeats similar themes in a later issue (68/19, September 1941). The dream about an undivided Finland was going to be fulfilled; it was God's will.

A. E. Jokipii, a well-known vicar, also uses the OT in an article titled "What Does God Think about Me?" (Kotimaa 45/1, July 1941), quoting Jer. 29:11: "For I know the plans I have for you, says the Lord, plans for welfare and not for evil, to give you a future and a hope." In the text, he affirms: "Our country will have a glorious future and a time of hope." He adds, however, that this also required sacrifices.

In August 1941, a writer using the initials L. P. writes twice in the section called "Daily Word" about a "Crusade" (issue 59/19) and "War" (issue 61/26). In the first writing, L. P. claims that the war has been called (by the army leaders) "a crusade: not only a fight for European culture but also against public and rude godlessness and all destructive atheism." L. P. also refers to the story about Ai, but not to the actual passage in Joshua 7. "Holy history describes how the Israelites could not occupy the small town of Ai because in the midst of them there was something dedicated to God to be destroyed." L. P. applies this to one's individual life: "Do you have in your life a secret sin that you have not confessed and you are not willing to give up? One such a sin alone can be a hindrance to victory. Will the victorious front break in front of you? Is it because of you that victory will not be achieved?"

In L. P.'s text, the story of Joshua 7 is transferred to an individual and pietistic level of life. This connection gives the impression that unless every Finn repents, confesses any secret sins, and asks forgiveness, the war could not be successful. One week later, the same writer, L. P., writes in the same section: "We are in a holy war against godlessness. But God's chosen people also fought against the pagans, and were destroyed. . . . Our fight is a holy war as long as and to the extent that we fight before God, humbly submitting to and accepting his will." L. P. also quotes Jer. 4:14 and Dan. 9:18, texts that the writer felt emphasize human beings' need for a clean and humble attitude before God.

In issue 69/23, September 1941, a writer using the initials A. W. K. has a short article titled "How Shall We Survive?" The writer summarizes the text of 2 Chronicles 20 and concludes:

This historic report is timely for us Finns, and instructive. ... However, we must not forget the condition on which the Lord gives us aid: that the people and their leaders humble themselves before God, regret, repent, and abandon the sins they are aware of. . . . The force which will help us survive comes from the invisible world of God.

In issue 73/7, October 1941, a writer known as "corporal K-o P-o" ("What Is the Holy War Like") points out that the expression "holy war" requires not only that the war itself and its goals be right but also that "the men who use the weapons strive to put their entire lives into the hands of God."

In issue 74/10, October 1941, an anonymous writer uses the title "Crusade." In the rather long article, the writer supports the use of the word "crusade" because "the defensive war" is a fight for Christianity.

In the "Today" section of issue 83/11, November 1941, E. Kilpeläinen writes about Saul's rejection in 1 Samuel 15. The story is interpreted as a personal and pietistic warning about what could happen if one does not wholeheartedly follow God. The writer warns readers not to have any secret areas of life, especially sins, which are not acceptable to God. Thus obedience to God requires as strict an attitude in the Finnish context as in the OT: it is "all or nothing." One month later, a writer using the initials M. P. ("Rejected by God;" 77/6, December 1941) refers once more to Saul (1 Samuel 15) and also to Samson (Judges 16). Both figures, writes M. P., are reminders that God could also reject the chosen ones. The stories of Saul and Samson are used in order to illustrate what could happen if believers do not adhere to all of God's demands or if they focus too much on material values.

In December 1941, *Kotimaa* published an Independence Day sermon delivered by Bishop Aleksi Lehtonen ("God's Help to Our Nation during the Last Stages"; 91/9, December 1941). Aleksi Lehtonen (1891–1951) was an influential figure in the Finnish context: a former professor of practical theology and a bishop of Tampere during the war (1939–1945). He was appointed archbishop in 1945. The text of the sermon was Ps. 107:19, 21:

> Then they cried to the Lord in their trouble,
>> and he delivered them from their distress; . . .
> Let them thank the Lord for his steadfast love,
>> for his wonderful works to the sons of men!

In the sermon, Lehtonen interprets Finnish history in light of this psalm.

Today when we celebrate our independence day in the middle of a raging war, we can only recognize in humble gratitude to God that, miraculously, he has helped the Finnish people so far. . . . Just recently, our nation has strangely been able to experience God's help. Within two difficult years the Finnish people have seen two wonders. In the Winter War, this small nation was left alone to struggle in the middle of a severe winter. . . . Elsewhere in the world it was told: In the north, David is fighting against Goliath. And it happened as in the biblical story. . . . Our people were rescued from destruction. And isn't there now another miracle taking place?. . . History is in God's hands. . . . We need not be concerned about God's righteous governance and the victory of the righteous. He cares for us and for our victory, if we lean on Him and want to live an entirely righteous life.

The sermon leaves no question that the bishop sees both wars as God's miracles. God has helped Finland in an extraordinary way, and all of history has been controlled by God. The context of the sermon is a mixture of religious and national elements: in the Lutheran cathedral in Helsinki on Independence Day, the bishop confirms that God and Finland have a special relationship. The text of the sermon, Ps. 107:19, 21, is part of the psalm describing various experiences in the history of Israel. Lehtonen uses the psalm *not* as a text about Israelites that could be applied also to the Finnish context; instead, the sermon directly describes the experienced reality in Finland and fully assimilates the textual level into contemporary history.

TAik (Finnish Journal of Theology) during the Second World War

Teologinen Aikakauskirja (*TAik*) did not remain nonpolitical or purely academic, but reflected on the two wars on several occasions (Laine 1997: 504–25; Seppo 1997: 526–55).

In 1941, *TAik* published two articles that are relevant for this study. A. E. Jokipii (1893–1968) wrote about wartime demands for a Christian proclamation (Jokipii 1941: 1–15), and A. F. Puukko (1875–1954) about the governance of God and world history (Puukko 1941: 349–66). Jokipii was a well-known vicar in the Finnish Lutheran Church, author of several theological books, and a doctor of theology. A. F. Puukko, professor of OT exegesis, represented the highest academic expertise. Puukko had studied in Leipzig, Germany, under the guidance of Rudolf Kittel during the early years of the twentieth century. His close connections with Germany were strengthened by his marriage to a German, Clara Maria Helene Füchsel. Later, Puukko joined the Academic Karelia Society, and was also known as an opponent of socialist ideas (Niemelä 1999: 7–41).

In his article, Jokipii expresses regret that a "general and deeper revival" is still absent in Finland. On the other hand, the Winter War has changed the traditional God-talk:

> God was felt to be very close compared to the remoteness which was experienced previously. The sense of God's closeness and reality was often astonishing. He was now in the true sense the God of history, who was involved in what has happened. The religion of the prophets became dear and comprehensible. Their books were read, and the eyes of faith saw the God who leads the destinies of peoples and individuals. . . . The glaring injustice of a great power attacking it [=Finland] could not be ignored. Faith in the victory of justice was a necessity. But justice was supported by the living God of history. (Jokipii 1941: 5)

Furthermore, Jokipii wonders if the Winter War had been "a punishment for sins or a call." Although the punishment was actually earned, Finland was also called to protect Nordic freedom and Western civilization. Thus Finland was partially an innocent victim. The true meaning of the war was "a call, given by the God of history. The war was expected to happen under God's guidance" (Jokipii 1941: 6). Jokipii also offers a summary of common patterns of wartime proclamation.

> God is with our people, because our mission is just, and because he has led us to this. Therefore, with a firm trust in God's help we shall courageously fulfill the tasks that the war has given us. God has prepared us for this. . . . Christianity has emphasized the importance of the moral relevance of each individual, the importance of a small nation becoming a bold weapon of God.

Jokipii quotes "The Lord kills and brings to life," but does not mention that the quote is from 1 Sam. 2:6. He also warns about speaking of God's defeat because God would always win, while nations and individuals could experience losses if they did not hear the call of God. Finally, he concludes the article by stating that "the Christian church has a task to proclaim the pure Gospel of Christ without letting weight of the wartime color and distort it" (Jokipii 1941: 10, 14–15).

Jokipii uses hardly any biblical references. Yet the article presupposes the use of the scriptures and their ideology. Thus God's protection can be taken for granted without any biblical references because it is possible to observe God's guidance, and there are moral grounds for it. The special value of the prophetic texts is also mentioned without any specific references. The author sees Finland not only as a poor and small victim but also as a mighty weapon in God's hands. The final comment in the article is the most interesting. Jokipii is aware that the Christian proclamation might on some occasions be colored by the context, but he seems to be sure that this does not occur in his interpretation.

Finally, an article written by A. F. Puukko deserves special attention. Originally, it was a lecture given at the synod meeting in the Mikkeli diocese on August 21, 1941. We can expect a scholarly approach combined with a pastoral application. Puukko begins by explaining the relationship between God and king in ancient Israel, based on 1 Samuel 8–12, and includes reflections on Palestine as a Holy Land and the governance of God. He supports the Israelite conquest of the land because of "religious and ethical reasons." According to Puukko, the central issue is:

> Baal was the god of lust, who preferred sexual excitement (cultic prostitution) and made his servants lethargic. The Canaanites also polluted the land with their unclean worship, which is why Yahweh, the God of chastity and sexual purity, took the land from the Canaanites and gave it to the Israelites, who had embraced the ethical religion of Yahweh through Mosaic revelation. The battle of the land of Canaan, the Holy Land, was thus a struggle between religions (Puukko 1941:352).

Puukko does not give any biblical references to the Israelite conquest or the Canaanite religion, but the connections to the books of Joshua and Judges are obvious. The article raises an ambiguous question since the conquest story in Joshua or Judges does not say much about the superior morality or sexual purity of the Israelites. Similarly, the idea that Canaanites were sexually wild and therefore lethargic is not mentioned in the conquest story. Moreover, this kind of black-and-white imaging makes it possible to claim that ethical reasons guide God's behavior in history. According to Puukko, the Holy Land was taken from the bad Canaanites and given to the good Israelites.

Puukko was not the only scholar to describe the Canaanites as representatives of low morals. Similar voices were heard widely among Finnish scholars (Gulin 1922: 9) and in the English-speaking world. G. E. Wright represented these views when he wrote that Canaanite civilization was "one of the weakest, most decadent, and most immoral cultures of the civilized world at that time" (Wright 1957: 108).

Even though Puukko does not refer openly to Finland, his audience was probably able to recognize the unarticulated but obvious connection. Finns represented the higher ethical nation, while the Soviet Union was identified with the bad Canaanites. Partly similar rhetoric was used in the same journal against the Soviet Union and Bolshevistic ideology (Mustonen 1941: 482–83).

In the major section of the article, Puukko focuses on the prophets and explains how Elijah, Ezekiel, Amos, Isaiah, Deutero-Isaiah, and others revealed the will of God. According to Puukko, the message of the prophets is that God rules in history and is able to use even large imperial powers for his own purposes. Imperial powers such as Assyria and Babylon were also under the judgment of God. The destruction of Jerusalem was not "caused by the will of the imperial power of Babylon but by the decision of Almighty God. The destruction of the holy city [Jerusalem] was decided in Heaven, not in the war camp of the Chaldeans. It was also executed from heaven: the angel of God was ordered to fill their hands with burning coals and scatter them over the city (Ezek. 10:2)" (Puukko 1941: 359).

However, Puukko is determined *not* to interpret the apocalyptic vision of Gog and Magog (Ezekiel 38) in reference to the contemporary Soviet Union. According to him, "such theories do not stand up in scholarly study" (1941: 360). Puukko concludes: "We Finns who are fighting for our homes, for the land of the fathers, and for faith in God, have a firm belief and living hope that the judgment of God is becoming real before our eyes" (1941: 361). According to Puukko, every generation "will experience in its own way God's power and guidance in its history." This happened in 701 BCE, when Sennacherib attacked Jerusalem, and the psalmist (in Psalm 46) has seen how it will happen at the end of time. Puukko concludes that the same message appears in the hymn of Martin Luther, "A Mighty Fortress Is Our God." Thus, "It is good to remember, in both the days of victory and defeat, that God is leading the history of our nation."

The article focuses on OT themes and is based on the general scholarly knowledge of that time. Puukko obviously hesitates to apply the OT texts directly to the Finnish context. This is especially apparent in the Gog and Magog section (Ezekiel 38–39). On the other hand, Puukko often assimilates the biblical text into ancient history: for him these texts more or less describe the real and experienced reality "behind" them: the prophetic texts describe, at least in some cases, the message of God as spoken through the prophets at certain historical moments.

Puukko does not clarify why the application of the OT texts to his contemporary situation is sometimes unacceptable (i.e., in the case of Gog and Magog) whereas at other times acceptable. Puukko's method is a combination of analogy and integration. Thus, since the Holy Land was taken away from the Canaanites, who had defiled the land, the readers could assume that if the Finns practiced high ethical norms they could beat the atheistic "Canaanite" powers, namely, the Soviet Union. However, he does not say this directly; one must read between the lines.

Summary of the Sources Analyzed

An analysis of the sources has revealed various OT texts that were used in *Kotimaa* and *Teologinen Aikakauskirja* during the latter part of 1941. The major results are as follows.

Biblical Texts and Images

First, the extensive source material contains many references to the Bible as well as quotes from biblical passages. A first impression after the analysis, however, is that the most likely texts, biblical references to the conquest stories and occupation of the promised land in Joshua and in Judges, did not have a specific role in the rhetoric examined. Actually, there are only few direct references to DH passages: one reference to the Achan story (Joshua 7) and two references to the rejection of Saul (1 Samuel 15). Thus only negative examples were used. All writers interpreted the stories in an individual and pietistic way, and warned Finns about unethical behavior. This also happened in cases when the text of the DH was not toward the individual but toward the collective. Obviously, the personal application resulted from the Finnish wartime context and Finnish religious traditions, and not from the biblical texts as they are, at least not to the extent of the Finnish transference.

Second, the chosen OT texts mostly represent warnings and threats, not promises about the land. Contrary to the preliminary research hypothesis, the national Finnish agenda concerning the conquest of land (as in Joshua and Judges) did not appear explicitly in the studied texts. This means that there are no direct references to or quotes from—first or second category of the reception—the conquest stories in the DH.

A study of the reception of the prophetic books and OT texts other than Joshua-Judges turns the expected pattern upside down. In several cases, explicit references to God and the promised land are used in the Finnish war context (for example Ezek. 36:33-35). Puukko quotes texts from several prophetic books. These included Amos, Isaiah, Deutero-Isaiah, and Ezekiel, as well as Ps. 107:19, 21. For one reason or another, there seems to be much more interest in using the prophets than historical books. This can be explained in several ways. The historical books may have been seen as past historical stories, not as analogies to be used or promises for the future. We must also remember that, in Kings, the DH ends with a national catastrophe. Moreover, the prophetic books were understood to contain special value: it was possible to read them easily as promises regarding the Finnish situation as well. This becomes clear, for example, in Hannes Anttila's text, quoting Ezek. 36:33-35. He openly speaks about Karelia's ruined cities and the promise of rebuilding them.

In the sources analyzed, several texts use expressions such as "holy war," God's guidance, God as the ruler of history. These references belong to the third and/or fourth category of reception (ideological or ambiguous connections). Though several authors use the expression "holy war," they never connect this expression with the OT; but the connection does exist. Nevertheless, in the OT, the expression "holy war" does not exist; the expression used instead is "war of Yahweh." Conceptually, the specific idea of a holy war does occur in prophetic texts, including Jer. 6:4 and Micah 3:5; and as a central idea it also appears also in passages such as Josh. 10:14: "For the Lord fought for Israel" (יהוה נלחם לישראל). The deuteronomistic ideology of the ban (חרם) is mentioned only once in the Finnish texts related to Joshua 7, whereas the (Priestly) tradition of cleanliness was common currency. Above all, the basic assumption of all the writings is the trust in God's power to help in a desperate situation (see Niditch 1993: 134–49). This view corresponds to OT texts such as 2 Chronicles 20, but also to Joshua and Judges in their entirety.

The same theme is continued in texts repeating the idea that God is the ruler of history and above all nations, and that Finland is a weapon in God's hands to punish the atheistic Soviet government. Furthermore, this view led to the idea that Finland was in a crusade against ungodly forces in order to protect Christianity and the freedom of the gospel.

A large share of the writings analyzed from *Kotimaa* and *TAik* belong to the fourth category of reception (ambiguous connection). A good example is A. F. Puukko's article, especially his description of the Israelite conquest of the land, in which he uses expressions not directly or explicitly connected to Joshua or Judges (for example, about the sexually wild but somehow also lethargic Canaanites). Although Puukko does not articulate a reference to the Continuation War, he seems to have a clear though implicit agenda to connect the Finnish war against the Soviet Union with the Israelite conquest story.

In several writings, various expressions about God as the ruler of history or ruler of nations are used in a way similar to their usage in the OT, although the connections are only implicit. In these Finnish texts, there are no direct references to Joshua or to Judges, such as stating that God would fight on behalf of us like he fought on behalf of the Israelites; however, all the writers assume this belief.

CONSEQUENCES AND AFTERTHOUGHTS

Two central concepts in this analysis have been "holy war" and "crusade." The first stems from biblical roots; the second, from medieval church history. The historical background of the terms is strongly political. Political and military leaders used biblical and religious terms as part of their ideological propaganda. In Finland, the terms were first used by the commander in chief of the Finnish army, C. G. Mannerheim, in June 1941. Mannerheim shared the usage with the German dictator Adolf Hitler, who used the expression "crusade against bolshevism" in a radio speech on the first day of the war (Vuori 2011: 161).

The Finnish media and a large number of writers followed this religious-political rhetoric. Instead of critical analyses, both the bishops and military pastors emphasized the divine character of the war. Thus the Lutheran church supported war activities; and religious ideas taken from the OT were interwoven with political rhetoric.

Reception analysis of how OT conquest stories are used in the present world is a tricky task for three reasons. First, the Israelite conquest stories in Joshua are—according to a "remarkable consensus" of scholars—not real historical events but myths (Collins 2005: 46). Whatever the context and the origin of the conquest myth, it aims to promote Israelite national coherence and stimulate the fighting spirit to have the land and keep it. These same elements can be observed in the Finnish reception during the Second World War.

Second, the usage of the conquest themes raises a question: How is it possible to decide that one particular war in the entire history of the world is a holy war, a just war supported and guaranteed by God? In Finland during the war, there were no serious doubts about the religious assumption that the war was just; consequently, the whole nation seemed to share the faith in a God who would protect it. Such a belief was not based on rational arguments or a historical similarity between ancient Israel and Finland. Such a belief meant that the God beyond the Bible was used in contemporary politics, and used to promote the country's own military aims.

Finally, the Continuation War ended on September 19, 1944. Finland had lost about sixty thousand soldiers and an essential part of its territory, and had to pay war reparations worth $300 million. In a way, these terms show that Finland lost the war. However, the Second World War did not lead to the annihilation of the Finns or even to the occupation of the country by the Soviet Union. Finland remained independent; but the "promised land," a large part of Karelia, was lost in these wars.

It is far beyond the limits of this study to evaluate whether the God-talk during the early months of the Continuation War was adequate, correct, or ethical. The Soviet attack in the Winter War was, from the Finnish point of view, unjust and wrong. In such a situation, there is a natural need to seek justice and support from God. The reasons for using God-talk are understandable. Connections to the political rhetoric are obvious as well. God and religion were used and abused by religious and political figures to raise the fighting spirit of the nation.

For some the result of the wars, although not the one hoped for, was a miracle performed by God. God's hands protected the small nation from the attack of an imperial power. And for those who are skeptical of such religious rhetoric in the context of war, one may say that the moral of the story is the opposite of what it seemed. Martti Nissinen (2008: 194) concludes in his article, "From Holy War to Holy Peace," thus:

> Religion can give rise to visions of peace and reconciliation, but it can also become "evil"; God can be invoked for the purposes of violent pursuits.

Following these lines, it is possible to say that using God-talk in the way it was done during the Second World War in Finland was simply a misunderstanding: Holy Wars do not exist.[4]

Notes

1. The term "Old Testament" (OT) follows the language of the studied sources.
2. All sources analyzed are in Finnish and translated by the author of this essay.
3. All quotes follow RSV if not otherwise indicated.
4. This article was revised by Nancy Seidel with care and skill.

6

Indigenous Helpers and Invader Homelands

L. Daniel Hawk

On the north bank of the Sandusky River, not far from the business district of Tiffin, Ohio, a bronze statue of the Indian Maid of Fort Ball keeps vigil over the city. She stands with relaxed serenity, her head bowed slightly so that her eyes welcome the onlooker. What appears to be a blanket hangs from her left shoulder and falls over her left arm, which lies folded across her midsection. The effect blends the indigenous with the classical. Although she is dressed in the attire of her people, her long blanket resembles a toga, and her pose is reminiscent of the statuary of ancient Rome. On a pedestal beneath her is a large bronze plaque with a relief and inscription. The relief depicts her in profile in the same pose, facing a man also in profile and in American colonial garb. The inscription reads, "This Indian Maid keeps ceaseless watch where red men and sturdy pioneers drank from a spring whose sparkling waters flowed within the stockade of old Fort Ball." The statue and its inscription hearken back with nostalgia to a time, at the beginning of the town's settlement, when the indigenous inhabitants of the land and the immigrant people who replaced them enjoyed the sustaining life of the land together. The maiden thus stands as a kind of autochthonous guardian spirit, both evoking the land's original inhabitants and blessing settlers who replaced them.

According to local folklore, the young woman—whose name is not remembered—assisted a detachment of American soldiers who had been sent to the area to build and garrison a military depot during the War of 1812. The Maid led the soldiers to the spring, which could be enclosed within the large stockade they wished to construct, thereby ensuring a protected water supply. In so doing, she implicitly worked against the interests of her people. The War of 1812 began in part because of a smoldering dispute over possession of the Ohio Country, which the Americans claimed, the British coveted, and the indigenous peoples inhabited. Seeking to maintain a buffer between Canada and an expanding American presence in the region, the British retained strong political and economic ties with the indigenous peoples, even after Ohio was admitted to the Union in 1803. At the time, indigenous peoples still possessed many areas within the state's boundaries, including the entire northwest quadrant within which the maid and her people lived. The British supported indigenous resistance to American encroachment with arms and economic aid. When hostilities erupted, most of Ohio's indigenous peoples allied with the British.[1]

Tiffin, where I spent my childhood years, lies about one hundred kilometers west and north of Ashland, Ohio, where I now live and teach. Like Tiffin—and virtually every locale in Ohio—Ashland has an Indian story associated with its settlement and early history. Ashland's story is also set in the War of 1812 and also revolves around a helper. In Ashland's story, however, the helper is a settler who unwittingly assisted the American military in a subterfuge. The Ashland story concerns Greentown, a large, predominantly Lenape (or Delaware) town situated due south of Ashland.[2] After the surrender of Detroit to the British in 1812, Greentown drew the attention of the U.S. military, which was concerned that the town might ally with the British. The Greentown elders' declaration of neutrality did not allay American anxiety, so a military force was sent to evacuate the town and remove its population west to a secure location. The citizens, however, refused to leave. Since the size of the town precluded the use of force, the military approached James Copus, a local preacher trusted by the Indians for his honesty and fair-dealing, and prevailed on him to convince the townsfolk to leave under military escort. Copus complied and succeeded. The citizens subsequently left their homes and followed the American soldiers westward, assured by a promise that their homes would be guarded and their possessions carefully inventoried. They had scarcely departed, however, when a contingent of militia rushed into the town, plundered their property, and burned the entire settlement to the ground.

Reading Joshua in Ohio elicits obvious parallels between the narratives of conquest that relate how Israel the people possessed Israel the land and how Ohio the people possessed Ohio the land. Joshua's portrayal of a rapid, comprehensive, and complete conquest of the land mirrors the story of the decisive campaign that subdued the peoples of the Ohio Country, with General "Mad Anthony" Wayne assuming Joshua's role as the invincible invader who easily defeats the assembled might of the peoples of the land. Reports that the Israelites slaughtered everything that breathed reverberate in the story of

Gnadenhütten, where ninety-six Christian Lenape men, women, and children were slaughtered by colonial militia in 1782, as well as many lesser-known accounts. The lionization of Joshua and Caleb as heroic icons of conquest can be traced in Ohio stories about frontiersman Simon Kenton and Indian fighters such as Ashland's Thomas Sprott. And finally, the sense of destiny that configures the biblical narrative—the conviction that Israel took the land because Yhwh willed and worked to make it so—resonates with the historical determinism that shapes Ohio's story of origins—that is, the view that the Indian was destined to be swept from the land by the ineluctable tide of civilization.

Ohio's narrative of origins is the American master narrative in miniature. The motifs, tropes, and figures that appear repeatedly in local tales and Ohio folklore are regional iterations of those that configure America's national mythology. In America's national memory, characters such as Andrew Jackson and Phil Sheridan reprise Wayne's role as the invincible Indian fighter. Sand Creek, Wounded Knee, and scores of other accounts bear witness to the fact that the slaughter of innocents at Gnadenhütten was not a singular incident. The removal of indigenous peoples from Ohio, cast as a historical inevitability, was replicated in an unrelenting program of ethnic cleansing as the American Empire expanded westward.[3] Frontiersmen like Daniel Boone, Davey Crockett, and Kit Carson stand alongside Simon Kenton as exemplars of the courage and attributes of the new nation, while literary counterparts like Natty Bumppo express the quintessence of the nascent American spirit.[4]

Reading Joshua in Ohio therefore opens a window into the symbolic architecture that configures both the biblical narrative and America's national mythology. Both biblical Israel and modern America construct national identity through narratives of conquest.[5] Cast as narratives of origin in the land, the conquest narratives in each case take up the artifice of story to depict and advance the values, attributes, and aspirations that define the nation. *Conquest* provides a particularly apt forum for exemplifying national character, as the ascription of positive virtues can be clarified by constructing indigenous Others who embody the opposing traits. In brief, conquest narratives as narratives of origin *unify* and *identify*, and they do so through the rendering of oppositions.

Joshua presents Israel as an integer, a single people united by covenant and wholehearted obedience to one God and under the leadership of a single leader.[6] "All Israel" crosses into the land as a unified body and in complete obedience to Joshua (Josh. 3:17; 4:1, 10–11). "All Israel" defeats armies and captures kings and cities with such uniform and total obedience that the nation and its leader become virtually one and the same: "Joshua took Makkedah" (10:28); "Joshua defeated [King Horam] and his people" (10:33); "Joshua took that entire land" (10:16). Joshua in turn exercises perfect obedience to Yhwh and the words of Moses (11:15, 23). "All Israel" gathers to make covenant at Shechem and hears all the words of the law (8:33-35). The peoples of the land, on the other hand, are a diverse plurality. They worship many deities, and many kings lead them. Even when they act in accord, as when the kings unite against Israel (10:1-5; 11:1-5), their separate identities are meticulously articulated. The conclusion of the conquest segment accentuates the scheme by summarizing the conquest with a recapitulation of Canaanite plurality through a listing of conquered kings, set in opposition to the repetition of "one": "the king of Jericho, one; the king of Ai, which is next to Bethel, one," etc. (12:9-24).[7]

A strong unifying impulse also configures American national mythology and finds expression in national symbols and rites. The national seal is inscribed with the Latin phrase *E pluribus unum* ("one out of many"). The American flag contains a "union" of fifty white stars on a blue field and is the focus of public rituals; citizens pledge allegiance to the flag and the national attributes it symbolizes: "one nation, under God, with liberty and justice for all." The attributes of liberty, justice, and equality unite present generations with those of the past and reinforce the conviction that the United States represents the apex of human civilization and the political realization of human aspirations.[8] Narratives of conquest, whether in national or local iterations, trace the origin and development of the national character via ascription and opposition, so that, for example, American industriousness is clarified by opposition to indigenous indolence, civilization in opposition to savagery, ordered society in opposition to lawlessness, and so forth.[9]

Conquest narratives as narratives of origin also lay claim to land. They may be regarded as constitutive political myths that express the deep sentiments that bind the nations to their lands. The idea of a "homeland" constitutes a potent and fundamental element of collective identity, whether it derives from ancient ethnic sentiments or modern nationalist ideologies. It reflects "an alleged and felt symbiosis between a certain piece of earth and 'its' community," wherein the terrain shapes the character of the people and the people shape the contours of the land.[10] The nation identifies with and is identified by its landscape, so that one may speak of Israel as a people and Israel as a land, or America as a people and America as a land, as one and the same. The identities of land and people are bound together. The symbiosis is evident, for example, in national hymns such as "America the Beautiful," which associates features of the American landscape (e.g., amber waves of grain, purple mountain majesties) with attributes prominent in Americans' sense of national self (e.g., liberty, law, self-control).[11]

The identification of a nation with its land is most often expressed through narratives that speak of the people as the original inhabitants of the land. Nations that cast their origin in the land through narratives of conquest, however, must do so with a deep sense of ambivalence. If indeed the identities of a land and its people are intertwined, how can the land be viewed as the homeland of an outsider group that bears distinctively different attributes from the indigenous people? If a people and its land share an inseparable bond, how can an immigrant people claim an attachment? The answer, I propose, is mediated through the construction of a myth that dissolves the organic relationship between the indigenous peoples and their land and forges a new attachment between the land and the immigrant people.

Both Joshua and the American master narrative construct identities and attachments through a mythic "regeneration through violence,"[12] designed to resolve the conqueror's problematic claim and attachment to the land. A "myth of the emptied land" transforms territory from indigenous land to invader homeland in four stages. First, it begins with the assertion that the land is defiled or misused by its indigenous peoples. Second, the invaders enter as an irresistible force that subdues peoples and breaks their hold on the land. Third, the conquerors order the land by setting boundaries, thus establishing a new association between the outsiders and the land. And fourth, the invaders complete the process by cleansing the land of the remnants of indigenous peoples and their deleterious influence. Indigenous helpers, such as the Indian maid, occupy a pivotal role in the scheme. They welcome the invader and announce the disappearance of the indigenous peoples and the land's reordering through conquest and occupation. By this artifice, the myth mediates the transformation of indigenous land into the invader's homeland. In the end, the land has been remade in the image of the invader.

THE LAND AS DISORDERED

Joshua and the American master narrative adopt the premise that the indigenous peoples somehow disorder or misuse the land. The reader who comes to Joshua by way of the Torah already knows that the practices of the peoples of the land have had a damaging effect on the land. As a result, Moses declares that both Yhwh and the land have expelled the indigenous peoples.

> Do not disorder yourselves by any of these practices, for the nations
> I expel before you disorder themselves by them. The land has been
> disordered, and I have held it accountable for its guilt. The land has

vomited out its inhabitants. . . . For the indigenous peoples did all these repulsive things you face. And the land has become disordered (Lev. 18:24-25, 27).[13]

Moses goes on to warn the Israelites not to adopt indigenous practices and so disorder themselves, lest the land also vomit them out for disordering it (vv. 28, 30). The residual indigenous presence in the land possesses such tenacity and power that it must be completely eliminated; the land must be thoroughly cleansed of the defiling peoples. If allowed to remain, their disordering influence will threaten the survival of the new community (Exod. 23:32-33; Deut. 7:1-4).

By contrast, Israel is a community born of deliverance and configured by boundaries. Much of the narrative from Exodus through Deuteronomy details the organizing of Israelite society, thought, and practice as the nation travels through a vast and unbounded terrain. Israel enters the land as an ordered and ordering people. Its communal life in the land is configured by boundaries established by Yhwh and the commands of Moses. The ordering impulse that configures Israel promises to benefit the land as well. The land will enjoy periods of rest just as the people do (Leviticus 25), and the nation's faithful obedience to divine commands and ordinances will bring seasonal rains, well-being, and ultimately a lavish fruitfulness that realizes the land's full potential (Lev. 26:3-13; cf. Deut. 28:1-14).

Similar thinking provided the warrant for Anglo-American confiscation and settlement of indigenous lands. From the perspective of the European settlers, vast tracks of wilderness lay vacant, unused, and unproductive. An early Puritan writer portrayed the land and its people as:

> A waste and howling wilderness,
> > Where none inhabited
> > But hellish fiends, and brutish men
> > That Devils worshiped.[14]

John Winthrop, the first governor of the Massachusetts Bay Colony, declared, "As for the Natives in New England, they inclose no land, neither have any settled habitation, nor any tame Cattell to improve the land by."[15] The notion that native peoples did not make good use of the land persisted throughout the duration of imperial expansion. Occupation and possession of indigenous territory was conceived as the establishment of a new order that benefited both the land and the people who settled it. Settlement enabled the land to achieve its full potential, so that it became fruitful and productive. Ohio in particular was to become a new Eden, "the garden of the world, the seat of wealth, and the centre of a great Empire."[16] The fulfillment of this potential would require the full measure of the settlers' energies for, in the words of an early historian of Ashland County, "the country was destitute of any of the moral or material resources that bear relation to civilized life" (Knapp 1863: 15). According to another early settler, the process of transforming the land would entail "reducing a country from a state of nature to a state of cultivation."[17]

Subduing the Indigenous Nations

The fiction that the indigenous peoples spoil the land and the invaders improve it provides the warrant for the former's elimination through a campaign of devastating war. The conquest narrative in Joshua (Joshua 2–12) portrays the subjugation of the Canaanites as a rapid campaign during which Israel, virtually without effective opposition, defeats the peoples of the land and slaughters "everything that breathed" (Josh. 10:40; 11:11, 14). The complete destruction of Canaanite cities and their populations is accentuated by the repetition of the verb ch-r-m (חרם Hif., "wipe out") throughout the account (6:21; 8:22; 10:28; 30, 33, 34, 36, 38; 11:20, 21). A list of conquered kings caps and confirms the conquest of the land's inhabitants (12:9–24), signaling the end announced at the beginning of the campaign (1:2–5). Israel wins victories because the nation is propelled by a power greater than itself. It is Yhwh who defeats the forces of the land and clears the way for Israelite occupation (6:2; 8:18; 10:12; 11:8). Overall, the narrative depicts Israel as an unstoppable force that enters the land and breaks the grip of its indigenous inhabitants.

Wanton slaughter and devastating warfare also marked colonial and federal campaigns against indigenous nations, in every region and at every phase of conflict, bracketed by massacres at Mystic Fort in 1637 and Wounded Knee in 1890. The first instance took the form of a preemptive strike against a palisaded Pequot town by a New England force that struck while the warriors were away; the strike resulted in the slaughter of virtually the entire population of approximately 500 people—mostly women, children, and elders. The last occurred when the 7th U.S. Cavalry attempted to disarm a band of peaceful Lakota; confusion led to the eruption of violence and the deaths of at least 150 men, women, and children. Campaigns of total war often included the destruction of towns and devastation of fields and food sources. During the

American Revolution, General George Washington sent Major General John Sullivan on a mission against those Iroquois who had allied with the British, with instructions to achieve the "total destruction and devastation of their settlements, and the capture of as many prisoners of every age and sex as possible . . . [and] to ruin their crops now in the ground and prevent their planting more . . . that the country may not be merely overrun, but destroyed" (Washington 1779). Sullivan undertook the campaign in late October, so as to deprive the Iroquois of food during the coming winter and seed for planting in the spring. Conquest by starvation took a later tack during conflicts with the nations of the Great Plains, when the federal government enlisted sharpshooters to hunt bison nearly to extinction.

The Ohio variation on the theme includes the aforementioned account of a massacre of ninety-six Lenape Christians at Gnadenhütten, a Moravian mission village. During the Revolutionary War, a contingent of Pennsylvania militia captured the townspeople while they were in the fields. The next day, the militiamen brought them into the village assembly hall by pairs, where their skulls were crushed with wooden mallets. Numerous campaigns to burn towns and destroy crops, often timed to reduce indigenous populations to starvation and so to submission and dependency, were undertaken throughout 1700s. The conquest reached its finale in 1794 with a lightning campaign led by General Wayne, which began with the burning of indigenous towns and fields and culminated in the defeat of an indigenous confederacy at Fallen Timbers.

Ordering the Land

The overwhelming defeat of the peoples of the land allows the invader to impose a new order on the terrain. Following the catalog of defeated kings in Joshua, Yhwh identifies vast areas of Canaan still in indigenous possession (13:1-7). The account then moves to a description of tribal territories, signifying the ordering of the land by the victorious Israelites (13:8—19:48). The repetition of three terms throughout the section establishes the connection between the land's ordering, the nation's claim to be the legitimate owners of the land, and the sense of destiny that authorizes the claim. Yhwh determines the boundary (גבול, gebhul) of each territory—and the area each tribe will settle—by lot (גורל, goral).[18] Each territory is labeled an inheritance (נחלה, nachalah), that is, an unassailable, permanent, and authorized possession.[19] The association of terms forges a strong connection between each tribe and the land it inhabits, affirming that each tribe lives in its land because it was *meant* to live in that land. Stories of heroes and failures intersperse the boundary descriptions (14:6-15; 15:13-19; 17:14-18; 19:47), and reports of remnant indigenous populations intimate that the ordering of land and people will not be completed until the disordering indigenes are no longer part of the landscape (13:13; 15:63; 16:10; 17:12). The erection of monuments, the establishment of shrines and altars, and burial of ancestors initiate a physical remaking of the terrain into a distinctive Israelite *ethnoscape* (22:10-12; 24:26-28, 29-33; cf. 4:5-9, 20-24; 5:9; 8:30-35). Through the chosen people, Yhwh now establishes his order in the land. Whereas the narrative previously affirms the conquest of the peoples, the delineation of boundaries now confirms the subjugation of the land itself (18:1).

American westward expansion followed a similar pattern of subjugation and ordering. Plans for the settlement of a region were often made well before the land was actually acquired from the indigenous occupants. A precedent was set with the passage of landmark legislation that established the process by which the lands of the Old Northwest would become states. The British had ceded the lands at the Treaty of Paris, and the American government claimed them, against the claims of the indigenous peoples, by right of conquest. Federal agents negotiated treaties at Fort Stanwix in 1784 and Fort McIntosh in 1785, in which indigenous leaders agreed to relinquish claims in the Ohio Country. The indigenous signatories, however, were individuals of dubious authority, and both treaties were rejected by the main bodies of the affected nations. Nevertheless, the government held that the treaties confirmed its claim to the territory. Shortly thereafter, Congress passed the Land Ordinance of 1785, which authorized government surveyors to organize newly acquired territory into townships of six miles square. The Northwest Ordinance of 1787 then established the process by which the land would be divided into territories and ultimately into states. The scope of the legislation extended beyond Ohio to all the land north of the Ohio River and westward to the Mississippi—land that at the time was occupied by the indigenous peoples. Article 3 of the ordinance declared that "the utmost good faith shall always be observed towards the Indians; their lands and property shall never be taken from them without their consent."[20] The underlying assumption, of course, was that their land and property *would* eventually be taken. Surveyors began their work in 1787 by establishing the Point of Beginning, on the west bank of the Ohio River, for the survey of all subsequent American land. When Ohio was admitted into the Union, the state boundary was drawn to the north and west of land still remaining in the possession of indigenous peoples. Mirroring the descriptions of tribal boundaries in Joshua, the state was thus defined and bounded while Indians still occupied significant territory within it.

a South Dakota newspaper a little more than a week before the massacre at Wounded Knee:

> The nobility of the Redskin is extinguished, and what few are left are a pack of whining curs who lick the hand that smites them. The Whites, by law of conquest, by justice of civilization, are masters of the American continent, and the best safety of the frontier settlements will be secured by the total annihilation of the few remaining Indians. Why not annihilation? Their glory has fled, their spirits broken, their manhood effaced; better that they die than live the miserable wretches that they are.[22]

After the delineation of boundaries for the new state, the cleansing of Ohio took place gradually over the course of forty years. Through more than a dozen treaties, the remnants of the nations ceded their lands to the federal government so that, by 1843, the process was completed by the Wyandottes' departure from their Grand Reserve in Upper Sandusky. From that point on, the fantasy acquired a markedly nostalgic tone. The Indians of Ohio became, in the memory of the descendants of settlers, "the noble sons of the forest" who populated an idealized past. An early Ohio historian, reflecting on the departure of the Wyandottes, could therefore encapsulate the myth in these words: "Thus every foot of the soil of Ohio passed from the red men, who had so long roved its savage wilderness, into the hands of the white man, who was destined to make the wilderness bud and bloom as the rose" (Abbott 1875: 675).

The Indigenous Helper

The Indian maid of Fort Ball is the local manifestation of a pivotal figure in the myth-symbol complex that configures the biblical and American conquest narratives: the indigenous helper who welcomes and assists the invaders. Her counterpart in Joshua is Rahab, who welcomes and shelters the Israelite spies and protects them from those of her people who seek them out (Josh. 2:1-25). The spies are harbingers of the new order that Yhwh will establish upon eliminating her people. Rahab, however, offers hospitality to the spies and proclaims Yhwh's praise and mighty deeds with words that take the form of a creed (vv. 10-11). As the story unfolds, she exhibits the attributes that characterize the daughters and sons of Jacob. She is cunning and opportunistic. She praises Israel's God. She aggressively secures an inheritance in the land for herself and her family (vv. 12-14). Rahab is a quintessentially liminal figure, both a personification of the land and the voice of the people who inhabit it.[23] Her name, "Rahab" (רחב, *rachab*, "wide, broad"), evokes the idyllic description that opens the story of Israel's journey to the land: "a good and *broad* land, a land flowing with milk and honey" (Exod. 3:8). Though indigenous, Rahab assumes the traits and goals of the invaders, even sharing with them, through association, the constitutive act of deliverance that defines the nation; the red cord in her window saves her family from destruction, just as the blood on the doorpost saved Israelite families in Egypt (vv. 17-21; cf. Exod. 12:7-13). Rahab is the bridge from the undefined terrain of the indigenous peoples to the bounded landscape of the invader. She plays a pivotal role as the invasion begins, mediating in her person the polarities that differentiate the peoples of the land's past from the peoples of the land's present.[24]

The Indian maid, attired in toga-like Indian raiment, is Rahab's alter ego for the citizens of Tiffin, the local manifestation of an iconic figure in America's national mythology. Indigenous helpers meet the colonists at the two great "beginnings" of the American national narrative of conquest. The story of the founding of Jamestown, the first permanent English settlement in America, is as much about Pocahontas as it is about the circumstances of settlement. The popular story scripts Pocahontas in ways reminiscent of Rahab. Pocahontas, as the story goes, intervened to save Captain John Smith from certain death at the hands of her father, Powhatan, who had the power to crush the fledgling settlement. No matter that the story about Captain Smith was likely a contrivance. The popular account shapes the story according to the contours of the myth, so that Pocahontas occupies a place in American imagination, literature, and cinema second to no other Native American.[25]

The second great beginning in the American story—the new nation's expansion across the Mississippi River—also features an indigenous helper. In May of 1804, the Corps of Discovery, led by Meriwether Lewis and William Clark, embarked on a journey westward to gather information on the vast Louisiana Territory recently purchased from the French, and on the indigenous peoples who populated it. Early in the mission, they were joined by a French trapper and his Shoshone wife, Sacagawea. The popular story of the expedition identifies Sacagawea as an indispensable guide and translator. Her presence with the party signaled to the nations throughout the territory that the party came in peace, and her intercession with the Shoshone nation enabled the corps to barter for the supplies necessary for crossing the Rockies.[26] Sacagawea interpreted for Lewis and Clark in their various encounters with indigenous nations, which generally began with the announcement to the people that their lands now belonged to the United States and that they had a new Great Father far to the east. Sacagawea's role in the mission is commemorated by no less than eighteen statues along the route of the expedition, and she remains the only Native American whose (imagined) visage appears on U.S. currency.

The indigenous helper is the pivot upon which the land turns away from the indigenous nations and toward the immigrant people. She greets the vanguard of the invading people without resistance, readily acquiescing to their claims, their dreams, and their superiority; her story is "a prescript bearing the projected desires of the colonizer."[27] Colonization, however, is a penultimate agenda within the myth she inhabits and advances, for the fulfillment of the myth's dream is not the domination of her people: it is their disappearance from the land altogether.[28] Whether in the guise of Rahab, Pocahontas, or the Indian maid, the helper's story constructs the land not as it *was* but as it has been *remade*. In the invaders' fantasy, her people have not just been colonized. They are *gone*. The Indian maid of Fort Ball keeps vigil over Tiffin as the avatar of a hybridized landscape. Through her, an immigrant people views the land as a hospitable entity—a homeland—now re-created in their own image.

Notes

1. The Native people in the area of Tiffin, however, remained neutral.

2. Although the tribe is better known as the Delaware nation, "Lenape" is the people's name for themselves in their language.

3. Although Americans rarely use the term *empire* today with reference to their nation, previous generations used it frequently and unapologetically; its imagery remains prominent in American iconography.

4. Natty Bumppo is the hero of James Fenimore Cooper's *Leatherstocking Tales* and the literary prototype of the American frontiersman, the personification of the new nation who melds the virtues of the settlers with the attributes of the land's indigenous inhabitants.

5. I use *biblical Israel* as a literary construct. I am not concerned here with Joshua's relationship to the actual origin of Israel, models for Israel's emergence, or the processes that eventuated in the final form of the text. Instead, my focus is on the canonical narrative and its construction of identity through a narrative of conquest. I therefore take the narrative's claim that Israel entered the land from outside as a given, irrespective of when and how this claim arose and developed. I use the phrase *master narrative* with reference to the American narrative of westward expansion. Although no canonical form of this narrative exists, its contours and content are well-established and constantly reiterated in public discourse and national catechesis. Interested readers will find accessible introductions in Stephanson 1995 and Hughes 2003.

6. The Hebrew term כל (*kol*), which signifies totality ("all," "whole"), occurs over 130 times in the book with reference to Israel or Joshua-as-Israel.

7. For comprehensive study of how Joshua constructs collective identity, see Hawk 2000.

8. For an elaboration of the myths that define America, see Hughes 2003.

9. Berkhofer 1978 offers a definitive study on this topic.

10. Smith 1986: 28; see also Smith 2003.

11. "America the Beautiful," Words by Katherine Lee Bates, music by Samuel Augustus Ward; in Barbour 1910.

12. The title of Richard Slotkin's classic study, *Regeneration through Violence: The Mythology of the American Frontier, 1600–1860* (1973: see particularly 3–56).

13. All translations are the author's. "Disorder" directly, albeit woodenly, captures the sense of the Hebrew verb repeated in this passage.

14. Michael Wiggleworth, "God's Controversy with New-England," in Cherry 1998: 42.

15. Quoted in Stannard 1992: 235. Stannard (233) writes that "the idea that failure to put property to 'good or profitable use' was grounds for seizing it became especially popular with Protestants." See his overview, 232–38.

16. Cutler 1787. Quoted in Cayton 2005: 2.

17. Varnum 1788. Quoted in Griffin 2005: 16.

18. The territories of the tribes in the Transjordan are not divided by lot. On the significance of this difference, see Hawk 2000: 177–90.

19. See the discussion in Habel 1995: 33–74.

20. "The Northwest Ordinance of 1787," in Prucha 2000: 9.

21. The Hebrew text of these references uses the synonymous verb גרש (*g-r-sh* Piel).

22. Quoted in Stannard 1992: 126. Ten years later, Baum wrote *The Wizard of Oz*.

23. Musa Dube (2000: 73) draws attention to the representation of land as a woman in colonial narratives. "Women's bodies," she writes, "become the prescripts and guide maps upon which the identity and desires of the colonizer, and the colonized too, are written and can be read."

24. The narrative also accentuates Rahab's liminality in spatial terms. She lives in the city wall, the space dividing the indigenous from the invader (Josh. 2:15); and later the story reports both that she and her family are put "outside the Israelite camp" (6:23) and that she "lives within Israel" to the present day (6:25).

25. For parallels between Rahab and a popular cinematic rendering of Pocahontas, see Rowlett 2000.

26. For an introduction and review of literature on the imperialist construction of Sacagawea, see Donaldson 2006.

27. Dube 2000: 77.

28. Writing of Rahab as the mouthpiece of the colonial agenda, Dube remarks (2000: 78): "The colonizer's ideal dream is that the colonized will proclaim the colonizer's superiority, pledge absolute loyalty, and surrender all their rights voluntarily." Within the context of the myth, we may add ". . . and then vanish."

PART II

Case Studies in Judges

7

Women Frame the Book of Judges—How and Why?

Athalya Brenner

Disclaimer: Context

This article was originally written for a Festschrift in honor of my friend and colleague Yairah Amit, published in 2012. Hence, its contents and context are primarily academic: the wish to honor a colleague, as is so often done, by presenting a piece of writing within that colleague's expertise, and utilizing her own scholarship for that purpose. But even at the original time of writing, in 2011, I intended to rewrite and expand it for the planned *Texts@Contexts* volume on Joshua and Judges. Subsequently a version of this essay was delivered as a paper in an SBL session of the Contextual Interpretation Consultation in San Francisco, in November 2011, and I thank the participants in the discussion for helping me crystallize my thoughts further on the topic.

Why write about women in Judges? Ostensibly Judges is a book about men, or mostly about men. Military men, so called "saviors." Male rulers. Excluding some female figures, of course. When you read the book, this is your first impression: a men's book. However, this impression cannot last for long. There are plenty of woman figures in Judges. Here as in other biblical passages, the overt and covert links made in the Hebrew bible between female figures and the *Hochpolitik* of government, nationalism, and territory do not cease to amaze me. On the one hand, at least theoretically, women are by and large removed from the political arena. On the other hand, they are described as saviors in cases of extreme urgency—or as victims in cases of a lost social order. In other words, they symbolize the social order that envelops them to the point of exclusion. A curious paradox, certainly.

Clearly, not all is confident and self-assured in the patriarchal world order that we often watch in the biblical stories, as if we were in a film unfolding unexpectedly to display (male) heroes and antiheroes as dependents, and politically active females as either non-females (non-mothers) or else as ethically deficient, even when they operate on "our" side. And also, somehow, somewhere, there is a nagging voice that tells me, pesters me, that similar paradoxical views of social maleness and femaleness are still inherent in my own culture, in your culture, at least to a degree, in spite of variances in time, space, and mentality. So please do help me, from your own contexts: why do women, actually female figures, mainly a certain type of female figures, actually daughters, frame the book of Judges at both ends and feature in its center, for better or—more often—for worse?

Ostensibly, the book of Judges is about "judges." These "judges," שופטים (shophetim), as is widely demonstrated in the book, are persons who effect collective deliverance from (military) danger[1] more than, as more usual for the verb שפט (sh-ph-t) Qal and its nominal derivatives, they engage in legislative and juridical activities.[2] Mostly the stories and short[er] notes about "judges" in this book, apart from one, are about male judges and their escapades. However, as has been noticed by many scholars, the book begins and ends with stories about women.[3] From Achsah (Judg. 1:12-15) and a reference to the Kenites (1:16) and to Jael's group, which will come to fruition in chapters 4–5, through to the abducted Shiloh women in chapter 21, woman figures are depicted again and again as major linchpins in the evolving drama of local stories made national: the drama of attempts to move from local leadership and its overriding discontents, in spite of occasional successes, to a more central government that would generate a greater success rate and greater security for its subjects, or partners.

The roles woman figures fulfill in the individual sections (such as the Achsah story) or in larger units (Samson's biography, chs. 13–16), as well as in the overriding plan of the book, the ideological "national" framework, vary. The figures may be defined in traditional terms, that is, as daughters, wives, or mothers; that is, as male-relational figures. Achsah, Jephthah's daughter, and the young women of Shiloh/Jabesh Gilead are introduced as daughters, as are Samson's Timnite wife and her sister, and the Levi's runaway wife (ch. 19). The latter is primarily a wife, albeit a secondary one פילגש, pilegesh); also wives are Achsah, Jael, Gideon's Shechemite wife (also defined as a pilegesh, 8:31), the wife of Jephthah's father, Manoah's wife; and according to many interpreters, ancient and modern, Deborah too—the only female "judge" in this book—is wife of Lappidoth, her textually absent husband, or of Barak (Valler 2012: 236–45). Let us not forget the mothers: Sisera's mother, Abimelech's mother (= Gideon's Shechemite wife), Jephthah's mother, Samson's mother (wife of Manoah), Micah's mother, and last but not least, the metaphorical mother, the "mother in Israel," Deborah again. Woman figures can also appear as independent agents, positive or negative, with no male filiation. Such are the wise women in the court of Sisera's mother, the woman from Thebez who kills Abimelech, the whore from Gaza, and Delilah. Most of these female figures are nameless as well as male-relational: they are important for the plot and message, may even assume male knowledge, functions, or roles (Deborah and Jael, Samson's mother), but are depicted as socially marginal because of their social dependency on males, of which their namelessness is a token. Whatever the individual story or case, all these descriptions are enveloped in two rubrics, both repeated several times, both editorial. The first repeated comment covers chapters 2–16 (end of Samson's biography): "And the *sons* of Israel [בני ישראל] did/continued to do what was bad in Yhwh's eyes" (2:11; 3:7,12 ; 4:1; 6:1; 10:6; 13:1). The second comment frames the last five chapters of the book, appearing at the beginning of the last section and also at its very end: "In those days there was no king in Israel, each *man* [איש] would do what was right in his eyes" (17:6; 21:25).[4]

Having described the relevant textual data, I shall attempt to assess the ways female figures and typecasts are used in Judges for the purpose of either supporting or else refuting the alleged need for central leadership, or kingship, so as to uphold a thriving social order. In this I wish to go beyond the basic recognition that woman figures indeed feature largely in Judges and in an evaluative manner, for instance as phrased by Tammi Schneider in her introduction to her commentary on Judges (2000: xiv):

> One of the major components affecting the evaluation of the judges is the role of women in their lives. With the exception of Ehud, Tola, Jair, Elon, and Abdon, the stories of the individual judges contain some reference to a woman, either by name or description of relationship to them, who heavily affect the judge's character and actions.

Or in her conclusion (288–89):

> Men in Judges often receive a negative evaluation because of the women in their lives, and the roles those women take, though the characters of the women themselves are not always seen negatively. . . . Achsah could be considered a vehicle for a slightly negative evaluation of Othniel. . . . In Judges the focus is not on the women

as characters evaluated in their own right but as foils through whom the men, especially the judges, are tested. . . Women also serve to reveal the impact of Israel's actions on the nation of Israel at large. . . . The Shiloh women's tragic plight demonstrates how Israelite society strayed so that women were institutionally raped and the system of protection was intentionally destroyed. . . .

I find Schneider's position absolutely correct and balanced, in as far as it goes, in that she de-marginalizes woman figures by clearly pointing out some of their functions as a literary device while simultaneously emphasizing their marginal status—basically just indicators for assessing males and their behavior—in the biblical text itself. Nevertheless, I would like to take the matter further, especially because, crucially, woman figures *open and close the book of Judges, framing it on both ends.*

That the book of Judges almost begins and certainly ends with woman figures is a given fact and an indication of their importance to it. They appear as individuals and in groups, in various roles, as agents and as objects, as autochtones (indigenous) and as allochtones (foreign), in stories as well as in short notes. Let us look again at the list of female figures earlier categorized into daughters, mothers, and wives, but this time from another perspective: that of the order they come into our view within the book. Achsah stars already in chapter 1, at least in the fragment about Judah, a rare reference in Judges (vv. 12-15). Then come Deborah and Jael as "national" saviors, as against the unnamed mother of Sisera and the group of her companions (chs. 4–5). Gideon has many wives, among them a secondary wife from Shechem, Abimelech's unnamed mother (8:31). This wife and mother from Shechem is not an actor or an agent in the stories depicting her husband and son. However, her community of origin is instrumental in Abimelech's attempt to secure dominance and eventually in his downfall and death—at the hand of a woman (9:50-55). Remember Dinah and Shechem (Genesis 34)? If you do, you know already at the beginning of chapter 9 that it will end in disaster. Abimelech is killed by an unnamed woman, and his attempt to institute kingship is thus aborted. Jephthah's mother is an unnamed זונה (*zonah*, "harlot")—which is difficult to understand, since with a harlot determining paternity is an issue, while it is implied in the text that Jephthah's paternity is recognized by his hostile half-brothers (11:1-3); Jephthah's daughter is nameless too (11:30-40). The daughter is sacrificed to Yhwh in accordance with Jephthah's vow, willingly on her part—believe it or not. In Samson's saga (chs. 13–16), women seem as important as Yhwh's spirit and the Nazirite condition, even more so perhaps, as motivation and cause for the stories to unfold: from his mother, so much more proper and intelligent than her bumbling but named husband (ch. 13); to Samson's first Philistine wife, the Timnite, and her barely mentioned sister (14:1-15:6); to the Gaza whore (all of them unnamed) (16:1-3), then to Delilah, who delivers him to his fate and glory in death (the rest of ch. 16). Micah's mother, of the Ephraim hills, uses her money, stolen then returned to her by her son, to establish a local temple around a statue and an *ephod*; these are eventually taken, together with the appointed Levite priest, by the Danites on their migration to the northern Laish/Dan (chs. 17–18). The secondary wife of the Levite, again unnamed (as is her husband, apart from his tribal tag), is raped by the men of Gibeah, perhaps ultimately murdered by her husband when she returns in the morning[5] (ch. 19). In the ensuing civil strife, the Benjaminites are nearly extinguished (ch. 20). To circumvent the decision not to allow exogamic wives to Benjamin men, two solutions are found: four hundred virgins (= daughters) are imported from Jabesh Gilead, after all other locals have been killed; and the other Benjaminites are encouraged to kidnap Shiloh girls (= daughters) dancing in the vineyards and to marry them. These last two groups are unnamed as well, and there is no doubt that the young women are illegally taken by the Benjaminites (the root גזל, *g-z-l* Qal, "to rob,"[6] is used in 21:23 for this action). This is the end of the civil war and of the book: "In those days there was no king in Israel; every man did what was right in his eyes." Thus we begin by reading about a well-established daughter in Judah, newly married and working for the success of her marriage (see Klein Abensohn 2012: 133–44), outside the natural habitat—so to speak—of the "judges"; and we end our reading with two groups of daughters—young women—coerced this way or the other to marry the corrupt Benjaminites, with neither their fathers nor they themselves having a say in this matter.

A quick analysis and summary of principal features will show that:

1. Most of the woman figures, be they individuals or groups, are unnamed. The only named female figures are Achsah, Deborah, Jael, and Delilah.

2. Most figures fulfill traditional, male-relational roles: mothers, wives, secondary wives, daughters, or a combination thereof. There are two categories of exceptions: saviors and sexual objects. Abimelech's killer, Deborah, and Jael are saviors—although, in the case of the last two, they may boast absent husbands in the biblical text and/or in its interpretation; Delilah is a temptress, another of Samson's women is a *zonah*, "prostitute," and others are sexual objects in addition to being wives and/or daughters (in the Gibeah story and in its aftermath).

3. A fair number are allochtones in some degree: so are Jael, Sisera's mother and her companions, Abimelech's mother and Abimelech's killer, Samson's women apart from his mother, and the Jabesh Gilead women.

4. All female figures are involved in events presented as of intertribal or national import.

5. Only a minority—the "savior" category together with Samson's mother, perhaps also Achsah, perhaps also Jephthah's daughter—are depicted as wholly or mostly positive characters. The others are painted either negatively or indifferently, or else as nameless victims.

On this occasion, I happily exempt myself from asking, or answering, questions about the historical *truth* content of such stories. The narrated time is indeed that of the last quarter of the second millennium BCE; but this has no bearing whatsoever on the historicity or veracity of the narrated tales, or—conversely—the lack thereof. The narrating time is what counts: and this is unknown although much investigated and much speculated on. To the connection between woman figures as framers and meaning-bearers of this biblical text, and the narrating or editing or composition time, we can now turn.

In what follows I shall use as guides, or hermeneutical keys, two sets of studies. The first is the work done by Yairah Amit on biblical literature in general and in particular on Judges, and especially on the book's editing, important work in Hebrew and in English that features largely in Judges scholarship (1999b [Hebrew 1992]; 2000 [2001]), and her work on biblical literature, polemics, and ideology (1999c; 2001; 2009). The second is the work in progress of my Ph.D. student Ingeborg Löwisch, first in Amsterdam and now in Utrecht, on female genealogies in the Hebrew bible, especially in 1 Chronicles 1–9 (and see Löwisch 2009).

Amit ultimately views Judges as the end product of a unified editorial composition displaying a method, a frame, a purpose, and a plan. She shows us that attributing parts of the book to deuteronomistic editorial activities, as done by many Judges scholars, is not enough to explain the book as a whole. Without going into her arguments or conclusions in detail, let me just state her position: she views *Judges "as extant,"* in her repeated phrase (that is, in its MT form), as anchored in the Assyrian conquest of the northern kingdom and the existential crisis it produced; that is, she attributes the book as edited principally to the last quarter of the eighth century BCE, and posits it as inspiration to the deuteronomic school rather than a derivative of the latter (Amit 1999: 358–83, especially 367–75; Amit 2009).

For my purpose here, leaving the actual date of composition/editing aside for the duration, accepting that Judges is a more or less unified editorial entity highlights the fact that it not only abounds in female stories (stories that have woman figures at their center) but also that such stories frame it at its beginning and at its end; and this, in turn, highlights the editorial status: it points to a premeditated decision to introduce a unifying element, be that decision conscious (as I think) or otherwise. Looked at from the other side of the same prism, that Judges begins and ends with female stories—let us be more precise again, with daughters' stories (Achsah at the beginning; the *pilegesh* and the daughters of Jabesh-Gilead and Shiloh at the end)—supports the idea of its compositional/editorial unity.[7] This framing, in a highly—even deliberately—organized and artistic composition, can hardly be incidental.

By way of illustration, let me compare this phenomenon of framing a biblical book by female figures to another biblical book, of another genre, where the situation is similar. In the book of Proverbs the first section, or collection (chs. 1–9) is indicated as such by its own title (Prov. 1:2) and by the title of the next section (10:1), among other things. This section has female figures—personified Wisdom in her various guises (Prov. 1:20-33; 2:1-15; 3:13-18; 4:5-13; 8:1-21; 8:22-36; 9:1-12), the זרה (*zarah* ["other"? "strange"? "foreign"?]) woman (2:16-19; 5.3-20; 6:24–perhaps to v. 35]; ch. 7), and Woman Folly (9:13-18)—at their center. The last section of Proverbs (chs. 30–31) also has various female figures and figurations: there are sayings about female matters or in which females play a prominent although not a positive role (30:15-28); instruction from the otherwise-unknown Lemuel's mother to her son-king concerning women and wine (31:1-9); and the last collection of Proverbs, as well as the whole book, culminates in the acrostic poem about the אשת חיל, (*'eshet chayil*, "woman of valor") that ends it.

Proverbs, beyond any scholarly doubt, is an *edited* work constructed of shorter and longer components, of various dates and provenances. Editing, as Amit has shown us, has ideologies to promote. An act of editing shapes a text, especially when the text harks back to variable sources, styles, and attitudes. Departures and accidents may occur but would not be expected in major points, such as the all-important beginning or end which, necessarily, require more planning. Therefore, neglecting to view the arrangement of female-figure frames as meaningful in some way, perhaps time- and place-related, may be an ideologically motivated mistake made by critics and readers for their own ends. This must be true for Proverbs, where the "female" content of its beginning and end and the significance thereof has been analyzed at great length (for instance Camp 2000). Having examined the "cosmic qualities assigned to both

Woman Wisdom and the Strange Woman," Camp suggests that "more than moral pedagogy is at stake. In these two figures lies a fundamental and multidimensional expression of religious self-understanding . . . a paradigm through which other literature may be read" (324).

Following Camp's advice, let us contemplate the possibility that the same consideration applies to Judges, again a many-layered composition eventually edited into a whole, presumably and ultimately according to a plan. Why does such an editorial plan require a framing by female figures, some of which are not simply reflections or refractions of bad, bad male behavior, even when the female figures are depicted as relational? Looking at some figures may afford a partial answer. At least Achsah, Jael, and Delilah are tricksters: they trick men. Is this only a reflection on men that is attributed to woman tricksters and to their actions, in view of trickster mythology (Tannen 2007, Landay 1998) out of and in the bible (Jackson 2002[8]) and in Proverbs? Tricksters have elements of godliness in them, apart from being liminal; this is common to many cultures. A female trickster, like a male trickster in this respect, is more than a reflection: she plays a transformative role as an agent for social change.

Furthermore, and this is another possibility, with a little bit of creative arithmetic, we can also arrive at *twelve* major individuals or groups of females in the book of Judges, discounting for the time being marginal figures such as Abimelech and Jephthah's mothers, and Samson's Gaza whore. Somehow and perhaps unconsciously, twelve woman figures over and against twelve judges? Or, perhaps consciously? At any rate, this is interesting.

So far, three factors point to a more prominent role, beyond reflections of male behavior, for female characters in Judges as an edited whole: the beginning-and-end framing, the trickster and savior roles, and the quantity of female figures. Let us move on with the investigation by discussing the implied editorial envelope of Judges not only in connection with, but also beyond, the woman-figures issue.

Is the edited Judges a propaganda manifest for the kingship, covertly for Davidic kingship to be more precise, assessing pre-monarchic modes of government as inadequate and leading to anarchy, to individual- rather than collective-motivated behavior that destroys the fabric of society? This is a distinct possibility, and such propaganda would be more apparent in chapters 1 and 19–21 because of the Judah storyline and pre-monarchic anarchy, respectively. (Is this another framing device? The tribe of Judah, hardly mentioned in the body of Judges, does appear at the book's beginning and end.) With such a possibility, with such an ideology that this Judean (Davidic) kingship as the only remedy to social ills, women will be foregrounded as a mostly negative example, in the sense that where women run society, or are allowed too much freedom, or motivate, or provoke male action, chaos ensues; and the women, ironically, are among the first to get hurt. Or, put differently: where men are weak, when women get a chance to prevail, catastrophe will not be late in coming and often will first affect the women themselves. This, then, would be a device for presenting the proper social order as being transgressed almost beyond repair. A reading such as this will be in keeping with general notions of morality and gender norms in the Hebrew bible. It will explain why most of the female figures in Judges are nameless—they are not in fact important enough to have names, even fictive ones (and see Schneider 2000: 289); or perhaps this is a pointed hint as to female intrinsic worth. Almost all of the female figures in Judges are traditionally male-related anyhow, or victims; and the large amount of "negative" or victim figures would support such a view. In that case, feminist scholars have argued, that female figures frame Judges is no reason for feminist celebration; it is just one more proof that women, in biblical times, were socially inferior and that their judgment in sociopolitical matters was considered suspect. Just by the way, the framing of Proverbs by female figures can be similarly explained as non-complimentary to women, by attributing the framing to the editorial claim of the book to be addressed to "a son" or "sons" who are the learning targets; what is better than positing sexual figures, or mother figures, as metaphors for learning or acquiring learning, for at least capturing the attention of the young, privileged, metrosexual "students"?

And this allusion to Proverbs may lead to yet another conjecture. Is perhaps the book of Judges, according to Amit a "history book" (1999b: 382–83), designed to teach "boys" such as those of Proverbs, again using woman figures to attract those presumably heterosexual privileged boys to the task of learning, this time with history rather than ethics on the curriculum? That the edited composition named Judges was later, at some time, posited as part of Israel's first Prophets cycle, which we call a "history" *cycle* (since it "covers," in Joshua to the end of 2 Kings, a period of several centuries), or "saving history" according to some, is a moot point. What was the "original" intention of this composition, for its primary audiences—to learn about history, or about religion, ethics, sacred and national identity? This too is worthy of consideration; but, according to my knowledge, has not been done seriously in biblical scholarship thus far.

And there are other possibilities still. Can Judges, or Proverbs for that matter, be read as female-authored literature, because of the emphasis on woman figures and the framing by such figures on both ends? Such a reading will be important, even empowering, for female readers but, because of the reasons listed—relationality to males, namelessness, victimization, largely negative or indifferent portrayal, ensuing social chaos more than positive portraits—such a possibility does not seem to this reader feasible, not to mention the difficulty of defining female authorship in the bible in general, including the most "natural" candidate for female authorship in the bible, the Song of Songs. So let us move further.

Ingeborg Löwisch reads genealogies in 1 Chronicles 1–9 and elsewhere for traces of female active participation in such genealogies, for fragments as well as for stories. In her understanding, genealogical narration about women—as wives, mothers, sisters, daughters, ancestors, leaders, builders of cities, and so on—signifies an act of memory, hence archival effort (Löwisch 2009: 228–56). This conscious act of memory dialogically supports the exclusive social order, a regular patriarchy, while also revealing its weaknesses and actual inclusivity. Furthermore, Löwisch assigns the composition or insertion of female material, an effective act of commemoration as well as memory creation, to times of social or political crisis, post-trauma times, when previous social orders are endangered and new ones need to be reformulated. Such is the situation, in her view, for 1 Chronicles 1–9, once again a collection of various materials carefully edited into a unified whole. In the later Persian period, say from the late fifth to the early fourth century BCE, a period of uncertainty politically and culturally and economically for the small, reformulated Jerusalem/Judah/Benjamin community, new memories must be found and recorded, all weapons must be enlisted for this effort. Women—even foreign women—may be considered more elevated community members in such emergencies; and information about them, authentic or invented, is included and recorded. Such is the situation in 1 Chronicles, as Löwisch shows, specifically in the case of past, long-ago Judah genealogies, where women play a relatively foremost role, because of the apparent need to [re]create Judahite memory for the present and future (and see the story about Achsah in Judges 1, again a Judah story).

Applying Löwisch's insights to woman figures in Judges will lead to the following tentative conclusions. The *narrated*, and edited, Judges collection is about crisis events as told, to be sure—whether they be political, military, ethnic, religious, or social crises. Women are always more visible in (narrated) times of crisis, then and now, whenever "then" might have been. Crises, local or otherwise, bring women to the foreground of social activity and even politics, then and now; and this will account for the presence of female figures in individual stories, or in cycles. But: Who and when would have been interested in spotlighting women to the point of framing the entire composition by woman figures? While assessing women's contributions as largely motivational for men or secondary in themselves, this framing nevertheless—even against its intended message—constitutes an act of de-marginalizing women, of recall, of inclusion as much as or perhaps more than exclusion. Clearly, a composition date of crisis, a *narrating/editorial* date of crisis, is to be sought for Judges, a time for memory, when the northern tribes that feature largely in the book, and the royal order ostensibly introduced to solve the problems of the era described, were no longer in existence.

Traditional bible scholarship points, almost by consensus, to a deuteronomistic or DtR editorial frame for Judges—that is, as composed in a time when the northern kingdom was no more and the memory of northern groups and locales would have already been necessary and subjected to Judahite purposes. This is certainly, once again, a possibility, with the Babylonian conquest of Jerusalem serving later as initializing a further crisis point. When both the territory (the North and Judah) and the monarchy are gone, it is urgent to memorize, recall, and manufacture their essence as imagined, or idealized, for present and future.

But there is one more option. Even Amit, who advocates the "art of editing" as the cohesive element that holds Judges together, admits to the possibility that the book's editorial frame could have been created in "waves," so to speak, that segments of it might have been younger than the tentative date she assigns to its main section. I would like to suggest that the final, last editorial effort for Judges, the one that posited chapters 17–21, or at least 19–21, at the end of the book, be considered alongside the similar frame of Proverbs, and alongside the inserted women's stories in the 1 Chronicles 1–9 genealogies. Let us reread Amit's assessment of Judges and its last chapters. For her, chapters 19–21 are not the proper editorial ending to the book, but are a departure, an "artificial" ending. She states the reasons for this analysis, then concludes:

> The editorial tendency, that appended Chapters 19–21, is not consistent with the implied editing of Judges. Hence the book is to be seen within the boundaries of Chapters 1–18, while Chapters 19–21 are an editorial deviation, whose purpose is to relate to the needs of the broader context. On the other hand, one should note that this appended editing used various sophisticated techniques in order to obscure the fact of its appending and to create the impression of a natural continuation (Amit 1999b: 357).

And, a little earlier on the same page—

> Their appearance is the result of editorial reworking that had an interest in connecting our story to the composition of the book, as if

Chapters 19–21 serve a compositional function of closing the circle of the entire book.

From the perspective that I have been attempting here, excising stories in whose center stand female figures, albeit victims in the case of the last chapters, would detract from the book's structure, in the same way that taking away chapters 30–31 in Proverbs would. Furthermore, judging three chapters (or five) out of twenty-one as an appendage that is somehow alien to an overall editing plan, or frame, makes the implied editing irrelevant to a large chunk of text; and if we add the number of verses that can be labeled deuteronomistic (especially but not only in chapters 2, 3, and 10), the implied edited section will become even smaller.

It therefore seems to me that, if "editing"/"implied editing" is to be retained as a cohesive factor for the book of Judges, it must be assigned to at least two "waves" of editorial activity. Amit may be correct in assigning the first "wave" to the last quarter of the eighth century BCE, a time of grave crisis; or, the proponents of the deuteronomic provenance for the book may in essence be correct in their attribution. At any rate, the hallmark of that first-wave editing is the assessment of a period as the period of "judges," and of theological disloyalty to Yhwh (chs. 2–16; or also with chs. 17–18, with no "judge" in the latter but through the associative connection with Samson's tribe, Dan, and its problems that lead to relocation). Be that as it may, a second editing "wave" that includes the factors concerning women figures—framing the collection at beginning and end, tricksterism, relationality, large-scale namelessness, negative as well as positive social roles (chs. 1, 17–21 or 19–21)—is implied not only from reading Judges on its own but also by reading it in parallel with Proverbs. And the principle of political/military crisis as a push for memory composition, also apparent in 1 Chronicles 1–9, is probably valid for Judges as much as it is valid for Proverbs and Chronicles—perhaps in the same early Second Temple period, a post-trauma (exile) period.

Quite a number of allochtonous women are mentioned in Judges, not always kindly. This may be in parallel to the exogamy/endogamy battles featuring in Ezra-Nehemiah, among other things. And creating a memory of what is no more is a third room, in Homi Bhabha's idiom, where women are allowed, in whatever capacity, whether or not they were ever in actuality allowed opportunities and influence in times past.

To summarize: I have tried to understand in this short essay why woman figures feature so largely in the book of Judges; moreover, why they actually frame the book front to back, as it is ultimately transmitted to us. Here are my main, tentative conclusions, which reach beyond "the woman's question" per se.

First, it is almost customary to view chapters 17–21 or at least 19–21 as "additions'" to the "original" book, since no "judges" are mentioned in them. My reading has shown that excluding those chapters from the as-is composition and defining them as "additions" would not undermine its framing by woman figures (Delilah in ch. 16, and the cheated and idolatrous mother in ch. 17!), but is hardly justified, among other reasons since no known version of Judges exists without those chapters.

Second, much material in this collection is indeed woman-focused. Far from being an "addition," the last chapters support the woman-focus as a literary structural device; the status of those chapters as understood in much Judges scholarship, then, should be revised.

Third, the book's name, together with the name's influence on its interpretation, is late-editorial and, in light of the above, tendentious although secondary or tertiary, or whatever, chronologically and otherwise. That the names eventually given to biblical books were at times arbitrary or non-descriptive, derived from their opening words, and then changed in translation according to contents is borne out by the Hebrew book names such as שמות ("names", = Exodus), ויקרא ("he called"= Leviticus), and so on and so on—who knows what the original name of Judges was, or its name in any stage of its edited coming-into-being? "Women and men in God's Service," or some such name? Or simply an attribution to a known or imagined redactor/editor, as in Samuel, or Isaiah, or Jeremiah, or Ezekiel for instance?

Fourth, the book's placing between Joshua and Kings makes it a "historical" book in our reception, whereas its original purpose, or context, might have been completely different, not to mention the purpose and content of its individual components, short or long.

Basically, while on this journey following Judges "women," I used five hermeneutical keys, two biblical and three bibliographic. The biblical keys were the textual data that woman figures abound in Judges and Proverbs 1–9, both complex and heavily edited collections, to the point of framing these two biblical books, and also pepper 1 Chronicles 1–9; and the varied roles those woman figures perform in those books. The bibliographical keys were studies by Amit on Judges and Löwisch on 1 Chronicles 1–9, considering editorial framework in the case of the former; issues of female inclusion in the latter; crisis, ideology, and memory in the work of both; and, to a lesser extent, Camp's work on Proverbs 1–9. Possibilities of interpretation were offered as reflections, the only rejected interpretation being—and regrettably so—that of female authorship/editorship for Judges (or Proverbs, for that matter).

Notes

1. So also in, e.g., 1 Sam. 8:5-6, when the Israelite elders ask Samuel to "Give us a king to govern us," according to the JPS and the NRSV, while the KJV has "to judge us."

2. The juridical and the military functions are at times coupled in biblical literature, viewed as required, complementary attributes of a leader's ability to fulfill the leading role (notably as in 1 Sam. 8.20b: "Let our king rule over us and go out at our head and fight our battle" (JPS), "and that our king may govern us and go out before us and fight our battle" (NRSV), "and that our king may judge us, and go out before us, and fight our battles" (KJV). Here too the term translated "govern" more recently and "judge" earlier is the Heb. שפט (sh-ph-t) Qal. And see *inter alia* BDB for the term (where both "judge" and "govern" are given unproblematically as head meanings, 1071). For this article, this is a minor point, worth referring to briefly simply because for decades now a shift judge>govern, rule or a certain contextual synonymity has been taken for granted in Judges research. It is perhaps worth noting that the only "judge" in the book of Judges to actually engage in juridical activity is Deborah: "She used to sit under the palm of Deborah between Ramah and Bethel in the hill country of Ephraim; and the Israelites came up to her for *judgment*" (Judg. 4:5 NRSV); "And she dwelt under the palm tree of Deborah between Ramah and Bethel in mount Ephraim: and the children of Israel came up to her for *judgment*" (KJV); and somewhat obscured in the JPS: "She used to sit under the Palm of Deborah, between Ramah and Bethel in the hill country of Ephraim, and the Israelites would come to her for *decisions*"; and the NIV: "She held court under the Palm of Deborah between Ramah and Bethel in the hill country of Ephraim, and the Israelites came to her to have their *disputes decided*."

3. See, e.g., Klein Abensohn 2012.

4. Both translations are mine.

5. It is not at all clear whether the woman is dead in the morning, or dies thereafter. The text is somewhat opaque: "Toward morning the woman came back; and as it was growing light, she collapsed at the entrance of the man's house where her husband was. When her husband arose in the morning, he opened the doors of the house and went out to continue his journey; *and there was the woman, his concubine, lying at the entrance of the house, with her hands on the threshold.* 'Get up,' he said to her, 'let us go.' But there was no reply. So the man placed her on the donkey and set out for home" (vv. 26-28 JPS; emphasis mine).

6. גזל (g-z-l) Qal and Nif. and derivative nouns such as גזלה (*gezelah*, "robbery" or "something robbed," BDB 159–60) appear in the Hebrew Bible over forty times. The English translations here seem to have shied away from the strong biblical definition of the Benjaminites' action. Thus the translations of this term are softer: "carried off" (JPS, NIV), "caught" (KJV), "abducted" (NRSV).

7. This of course does not imply a denial of the probable history, perhaps a long one, for oral and/or written, individual sections, or even a proto-Judges composition.

8. Jackson, meanwhile, completed her Oxford Ph.D. about comedy and feminist criticism of the Hebrew bible (degree awarded 2008), with elaboration of the 2002 article. Although I have seen the dissertation, I was unable to consult it at the time of writing. The revised dissertation is now published (end 2012) but I have not been able to consult it either.

8

Jael, *'eshet heber* the Kenite: A Diviner?

Ora Brison

This essay is dedicated to the memory of my late friend Shery Curiel, whose support and insightful input of an earlier draft were invaluable to me, and especially for her friendship that I miss so much.

A Personal Introduction

My experience in volunteering at an abused women's shelter in Tel Aviv gave me firsthand acquaintance with violence against women in the Israeli community of the twenty-first century. I could hardly understand how it was possible for a woman in our "modern, democratic, egalitarian, and liberal" society to undergo and accept abusive, humiliating, and painful situations. Meeting with and talking to women who were subjected to continuous abuse and violence, and whose self-esteem was at the lowest possible level, influenced the choice of subject for my Ph.D. thesis. After spending so much time with intimidated and dependent women, I wanted to counterbalance that disturbing experience by spending time in the company of some resilient and independent women. So I decided to examine the reverse phenomenon: that of literary female figures portrayed as strong, independent, and aggressive.

My thesis, "Between Biblical Heroines and Heroic Goddesses: Female Heroines in the Hebrew Bible and Ancient Near East Literature," focuses on narratives of mythological and biblical heroines who, by performing dramatic and sometimes violent acts, and while endangering their lives, save people close to them.[1]

Among the heroines in my research are Zipporah, Deborah, and Jael of the Hebrew Bible, and Judith of the Apocrypha. In the course of my research, I came to realize that the heroines whose conduct is unconventional and characterized by gender role-reversal, and who are portrayed as having independent and sometimes aggressive behavior, are also linked to cultic activities and religious practices. I therefore suggest analysis and examination of various lacunae in those heroiness narratives, as well as dealing with unanswered questions, from cultic and religious perspectives. This research approach might help finding cultic traces that are embedded in the stories, and could contribute to a better understanding of the heroines' *Sitz im Leben*, as well as provide clearer insight into the "femininity paradigm" of patriarchal ideologies. Looking at the limited and restricted status of (contemporary) Orthodox Jewish women in Jewish Orthodox religion and cult, and coming from an Orthodox family background myself, I would like to give these women their rightful place in the Israelite cultus.

The Encounter between Jael the Kenite and Sisera

For this essay I have chosen the story of the ambiguous encounter between Jael the Kenite and Sisera, the army commander of Jabin king of Hazor, described in the book of Judges in two versions: prose (4:17-22) and poetry (5:24-27).[2] This war story portrays two heroines who are involved in violent actions:[3] Deborah and Jael. Deborah initiates the war against the Canaanites, is responsible for recruiting Barak and gathering the Israelite army, and participates herself in the battle. She delivers the prophecy that will determine the war's outcome by selling Sisera "into the hand of a woman" (Judg. 4:9).[4] Jael seemingly acts on the prophecy and fulfills it by killing Sisera (4:21; 5:26-27).

Most scholarly interpretations and readings present the encounter between Jael and Sisera as a variant story of the cross-cultural literary genre on the themes of seduction, trickery, violence, and death, portraying a female figure that deliberately lures an enemy to his death with food and drink and, most significantly, sexual enticement.[5]

Prevailing Commentaries and Interpretations

The commentaries regarding the Jael-Sisera story as a sexual encounter go back to the early interpretations of Pseudo-Philo (*L.A.B.* 31.3) and talmudic scholars (*TB Yeb.* 103a and *Naz.* 23b). Currently, those holding this approach include Fewell and Gunn, who claim that a man's entering into a woman's tent was almost always for sexual purposes (1990: 392). Niditch finds the story rich in images of sex and death (1989: 43–57; 1993: 113–15). Similarly, Fuchs (1985: 137–44; 1999: 77–84), Bird (1997: 34), and Sharon (2007: 249–69) consider this to be a story of sexuality, trickery, and violence. Reis (2005: 24–47) finds that the story "smolders with sex" and explains Jael as a "femme fatale" (25). Halpern says that Judg. 4:17-22 stands without doubt among the most lurid texts in the Hebrew Bible (1983: 388). Soggin suggests that Sisera forced his presence upon Jael, but condemns her behavior for disregarding the rules of hospitality (1981b: 77–78). Zakovitch contends that while most of the sexual innuendoes have been excised, there are enough clues to read the story as one of rape and vengeance (1981: 364–74). Yee finds the killing scene a reversal of rape, where the rapist becomes the victim (1993: 116). Matthews says that the story is about hospitality (1991: 13–21). Klein finds that Jael is a woman "devious with sexuality," who breaks the code of the host (1988: 42). Alter remarks that although "Jael's initial words to Sisera might almost be construed as a sexual invitation . . . she at once assumes a maternal role toward her battle-weary guest, tucking him in like a child, giving him milk rather than the water he requested" (Alter 1983: 615–37; also 1985: 48). Bal (1988c: 145–46; 1988b: 208, 213) proposes that the stories are not about sex, but rather that Jael offers Sisera the basic attributes of maternity: protection, rest, and milk. Brenner, too, finds maternal imagery in the description of Jael, but says it is combined with some sexual connotations (1985: 119; 1994: 46). Brenner adds that the elements of hospitality are dominant in chapter 4; in chapter 5, she points to some elements reminiscent of a natural birth scene (1993a: 103–5).

It is worth noting that throughout the centuries the responses to Jael's deed have been ambivalent, and have oscillated between praise and condemnation.

AN ALTERNATIVE READING

I shall offer another interpretation to this enigmatic encounter, arguing that various elements, details, and intertextual patterns in Judges 4 and 5 indicate that the texts, though reworked and edited, embed traces of aspects associated with cultic practices of magic and divination. The setting, atmosphere, imagery, and dialogues point to a different picture: not of a chance encounter of a defeated general looking for shelter with a woman in front of her tent, but of a military leader seeking an audience with a (female) cultic intermediary/diviner in order to learn about his future fate.

The proposed interpretation will be demonstrated by comparing the Jael-Sisera story to two other biblical stories that, according to my reading, belong to the same literary genre, both sharing the same theme and taking place in times of war and community distress. The first is the encounter between King Saul, the medium (אשת בעלת אוב, *'eshet ba'alat 'ob*)[6] of En-dor, and Samuel's spirit, on the eve of Saul's final battle with the Philistines (1 Sam. 28:5-25). The second story occurs during the Israelites' sojourn in the wilderness and recalls the prophet-diviner Balaam and Balak king of Moab (Numbers 22–24). The two military leaders seek advice from cultic intermediaries/diviners. The diviners unwillingly foretell the protagonists of their impending defeat in battle and, moreover, King Saul then learns of his own impending death.

These two encounter stories share themes of prophecy and divination. I suggest a similar reading of the Jael-Sisera encounter story, a reading from a cultic perspective. The main similarities and differences between the stories, together with the Deborah-Barak encounter, are compared and presented in table 1 at the end of this essay.

My proposed interpretation has been formulated through a close reading of the relevant biblical text and its literary analysis.

Preface and Background

The two versions in Judges 4 and 5 share the same basic plot, the same background, and the same characters; the events portrayed in both are similar, and so are many parallel elements (Amit 1999: 218–20; Brenner 1993: 98–99). These texts, although different, do not contradict but rather complement and harmonize with each other.[7] In this article, these two texts will be treated as a single story. The two versions contain lacunae, puzzling expressions, and unique words (*hapax legomena*), and pose long-standing questions: Why, after losing the battle to Israel, does Sisera flee to Jael's tent? What happens in the tent? And, above all, what motivates Jael to kill Sisera? It is striking that Jael, a Kenite, not an Israelite, is chosen to deliver the *coup de grace*, vanquish the foe, and complete the victory of the Israelites over the Canaanites. Neither the prose nor the poetry text provides answers or solutions to these conundrums.

Background: Proleptic Exposition

Prior to the meeting between Jael and Sisera, two retrospective details about the Kenites are introduced.[8] Put together with Deborah's enigmatic prophecy/oracle that "the Lord will sell Sisera into the hand of a woman" (Judg. 4:9), those details foreshadow events that lead to the fatal encounter.[9] Thus on the narrative level, the readers get to know, first, something the protagonists do not (Alter 1981: 20). The first informative detail is, "Now Heber the Kenite, of the children of Hobab the father-in-law of Moses,[10] had separated himself from the Kenites and pitched his tent near the terebinth tree at Zaanaim ('Elon-beza'anaim), which is beside Kedesh" (Judg. 4:11).[11] Biblical places that bear names related to sacred trees, such as 'Elon Moreh (Gen. 12:6) and 'Elon-Me'onenim (Judg. 9:37), were associated with cultic sites (Mazar 1965: 301; Ackerman 1998: 96–97). The second piece of information is: "For there was peace between King Jabin of Hazor and the house of Heber the Kenite" (Judg. 4:17). "That expression means not just friendly relations but an alliance," says Soggin (1987: 66–67).

Similarly, in Saul's encounter with the medium of En-dor, foreshadowing informative details are provided. One tells of the death and burial of Samuel (1 Sam. 25:1), and the other reminds the reader, "And Saul had put the mediums and the spiritists out of the land" (1 Sam. 28:9).

The poetic version mentions one more informative detail: "In the days of Jael" (Judg. 5:6) suggests that Jael was very likely a known public figure (Hackett 1985: 22–23). The relevance of positioning these expositional background details here is of a proleptic nature (Murray 1979: 159), and will be discussed later.

קינים *(KENITES)*, חבר *(HEBER)*, אשת *('ESHET)*

THE KENITES

The links between the Kenites of Midian and the Israelites stretch back to Moses and his father-in-law, Jethro, the priest of Midian (Num. 10:29–33). Traditions about ties between the Kenite priests and the priests of the tribe of Levi were reinforced (from the archaeological perspective) when an altar and a high place were discovered in an archaeological dig in Arad. Mazar surmises that the Kenites were Midianite priestly clans that first settled in the Negev-Arad area and later migrated elsewhere, also northward, establishing additional ritual sites in their newer encampments. He regards the relationship with Jethro, noted in the Jael-Sisera story, to be of a cultic context. Mazar proposes that Sisera fled to Jael's tent to seek sanctuary (1965: 297–303). His argument is extended by Cross (1997: 200–201) and Ackerman (1998: 93–102). One does reasonably assume, then, that 'Elon-beza'anaim might have been a Kenite cultic center.

חבר (HEBER): IS IT A PROPER NAME, A TRIBAL NAME, OR AN OCCUPATION?

The etymology of the root חבר, (h-b-r, pronounced *ch-bh-r*), might be understood as of West-Semitic or Akkadian origin, both with a wide semantic field (O'Connor 1986: 77). The range of the uses of *h-b-r* in the Hebrew Bible includes different terms and verbs stemming from this root. For example: "to associate" (Qal: Gen. 14:3 Hithpael, 2 Chron. 20:37; cf. also the noun *haber*, "friend, colleague" Prov. 28:24), "to bind" (Piel: Exod. 26:3-10), and "wound" (noun: Isa. 1:6; Prov. 20:30). Finkelstein interprets the root *h-b-r* as "to be noisy" following the Akkadian *habaru* (1956: 328–31). In past scholarship, the *heber* mentioned in Judges 4 and 5 has been mostly understood as the name of Jael's husband. *Heber* appears as a proper name of other individuals in Gen. 46:17=1 Chron. 7:30-32; Num. 26:45; 1 Chron. 4:8; 8:17. In Num. 26:45 also, a derivative form, "the Heberite," is used. The accepted current explanation for the *heber* mentioned in Judg. 4:17, 21, 24, and in Hos. 6:9, following the Akkadian *hibru(m)* in the Mari texts, is that *heber* indicates a small tribal subdivision, a group or a clan of families (Malamat 1962: 144–45; Gray 1986: 258.

The religious associations of *h-b-r* are generally of a negative nature. In Hos. 4:17, the prophet says that Ephraim is חבור עצבים, *habur ʿatzabim*, "an assembly of idols"; and Isa. 44:11 alludes to a פסל, *pesel*, "idol," and חבריו *haberaw*, "its assembly of idols" (O'Connor 1986: 78). The joining of *heber* and *hober*, חובר חבר (*hober heber*) as a noun phrase occurs in Deut. 18.11 in the list of diviners and magicians. *Hober heber* is explained as a cultic functionary who ties magical knots, a spell-binder, following the Akkadian *ebēru*, meaning to "bind, join." In Mesopotamia, tying knots in colored wool was thought to ward off evil spirits and curses. Jeffers (1996: 32) proposes that the *hober heber* could be connected not only with the principles of sympathetic magic (tying of knots), but might also be regarded as מלחש (Ps. 58:5), a spell-caster: "a person who binds his victims by the use of words, mutterings, incantations and curses." *HALOT* (287–88) adds that *heber* may be a common noun meaning magic, sorcery, or incantation, generally in the plural, as mentioned in Isa. 47:9, 12 and Ps. 58:5. The root *h-b-r* appears in a list of evildoers, *hbrm*, in an Ugaritic inscription (Avishur 1981: 16). The root *h-b-r* is also found in a Phoenician inscription from Seville, Spain (dated c. 730 BCE): *bny sʿf lʿstrt hbry tnt*. This is interpreted by Solá-Solé (1966: 97–108) and Vattioni (1967: 178–80) as "mediums/oracle priests of Astarte, spell casters of Tinnit," following Deut. 18:11. This may indicate the use of *h-b-r* derived terms by the Phoenicians as well. It seems that the interpretation of *h-b-r* in its religious/

magical connotation is quite relevant, and I, therefore, adopt this explanation for this proposed reading for Judges 4 and 5.[12]

אשת ('ESHET): WIFE OF HEBER? A FAMILY/GROUP RELATIONSHIP OR CULTIC OCCUPATION?

In biblical literature, the form אשת, 'eshet (construct state of אשה, "woman, wife") generally refers to a married woman, hence another reason for the majority understanding, "Jael *wife* of Heber the Kenite." Seeing that *heber* in the role of Jael's husband has no independent function in the story, another interpretation might be considered. Syntax analysis shows that Hebrew *'eshet* joined with an apposition in a construct state can be descriptive, such as in *'eshet kesilut* ("woman of folly," Prov. 9:13); *'eshet chayil* ("woman of valor," for instance Prov. 31:10; Ruth 3:11); or *'eshet zenunim* ("woman of harlotry," Hos. 1:2). A parallel formation has "woman" and an adjectival modifier, not in the construct state, for the same designatory purpose. Examples are *'ishshah zonah* (once again "woman of harlotry," for instance, Judg. 11:1) and *'ishshah neb'iah* ("woman of prophecy" = "prophetess," Judg. 4:4). Following HALOT (43–44), such constructs may indicate occupation or public office, in parallel to the noun formation איש אלהים, *'ish 'elohim* ("man of god," 1 Sam. 2:27) and איש כהן, *'ish kohen* ("man of priest[hood]" = "priest," Lev. 21:9). Therefore, *'eshet heber* can be considered the counterpart of *'eshet ba'alat 'ob*, "medium," as used in the Saul-medium story (1 Samuel 28).

THE ENCOUNTER

This is a dramatic story in three acts, portraying three protagonists, Jael, Sisera, and Barak, with Deborah's prophecy in the background. There is symmetry between the first and third acts: both take place outside Jael's tent. In the first act, Sisera arrives at Jael's tent; and in the third, it is Barak who arrives there. The second act, which takes place within Jael's tent, is the centerpiece.

ACT 1: OUTSIDE JAEL'S TENT: "AND JAEL WENT OUT TO MEET SISERA";
"DO NOT FEAR!

SISERA'S ARRIVAL

Defeated in the war against Israel, Sisera abandons his chariot and flees the battlefield. His soldiers retreat toward their own city, Harosheth Hagoyim, where they hope to find shelter and protection (4:15). The reader expects Sisera to go with them, but, behold! Sisera goes in the opposite direction, toward the tent of Jael *'eshet heber* the Kenite, located within Israelite territory. The accepted explanation for his chosen direction is the peace treaty between Jabin King of Hazor and the Kenites, with whom he sought shelter, as mentioned in Judg. 4:17 (Murray 1979: 159–60).

When this information is taken literally, some questions arise. If such a treaty did exist, why then did the other soldiers not seek shelter in the same direction? Why does the text not state that Sisera sought help from his Kenite allies? Why does Sisera flee explicitly to the tent of Jael? Matthews adds another question: If Sisera was indeed seeking sanctuary, should he not have approached the tent of the head of the household, rather than that of his presumed wife (1991: 15)? Did he have an ulterior motive? It is possible to assume that Sisera's reason was unrelated to military help or search for shelter. He may have chosen his destination deliberately—the tent of a known woman, "*'eshet heber* the Kenite," in the sacred place 'Elon be-za'anaim. By designating the tent to Jael herself, the author implies that it may have had a special significance and that she might have been an independent woman, therefore a professional working for her livelihood. Sisera probably understood that he had not been defeated by the small, unprofessional Israelite army, but that the God of Israel had determined the fate of the battle (Judg. 5:20-21). One also may assume that Sisera, defeated and humiliated, had abandoned his chariot and fled on foot so that he would not be recognized, wishing to avail himself of Jael's known abilities. In his distress, he sought a known diviner/cult practitioner to reveal what his future held.

The similarity to the story of King Saul and the medium of En-dor is apparent. King Saul, too, is presented in a humiliating state. Stealthily, in disguise, and under cover of the night, he comes to consult with the medium after all other efforts to obtain divine guidance through legitimate channels have failed (1 Sam. 28:6, 15).[13]

"AND JAEL WENT OUT (OF THE TENT) TO MEET SISERA"

This phrase opens both the first and third acts (4:18; 22), and is one of the important keys to the understanding of the story. In the ancient Near East, a woman leaving her tent to greet a man not of her kin deviates from all customary norms of female conduct. All norms and conventions of modesty in such societies contravene Jael's independent and improper behavior when she exits the tent to welcome Sisera and, later, Barak (Frymer-Kenski 1992: 53, 86, 232). Furthermore, Jael tells Sisera, אל תירא, 'al tira', "Do not fear!" (4:18). One would think that as an unprotected woman who left her private domain for the public she should be fearful for her life vis-à-vis Sisera, portrayed in the poetic version as a warrior who seizes women as spoils of battle (5:28-30). Why would he fear one solitary woman?

JAEL'S TENT

The word אהל, 'ohel ("tent") occurs often in the Hebrew Bible in a cultic context, describing the dwelling of God during the Israelite sojourn in the desert (Exod. 39:32; 40:2, 6): the terms משכן, mishkan, or אהל מועד, 'ohel mo'ed ("tabernacle tent") were apparently retained for many generations after the settlement in Israel (Ps. 15:1; 78:60).[14]

If we accept the proposal that Jael's tent was no ordinary tent but had a distinctive cultic function,[15] then there is another argument for understanding Jael's unusual behavior in going out of the tent and her welcoming conduct toward Sisera and Barak. In the ancient Near East, a cultic tent or temple had an open area—a courtyard attached to or surrounding it. That courtyard (Greek, temanus) was also regarded as a sacred place into which only cultic functionaries and priests were allowed to enter (Meyers 2005: 235–37; see, for example, Exod. 27:9-19; Lev. 6:9; 1 Kgs. 8:64). In addition, the expression "the door [entrance] of the tent," mentioned later, occurs several times in the Hebrew Bible, mainly in the context relating to the appearance of God or God's emissaries (Gen. 18:1-2; Exod. 33:9-10; 39:38; Num. 12:5). If so, we may understand why Jael comes out of the tent, stays within its sacred boundaries, and is not afraid to talk to Sisera or Barak.

אל תירא ('AL TIRA'), "DO NOT FEAR"

This initial statement is the only time Jael speaks to Sisera, and it is worthy of special attention, as it is important for the exposition of the character in the story (Alter 1981: 90). The expression that Jael utters, "Do not fear" (4:18), is cardinal to the narrative and appears in the Bible dozens of times. In several revelations, God exhorts such chosen ones as Abraham, Jacob, and Moses not to fear, using these very words (Gen. 15:1; 46:3; Num. 21:34). The literary formulas: "Have no fear," "fear not," or "do not fear" are also known from other literary texts of the ancient Near East, notably from prophecies and oracles delivered to kings. As a statement of encouragement from the gods, it is frequently found in prophecies to the Assyrian king Esarhaddon (681–669 BCE), often delivered by women diviners (Parpola 1997: 5; Weinfeld 1977: 183–84). The goddess Ishtar of Arabela uses the same expression, "Have no fear!," when she appears to the Assyrian king Ashurbanipal (669–627 BCE in a message-dream (Gafney 2008: 65). Koehler (1919: 33–39) maintains that the expression is a type of prophetic introduction also in the Bible. In this initial dialogue the authoritarian figure, Jael, uses the expression vis-à-vis the weaker figure, Sisera.

It is reasonable to assume that Jael's tent stood apart from the other Kenite tents, since we are not told that anyone else comes out to meet Sisera.[16] One may also suggest here that Sisera was afraid of the tent itself—which may have been no ordinary tent—or of something inside it. Based on the assumption that Jael's tent was sacred and on Jael's authoritative image, one may reasonably assume that she might have been a cultic functionary and a public figure, and probably enjoyed freedom of speech and freedom of movement beyond that of an ordinary woman. As a woman who might have had a role in the community, she was probably used to receiving strangers in her tent. The invitation to enter the tent makes it is quite clear that Jael is not afraid of Sisera. We know nothing of what Sisera says to Jael. He does not explain why he has come, nor does he reply verbally to her invitation. The reader feels that fragments of an introductory dialogue may have been omitted. Jael probably did not recognize Sisera, but she clearly knows why he has come. This opening scene shows an image of welcoming and protection (Alter 1985: 48–49). Here, it is worth mentioning that the initial dialogue between King Saul and the medium of Endor, in comparison, presents a completely different situation. In 1 Samuel 28 the medium is the one who is afraid and suspicious of King Saul and is reluctant to perform her task. Furthermore, whereas Saul declares, from the beginning, the purpose of his arrival at the medium's place, there is no mention of Sisera's intentions.

ACT 2: INSIDE JAEL'S TENT: שמיכה (SEMIKHA) ספל אדירים (SEFEL 'ADDIRIM), קרב (Q-R-B)

Once Sisera and Jael enter the tent, she performs several actions, employing different materials and unique artifacts. Occurrences within the tent are very intensive and dramatic; therefore, one might consider that the description of all these seemingly trivial elements serves an essential function in the narrative. Are these artifacts ordinary household items?

שמיכה, SEMIKHA

Jael's first act is to cover someone or something with a *semikha* (4:18–19), a noun that appears in the Bible only in this one instance and whose etymology is unclear. Bible scholars concur, from the context, that this word means "blanket, rug," or "mantle." The accepted interpretation is that Jael covers the weary Sisera with a blanket/rug to hide him from his pursuers. This raises questions.[17] In no other act of covering someone who goes to sleep does the Bible use the word *semikha*. A person who is cold or asleep is covered with clothes, as with the aged King David (1 Kgs. 1:1) and the drunken Noah (Gen. 9:23); and Michal, wishing to conceal David's flight, uses clothes to cover the figure lying on the bed (1 Sam. 19:13). Besides, covering Sisera seems to interrupt the sequence of the previous activities. Furthermore, try as I may, I cannot recall anywhere else in the Bible where a military hero lies down to sleep while being pursued by his enemies!

The Bible frequently mentions the coverings of ritual objects—the ark of the covenant, the altar, and various implements used in the sanctuary. These covers were made of expensive woven textiles and animal skins intended for the sacred objects used for rituals only, and they are not mentioned in any other context (Exod. 35:12, 40:21; Num. 4:5). We may assume that the *semikha* is some kind of cultic cover. Now, let us examine the other elements and objects in the story.

ספל אדירים, SEFEL 'ADDIRIM

The noun *sefel* ("bowl") occurs in the Bible only here and in one other time, in the story of Gideon and the sign/omen of the fleece (Judg. 6:35). The *sefel* as a sacred drinking object is also associated with the Ugaritic gods (Cassuto 1952: 26, 63; Parker 1997: 60; Smith 1997: 106). Occurrences of using the "bowl" reinforce the assumption that the *sefel 'addirim* ("lordly bowl"), in which Jael offers curds/cream might have been a ritual object (a libation vessel) designed for cultic purposes, and not a household utensil. "Please let me have some water for I am thirsty," Sisera asks of Jael (4:19). She serves him חלב ("milk"), and "she brought out cream (חמאה) in a lordly bowl" states the poetic version (5:25). Both written and iconographic sources of the ancient Near East emphasize the importance of milk and curds (often paired), which were considered a source of vitality and were offered to the gods.[18] Reis says that in giving Sisera milk, instead of the water he requests, Jael gives the drink she wants to give, and not the drink he wants to get, which shows Jael's continuing control over him (2005: 30). It is possible that Jael does give him water to drink, and that the milk and cream/curds were not intended for Sisera but rather served as libation and offerings.[19]

THE VERB קרב, Q-R-B HIPHIL

The use of the verbal root *k-r-b* (pronounced *q-r-v*) in the Bible is mainly in association with offerings (Hiphil: Lev. 1; 3). The use of the root in the Hiphil stem here, in the active form, points to several other instances connected to revelations of God and repasts for his messengers (Genesis 18; 19; Judges 6; 13). It is important to note that in the encounter at En-dor, too, the Hebrew root *z-b-ch* Qal, "offer a cultic meal" is used in association with the meal prepared by the medium (1 Samuel 28).

The encounter between Jael and Sisera is full of imagery rich in cultic atmosphere and includes an accumulation of ritual elements—milk, curds, the lordly bowl, and the use of *q-r-b* Hiphil—giving the impression of a repast or an offering ceremony, presented to the household gods or possibly intended to summon some divine being to disclose the future in a dream or vision.

Assuming that the *semikha*, too, is among the other ritual objects in the tent, then the first phrase, "she covered," refers not to Sisera but to an image or a cultic object in the tent. The second occurrence of "she covered" might refer to Sisera, who lies down to sleep in Jael's tent, but not because he is tired. Covered in a sacred *semikha*, he hopes to receive a message from the gods about his future in a dream, vision, or oracle.

INCUBATION DREAM: A MESSAGE-DREAM?

In ancient Near Eastern cultures, dreams were considered primary venues for communication between humans and the divine. Incubation—the practice of sleeping in a sacred place—and making ritual offerings were thought to facilitate divine message-dreams, and were claimed to be widely practiced (Faber 1995:

1899). Divine revelations by dreams required interpretation (oneiromancy):[20] since not everyone could interpret dreams and apparitions, intermediaries had to be consulted. Necromancy also required some technique in order to conjure the dead and converse with them (van der Toorn 1994: 122).[21]

The Mesopotamian custom was for the seer, often a woman diviner, the *šā'iltu* (Akk.), to sit near the head of the dreamer to explain, interpret, and "translate" the dream (Akk., *mupaššir šunat*; Oppenheim 1956: 221–25).[22] The earliest known reference to the "incubation dream" is mentioned in an incantation text (TH 80.III) from Mari (Bonechi and Durand 1992: 151–59). It tells of a woman who lay down to sleep in a sacred place in order to receive a message in a dream. Another example from Mesopotamia is the dream of Gudea, ruler of Lagash (c. 2144–2122 BCE), which was interpreted by his mother, the goddess Gatumung (Oppenheim 1956: 211–12). Likewise, the goddess Ninsun, Gilgamesh's mother, interpreted his dream (van der Toorn 1994: 128); and also Geshtinana, Dumuzi's sister, interpreted his dream (*Dumuzi's Dream*; Black et al. 2004: 78). There are also recorded examples of Mesopotamian female cultic prophetesses going into trances, in which the gods speak through them (Moran 1969: 52–54; Gafney 2008: 58). That practice is also known from Ugarit. In the epics Aqhat (Parker 1997: 51–56) and Kirta (Greenstein 1997: 48–49), message-dreams are also described. An incubation dream from Egypt tells of king Thutmose IV (c. 1401–1391 BCE), who slept between the feet of the sacred sphinx and is described in the "Sphinx Stele" (Oppenheim 1956: 251). The Hittite king Murshili II (c. 1321–1285 BCE) asks for a message-dream in his Plague Prayer to the Storm-god of Hatti (CTH 378.II), (Singer 2002: 57–58). More examples can be found in Ackerman's article on Jacob's dream at Bethel (1991: 92–120). The message/oracle is generally short, concise, laconic, and often foretells the future in a cryptic form.

The Bible, too, recognizes the dream as a legitimate mode of divine communication (Num. 12:6; Job 33:15-17), and dream interpretation as divinely inspired (Gen. 40:8; Dan. 2:28) (Noegel 2007: 178). Among such well-known visions are Jacob's vision at Bet-El (Gen. 28:11-18) and Solomon's incubation dream in Gibeon (1 Kgs. 3:3-15), both recognized as divine communications. Joseph functioned as a dream interpreter and diviner in Egypt (Gen. 40:5-19; 41:1-32) and Daniel in Babylon (Dan. 2: 25-45). The issue in the Bible is who interprets the dreamer's vision—is he or she an endorsed prophet or a diviner?

Sisera may be assumed to have gone to sleep in the sacred tent covered with a cultic cloth in order to receive a divine message as to his future, and to have it interpreted. At En-dor, too, Samuel's apparition is raised by the medium while

Saul is described as having flung himself prone on the ground (1 Sam. 28:20), and it is to the medium that Samuel's spirit is visible during the séance.

In conclusion, we can assume that Sisera, defeated by the Israelite army, reached Jael's tent, located in a sacred place, to consult the gods. Textual and contextual evidence presents Jael as a recognized figure, a diviner, a cultic practitioner who, it would seem, interprets dreams and foretells the future.

The interpretation of the sequence of events until now answers the question: Why has Sisera fled to Jael's tent? However, it does not answer the intriguing question: What was Jael's motivation for killing Sisera?

IN THE TENT: A REVELATION? A MESSAGE DREAM? A PROPHETIC VISION? AN ORACLE?

> He said to her, Stand at the door of the tent, and if any man comes and inquires of you, and says, Is there any man here? you shall say, No [אִין, 'ayin]! (4:20)

Who is speaking? What does he mean? Who could come to Jael's tent, and why? Notably, the foreshadowing statement in 4:16, describing the destruction of the entire Canaanite army, "not a man was left," echoes in the background.[23]

This command and its speaker, appearing after the repetition of "she covered him," are obscure and cryptic. It can be interpreted in multiple ways. The accepted explanation is that Sisera gives the order to Jael to stand at the entrance of the tent, using the term "anyone" both for himself and for whoever might be looking for him. This, again, is not consistent with the sequence of events that take place within the tent. Why does he not say this before he lies down to sleep? It is not likely that Sisera would knowingly describe himself as "any man." The formulation here appears to refer to someone specific, not used in its general sense. Repeating "any man" twice is puzzling as well. This manner of speech is in complete contrast to Sisera's initial dialogue with Jael. At the beginning, he humbly pleads with her, while now he commands. Sisera's circumstances do not give him the authority required for giving orders (Bal 1988c: 144). This sentence, so out of character and out of place, will be considered later.

IN THE TENT: THE KILLING: בלאט, BALLA'T ("SECRETLY"), וחלפה מחצה וחלפה ("STRUCK, CRUSHED, AND SMASHED")

The climax is reached when Jael kills Sisera. What motivates Jael the Kenite to kill Sisera, commander of the Canaanite army? This is the crux of the whole tale. Neither text answers this question. The gap in the narrative sends one searching for missing links between the killing, the command, and Deborah's prophecy. Using the analysis above, I attempted to uncover additional textual clues. Now I will propose my answer.

The expression "she went to him softly" (4:21)[24] indicates that Sisera is probably kneeling or lying down when Jael approaches him quietly, as in the case of David approaching the sleeping Saul "softly" (1 Sam. 24:4). This description shows that Jael goes to him as the dominant figure, and that this refutes any idea of rape, as suggested by some commentators. As pointed out by Alter, the usual formula "he came to her" (Gen. 29:23; 30:4; Judg. 16:1; 2 Sam. 2:24) is used in the Bible for a male initiator of sexual activity (1985: 49). Lewis (1989: 160, 162–63) argues that the adverb בלאט, balla't is a synonym for בסתר ("secretly") and is applied in connection to necromancy, as mentioned in Isa. 45:18-19 and 66:4. Lewis's explanation for balla't is in accord with the description of Jael's cultic conduct throughout the encounter.

The poetic text states that she "pounded Sisera, she pierced his head; she split and struck through his temple" (Judg. 5:26). These verbs are associated with the wars of the God of Israel (Exod. 15:6; 14:24; 2 Sam. 22:15; Deut. 33:11; Num. 24:8). To say, finally, that he "sank" and "lay still" is to describe him as one whom God had struck down. The verbs "struck," "pierced," "split," and "sank" are also commonly used in describing the wars of the Ugaritic gods, especially those of the goddess Anath (Cassuto 1952: 29; Parker 1997: 70–71). Their use here affirms that this was probably a ritual slaying. Furthermore, one could explain "at her feet he sank" (5:27), as well as "knelt," "fell," and "lay," as part of the divination sequence of events taking place in the tent.[25] If we assume that the message would have come in a dream, a séance, or an oracle, then "at her feet he fell . . . lay" (5:27) could describe the instant when Jael takes her place beside Sisera's head as he lay in a kind of incubation-dream or a divination séance, to interpret the dream for him.

Now we return to the expression, "He said to her, Stand at the door of the tent, and if any man comes and inquires of you, and says, is there any man here? You shall say, No!"

One should note that, when several characters—some unnamed—are quoted, and the Hebrew verb for "say" (אמר, 'a-m-r Qal) is emphasized by repetition, as it is here, the repetition points to the subsequent phrase as being the words of another character (Gen. 3:9-13; 22:7; 1 Sam. 20:9-12; 1 Kgs. 20:14). Thus one might read that sentence not as the words of Sisera, who appears to have fallen asleep, but as the words of a third presence in the tent, part of the message-dream revelation, or an oracle addressed to Jael in the imperative.

THE PRIME MOVER: REVELATION OF GOD AND OF GOD'S EMISSARIES (JUDGES 4–5)

In the war of Deborah and Barak against the Canaanites God is an active partner—the instigator who guides the narrative and determines its outcome (Brenner 1993a: 103–4). In Judges 4 and 5, there are numerous divine revelations and manifestations of God and God's emissaries. This seems to support my proposed interpretation of the encounter between Jael and Sisera.[26]

Amit comments on the divine revelations in Judges: "The reader of Judges finds, at every reading stage, that God intervenes directly in history. God's messengers arrive and signs are seen. Even events where no clear and visible signs seem to lead to the same conclusion. (1997: 33). Given that chapters 4 and 5 describe several divine revelations, I suggest that a revelation of some sort, a message-dream, an oracle, or a prophecy, occurred in Jael's tent.

That command, "stand!" (4:20), is similar to the instructions given to prophets in Mari, "Stand!" and "Stand up!" during a revelation, and also recalls the prophet Ezekiel's visions (2:1; Weinfeld 1977: 181–82). The verb עמד, '-m-d ("stand") is used frequently, especially in connection with standing before God and his divine messengers (Gen. 18:8, 22; Exod. 17:6; 33:10; Lev. 14:14; Ezek. 2:1).[27] Notably, the expression "the door of the tent" in the Pentateuch denotes a place of special importance at which God appears and from which he speaks (Exod. 33:9-10; Num. 12:5; Deut. 31:15). This command (Judg. 4:20), given to Jael during the event (a revelation? an oracle?) that happened in the tent, refers to the future and is constructed as a cryptic riddle, characteristic of oracles. The command is spoken in the masculine imperative form and foretells the future events in an ambiguous way. The command, ordering Jael to deny the presence of a man in her tent, leads to the most crucial moment of the encounter; it is at that point the transformation in Jael's behavior occurs.

At this stage, perhaps, the main question, Why indeed did Jael kill Sisera? may be answered. Jael is not ordered to conceal the presence of Sisera in the tent from just "any man" (used here as a common noun): "And if any man comes and inquires of you, and says, 'Is there any man here?' you shall say, 'No'" (4:20). The meaning of the Hebrew word אין, *'ayin* is "none-existing," as in Exod.

17:7. This command may be a remaining part of a longer, hidden dialogue spoken in the course of the message-dream/oracle session. It might be meant for Jael to find out how Sisera can be turned into a non-man, how he might cease to exist, and to act on it.[28] It is possible that, in the course of the revelation or the séance session, Jael understands that she is ordered to kill Sisera, while the object of that phrase, Sisera, is unaware of the proceedings that lead to his death.[29] In her act, Jael brings to completion the destruction of the Canaanite army, as stated in 4:16: "not a man was left." Amit says that "the absence of obvious motives for Jael's action, and the fact that she is a woman—as Deborah's prophecy required—all these reinforce the impression that Jael is activated by whoever controls the entire set of happenings" (1987: 97–98).[30] In the parallel story of 1 Samuel 28, during the séance, Samuel's ghost raised by the medium tells Saul of his imminent defeat and death in the war that will take place soon after that encounter.

IN THE TENT: POST MORTEM

After the command had been fulfilled, the text recounts that "she fell to the ground" (4:21).[31] This phrase, written in the feminine form, most probably refers to Jael (Grossfeld 1997: 348-51; Klein 1988: 42) and not to the hammer (Hebrew *maqqebet*, grammatically fem.) she held in her hand, like some commentators propose (Fewell and Gunn 1990: 393-4). The physical act of falling down uncovers the turmoil and mental situation.[32] One may assume that it describes Jael's reaction, shocked and troubled by the sense of the presence of the divine and the events that transpire in the tent.[33]

Likewise, in the parallel encounters, King Saul (1 Sam. 28:20) and Balaam (Num. 22:31) fall on the ground, and in Numbers 24:16 Balaam explains that falling down is part of a visionary trance.[34]

Jael's action might be compared to Balaam's: like him, she is an instrument of the will of God, and (maybe), like him, she is forced to act against her own will. Deborah respects and acknowledges Jael and her status, and blesses her for her deed (5:24).

ACT 3: OUTSIDE JAEL'S TENT

The circumstances of Barak's arrival mirror those of act 1. Barak, pursuing Sisera, arrives at Jael's tent; she goes out to meet him, and it is she who addresses the Israelite military commander. Her speech is different from that used to address Sisera: it is in the imperative—לך ואראך ("Go and I will show you,"

4:22)[35]—and resembles Deborah's dialogues with him (4:6). לך ואראך is an expression rarely found in the Bible, notably, when God tells Abraham: "Go forth from your native land . . . to the land that I will show you" (Gen. 12:1), and when God speaks to Moses in the burning bush revelation (Exod. 3:10). The other instances, too, are either direct divine orders or commands through the prophets and God's other messengers. Jael's use of it intensifies the sense that she acts on a divine command. The encounter between Jael and Sisera, then, mirrors and also connects to the encounter between Deborah and Barak.[36]

The story that began with Deborah's prophecy, "The Lord will sell Sisera into the hand of a woman," ends in the third act of the drama with, "and there Sisera was lying dead."

Conclusion

Two heroines have an important share in the events that lead to the victory of the Israelites over the Canaanites. Deborah is the acting leader, responsible for recruiting Barak, gathering the Israelite army, and giving the sign starting the war. She delivers the enigmatic prophecy/oracle predicting that "God will sell Sisera into the hand of a woman" (Judg. 4:9). Jael receives her own prophetic message and carries out the sentence (4:20-21).

It is Jael's hand that kills Sisera and thus brings about the fulfillment of the oracles. It is both important and a pleasure for me to note that, in this biblical war story, two empowered women, the representatives of religious and cultic practices, rather than the military commanders, are God's emissaries that act on his behalf and have a major role in the deliverance of the Israelites.

	The Deborah-Barak encounter (Judges 4–5)	The Jael-Sisera encounter (Judges 4–5)	The Encounter of Samuel, Saul, and the medium of En-dor (1 Samuel. 28)	The Encounter of Balak and Balaam (Numbers. 22–24)
Military commanders	Barak ben Abinoam leads the northern tribes	Sisera leads the Canaanite army	King Saul leads the Israelite army	Balak ben Zippor, king and army leader of Moab

Prophets and diviners	Deborah, Israelite prophetess, 'eshet lapidot, and judge	Jael of heber the Kenite, probably a foreigner and a diviner	Samuel's spirit and the medium of En-dor, name and origins unknown	Balaam ben Peor, prophet and diviner from Pethor by the Euphrates.(22:5)
Time frame: war and distress	Deborah chooses Barak to lead the Israelites against the Canaanites.	Sisera defeated in the war with Israelites	King Saul fears war with the Philistines attacking Israel	Balak fears an attack from the Israelites that arrived at his borders
Place of the encounter	Palm of Deborah—Kadesh, Jezreel Valley	'Elon-beza'anaim, Jezreel Valley	En-dor, Jezreel Valley	
Disguises		Sisera left his chariot and fled on foot (4:15).	Saul "So Saul disguised himself and put on other clothes" (28:8), andsnuck in atnight	
Reasons for consulting and seeking divine aid	Barak says: "If you go with me then I will go" (4:8).	Sisera, defeated, flees to Jael's tent to learnof his future from the cultic intermediary, Jael.	"Saul inquired of the Lord, the Lord did not answer him, either by dreams or by Urim or by the prophets" (28:6). He then goes to the medium of En-dor.	Balak chooses Balaam, a well-known but non-Moabite prophet and diviner, to confront and curse Israel.
Messages, signs, and divine revelation	Deborah receives prophetic messages from God	Jael in her tent appears to have had a revelation and receives a prophetic message.	The medium raises Samuel's spirit who delivers his last prophecy to King Saul.	Balaam receives messages directly from God and his angel.

Offerings and sacrifices		Jael offers milk and "sacrifices" curds (5:25).	The medium of En-dor "sacrifices" a stall-fed calf (28:24).	Balak and Balaam offer numerous sacrifices.
Announcing the prophetic oracle	"The Lord will deliver him (Sisera) into your hands" (4:7). ". . . for the lord will sell into the hands of a woman" (4: 9).	"If any man comes and inquires of you, and says, Is there any man here? You shall say, No ('ayin]! (4:20)	"For the Lord has torn the kingship out of your hands . . . will deliver the Israelites. . . into the hands of the Philistines" (28:17-19).	"Come, I will advise you what this people will do to your people in the latter days." (24:14).
Realization of the prophetic oracle	"And there lay Sisera dead (4:22). "On that day God subdued King Jabin of in the presence of the children of Israel" (4:24).	"Go and I will show you the man you are looking for" (4:24).	"And Saul grasped his sword and fell upon it"; "the men of Israel fled before the Philistines" (31:4-7).	"A Scepter shall rise out of Israel And batter the brow of Moab," (24:17). Under Ehud ben Gera, "Moab submitted to Israel" (Judg. 3:30).

Notes

1. By the term *heroine* I define female figures human and divine, characterized by gender role-reversal, who show courage in dire and dangerous situations. This is in accordance with Fuchs, who defines the *heroine* as a feminine parallel to the masculine term *hero* (1982: 149–60).

2. It is one of two narrative poems in the Hebrew Bible juxtaposed to a parallel prose account. The other is in Exodus 15 (Cross 1997 [1973]: 86).

3. In military contexts, women were generally associated with marginal roles and depicted as the victims of wars. Therefore, a story presenting female heroines as active participants in a military conflict is exceptional.

4. All biblical translations in this essay are according to the NKJV.

5. On similar encounters belonging to that literary genre in Near Eastern mythological texts, see Fontaine 1988: 84–102; Brison 2007: 67–74.

6. On necromancy and *'ob*, "spirit," see Hoffner 1967: 385–401; 1974a: 130–34; Tarragon 1995: 2071–81.

7. De Moor and Watson regard Judges 4 as the prose introduction to the *Song of Deborah* (1993: xi). See also Fewell and Gunn 1990: 389–91.

8. This literary technique is described by Sternberg as "proleptic exposition or future-directed retrospect—where the Bible's strategies of economy, sequence, and foregrounding meet" (1985: 280).

9. On "foreshadowing events," see also Polak 1994: 167–91.

10. On "Jethro," see Albright 1963: 1–11.

11. *'Elon be-za'anaim* is identified in the Bible with 'Elon-beza'anannim (Josh. 19:33). Kedesh is mentioned as a Levite shelter town (Josh. 21:28; 1 Chron. 6:57). Mazar 1965: 297–303; Aharoni 1968: 2–32.

12. I am currently working on the more complex biblical picture indicated by the interesting occurrence in close proximity of *beit heber*, and *'eshet midyanim*. ("Midianites"?), Prov. 21:9 and 25:24, and plan on showing the connections between them and Jael *'eshet* Heber.

13. Consultations and questions for divine guidance presented to cult intermediaries—prophets, diviners, and oracles—on military matters, before going to war, were a widespread custom in the ancient Near East. In the Bible, God's word was sought before the ark of the covenant, through priests and prophets, the *ephod*, the *Urim* and *Thummim*, and through message-dreams. Some biblical examples are Moses consulting Eleazar the priest (Num. 27:21) and David consulting priests (1 Sam. 23:9-12). See also Exod. 14:18; 28:6; Judg. 7:13; 18:5-6; 1 Kgs. 22:5, 15; 2 Kgs. 3:11. There are also numerous examples of inquiries concerning wars in texts from Mari: ARM 10:8; ARM 10:4 (Weinfeld 1977: 184; Malamat 1998: 88–89). The Assyrian kings, too, did not rely only on military expertise, but consulted the diviners for oracles and omens (Oppenheim 1960: 136–38). We learn of the importance of the prophet/diviner during war times from Esarhaddon's (681–669 BCE) vassal treaties. He demanded a pledge of loyalty not just of the vassal king and his sons but also of their diviner (Parpola and Wattanabe 1988: 33).

14. Cultic tents were known also in the different cultures of the ancient Near East: Midian (Num. 25:8); Ugarit: Aqhat, CAT 4.1.17 V: 31-33 (Parker 1997:59); Mari (Fleming 2000: 484-98).

15. Mazar suggests that Jael's tent was a Kenite sanctuary (1965: 302). Ackerman proposes that Jael had a cultic function (1998: 93–102).

16. "The Tent of Meeting" also stood apart (Exod. 33:7-11; Num. 11:16).

17. The LXX (A) interpretation of the problematic phrase suggests that Jael covers Sisera's face.

18. In the Bible: Gen. 18:8; Deut. 32:14; Prov. 30:33. In Ugarit: CAT 23.1.23 V.14-15 (Lewis 1997: 208). In Mesopotamia: Black et al. 2004: 226 (*The Debate between Sheep and Grain*). In Anatolia: *KUB* 17.10 I 25-27; *KUB* 15.34iii26-27 (Hoffner 1998: 35).

19. In the Hittite text KBo 11, 3iii 12, the MI.ŠU.GI; Hittite: *Hasuwas* (the title for old woman/wise woman) holds out an offering of curds and cheese (Hoffner 1974b: 121).

20. On oneiromancy in Mesopotamia, see Bottéro 1992: 105-25; in Israel, Noegel 2007: 113–89.

21. In a Mesopotamian lexical list, the female necromancer (Akk. *mueślitu silli*) occurs between sorceress and midwife (van der Toorn 1994: 124).

22. The *ša'iltu* belonged to a class of diviners whose function was to answer mantic inquiries by seeking oracles from the gods. The oracle-priestess is mentioned not only in religious texts but also in certain documents of daily life (Oppenheim 1956: 221).

23. Some commentators say that Sisera here ironically foreshadows his own death (Murray 1979:183; Bal 1988b: 121-22).

24. A more adequate verbatim translation would be "secretly" or "quietly."

25. Niditch (1989:48), Fewell and Gunn (1990: 404), and others attach sexual connotations to "fell" and "lay."

26. The LXX adds to Barak's reluctant answer to Deborah in 4:8: "I do not know the day when God will send his angel with me" (4:8). Deborah delivers other prophecies to Barak and commands him to go forth to war (4:14). The poetic text also contains divine revelations and interventions in the course of nature. The heavens, too, are engaged in the war (5:20). Three verses later, the angel of God doubly curses those who failed to support God's army (5:23). Moreover, God's angel, through Deborah, doubly blesses Jael (5:24).

27. Also: Deut. 5:5, 28; 29:14; Josh. 5:13, 15; Judg. 2:28; 1 Sam. 19:20.

28. See Bal 1988b: 144.

29. The medium of En-dor discovers Saul's identity only when Samuel's dead spirit appears. Similarly, one may assume that Sisera's identity is revealed to Jael during the message-dream/oracle session.

30. Amit maintains that the reason for Jael's action is her identification with Israelites (1987: 94, 108n20).

31. Here, I prefer using the verbatim translation: "and she went down onto the ground."

32. A state described by Otto *mysterium tremendum et fascinans* ("awe-full mystery and fascination") (1936: 12–41).

33. The other two instances in the Hebrew Bible of צנח, *tz-n-ch* Qal ("fall"), the verb used here, have a woman as the verb's subject as well (Josh. 15:18; Judg. 1:14).

34. See also Ezek. 1:28.

35. Here, I prefer using the verbatim translation: "Go and I will show you."

36. On the triangular structure of the protagonists in the story, see Brenner 1993a: 98–109.

9

Choosing Sides in Judges 4–5

Rethinking Representations of Jael

Ryan P. Bonfiglio

INTRODUCTION: CONTEXTUAL READINGS OF JUDGES 4–5

Judges 4–5 juxtaposes two accounts of Jael's murder of Sisera, one in prose (Judges 4) and the other in poetry (Judges 5).[1] These texts, which describe an Israelite victory over the Canaanites, have long since attracted the interest of biblical scholars. While past interpretive approaches tended to concentrate on how these texts might provide clues about the historical background of early Israel, more recent studies have surfaced important ideological concerns about the role and function of a non-Israelite heroine in a book that predominantly focuses on Israelite heroes.[2] Such interests are notably on display in Katherine Doob Sakenfeld's 2007 presidential address at the annual meeting of the Society of Biblical Literature. Sakenfeld challenged her fellow scholars to open biblical texts to a diverse array of contextual perspectives and, as a test case, offered her own postcolonial reading of the story of Jael in Judges 4–5 (Sakenfeld 2008: 12). In Sakenfeld's view, Jael, as neither Israelite nor Canaanite, functions as a type of borderland figure in the overarching drama of Israelite-Canaanite conflict and, as such, offers a potential point of contact for contemporary postcolonial subjects who likewise find themselves caught between competing sociocultural or political forces.[3] Be it from the vantage point of readers from the developing world who face the lingering specter of colonialism or immigrants in industrialized nations who must negotiate complex issues surrounding assimilation and acceptance, Sakenfeld's research is suggestive of the variety of ways in which Judges 4–5 might be read from different contextual perspectives.

In the course of this essay, I hope to join in the conversation Sakenfeld and others have already begun about contextual readings of Judges 4–5. I choose to do so with an awareness that I might be a somewhat unusual—or at least unexpected—conversation partner. As an American-born white male, I do not claim firsthand knowledge of the sorts of contexts mentioned above, and my own place as a reader can only be described as being pro-postcolonial in terms of my theological convictions and political commitments. Nevertheless, as a second-generation Italian American, I do come to the text bearing countless stories about how my maternal grandparents, Dominic and Florence, struggled to forge a life together in a steel town outside of Philadelphia in the early 1900s. Although I do not claim their experiences as my own, I find that my contextual concerns as a reader of Judges 4–5 are informed by this history and how it has come to shape what it means for me to occupy an advantaged place in a country once so foreign to my grandparents.

Like many other European immigrants who came to America in the early twentieth century, my grandparents felt the pinch of discrimination in a variety of ways. They were ridiculed for their broken English, limited to certain jobs, and marginalized for being one of the few Italians members of their Catholic parish. Their "hyphenated condition" as Italian Americans at times entailed being caught between competing sociocultural forces, torn between loyalty to their old Italian heritage and integration into their new American context.[4] Even as my grandparents' experience might only partially overlap with that of contemporary immigrants, the stories they told and the struggles they had bear witness to the conflictual nature of being cultural outsiders.

Yet the difficulties my grandparents faced in their early years in America eventually gave way to numerous successes. They started and ran a profitable small business, and my grandfather was elected to various political offices over the course of two decades—not a small feat for an Italian Democrat in a staunchly Republican town with a sizable Irish population. But in their view, the most tangible realization of the "American Dream" was the fact that they had three children—and eight grandchildren—who became thoroughly assimilated into and accepted by the dominant culture. For us grandchildren, whatever tension might remain in our hyphenated condition all but fully has been resolved in favor of being full-fledged Americans. We are now the "us" in contrast to the "them" of present-day immigrants. In just two generations, what was once a foreign land to my grandparents is now our entitled home.

Thus my own family's history reflects competing stories of difficulty and triumph, discrimination and assimilation. In fact, I find that my own contextual perspective is informed as much by questions concerning my grandparents' successes as it is by those about their struggles. If my grandparents are examples of immigrants who successfully attained the American Dream, at what cost did such a dream come? What did they have to leave behind in order to gain a surer footing in their new context? How is my own place as a member of the dominant culture the result of my grandparents' choosing the American side of their Italian American identity? As a generative example, not long after arriving in the states, my grandmother was forced to drop out of school because her knowledge of English was severely limited. Years later, she and my grandfather refused to teach their children Italian and prohibited it from being spoken at home. I can only imagine how much my grandparents wanted to spare their children from standing out or being denied any opportunity because of their accent or language. For all intents and purposes, this strategy worked—though their children were fully accepted as "real" Americans, knowledge of the Italian language was left behind. Though it would be difficult to fault my grandparents or others who have made similar decisions based on what they believed to be best for their families, it is hard not to notice the dilemma they faced: acceptance by the dominant culture was contingent on assimilation.

This is the sort of dilemma that other immigrants, both past and present, face when they are pressured to choose sides with regards to their sociocultural loyalties and identities. While retaining strong ties to one's cultural roots, or even refusing to choose sides at all, often results in marginalization, choosing to assimilate into the dominant culture is typically rewarded with approval and acceptance. In other words, for many immigrants, the dilemma inherent in choosing sides is not only that the dominant culture compels them to choose (that is, to be Italian *or* American) but that only the side of assimilation leads to acceptance.

It is with these concerns and contexts in mind that I turn to my own reading of Judges 4–5. Specifically, I find myself approaching these texts wondering if Jael, as a type of non-Israelite, non-Canaanite outsider, also faces the dilemma of having to choose sides. If Jael is indeed represented as a "most blessed" heroine in Judges 4–5, in what ways do the two versions of this story construct her heroism in different ways? What possibilities or problems surface if Jael is read from the contextual perspective of cultural outsiders such as my grandparents or first- and second-generation immigrants of today? In pursuing such inquiries, I will develop my interpretation of Judges 4–5 in two ways. First, whereas other scholars tend to infer a composite picture of Jael from an integrative reading of Judges 4–5 as a whole, my intention is to assess how these two accounts of Jael's murder of Sisera might construct different profiles of Jael's actions and, as a result, prompt different assessments of how she functions as a heroine.[5] Second, by drawing on postcolonial theories about mimeticism and model minorities, I will explore how the subtle differences between the Jael of

Judges 4 and the Jael of Judges 5 might become quite significant when viewed from the perspective of contemporary immigrant populations that likewise face the dilemma of choosing sides. While my own contextual reading does not aim to capture or reflect the diverse experiences of all immigrant families (nor even the other members of my own family!), I hope that the sorts of issues raised below might spark further thought and reflection on contextual readings of Judges 4–5.

The Jael of Judges 4: A Heroine for Israel

Judges 4 situates Jael's encounter with Sisera within the formulaic pattern of rebellion, punishment, repentance, and deliverance that recurs throughout the book of Judges: In 4:1, the Israelites rebel by doing "evil in the eyes of the Lord" (cf. 2:11; 3:7, 12; 6:1); in 4:2, they are punished by being sold into the hands of the Canaanites (cf. Moabites in 3:12, Midianites in 6:1, and Philistines in 10:6-7); and when they "cry out to the Lord" in 4:3, God raises up a deliverer to free them (cf. 3:9, 15; 6:7; 10:10). If the first three verses of this chapter seem to adhere to the characteristic narrative pattern of the book as a whole, then it is all the more striking how v. 4 subsequently subverts the expectation that the anticipated deliverer will be a man. The one who is judging Israel at that time is Deborah, and she is introduced as אשה נביאה אשת לפידות ('ishshah nebi'ah 'eshet lappidot), "a woman, a prophetess, the wife of Lappidoth" (my translation).[6] According to Robert Alter, the piling on of these three appositional terms, each feminine in gender, produces a type of "purposeful awkwardness" that drives home the surprising fact that a woman, not a man, will deliver Israel (Alter 1992: 41). Furthermore, in v. 9, Deborah explicitly tells Barak that the Lord will give the Canaanite military leader, Sisera, "into the hand of a woman." At this point in the narrative, the reader might well suspect that this woman is Deborah herself. In fact, a host of modern interpreters assume that Deborah is the true hero of Judges 4.[7] Thus, if Deborah's prediction in 4:9 unsettles expectations about the deliverer's gender, it does little to disturb the notion that the hero will be an Israelite.

Yet here the narrative takes a surprising turn. Deborah quickly fades to the background just as another woman, Jael, appears. She is the focus of the rest of the prose account: When Sisera flees on foot to her tent after being defeated in battle (v. 17), Jael hospitably invites him in before slaying him in his sleep (vv. 18-21). By the time Jael shows Barak the dead body of Sisera (v. 22), it is clear that God has delivered Sisera, and thus the Canaanites, into Jael's hands. Yet what is so striking is that while Jael seems to play the role of Israelite deliverer in the prose account, she herself is not an Israelite. In fact, in a drama about Israelites and Canaanites, Jael appears to be neither. Rather, Judg. 4:17 describes Jael as "the wife of Heber the Kenite" (אשת חבר הקיני, *'eshet heber haqqeni*). Susan Ackerman rightly notes the possibility that *heber* might not be a proper noun but rather a common noun meaning "clan" or "community" (Ackerman 2000: 37–38). This understanding would imply that Jael is "the woman of the Kenite clan." In either case, it remains unclear whether Jael is a Kenite herself, is married to a Kenite, or both.

However Jael's Kenite connection might be construed, mention of it seems to play an important role in the prose account. Specifically, vv. 11 and 17 remind the reader that the Kenites had ties both to the Israelites and to the Canaanites. On one hand, by referring to the Kenites as the descendants of Hobab, Moses' father-in-law, v. 11 activates a tradition in which the Kenites and Israelites are linked through ancient kinship. On the other hand, v. 17 explains that Sisera flees to the tent of Jael because there was some sort of peace—perhaps a political allegiance—between the Kenites and the Canaanite king Jabin. In both cases, it is not entirely clear what these different connections have to say about the loyalties of the Kenites, let alone Jael herself, other than the fact that they are not entirely pro-Israelite or pro-Canaanite.[8] Nevertheless, what is important to note about Judges 4, as Sakenfeld points out, is how the main events of the story thus far—Israel's victory and Sisera's flight to Jael's tent—force Jael to choose sides (Sakenfeld 2008: 16). When Sisera arrives at her tent, Jael cannot simply remain above the fray. She faces an unavoidable dilemma: if she offers safe haven to Sisera and maintains the existing peace between the Canaanites and the Kenites, she becomes a Canaanite accomplice; if she turns against Sisera and helps secure Barak's military victory, she solidifies an alliance with the Israelites that is already implicit through kinship ties.

The subsequent narrative leaves no doubt about which side Jael chooses. Her actions hint of a premeditated plot to assassinate the Canaanite commander and thus secure Israelite victory. By calling Sisera to "turn aside" (סורה, *sura*, 4:18), from *s-w-r* Qal, a verb used elsewhere in the Hebrew Bible (HB) to express a hospitable invitation (cf. Gen. 19:2; Judg. 19:15; Ruth 4:1), Jael leverages a social convention to lure Sisera into her tent. Likewise, by urging Sisera to "have no fear" (אל תירא, *'al-tira'*, in the same verse) Jael draws on language often used to express reassurance in military contexts (cf. Deut. 31:6; Jer. 30:10; 46:27-28) to lull Sisera into a false sense of security. Jael then gives Sisera milk and covers him with a rug to help him sleep, not unlike a mother caring for a baby. This ruse has infantilizing—if not emasculating—implications.[9] The reader can hardly miss the ensuing irony:

when Sisera instructs Jael to tell any visitor that there is no man in the tent, Jael need not lie.[10] Once Sisera is put to bed and is "lying fast asleep" (v. 21), Jael is able to carry out the murder.

Whatever objection the reader might have concerning Jael's violation of conventions of hospitality is quickly ameliorated by the concluding two verses of the prose account.[11] By informing the reader that God subdued the Canaanites on the very same day Jael killed Sisera, it becomes clear that if Jael is a morally suspect assassin, then Yahweh is culpable for ordering the "hit." As the instrument of God's deliverance, this non-Israelite heroine seems to enact the common proverb, "The enemy of my enemy is my friend." This form of political allegiance is not unfamiliar in biblical literature, as is especially evident in Yahweh's promise to Israel to be "an enemy to your enemies and a foe to your foes" in Exod. 23:22. This does not imply that Jael's actions lack self-interest at a more personal level. To be sure, when news of the Israelites' rout of the Canaanites reaches her tent, it might well have become a matter of personal safety for Jael to side with the winners. Nevertheless, Judges 4 underscores the fact that Jael faces a choice between siding with the Israelites or with the Canaanites. By virtue of choosing the former, Jael becomes a heroine for Israel in a manner not unlike the various Israelite deliverers found throughout the book of Judges.

The Jael of Judges 5: A Heroine Among Women

In his study of the function of ambiguity in Judges 4–5, Eric Christianson contends that the cumulative effect of the two distinct retellings about Jael's murder of Sisera is to prompt us readers "to question our grasp of the narrative" (Christianson 2007: 531). To be sure, the numerous differences that exist between the prose and poetry accounts cannot readily be harmonized. Specifically, Judges 5 represents Jael as a different sort of heroine than is found in Judges 4. Several important differences are of note.

First, although Judges 5, like Judges 4, introduces Jael as "the wife of Heber the Kenite" (5:24; and see above for this choice of understanding אשת חבר הקיני, 'eshet heber haqqeni), the poem says nothing more of the Kenites or their possible connections to the Israelites and Canaanites. Even if the audience already knows the backstory of the Kenites and their genealogical and political ties, that the poem does not include these details has significant implications for the reader's understanding of the rest of the story. For one, it is less clear in Judges 5 why Sisera might have approached Jael's tent in the first place: is Sisera intentionally seeking refuge from a political ally, or does he simply have no better option at the moment? In addition, while Jael's actions still ultimately advance the cause of the Israelites, the poem does not as explicitly frame Jael's action as a choice between two opposing sides. In other words, the lack of reference to the Kenites' genealogical and political ties creates an ambiguity that somewhat diffuses the side-choosing dilemma that Jael more clearly faces in Judges 4. As a result, the reader is left more room to see in Jael's actions a different sort of choice.

Second, Judges 5 provides fewer details about key aspects of Jael's encounter with Sisera. For instance, in the poem, Jael neither invites Sisera into the safety of her tent nor lulls him into a vulnerable sleep. Rather, Sisera simply appears in v. 25 and then is murdered in vv. 26-27. As a result, whereas Jael's actions seem planned and purposeful in Judges 4, there is no clear sense of premeditation in Judges 5. Furthermore, in chapter 5, Jael never announces her deed to Barak as she does in 4:22, and no narrative comment is provided that links Sisera's death to God's subduing of the Canaanites (cf. 4:23-24). Because of this, even though the poem clearly celebrates some sort of Israelite military victory, it is far less clear that Jael is cast in the role of Israel's deliverer. In fact, Judges 5 more explicitly emphasizes the role of the divine warrior Yahweh (cf. 5:3-5) as Israel's true deliverer.

Perhaps most significantly, Judges 5 seems to provide a slightly different account of the circumstances surrounding Jael's murder of Sisera. For instance, 4:21 implies that Jael kills Sisera while he is lying fast asleep on the ground. This would explain not only why Jael must approach him "softly" or surreptitiously (בלאט, balla't) but also why the tent peg ends up in the ground after being hammered through his temple. A different description obtains in Judges 5. In the poetic account, it is only after the fatal blow is struck that Sisera sinks and falls to the ground (v. 27), implying that Sisera is not lying down—and indeed might not be asleep—when Jael administers the fatal blow.

How, then, does Judges 5 depict the scene just prior to Sisera's death? Although the poem is certainly not explicit on this matter, v. 27 might provide a clue. It describes Sisera's death using several verbs in the Qal formation—"kneel" כרע, k-r-'), "lay" (שכב, sh-k-b), and "fall" (נפל, n-ph-l)—that can each carry sexually connotative double meanings. In fact, Susan Niditch persuasively argues that the language in 5:27 simultaneously evokes death and eroticism (Niditch 1989: 51). For instance, sh-k-b is often used in sexual contexts to refer to rape, as is the case with Dinah (Gen. 34:2, 7) and Tamar (2 Sam. 13:11, 14). At the same time, sh-k-b can also be associated with death, as in the common idiom for dying "he slept with his ancestors," (וישכב עם אבותיו, wayyishkab 'im-'abotayw). Likewise, k-r-' is used in Job 31:10 to imply kneeling over a woman in a sexual posture, while in Ps. 20:9 the same verb, coupled with *n-ph-l* (as in Judges 5), indicates death and defeat (Niditch 1989: 48). Various other scholars also contend that the double meanings implied by these terms creates the possibility that some form of sexual violence is in view.[12]

While this reading of Judg. 5:27 is compelling, the conclusions that Niditch draws from it are less persuasive. She contends that the verse depicts a type of reversed rape in which Jael acts the part of a femme fatale (Niditch 1989: 50–52). In other words, Jael intentionally turns the tables of sexual violence on her male victim. Such a view is plausible, though it is not the only interpretive option. In fact, this conclusion seems to depend on certain details—such as a premeditated plot to lure Sisera into the tent—that are only found in Judges 4. If one resists the tendency to harmonize Judges 4–5, then another interpretive option emerges. Jael's actions in Judges 5 might just as well be understood as a form of self-defense, or as Sakenfeld says, a way of "say[ing] 'no' to rape in the context of war" (Sakenfeld 1997: 20). Indeed, it is hardly difficult to imagine the possibility of sexual violence looming in the background of ancient (or modern) accounts of war. This possibility might even be implied in the lament of Sisera's mother in 5:28-30. She imagines her son, along with the rest of the Canaanite army, returning victoriously with "a womb [= girl] or two" for every man (v. 30) as their rightful spoils of war. Sisera does not return as his mother hopes, and so perhaps Niditch is right to imply that Sisera himself had become the victim of Jael's violence (Niditch 1989: 50). But in my view, Sisera's lack of success on the battlefield would not make him any less inclined toward carrying out his own acts of sexual violence. In fact, Sisera might have seen Jael as a type of consolation prize: what he cannot win on the battlefield he attempts to claim in Jael's tent. If this interpretation is correct and Sisera is the subject, not the object, of sexual violence, then what Jael does in Judges 5 might be understood as resistance to rape, not reversed rape. This possibility might make sense of why Judges 5:24 hails Jael as "most blessed *among* women" (תברך מנשים, *tebhorak minnashim*, my translation). In other words, in situating Jael's murder of Sisera as resistance to rape, Judges 5 represents Jael more as a heroine *among women* than as a heroine *for Israel*.

MIMETICISM AND THE MODEL MINORITY DILEMMA: THE COST OF JAEL'S HEROISM

As Sakenfeld has suggested, these representations of Jael might offer numerous contemporary readers an intriguing point of contact. On the one hand, as

Israel's triumphant deliverer, the Jael of Judges 4 might well function as a resource for readers who wish to resist a long history of interpretive conclusions that essentialize all non-Israelites as the adversarial Other. On the other hand, as a woman who says no to rape in the context of war, the Jael of Judges 5 might stand as a model of courage and agency among contemporary readers who have faced sexual violence (Sakenfeld 1997: 17). While such readings are not to be denied, questions remain. In what ways—and at what cost—does Jael become a heroine in these stories? How can the different profiles of Jael in Judges 4 and 5 be understood from a contextual perspective? In this section, I will briefly evaluate these questions by turning to theories developed within postcolonial studies about mimeticism and the "model minority" paradigm.

One of the ways postcolonial theory frames the interaction of dominant (colonizer) and marginal (colonized) groups is through the concept of mimeticism. In an article on Asian American biblical hermeneutics, Gale Yee draws on the work of cultural theorist Rey Chow to highlight the various levels of mimetic pressure experienced by marginal groups, be they colonized nations or immigrants and refugees in industrialized countries such as America (Yee 2006: 153–54).[13] At one level, the marginal group might be legally forced to imitate the language, values, and customs of the dominant group. Such coercion is a part of everyday life for many immigrants in America today. Yet marginal populations face mimetic pressure at a second level. Many cultures construct a system of rewards and affirmations that are selectively granted to those outsiders who live in accordance with the values and norms of the dominant group. Those who choose to assimilate into and align with the dominant culture are often referred to as "model minorities" insofar as their choices provide a template for how the dominant culture would want other minorities to act.

The term "model minority" took hold in the 1960s, most notably through the work of Berkeley sociologist William Petersen. Petersen applied this term to Asian Americans who achieved a high level of success relative to other minority immigrant populations in the United States (Petersen 1966; 1971). While at first glance this term might appear complimentary, law professor Frank H. Wu rightly exposes the model minority paradigm as yet another level of the marginalizing influence by the discourse of the dominant culture (Wu 2002: 37–77). In fact, the model minority paradigm is problematic on several levels. First, this paradigm tends to make the acceptance of minority groups contingent on assimilation. Thus a minority group is deemed to be a "model" only insofar as they become like the majority population, a process of imitation that often demands the severing of ties with alternative cultural and political identities. Second, the model minority paradigm proves to be problematic in that the existence of a model minority often implies the existence of a "problem minority" to whom the dominant group can say: "The model minority made it—why can't *you*?" (Wu 2002: 49). Behind this logic is a blame-shifting mechanism that tends to frame the struggles certain immigrants face in their new context as a direct result of their own failure to choose assimilation over and against maintaining sociocultural ties to their past. Thus, while the presence of model minorities is often used as evidence for the inclusivity and tolerance of the dominant culture, this paradigm belies the effects of systemic patterns of oppression.

How might this assessment inform an understanding of the different portrayals of Jael's heroism in Judges 4 and 5? The Jael of Judges 4 might be understood as a type of model minority. Put differently, Jael is a heroine for Israel because she plays the role of the faithful outsider, a trope found occasionally in the Hebrew Bible in which the actions of certain non-Israelites, such as Ruth and Rahab, are shown to serve the interests of the Israelites. This much seems to be true of Judges 4, where Jael's actions are framed as a choice for Israel and against Canaan. While it would go too far to suggest that the prose account represents Jael as somehow assimilating into Israelite culture or religion, it nevertheless underscores that when faced with the dilemma of choosing sides, Jael makes a choice for Israel. Furthermore, in Judges 4, the nature of Jael's actions, not just the results, hints at mimicry. For instance, the Jael of Judges 4 seems to be made in the image of the Israelite deliverer Ehud in Judges 3. Ehud intentionally approaches the enemy Eglon (3:16-17), uses deception and secrecy to set a trap (vv. 19-21a), thrusts (*t-q-* 'Qal) a sword all the way through the enemy's body (vv. 21b-22), leaving him lying (*n-ph-l*, v. 25) dead on the ground. Ehud then announces his triumph (v. 28), and the story concludes with the enemy forces being subdued (*k-n-ʿ* Niphal, v. 30). Similarly, Judges 4 describes how Jael intentionally approaches the enemy Sisera (v. 18a), uses deception and secrecy to set a trap (vv. 18b-20), thrusts (*t-q-ʿ*) a tent peg all the way through the enemy's body (v. 21) until it goes down (*ts-n-ch*) into the ground. Jael then announces her triumph (v. 22), and the story concludes with God subduing (*k-n-ʿ* Hiphil, v. 23) the enemy forces. This close parallel suggests that in Judges 4 Jael is portrayed as a heroine for Israel by virtue of behaving like an Israelite hero. This observation is not intended to critique Jael's action or imply she "sold out" to Israelites interests. Rather, my aim is to provide one way of understanding how Judges 4 frames Jael's actions as an act of heroism *for Israel* and what this might mean for contemporary readers who likewise face the dilemma of choosing sides.

In contrast, Judges 5 seems to offer more resistance to this hero-as-model-minority paradigm. By leaving details about the Kenites offstage and giving a different account of the murder itself, Judges 5 neither situates Jael's actions as a choice for the Israelites nor describes them in terms characteristic of other Israelite deliverers. If Jael still faces a choice in the poem, it is less about siding with the Israelites or Canaanites. Rather, the choice Jael makes to kill Sisera is one that seems to prioritize her own self-protection. At the very least, the ambiguity surrounding the murder in Judges 5 diffuses the side-choosing dilemma that is so prominent in Judges 4. Without denying the fact that the actions of Jael in Judges 5 still advance the cause of the Israelites, the poem creates space for understanding Jael's actions as a triumph "among women." In this way, the Jael of Judges 5 is less a model minority than she is a model of agency and resistance for women—both ancient and modern—who likewise face sexual violence.

Conclusion: Reading Texts, Rereading Contexts

What is gained by bringing postcolonial theory about mimeticism and the model minority paradigm into conversation with Judges 4–5? For one, these perspectives can raise an awareness that what needs to be examined in contextual readings of biblical texts are not only the *negative* portrayals of non-Israelite "Others" but also the *positive* portrayals that require these "Others" to assimilate into or align with the dominant culture. Such an awareness would not sever the point of contact Sakenfeld and others see between Jael and contemporary postcolonial subjects. Rather, it would prompt a more critical reading of the text, mindful that "success stories" do not always represent the whole story. Although Jael is never again mentioned in the Bible, one might wonder about the collateral costs of her deciding to side with the Israelites (especially in the prose account): Was she alienated from her Kenite friends and family? Did she (or the Kenites) later come under the protection of the Israelites, and if so, did this require leaving behind certain practices, customs, or beliefs? Though speculative in nature, such musings might prompt immigrant (or postcolonial) readers to see a stronger resonance between the implicit complexity of Jael's heroism and the conflictual dilemmas they face as outsiders in a dominant culture.

Second, reading the biblical text in light of theories about mimeticism and the model minority paradigm can conversely prompt us to reread our own contexts in a more self-critical fashion. In my case, the stories my grandparents told about their struggles and successes in America always seemed far removed from my life experiences. But as I come to reflect on the sorts of dilemmas they faced and the kinds of decisions they made, I realize that their stories have much to do with me and why I am an insider in the dominant culture today. My surname, Bonfiglio (which comes from my father, whose parents were also Italian Americans), literally means "good son" in Italian; and in many ways, I have played the role of the good *American* (grand)son that Dominic and Florence (and Paul and Rose), as cultural outsiders, would have wanted to have. I now see more clearly that being this sort of "Bonfiglio" entailed a certain cost to those who came before me: I am no longer considered a minority in this country in part because my grandparents chose assimilation, and in effect, became a type of model minority. Yet, on the other hand, I also am becoming more aware of the textures in their stories, of the ways in which my grandparents, like the Jael of Judges 5, refused to choose sides and instead took on the risk of maintaining the heterogeneity of being Italian Americans. In fact, the stories I remember so well were often shared in and around food, celebrations, and customs that richly preserved our Italian heritage in this new American context. Thus, just as the two representations of Jael in Judges 4 and 5 are closely and inseparably linked, so too are moments of assimilation and resistance closely and inseparably linked in the fabric of my own family's history. It is in this encounter with both Jaels—and perhaps the multiplicities of our own histories and contexts—that one can more clearly bring into focus the promising and problematic complexities of reading Judges 4–5 from the context of cultural outsiders.

Notes

1. I would like to thank Jacqueline E. Lapsley, Katherine Doob Sakenfeld, Carol A. Newsom, and Joel M. LeMon for their insightful feedback on earlier versions of this project. Any errors or omissions remain my own.

2. One of the earliest and most significant ideological-critical studies of Judges 4–5 is Mieke Bal's *Murder and Difference* (1987a). Bal's *Death and Dissymmetry* (1988a) also makes an important contribution to ideological concerns in the book of Judges more broadly. Subsequently, a host of other scholars have likewise studied Judges 4–5 with certain ideological concerns in view (Fewell and Gunn 1990; Yee 1993; Sakenfeld 1997; Ackerman 2000; Assis 2005; Guest 2005; and Reis 2005). Most recently (2011), Carolyn Sharp takes up the story of Jael (and Sisera) in Judges 4–5 as a test case in her exploration of a wide variety of interpretive methods.

3. Similar postcolonial reflections have been offered on other biblical figures, such as Rahab (Dube 2006) and Ruth (Dube 2001; Donaldson 1999). Though not addressing Jael specifically, Kim's essay (2007) offers a helpful entry point for postcolonial readings of Judges 4–5.

4. Gale Yee uses the term "hyphenated condition" to describe her experience as an Asian American of the pressure to identify with one of the two sides of the hyphen (2006: 159).

5. Several insightful examples of these integrative readings of Judges 4–5 can be found in the work of Sakenfeld 1997 and Brenner 1990. While these readings are rich and helpful, my own

work explores how the distinctive literary features of Judges 4 and 5, including their generic conventions and lexical choices, function to construct two related, though different, profiles of Jael's murder of Sisera. This perspective is not without precedent. See, for instance, Bal 1987a; Zakovitch 1981, and Fewell and Gunn 1990.

6. Though the Hebrew *'eshet lappidot* is typically translated "the wife of Lappidoth," it might also be read as "the woman of torches" (or the like) since elsewhere the singular noun *lappid* can mean "torch" (cf. Judg. 15:4). However, the former translation is to be favored for two reasons. First, when referring to torches, the plural form of *lappid* typically appears as *lappidim* (cf. Judg. 7:16, 20). Second, the only other woman specifically identified as an Israelite prophet, Huldah, is introduced with a similar formula that includes *'eshet* in construct with a proper noun: "the prophetess Huldah the wife of Shallum" (2 Kgs. 22:14; 2 Chron. 34:22).

7. For instance, Gore, Leighton Goudge, and Guillaume claim that "the heroine of the story is Deborah, a prophetess with the power of a Joan of Arc, who rouses Barak to lead the Northern tribes against Sisera" (1928: 156). Likewise, McCann believes that Deborah is referring to herself in 4:9 (2002: 51-53), while more recently Assis contends it is Deborah who is Israel's deliverer, and thus the true focus of the story (2005: 11).

8. On this point, I disagree with Yairah Amit, who understands the Kenites as a neutral party in the Israelite-Canaanite conflict (1987: 97). In my view, rather than having no allegiances, the Kenites have conflicting ones.

9. Reis (2005), and to a lesser extent Assis (2005), understand the imagery of Judges 4 as sexually explicit. However, in my estimation, this reading conflates the motherly imagery of Judges 4 with the more sexually connotative language of Judges 5. Especially in the case of Reis, her "erotic reading" of Judges 4 seems to arise from a methodological commitment to reading Judges 4 and 5 as "an integrated, unified exposition" (2005: 44).

10. The NRSV's rather tepid translation, "Is anyone here?" (4:20) for the Hebrew היש פה איש, *ha-yesh po 'ish*, tends to obscure any sense of irony present in these verses.

11. Nevertheless, some modern commentators refuse to see in Jael anything but an example of immoral behavior. Keil and Delitzsch contend that Jael's "heroic deed cannot be acquitted of the sins of lying, treachery, and assassination" (1996: 306).

12. See, for instance, Fewell and Gunn 1990: 393–94, Sakenfeld 1997: 20, and Wansbrough 1992:101–22.

13. See also Chow 2002.

10

The Woman Warrior Revisited

Jael, Fa Mulan, and American Orientalism

Gale A. Yee

I purchased the paperback version of Maxine Hong Kingston's *The Woman Warrior* when it appeared in 1977. The irony is that I never read it until I had to teach it for a women's studies class in the late 1980s. It was the concept of a Chinese woman warrior, not the book itself, that intrigued me as a Chinese American female: the ancient legend of a powerful woman who, like many in the U.S. Women's Liberation Movement of the 1970s, defied the conventions of the weak, obedient womanhood of traditional Chinese patriarchy. She was for me a female counterpart of Superman who fought for truth and justice, but perhaps not for the "American way." It was this concept of a female warrior that drew me to write on Jael in Judges 4 for a *Semeia* volume devoted to women, war, and metaphor (Yee 1993). My fascination with her continued as I speculated on what I would do for an Asian American reading of Judges 4–5 (Yee 2006: 162–63). My contribution to this *Texts@Contexts* volume therefore offers me a welcome opportunity to delve once more into the woman-warrior motif through an intercontextual comparison between Jael[1] and Fa Mulan, the Chinese woman warrior who inspired Kingston's work. Intercontextual features can be found in their shared warriorhood, their respective ethnicities, their (trans)gendering, and the reception history of their narratives. Particularly with respect to Fa Mulan's reception history, I will focus on the American Orientalism that plays a significant part in the mass-marketed Disney production *Mulan* (1998) and my own conceptualization of my ethnic heritage.

Warriorhood

Both Jael and Mulan can be considered warriors, although in differing ways. In my 1993 article on Judges 4, I argued that the social structure of pre-monarchic Israel offered possibilities for women to engage in informal wartime operations. Because the family household (*bet 'ab*) was the basic socioeconomic unit and because women held critical leadership positions within this unit, albeit informal ones, women like Deborah had opportunities to emerge as leaders during times of war. Furthermore, if one extends the definition of warriorhood beyond those who fight on the battlefield to those who work in covert operations and intelligence, then Jael would be considered a warrior. Her assassination of Sisera, the enemy's top-ranking general, already classifies her as a warrior, more broadly defined. The fact that she uses trickery is no different from the guerilla tactics already employed by the Israelites (Yee 1993: 109–14).

A significant number of myths of heroic Chinese women, of whom Fa Mulan is the most well known, defy the stereotype of women as victims of Chinese patriarchy (Dong 2011: 9–50; Mann 2000: 835–62). Although originating between the fourth and sixth centuries CE, an anonymous folk song, "The Ballad of Mulan," was published in a thirteenth-century anthology of lyrics, folk songs, and poems.[2] The song describes a young woman at a weaver's loom, anxious about her father's conscription into the khan's army, because he had no older son who could be drafted in his place. Mulan decides to purchase a horse and other equipment "to take my father's place to go on a military expedition" (Dong 2011: 54). Bidding farewell to her parents, she fights valiantly for twelve years alongside her fellow male warriors, who take her to be one of them. When she is presented in the emperor's court, she eschews a promotion in rank and honor, preferring a fast camel that would whisk her back to her hometown. Upon her arrival, she enters her boudoir, removes her military attire, puts on a dress, fixes her hair, and applies makeup to her face. When she emerges as a lovely woman, her comrades, who evidently came home with her, are amazed: "We spent twelve years fighting together, but didn't know that Mulan was a woman" (Dong 2011: 55).

Lest one regard Mulan as some proto-feminist heroine, stories about Mulan and her kind were written and transmitted primarily to illustrate how Confucian patriarchy should function. Patriarchal Chinese values celebrated and hinged on powerful women. A distinctive feature of Confucian patriarchy is the separate realms of *yin/yang* cosmologies, the male, the public "outer," and the female, the domestic "inner" (Mann 2000: 842). Although Mulan transgresses these boundaries by her warriorhood, she adheres to the Confucian codes of duty, loyalty, and filial piety that did not threaten, but rather upheld, the dominant rule of men (Dong 2011: 13–15; Li 2003: 4–5). The poem opens with Mulan weaving at the loom in her house, a domestic task performed by women. The so-called masculine aspects of her life—her many years as a soldier—are simply compressed into a few lines. The poem focuses instead on the honors the emperor bestows on her for her valor and her eventual return to the domestic sphere. After her turn as a loyal warrior for the empire, she resumes the traditional roles of daughter and potential wife/mother.

Tropes of inner/outer and domestic/public also figure in the story of Jael. Jael differs from Mulan in that she eliminates her enemy secretly: not on the open battlefield, but in the private sphere of her tent. Jael does not disguise her gender in her "combat" with Sisera, as Mulan does. In fact, she "performs" some of the traditional behaviors of her female gender (Butler 1999: 179). She invites Sisera into her personal space, which some have likened to a womb (Fewell and Gunn 1990: 393). Like a mother, she covers him with a rug, gives him milk to drink, and protects him from the dangers without (Judg. 4:18-20). Mulan, on the one hand, displays her womanliness after her time in battle, when she returns to her family and reveals herself as a female before her fellow soldiers. Jael, on the other hand, exhibits her martial prowess only after she performs as a traditional woman. Both heroines in their own different ways share the incongruity of being a female warrior in the male arena of war.

Ethnicity

In my 2006 article, "Yin/Yang is Not Me," I posed the following questions about Jael, inquiring into the nature of her ethnicity, as I contemplated my own as a Chinese American biblical scholar: Was Jael a foreigner (non-Israelite) like her husband, Heber the Kenite? Was Jael a Kenite like her husband? What was the nature of Kenite/Hebrew ethnic, political, and/or economic relations? How does Jael's ethnicity influence her status as a woman warrior? (Yee 2006: 162–63). I return again to some of these questions, as I consider Jael's ethnicity from an Asian American perspective and compare it to Mulan's.

A major problem is that we cannot easily pinpoint Jael's ethnicity or even her marital status to a Kenite male. First of all, ambiguity surrounds the ethnicity of the Kenites themselves as kin-group relatives to Moses in Judges. According to Judg. 1:16, the descendants of the Kenite father-in-law of Moses—whom the LXX and Judg. 4:11 name Hobab—"went up with the people of Judah from the city of palms into the wilderness of Judah, which lies in the Negeb near Arad" (NRSV, here and in further bible citations). The text relates that these Kenite descendants settled with the Amalekites, raising the possibility of intermarriage between the two ethnic groups. Judg. 4:11 then explains how a group usually situated in the southern wilderness now resides in the far north: "Heber the Kenite had separated from the other Kenites, that is the descendants of Hobab the father-in-law of Moses, and had encamped as far away as Elon-bezanannim, which is near Kedesh." In Num. 10:29, Hobab is not Moses' father-in-law, but the son of Reuel the Midianite, not a Kenite (cf. Exod. 2:18). Another tradition names Moses' father-in-law Jethro, although still affirming the Midianite, rather than Kenite, connection (Exod. 3:1). Uncertainty regarding the name (Hobab/Reuel/Jethro) and ethnicity (Midianite/Kenite) of Moses' father-in-law and the possible Kenite/Amalekite intermingling complicates the ethnicity of the Kenite descendants described in Judges 4 (Halpern 1992: 20–21; Ackerman 1998: 94–95).

If we take *heber* as a proper name, Heber is the husband of Jael and belonged to a Kenite clan that had separated from the Kenites, who had settled in the south and had moved far north (Judg. 4:11). Because "there was peace between King Jabin of Hazor and the clan of Heber the Kenite," Sisera flees to the tent of Jael, wife (*'ishshah*) of Heber the Kenite (Judg. 4:17). This detail implies that the allegiance of Heber's northern clan to the Canaanites differed from the allegiance of the southern Kenites, who were allied with the Israelites. However, if Heber's clan had friendly relations with Barak's Canaanite enemies, then why did the Israelite leader respond freely to Jael's invitation, "Come, and I will show you the man whom you are seeking" (4:22)? "Would not the logic of the peace treaty suggest that this *Israelite* general should be wary of a *Canaanite* sympathizer?" (Ackerman 1998: 92). Robert Boling remarks that it was providential that a Galilean Kenite chieftain had a loyal Yahwist wife (Boling 1975: 97). However, this raises the question of whether Jael was a Kenite convert to Yahweh or an Israelite Yahwist who married a Kenite, which might have lessened Barak's suspicions about entering her tent. The text is not clear regarding Jael's ethnicity or her religious and political alliances apart from her husband.

Furthermore, Heber the Kenite may not have been Jael's husband. If one does not read *heber* as a proper name but as an ethnic "group" or "clan," *heber haqqeni* in 4:11, 17 could simply refer to the Kenite group or community. By moving north, this group had detached itself from the southern desert Kenites, who were distantly related to the Israelites through Moses' Midianite father-in-law Hobab. Jael would then be a woman (*'ishshah*) belonging to this indeterminate group of Kenite origin who had moved far north near Kedesh (4:11) (Soggin 1981: 65–66, 74–75; Halpern 1992: 18). In this case, Jael would be a non-Israelite, an ethnic foreigner from the Israelite perspective (Ackerman 1998: 99–100).

The slipperiness in pinning down Jael's ethnicity and its geographical loci has some analogues with the Asian Fa Mulan. Mulan's tale probably originated from a non-Han ethnic tradition.[3] The poem resembles some of the folk songs about the heroic women of a foreign nomadic tribe known as the Xianbei who conquered and controlled northern China between 386–534 CE. Xianbei women were skilled in horseback riding and in archery. If the "Ballad" came from a similar milieu, the martial features of these women would have been appropriated by the Han Chinese, who infused them into their own heroine Fa Mulan. Thus the character Mulan most likely had a foreign ethnic origin at the earliest stage of her literary history (Dong 2011: 53; Lan 2003: 229–33). Nevertheless, because her story of gender defiance was so fascinating and engaging, various parts of China over the years wanted to claim her and incorporate her into their regional histories, augmenting the different traditions surrounding her (Dong 2011: 85–86).

Jael's ethnicity also has intriguing analogues with the Asian American ethnic experience. Consider the description of Bobby, a resident of Koreatown in Los Angeles, in Karen Te Yamashita's imaginative and brilliant novel on the clash of cultures and hemispheres, *Tropic of Orange*:

> That's Bobby. If you know your Asians, you look at Bobby. You say, that's Vietnamese. That's what you say. Color's pallid. Kinda blue just beneath the skin. Little underweight. Korean's got rounder face. Chinese's taller. Japanese's dressed better. If you know your Asians. Turns out you'll be wrong. And you gonna be confused. Dude speaks Spanish. Comprende? So you figure it's one of those Japanese from Peru. Or maybe Korean from Brazil. Or Chinamex. Turns out Bobby's from Singapore. You say, okay, Indonesian. Malaysian. Wrong again. You say, look at his name. That's gotta be Vietnam. Ngu. Bobby Ngu. They all got Ngu names. Hey, it's not his real name. Real name's Li Kwan Yu. But don't tell nobody. Go figure. Bobby's Chinese. Chinese from Singapore with a Vietnam name speaking like a Mexican living in Koreatown. That's it. (Yamashita 1997: 14–15)

Here, stereotypes of Asian Americans are disrupted by reality, reflecting the diverse contexts of many Asian Americans.[4] Similarly, Jael's ethnicity has also been difficult to determine. She was part and parcel of that "mixed multitude" (see Exod. 12:38) that constituted early Israel: "a collection of loosely organized and largely indigenous, tribal, and kin-based groups whose porous borders permitted penetration by smaller numbers from external groups" (Killebrew 2004: 184–85).

(Trans)Gendering

In my 1993 article, I maintained that the woman warrior occupies a structurally anomalous position in the human domain. She is neither male nor female as they are normally understood, but shares features of both. She is a liminal figure and thus a threat to the dominant structures of power. In order to mitigate this threat, the author of Judges constructs Jael through syndromes—shame and sexual voracity—that reinforce his androcentric interests. Jael primarily becomes a means to shame the men associated with her. She shames Sisera, because he suffers a humiliating death by the hand of a woman, and Barak, because he could not carry out Sisera's death himself. In keeping with the unbridled lust characterizing warrior queens, Jael lures Sisera to his death through her sexuality (Yee 1993: 99–117). We have already seen the way the warrior woman Fa Mulan was portrayed in ways that bolstered Chinese patriarchy. Both women transgress the societal dictates of their gender while still remaining paradoxically within their confines.

In the "Ballad of Mulan," Mulan violates gender norms through cross-dressing and through disguising herself as a warrior by securing the accouterments of battle—a horse, saddle, bridle, and long horsewhip. It is significant here that "clothes do *not* make the man," but the supplies needed for military transport do. Clothing comes into play only when Mulan returns home and slips on a dress, highlighting her femininity and her return to the traditional order. Every development of her story over time and region will imprint on her its own ideology of maleness and femaleness and the contradictions therein for a woman warrior. For example, in the sixteenth-century play by Xu Wei, "Female Mulan Joins the Army Taking Her Father's Place," the heroine actually does dress in men's clothing, but paradoxically also has bound feet, a key signifier of femininity and the erotic of the time. The eroticism of bound feet emanates from the fact that men rarely see a bound foot without the white bandages covering it (Jackson 1997: 103–22). Thus when Mulan must loosen the bandages binding her feet as she dons her military uniform, especially the male footwear to accommodate these feet, it becomes an erotic moment. Mulan figures out a way to restore the damage to her "lotus feet" when she returns home to get married, all of which underscores the fact that Mulan does not deviate completely from the established male order (Dong 2011: 66–72).

Gender contradictions become particularly apparent when Mulan's story is staged in Chinese opera, where even up to the twentieth century the most popular actors playing female leads were men (Li 2003). The role of Mulan would be performed by a boy or a man, playing a woman who disguises herself as a man and then returns to being a woman. Shades of *Victor/Victoria* in reverse! Because the potential audience of Xu Wei's play is the male elite class, the addition of foot-binding to Mulan's story takes on a (homo)erotic subtext, when a male actor plays a part of a woman unbinding her feet, while getting dressed as a man (Dong 2011: 70–71). From the perspective of queer theory, Li expresses these contradictions in Chinese opera succinctly:

> The engendering of the spectacle and spectatorial gaze, and the circulation of the sexual and the homo/hetero-erotic in a multiple crisscrossing within and across the binary hierarchies of man/woman, sex/gender, (male) gaze and (female) object, erotic desire/object of desire—all subsumed within a heterosexual matrix (Li 2003: 20).

One of the most provocative examinations of Jael's (trans)gendering to date is also a queer reading, one by Deryn Guest on Judges 4–5 (Guest 2011: 9–43). Guest rejects interpretations of Jael that persist in confining gender to the binaries male/female, masculine/feminine. As long as scholars remain within this closed dichotomous system, Jael's transgressive acts can only be seen as gender "reversal" that for Guest simply shifts the ground from one gender to the other. Guest prefers instead to resist, subvert, undo, and deconstruct these binaries to reveal them as social constructions (9). She finds my 1993 article on Jael to be the most promising study on which to build such a queer reading, because its focus on the liminality of Jael opens the way to gender destabilization (Guest 2011: 16–19). Nevertheless, she critiques my use of female pronouns to describe Jael, thus bypassing a syndrome that would have strengthened my argument for Jael's liminality, namely, the tomboy syndrome. This syndrome "catches the eye of a lesbian reader who can resonate with such preferences and the subsequent stigma" (16–17). According to Guest, *all* commentators have not been able to break through the male/female binary in consistently referring to Jael as female, because they fail to see, à la Judith Butler, that gender is a performance (20).

Along with Jael's transgressive warrior actions, Guest senses "gaydar bleeps" in Judges 4 that hint at Jael's genderqueerness: Jael's masculine name and the masculine imperative of Sisera's command to Jael to stand at the entrance of the tent (20–21). While several scholars, including myself, have described Jael's violent assassination of Sisera with a phallic tent peg as a reversal of male rape, Guest maintains that

> Jael is not a *woman* warrior and equally Jael is not a *male* rapist. . . . Jael is a figure who unsettles and destabilizes, whose performativity provides one of those unintelligible genders that give the lie to ideas of sex as abiding substance (26, emphasis in original).

Jael's gender is not-man/not-woman.[5] Although ill at ease with the female pronouns in the following citation from Robyn Fleming, Guest thinks that Fleming comes close to explaining why Jael provokes such anxiety in her genderqueerness:

> Jael is almost the personification of gender blur, that force most threatening to the hierarchical structure of patriarchy. If you can't tell for sure which people are men, and which are women, how can power structures based on gender inequality be maintained? This then is the source of the phallocentric reader's unease about the character of Jael. The problem is not that she breaks with laws of hospitality, or even that she is a rapist, quite. The problem is that in doing those things, and in order to do those things, she destabilizes both her own gender construction and the gendered identities of others. (Fleming 2005, cited in Guest 2011: 29–20).

It is this gender blur, this gender confusion that aggravates and provokes the dominant structures of patriarchy in the Jael narrative.

As other regions and populations in China have wished to claim Mulan for their own, so does Guest desire to claim Jael for genderqueer readers who identify themselves as not-man/not-woman. "Jael seems to provide an unforeseen biblical character for those butch lesbians who desire to wear their genderqueerness with pride" (31). In commenting on Guest's article, Kamionkowski remarks that Guest's agenda is *"not just to break down heteronormative structures but to create a place for herself within biblical readings"* (Kamionkowski 2011: 134, emphasis in original). Even in such a patriarchal text as the Bible, Guest is able to find something constructive in the person of Jael for those who occupy a space outside of heteronormativity.

RECEPTION HISTORY

Because the woman warrior occupies such a liminal position, betwixt and between dominant conceptions of gender, my 1993 article discussed a number of different and contradictory ways in which Jael (and Deborah) have been taken up and represented in the course of their long reception history (Yee 1993: 121–26). For example, in his first-century work, Pseudo-Philo depicts Sisera as a predatory collector of beautiful women as concubines in the spoils of war. For this reason, Deborah prophesies that "the arm of a weak woman would attack him and maidens would take his spoils and even he would fall into the hands of a woman" (*Bib. Ant.* 31:1).[6] Pseudo-Philo's Deborah becomes the champion of female honor that has been disgraced by Sisera. The vehicle of Sisera's demise is one of these women upon whom Sisera preys. Sexualizing the confrontation between Jael and Sisera, Pseudo-Philo describes Jael as "very beautiful in appearance." She "adorns herself" and goes out "to meet" Sisera to invite him back to her tent. Unlike Mulan, who cross-dressed as a man, Jael highlights her femininity by getting dressed to kill in seductive attire. Upon seeing her bed festooned with roses, Sisera declares, "If I am saved, I will go to my mother, and Jael will be my wife." The net effect of Pseudo-Philo's sexual expansions is to make Jael an agent of revenge for the rape of women. Instead of seizing beautiful women as spoils for himself, Sisera becomes undone by one.

The study of the reception history on Jael has been enhanced by David Gunn's commentary on Judges (Gunn 2005: 53–92).[7] Gunn examines ancient, medieval, modern, and contemporary religious and secular literature, paintings, engravings, and poems that depict Jael. His study reinforces my own earlier conclusions regarding the contradictory interpretations of Jael from the earliest times, because of the liminal position she occupies as a woman warrior. On the one hand, she can foreshadow Jesus, the church, or the Virgin Mary in that her assassination of Sisera anticipates Jesus', the church's, and Mary's triumph over sin or the devil. On the other hand, she is the quintessential femme fatale, a mother snake who lures one into her tent, soothes him into a false sense of security, and "slid like snake across the tent—struck twice—and stung him dead" (Gunn 2005: 77). Jael has been a particular favorite in the visual arts (Bohn 2006: 107–27; Haber 1995: 87–92; Christiansen and Mann 2001: 344–47),[8] music (Leneman 2007: 428–63), poetry (Robnolt 1995: 1), film (Christianson 2008: 39–60), and children's literature (Bottigheimer 1996: 142–51).

Lan Dong thoroughly documents the reception history of Fa Mulan, which she describes as a palimpsest, an evolving interplay of continuity and erasure in which Mulan's tale is written and rewritten into multiple layers that efface and erase previous versions (Dong 2011: 5). Mulan is transformed from a foreign nomadic warrior into several iterations of an idealized Han Chinese heroic maiden. She becomes the avatar of Maxine Hong Kingston, the warrior avenger in Kingston's autobiography (Kingston 1977). She morphs into several different incarnations in a number of American children's books, culminating in a major Disney animation, *Mulan* (Madacy Entertainment Group 1999). It is the Disney production of Mulan's story that interests me as an artifact of American Orientalism.

In my 2006 article, I examine my own process of becoming an Asian American, a totally different breed from one who is born and bred in Asia. Even though I look Chinese, I do not have the usual markers of Asianness. As a third-generation Chinese American, I cannot draw on immigrant experience from a previous time in China. Unlike Maxine Hong Kingston's mother, my own never told me Chinese legends of ghosts and woman warriors, most likely because as a second-generation Chinese American she didn't know any herself. Even though I was raised in a Chinese-speaking household, my parents did not teach their twelve children Chinese, so that we would assimilate more easily into American culture. I also suspect that they spoke Chinese whenever they didn't want us kids to understand what they were talking about. I did not grow up in Chinatown but in the slums of Blackstone Ranger Chicago, with blacks and Puerto Ricans. My parents were devout Roman Catholics, and did not practice the traditional Asians religions: Buddhism, Taoism, and Confucianism. So I can confidently declare that, with respect to my Chinese ethnicity, "Ying/ Yang is not me" (Yee 2006: 152–63; 1997: 108–12). I am a Chinese American inside and out.

Nevertheless, I've had to explore the Asian side of the hyphen in figuring out what an Asian American reading of the biblical text looks like. I discovered that during my formative years, my understanding of Asian was refracted through the prism of American Orientalism: the representation of Asia as a geographically distant, foreign land filled with exotic and dubious characters and cultural practices that must be subdued and domesticated (Ma 2000; Lee 1999; Okihiro 1994). My early exposure to China and its culture was through Charlie Chan and Pearl Buck movies, where white actors played Chinese characters. My Chinese icons were Fu Manchu, Dragon Lady, and Ming the Merciless from the planet Mongo of the *Flash Gordon* TV series. I was mesmerized by the martial arts of Mrs. Peel in the TV series *The Avengers*, until after years of karate and kung fu myself, I realized that she knew very little about these skills. I actually enjoyed reading James Clavell's Asian Saga novels! I was one of those Chinese Americans "who got their China and Japan from the radio, off the silver screen, from television, out of comic books, and from the pushers of white American culture" (Chin 1991: xi–xii). The Orientalist features of Disney's *Mulan* have already been examined at length (Dong 2011: 159–87; Ma 2003: 149–64; Chan 2002: 225–48; Wang and Yeh 2005: 175–93; Tang 2008: 149–62). Because of my own early racial formation, I want to explore the Americanization of Fa Mulan by Disney, and how it may affect the formation of racial and gender identity for young Chinese American females as they encounter this woman warrior of their ethnic heritage.

Disney's *Mulan* transforms the legend of our ancient Chinese heroine into a Western animated family feature film for a global market. Although she has Chinese features, Mulan seems to be a typical American teenager, facing issues of identity and purpose. Like all Disney females, she sets out on a journey to discover her true self, one that involves plenty of adventure and a little romance. The cross-dressing aspect of the legend is particularly highlighted and conflated with the Confucian ideals regarding gender and family honor. In order to make a good impression on the matchmaker, Mulan is forced to undergo an extensive beauty treatment and complete clothing makeover. Playing during this makeover, the song "Honor to Us All" is replete with Chinese gender stereotypes:

> Men want girls with good taste,
>> Calm,
>> Obedient
>> Who work fast-paced
>> With good breeding
>> And a tiny waist.
>> You'll bring honor to us all.

After she blows her interview with the matchmaker, she expresses her search for identity in singing "Reflection":

>> Who is this girl I see
>> Staring straight
>> Back at me?
>> Why is my reflection someone
>> I don't know?

Somehow I cannot hide
Who I am
Though I've tried
When will my reflection show
Who I am inside?

In contrast to the "Ballad of Mulan," Disney's Mulan makes a big display of seizing her father's sword, cutting off her hair, putting on her father's armor, and replacing her father's military summons with her decorative hair comb. The cross-dressing makes the transformation from female to male visually explicit.[9] Although Mulan struggles to play the part of a man, it is also clear that her male comrades fall short of the ideal manhood. General Li Shang, Mulan's potential love interest, scornfully sings at his troops:

You're a spineless, pale pathetic lot,
And you haven't got a clue
Somehow I'll make a man out of you.

The cross-dressing acquires a humorous reversal toward the end of the movie. In order to infiltrate the palace and save the emperor from the evil clutches of Shan Yu, Mulan's comrades deck themselves in female clothing and pose as concubines.[10] While Shan Yu's thugs drool over and are beset by these cross-dressers, "I'll Make a Man Out of You" ironically plays in the background.

In contrast to other Disney films where the male hero rescues the female lead, Mulan actually saves Li Shang at several points in the film. She, not Li Shang, also disposes of the film's villain. In the slaying of Shan Yu, Mulan snaps open her fan (a feminine artifact) to catch and twist Shan Yu's sword (a masculine one) out of his hand. Reminiscent for me of Jael's killer tent peg, Shan Yu is then blown away by a giant phallic firecracker that hits him in his groin.

Plenty of academic articles examine the influence of Disney on gender and race (see Bell, Haas, and Sells 1995; Brode 2005; Ayers 2003), but none is on the influence of Disney's Mulan on the racial formation of young Asian American girls specifically.[11] I therefore combed the Web and blogs of Asian Pacific Americans. One in particular stands out, because it echoes some of the themes in Deryn Guest's queer study of Jael. Twenty-four-year-old Mimi Nguyen describes herself as a Vietnamese refugee-tomboy from "the swampy environs of a Midwestern small town" (Nguyen 1998: 1). As children, she and a fellow Latina migrant assimilated the identities of strong female icons, such as the Bionic Woman and Wonder Woman, to help them survive as strangers in a strange land. However, all of these icons were "white as snow." Nguyen eventually finds her ethnic avatar in the Disney Mulan—"an Asian tomboy too butch for the bride gig"—and reads the film as gender subversion:

> What's amazing is the sly acknowledgement that gender norms are socially constructed—both masculinity and femininity are exposed as elaborate performances—while concurring that these same gender norms prove to be the source of much injustice. Never mind feudal China, it's a critique that resonates in contemporary U.S. society. So throw in lots of drag and transvestitism, "Mulan" becomes a veritable boiling pot of gender trouble (Nguyen 1998: 2).

Nguyen tackles the question whether one should dismiss Disney's *Mulan* simply as a consumerist ploy to cash in on the global multicultural market or see it as a validation that Asian American has finally made it culturally on the big screen. Nguyen opts for neither:

> So let's get over the obvious, the bad dog/good dog scenario. We give too little credit to the power of the imagination if we believe either that until 'Mulan,' little Asian-American girls floundered without inspiration or, on the other hand, that with 'Mulan,' little Asian-American girls are ripe for conglomerate-sponsored consumer conformity (Nguyen 1998: 4).

Instead, for Nguyen there is a third space, a place in-between, where "we can juggle our critiques and our pleasures with the complexity of analysis they deserved," even though she acknowledges that she would have killed for a Mulan action figure when she was ten years old (Nguyen 1998: 5).

And so would I!

CONCLUSION

Intercontextual overlaps exist between Jael of Judges 4 and the Chinese heroine Fa Mulan. Both women are warriors, one on the formal battlefield, the other in the informal arena of her tent. Their ethnic origins are a little suspect. Mulan may have been originally a non-Chinese heroine. We do not quite know Jael's ethnicity. Was she Israelite or Kenite? Both share that slippery gendered space between male and female. As a result of this "gender blur," contradictory and conflicting interpretations of their narratives abound. Because of my own racial formation by American Orientalism, I have particularly focused on the representation of Fa Mulan by Disney, in which she becomes a spunky independent teen searching for her true self.

I have now come full circle in my study of Jael in Judges 4. This essay allowed me to catch up on interesting research on Jael. But more importantly, it gave me a great excuse to examine contextually the Chinese woman warrior Fa Mulan, something that I have been wanting to do since my 1993 article. And let's face it, since enjoying the Disney production *Mulan*, in spite of or maybe because of its American Orientalism. Perhaps if I had a Mulan action figure during my tender years, I would not have gravitated so readily to the woman warrior Jael.

Postscript

I was fortunate to participate in the China study tour sponsored by my institution, Episcopal Divinity School, in May 2012. One of the stops was the important ancient capital city of Xi'an, where the Nestorian stele (781 CE) documents the presence of 150 years of Christianity in China. Also found in Xi'an are the famous terra cotta warriors of the first emperor of China, Qin Shi Huang. I took a detour to the exhibit and, in tourist mode, had the following picture taken to embody what Fa Mulan might have worn in one of her literary incarnations.

Notes

1. The bibliography on Judges 4–5 is extensive. For research since 1990, see Mayfield 2009: 306–35.

2. For an English translation of the poem, see http://www.yellowbridge.com/onlinelit/mulan.php.

3. The Han was and is the largest ethnic group in China.

4. I remember being in a diner in Chicago and seeing my waitress and the cook arguing with each other. The waitress came over and told me that she and the cook had a bet with each other to identify which Native American tribe I belonged to. I don't remember the tribe, Apache, Sioux or whatever, but I had to disappoint both when I told them that I was Chinese. Furthermore, in this era of racial profiling, the Asian ethnic group most people think I'm from is Filipino/a.

5. Guest has explored this description of not-woman/not-man with the butch lesbian experience (Guest 2008: 254–58).

6. Following the translation of Harrington 1985: 296–377.

7. In the Blackwell Bible Commentaries series, which is devoted to the reception history of the Bible.

8. A number of paintings about Jael can be viewed at http://www.biblical-art.com/biblicalsubject.asp?id_biblicalsubject=131&pagenum=1. For art and music, see http://catholic-resources.org/Art/.

9. A Disney movie poster, in dramatic Chinese red featuring Mulan in full military garb, astride a noble horse, with both staring fiercely at an unseen enemy, can be viewed at http://en.wikipedia.org/wiki/Mulan. See also http://www.nytimes.com/imagepages/2006/03/19/arts/19solo_ready.html for a scene where Mulan leads a cavalry charge. Her love interest, Li Shang, in on the white horse to her left.

10. The cross-dressed concubines can be seen at http://wwww.fanpop.com/spots/disney-princess/images/16075306/title/mulan-photo.

11. Among white audiences, Mulan seems to rate very highly. After researching many parents, dweeb posts an opinion on *fanpop!* ranking the nine Disney Princesses on terms of being good role models for young girls. Mulan was the number-one choice—"the ultimate Disney hero, male or female!"—and many responses to her blog concur (Dweeb 2010). For the opposite opinion, see Wilson (2011), who regards Disney's Mulan as a role model for a generation of "Twinkies," girls who are yellow (Asian) on the outside and white (American) on the inside, many of whom are adopted.

11

This Season You'll be Wearing God

On the Manning of Gideon and the Undressing of the Israelites (Judges 6:1—8:32)

Meir Bar Mymon

In this essay I shall examine the process that shaped Gideon into being a *Man*. The process that made a *Soldier Man* out of him did not end until Gideon wore God the warrior, and God wore Gideon (Judg. 6:34); moreover, the process was fully realized only when Gideon undressed himself from Yhwh by creating the *ephod*, reducing God to the level of a scorned image and shifting his own male image from a fighter back to a *Man*, self-made. By so doing, Gideon reduces God to the status of uniform, the temporary clothing that has shaped him to a certain category of masculinity. In other words, I wish to shift the cultural signification of the image of Gideon from a soldier back to a citizen, hoping that one day I too can finally undress myself from my uniforms in the hope of becoming a civilian.

WHEN MEN WERE WARRIORS

The winter of 1996 was the winter that altered my life, or at least nearly did. It was the winter in which that fragile "I" of mine—the "I" of an Israeli teenager who had just finished high school and was clueless about his identity or the world of identities that surrounded him—entered the Israeli identity pressure cooker for a fast cook-and-serve of the new Israeli "I," the "I" that will cling to the body forever, the "I" that will mark any Israeli wherever he is, the mark of Cain, the "I" of the soldier.

The damp winter day and the irritating tiny drops of rain that fell on the olive gray military compound did not discourage the thousands of cheerful Israeli children who hopped onto the buses that would take them to the בקו״ם, BAQUM, the acronym of the army "absorption and categorization camp," the almighty Israeli army base in the center of the country that classifies most of the Israelis, men and women, and puts them into the שרשרת חיול, the preliminary "chain of soldiering." This process gives the new recruits uniforms, vaccinates them, takes x-ray shots of their teeth in case this is all that's left of them in battle, and has them sign an insurance policy that grants their parents money and benefits if their soldier offspring dies.

I was neither exactly cheerful nor quite gloomy. I was shocked, perhaps even terrified, of this unknown process, at the end of which awaited a monster whose name I did not know, but whose presence hovered above me all my life, a monster that for years was hiding in the closet, under the bed, in the classroom, and in the Israeli history books, and was waiting quietly and patiently to be uncovered. And this monster was revealed indeed; by the end of the soldering process, after I had put on my uniform and learned how to cuff the low hem of the pants to the boots, I dared to look forward. There I saw an image reflected in the mirror and looking at me; and on the mirror frame, there was an engraved sentence emphasized with yellow paint: "Soldier, improve your outfit!"

At that moment I saw a new "I," an "I" that had been dormant in me for eighteen years, carefully fed and nursed by the Israeli Zionist cultural system: a self that had been an "I" cocoon was now articulated and ready to take control over me. During the neophyte process I felt how my breath was sucked out of my life, how the blood left my veins, how my body turned docile and united with a greater body, the body of the Israeli army, controlled not by my own mind but by the collective mind. I saw how this "I" took control over the newly born soldiers, I saw how it was fed and nurtured, and how, gradually, the previous "I," the childish, playful "I" had been changed into a different one, still childish but with a mission: to guard the beloved country and its Holy City, the Woman Jerusalem; and I was determined to resist.

THE GUARD OF THE WALLS

I am standing on the wall
Standing in the rain, all by myself
And the entire old city

Is laid on the palm of my hand
I gaze at her, in love
I always climb these walls to gaze
But this time I am here on a mission.[1]

This song was first performed by the army Central Command band (Hebrew: *piqqud merkaz*) in 1977 and describes the emotions of a young soldier who is positioned to guard over the walls of the old city of Jerusalem, portraying the city as a woman and the first-voice singer as a brave soldier, but still a child intoxicated by the beauty, sounds, and smells of Jerusalem, still trying to be alert and keep guard. In the chorus, the soldier reflects on his days as a young boy:

Whoever dreamt back in class at school
When we learned to recite:
"Upon your walls, O Jerusalem, I have set watchmen,"[2]
That one day I will be one of them?

And indeed, this day had come. This soldier that was a boy was a man now, a member of a grand nation, watching over his beloved Jerusalem. Twenty years after this song had been written and first sung, and I too had to go through the same process: I learned to recite the exact phrases in the book of Isaiah and went the exact route of the song's child/soldier, including taking an army oath of allegiance at the Wailing Wall, holding my rifle in my right hand and a Bible, close to my heart, in my left hand.

At that moment, the process of my masculinization and cultural/national becoming had come to its climax; from now on I could call myself a true Israeli and be part of an institution that could not survive without me, an institution that had shaped me so I could be part of it: a society of soldiers/civilians whose one hand guards the nation and the other creates its past, present, and future.

COME ON BOY, BE A MAN

Up until a few decades ago, especially until the 1990s, a *Man* was a solid building, a rock-hard figure of one image, untouchable and unbreakable. Studies on masculinities have changed this point of view and are now showing that what we tend to see as a monolithic configuration is a highly complex and very fragile, multifaceted structure. This structure is built by many different myths of masculinities that are constantly shaped and reshaped in order to fulfill a cultural-historical end. Masculinities studies[3] seeks to understand how these myths are constructed and how power relations between men and women, as well as among men, are sustained. However, *masculinities* can also be perceived non-essentialially as a set of behaviors and practices that do not necessarily require the male body in order to exist, and can be adopted by anything and anyone. Therefore, we can also implement this term with regard to spaces, places, and realms that can have a major role in producing the gendered identity in a text.[4]

In this essay, I will focus only on the construction of the *Man*, meaning the mainstream image and not the marginal aspects, showing how a *Man* is being born and the purpose of the creation of such a *Man*, and especially the twist in this becoming-a-*Man* story of Gideon.

Be a Man, So that I Can Be One Too

An example for a masculinization process, and how the image of *Man* is constructed, can be found in Barrett's article about the establishment of hegemonic masculinity in the U.S. Navy (Barrett 1996: 129–42). The U.S. Navy makes the novices ("boys," as they are called initially) undergo a masculinization process so that, eventually, they will become part of the hegemonic masculinity and will be warriors, a true army of *Men*. The novices go through a very severe masculinization process that strips their previous images of masculinities and creates a new one. This process includes head shaving, receiving uniforms, violent training, harassment, humiliating initiation ceremonies, and sex tutoring and control via the establishment of fear from STDs (sexually transmitted diseases). The process ends in creating a *Man*, a model that no other man can claim unless he has been in the Navy, a model that no woman can claim, for she will never be a *Man*; nor a gay man since, at the time of Barrett's research openly gay men, and women, were not able to serve in the U.S. armed forces.[5] The masculinization process continues to be a challenge for those women and men in the Navy who do not fit into such a strict model of what it is to become a *Man*. This strict model penetrates civilian society and influences its behaviors and male models, making the Navy an overall gendering institution for American society.

I wish to add to Barrett's research that this process not only genders the "boys" and makes them into *Men* but also reconfirms the Navy as an all-hegemonic male establishment that requires its men to be hegemonic over other models of masculinities, and is accountable only to itself. One cannot survive without the other, and this process and symbiotic relationship always change according to historical events. The reference point (which could be an institution, hegemonic idea, religion, dictator, corporations, God, and so on) will always re-create itself in order to survive and, in turn, recreate the *Man*.

GIDEON AND THE FORNICATION OF THE *EPHOD* (JUDG. 6—8:33)

The reference point in our biblical story of forming a *Man* is of course Yhwh. But first, this God needs to clean up his act before he can be (or maybe reclaim) a reference/focal point.

CHAPTER 6—THE BIRTH OF THE NEW MAN

The situation described at the beginning of Judges 6 (vv. 1-6) portrays a devastating reality of a submissive Israelite masculinity. The Midianites have been oppressing Israel for seven years; the Israelis, fearing the Midianites, dig tunnels and hide in caves, work hard on sustaining their land only to see its crops harvested by others, and are facing the risk of famine. God's answer to the situation, which he himself has brought upon the Israelites, is a savior according to the known formula of the book of Judges. However, before this savior comes and averts the catastrophe, he is first carefully constructed in a long process of masculinization that affects not only him but also Yhwh himself.

In v. 11, Gideon is presented to us as a young boy who hides wheat from the Midianites. To this boy Yhwh says: "The Lord is with you, valiant warrior!" (6:12b). One must stop and ask, how come Gideon is a גבור החיל, "man of valor?" And Gideon asks the same question: "Please, my lord, if the LORD is with us, why has all this befallen us? Where are all His wondrous deeds about which our fathers told us, saying, 'Truly the Lord brought us up from Egypt'?" (6:13) And here, for the first time, a biblical hero undermines not only the capacity of Yhwh to lead but also the ability and power of God himself. Gideon affirms in front of God's messenger the known reality: Israel is a weak nation with a weak God and no leader. This matrix is not conducive to Israel's survival, and this is what Yhwh wishes to change now: he wants to recruit the weak Gideon and transform him into a *Man*, thus changing the matrix into a new equation: strong leader = strong nation = one strong God.

In the first dialogue between Gideon and Yhwh (6:12-24), Gideon wants proof. First, he questions the abilities of his God; and second, he questions his own abilities, since he is the youngest and the poorest of his clan. Gideon understands how the male hierarchy works: in order to be dominant you must be rich, powerful, and of course not the youngest in the family. The answer Yhwh gives is repeated in 6:12, 14, and now in v. 15: "I will be with you." But this is not enough for Gideon; he wants proof. The first test Gideon puts Yhwh through is the first in a series of tests, in all of which Yhwh prevails. After every success, Gideon becomes more of a *Man*, and Yhwh also becomes more of a (*Man*) God. This symbiotic relationship between both *Men* is the thread that weaves this narrative together: Yhwh needs Gideon in order to show his own hegemonic masculinity, and Gideon needs Yhwh in order to become a warrior *Man*; similarly, in the American Navy, the Navy needs its soldiers to be fearless *Men*, and they need the institution that makes each one of them into a *Man* in order to be transformed.

After the first test, Gideon starts to believe again (or maybe believes for the first time) in God, and in 6:22 he admits it: "Alas, O Lord God!" Now, after Yhwh has established Gideon's faith, he asks Gideon to do something for him: to destroy his father's altar, demolish the pole of Asherah, build a new altar for Yhwh, and offer a burnt offering with the same wood of the Asherah (vv. 25-26). By destroying his father's altar, Gideon increases his and God's male image by performing on two levels. First, he destroys Baal, cleans his house from the influence of a different male deity—Baal the god of fertility—and sacrifices a bull, the symbol of Baal, on the ruins of this deity's altar with the wood of the Asherah, Baal's phallus. This act diminishes Baal and his masculinity and goes further: Gideon also intensifies his own masculinity, and that is the second level. Baal's altar is located at his father's house. By acting as he does, Gideon actually attacks his father and his father's relationship with a different masculinity. In fact, he is the only judge in the book of Judges that opposes his father. This act represents Gideon's embarking on a new path, a path that will result in his becoming stronger and more of a *Man* than his father, with the guidance of the ultimate *Man*—Yhwh. The old generation of a *Man*-Baal relationship is over now, making room for a new *Man* and a new God.

Lillian Klein claims that Gideon is a coward: he obeys Yhwh, but at night, out of fear of the townspeople (Klein 1988: 55). I wish to claim the reverse. Gideon does not believe God and wants evidence, time and again. This does not make him a coward or less of a *Man*, but exactly the opposite. Gideon is a different hero, a different *Man* prototype if you wish; he is rational, independent, self-sufficient, and—as we shall see at the end of the narrative—also a self-made *Man* who thinks for himself; and even though he follows Yhwh's commands, he still has his own thoughts.

The story continues with the intention of the townspeople to kill Gideon, for they consider his act a sin (6:30). Joash, Gideon's father, answers back that if they wish Gideon dead, then they should ask Baal to do so, and since Baal does not kill Gideon, Joash gives his son a new name: "That day they named him Jerubbaal, meaning 'Let Baal contend with him, since he tore down his altar' (6:32). Not only has Gideon fought with Baal and won, but he also, and most importantly, has fought with his father and won. Gideon is now a head of family, stronger than his father and the representative of the true *Man*-God figure. He is named by Yhwh גבור החיל ("man of valor"), and by his father ירבעל (Jerubbaal). With these two names and with an improved male image, Gideon heads out to battle.

GOD SUITS YOU

Judges 6:33 starts the war cycle. Here, like in the other stories in the book, we expect the war to be won by God and that good times will follow. That indeed will happen, but something else happens here as well. 6:34a is a very scandalous verse that, if connected to the end of the Gideon cycle, will foreground an outrageous outcome. The Hebrew phrase ורוח יהוה לבשה את גדעון does not translate clearly enough in the JPS, which has: "And the spirit of the Lord enveloped Gideon," even though it seems that the verb "to envelope" is semantically close to the Hebrew verb לבש (*l-b-sh*), "to wear." The ASV and KJV, as well as the commentaries that discuss this matter, are also semantically far from the meaning "to wear":

But the Spirit of the Lord *came upon* Gideon. (KJV 6:34a)

But the Spirit of Jehovah *came upon* Gideon. (ASV 6:34a)

Yairah Amit writes that the verb לבש (*l-b-sh* Qal) here is basically similar to occurrences of פעם (*p-'-m*) Piel or צלח (*ts-l-ch*) Qal, both with the רוח ("spirit") of Yhwh as the verb's subject, which are used in the book of Judges to emphasize the connection between God and the hero (Amit 1999: 132). Alberto Soggin claims that the meaning of this verb in this story is "to strengthen," semantically probably a late exilic form, since it can be found in that sense in the book of Chronicles and Job (Soggin 1987: 129). According to Boling, the spirit of Yhwh is a force that takes control over the judge and extracts great power; normally, the spirit "comes upon" Othniel (3:10) and Jephthah (11:29), or "prods" Samson (13:25; 14:6, 19; 15:14). On Gideon, Boling says: "On one occasion, it was recalled, this spirit so completely took charge of Gideon that the latter mobilized far more fighting men then were really needed" (Boling 1975: 25). And yet, I feel that something is neglected here, and one cannot just blame negligence on the editor/writer.

First, in other places in the book of Judges, when we see the verbs צלח (ts-l-ch) Qal or פעם (p-'-m) Piel, a battle ensues. In the case of Gideon, the war comes only after three scenes: (1) 6:35-40 (two tests of God); (2) 7:1-8 (Gideon's reconnaissance force); and (3) 7:9-15 (the foreign man's dream).

Second, there are over a hundred verses in the Hebrew Bible in which the root לבש (l-b-sh) appears and, in all of them, someone is putting some sort of clothing on another in the Hiphil stem (although admittedly not in the Qal stem, as in our verse). In all these instances we have the same grammatical formula: x makes y wear z, with y as the direct object and the clothing (z) as the second direct object. The Hebrew הלביש (hilbish, לבש Hiphil) is a causative verb—a verb that indicates doing something to somebody (Yarkoni 2004: 75). An example is וילבש שאול את דוד מדיו, "and Saul clothed David in his own garments" (1 Sam. 17:38; JPS adds the preposition "in" before the second object of the word). In Gideon's case, we have the spirit of God clothing Gideon, making him a man who actually wears God through an almost impossible linguistic form. And yet, this linguistic usage has several parallels, biblical passages that contain the wearing of an abstract quality, indicated by l-b-sh Qal: the wearing of a "spirit" (רוח) by 'Amasai in 1 Chron. 12:19 (once again, in a military context); the "spirit of God" that clothes Zachariah the priest in 2 Chron. 24.20; and the "justice" that Job wears, and that "wears" him, in Job 29:14. The case of Zechariah must be different from Gideon's, who is no priest but a soldier with no spiritual attributes. Still, the verb formation of לבש (l-b-sh) Qal with a spiritual attribute as subject, and the human as object, is common to all three occurrences. BDB explains the form as: "*and the spirit of י clothed itself with Gideon, i.e. took possession of him*" (BDB 528); and so does James Martin, who employs the BDB explanation in his commentary on the verse (Martin 1975: 90). This means that the divine spirit does not just prepare the hero for battle but literally takes the hero's form or is shaped according to his form, since the equation of "*x made y do z*" does not exist here. Yhwh is Gideon now, and the stronger Gideon becomes, the more Yhwh will be too, and vice versa; Gideon is the expression of Yhwh's performance in terms of leadership and military abilities. The same way that I, as a soldier, was wearing the uniforms of the IDF (Israel Defense Force), so was the IDF wearing me; I became the Force's physical manifestation, the materialization of its myths of masculinities and of Israel, if you will.

At the beginning of the Gideon story we have not only a weak Israel and a weak Gideon but also a weak God. Yhwh needs his people to be strong in order to be strong himself. No strong leader can have a weak nation; no powerful father can have loser sons. (The firstborn, at the very least, cannot be a loser.) This is the process that Yhwh is putting Gideon through: making him stronger, and by so doing also making himself much more powerful. Just as in the process that the boys in the U.S. Navy undergo, the more they are *Man*, the more the Navy is a *Man*. They are *Manning* each other. Hence, Gideon is all God, and God is all Gideon. The "I" that called Gideon is now replaced with a different "I," an "I" that can be called Gideon/Yhwh.

If we go back to the first dialogue between Yhwh and Gideon (6:11-23), we see that God's messenger speaks to Gideon in the second person singular, and Gideon answers in the first person plural, meaning Gideon speaks for everyone. Hence, making a *Man* out of Gideon makes the entire Israel into a *Man*. God's wars are Israel's wars; Israel's victories are God's victories.

THE MYTH OF MASCULINITIES

Gideon goes through both a masculinization and a *mythologization* process. He becomes a soldier, and a soldier needs a uniform: in this case, the uniform is no less than the spirit of Yhwh. On the political-cultural level, such uniforms act as a myth. Once Gideon is wearing God, his actions are actions of God. Both *Men* are now attached together, and two correlated models are formed: (1) The earthly *Man*, the leader, the *Man* of the year/day/hour that can be a role model to other men, the brick that can be a cornerstone for forming a society; and (2) the ultimate *Man*, the unattainable one—God, the truly hegemonic male, a model to emulate and strive for, knowing that we will never succeed; an institution, if you wish, that forms a reference point that will keep producing myths of masculinities for social/political/historical ends.

According to Roland Barthes, myth is a mode of signification, a form that is defined not by the object of the message but by the way the message is uttered. Myth is a type of speech that is chosen by history for a social end (Barthes 1972: 109). History determines the life and death of a myth according to the shifting circumstances of power and changing modes of representation. Barthes sees myth as a metalanguage that is constructed from a prior semiological system and consisting of more than just written discourse. Cinema, advertising, and photography all support myth, whose materials are objects appropriated for social usage, which Barthes calls "ideas-in-form," including flags, signboards, clothes, and other objects that bear messages (Barthes 1972: 112, 115). In the present case, Barthes's insights are applicable both to the Hebrew Bible and to the Israeli army.

The Israeli army functions not only as the military force that protects Israel but also as a socialization agent, producing myths of Israelis and of the Israeli *Man*. The IDF is not a mercenary army, but an army that every healthy Jewish (and some Arab) Israeli citizen is obliged to serve in; hence, it is bound to be part of the Israeli identification procedure. The "IDF spirit" "feeds [literally: suckles] on the tradition of the state of Israel and its democratic principles, laws and institutions; and on the traditions of the Jewish nation throughout its history."[6]

Gideon is a part of that tradition, and the Israeli army uses the tradition to produce its own myths. An Israeli citizen pledges allegiance to the nation only once in his or her lifetime, and that happens at the end of his or her military basic training period. The pledge is performed mostly, but not always, either at Masada or at the Wailing Wall, while the new Israeli soldier is in uniform. This ceremony is a myth-making institution: it links the young Israelis to their nation by telling them that Israel is first and foremost a nation that has an army, and sometimes vice versa—an army that has a nation. Those army uniforms worn by the sworn-in novices *are* Israel. Similar to the way that Gideon wears Yhwh and, in exchange, has Yhwh wear him, so the young contemporary Israeli becomes part of Israel in that myth-making ceremony; he (in this case he, since the Israeli army is constituted of males much more than females, even though females must do obligatory military service as well) has been preparing for this his whole life, and in that moment of swearing allegiance to the army, he sees Israel in all its glory: a strong nation with a Bible (history) and a gun (the means to protect it). And by accepting the myth, he gives Israel its existence and an acknowledgment of its ethical path.

I Love the Smell of War in the Morning

God proved to Gideon that he could function as a focal point for *strength* and *courage*, both myths of masculinities. Now God wants to prove that same thing to the people: "Israel might claim for themselves the glory due to Me, thinking, 'Our own hand has brought us victory'" (7:2b). God wants to make sure that Israel knows that he is the one behind the battles, the one and only ultimate warrior, the focal point, the blueprint of masculinities. After a careful examination, Gideon forms his סיירת, *sayyeret*, Hebrew for "reconnaissance troupe," a select group of three hundred males. And here we see how Gideon becomes not only a leader but also a general, the head of a selected group of men that are not only the most courageous but also the most intelligent of the available fighters. (This word, סיירת , was adopted by the modern Israeli army to represent the elite forces of the IDF.) Now Gideon becomes a tactical and smart leader; let's note the following IDF commentary: "The origin of the name of regiment 13 [the Gideon regiment] is the commander and Judge—Gideon. Gideon had a clear and precise goal; he was calculated, decent and knew how to use his advantages and disadvantages. So is the Gideon regiment of the Israeli army of our time."[7]

Everything is ready. Gideon believes in God, the Israelites are ready for war, the *sayyeret* has been chosen, the tension is built, and we expect the drama to unfold and the war to start. But just a breath away, the climax dissipates and we have another scene of persuasion, another delay of the war scene (7:9-19). This time, it is not Gideon who is asking for reassurance, but God is doing it himself. God asks Gideon to go to Midian's camp and tells him that if he is afraid he can take another man with him. In Midian's camp, Gideon hears a conversation between two Midianites, the first recounting his dream and the second interpreting it: "That can only mean the sword of the Israelite Gideon son of Joash. God is delivering Midian and the entire camp into his hands" (7:14b). The dream interpretation brings all masculinities models together: first, we have the sword, then Gideon, son of Joash, man of Israel. Not only his people, his father, and God crown Gideon, but he also gets the full recognition from the foreign *Man*, the enemy, the other *Man*, who reflects the self. And this other *Man* not only acknowledges Gideon's supremacy but also acknowledges Yhwh as the real God. Both Yhwh and Gideon are getting stronger and more powerful and fully ready to show it to the world.

In Midian's camp, Gideon receives his reassurance; the foreign men tell each other that the sword that God gave Gideon will kill the entire Midianite army. But where is this sword exactly? Gideon goes back to the camp and encourages the Israelites to go and fight by telling them: "When I blow the trumpet, I and all that are with me, then blow ye the trumpets also on every side of all the camp, and say, 'For the Lord and for Gideon!'" (7:18). The Israelites do not exactly say what he told them to and, instead, they say: "A *sword* for the Lord and for Gideon!" (7:20b). Gideon cannot see what the Midianites and the Israelites see: namely, that he has a "sword," that he is a militant leader who runs a full-scale war that will result in ethnic cleansing, all according to Yhwh's master plan. Gideon has the intelligence and rationality and also the "sword," the great male phallus. He cannot see it because he is wearing it, because the spirit of God, the spirit of the warrior, is so strongly attached to him that he has become one with it. (Similarly, young contemporary Israelis cannot see that their uniforms are still attached to them even after their three years of compulsory army service are over.)

TAKE OFF YOUR CLOTHES AND LET'S GO HOME

I will not discuss the whole of chapter 8 and the aspects of Gideon's actions vis-à-vis Ephraim and the leaders of Midian,[8] but will go straight to the ironic and surprising scene that is the culmination of this cycle—namely, 8:22-28. Israel asks Gideon and his dynasty to rule (משל, *m-sh-l* Qal) over them; Gideon answers that neither he nor his sons will rule over Israel but only Yhwh, then commences to create an *ephod* from the gold that Israel has looted during the war.

What is this *ephod* exactly, and what does it look like? Boling sees the *ephod* as "an elaborate priestly vestment, the visible heavenly glory of the invisible God of Israel" (Boling 1975: 160). Amit seeks an answer from the writings of medieval Jewish commentators, such as Radak and Rashi, and comes to the conclusion that the *ephod* is a kind of a statue; and that if we keep on reading the second part of this verse, "There all Israel went astray after it" (8:27b), we will witness the similarity to the story of the golden calf (Exod. 32:2-6), linking the collection of Israel's gold in Sinai to the collection of the looting in Ophra (Amit 1999: 155). Butler describes the *ephod* as "an elaborated priestly apron much like that worn by the high priest in Israel's true worship but sometimes interpreted as a cultic image or idol" (Butler 2009: 222).

Younger's explanation for the *ephod* is much closer to what I wish to point out. Younger writes:

Perhaps Gideon's Ephod refers to a high-priestly type garment. . . . However the amount of gold and the verbs used to describe Gideon's action ("made," "set up") mitigate against this understanding. Here "ephod" is perhaps used figuratively to represent not only the garment that clothed a sacred image but also the image over which the garment was draped (Younger 2002: 205–6).

What is this image exactly, and for what purpose did Gideon create the *ephod*? Why not simply build a golden calf? In my opinion, the *ephod* is a form of clothing, a sort of uniform if you wish. But before I fully elaborate my take on the *ephod* as a form of clothing, we must stop here and think about two important elements: the symbolic meaning of the *ephod* and the use of the verb מָשַׁל (*m-sh-l* Qal, "to rule") in speech by Israel and by Gideon. A close consideration of these will bring us back to the beginning of the narrative.

The Verb *m-sh-l* Qal does not refer to God as its subject in most of its occurrences in the Hebrew Bible;[9] furthermore, it never refers to God's rule over Israel. God leads Israel and shepherds them, but never rules over them with the verb מָשַׁל Qal. Only twice outside our story is God the subject of the predicate *m-sh-l* (2 Chron. 20:6; 23:20), and in both occurrences he "rules" over foreign kings. This, and the use of this verb in Gideon's answer *three times* in relation to the ruling of Gideon, reduces Yhwh's importance as the ultimate leader and makes him just one more ruler. After close consideration, what seems as a good, modest answer by Gideon to Israel can be perceived as tricky and ridiculing: God is not a big *Man*; he is just one ruler among others, and he looks like an *ephod*.

Gideon does what no judge has done before: he leaves his office and goes back home, leaving this post in God's service. But that is not the end of our story. Gideon needs to undress himself from the spirit of God, and he does so with the creation of the *ephod*.

Clothing or uniforms act as a temporary symbol to fulfill a task or goal, a symbol that transforms the wearer from one cultural image to another: an office suite, a kitchen chef's hat, a construction worker's helmet, army uniforms, a priestly *ephod*—these are all cases in point.[10]

Gideon may not have understood that he had a sword, but may have just realized that he was wearing God. And after he declines ruling over Israel, he undresses himself from the spirit of Yhwh; builds the *ephod* in the center of his town, the same town where he has destroyed Baal's altar, scorning Yhwh; and goes back to his home, probably to make money, build a house, and have children—in short, to be a civilian. His punishment for the creation of the *ephod* is a small annotation from the narrator: "And it became a snare unto Gideon, and his household" (8:27b); and this annotation can be seen also as a hint for the story of Abimelech that follows.

The first time Gideon becomes a *Man* is after destroying his father's altar and overcoming his father, Baal, and the people of the town. His masculine identity becomes stronger the more the story progresses: he fights, rules, and controls until receiving Israel's request to reign over them. His full realization of his own self, of his *Manhood*, though, occurs after he takes God off and places him in the center of town, undressing himself from God's spirit and in return freezing God's image in the shape of a golden *ephod*. Then Gideon becomes the one and only self-made *Man*, a man who creates his own image, a *Man* who not just fights God and wins without any bodily or mythical defects (like Jacob, Gen. 32:32), but a *Man* who vanquishes God altogether.

Gideon does the impossible: he manages to cast off the responsibility of being a leader and warrior for Yhwh, producing his own myth and becoming a self-sufficient *Man*, with no need for God. By so doing, he mocks God the Lord of Hosts and his games of wars and sovereignty, reducing him to an *ephod* made from war booty.

Let us not forget that Gideon does not stop by merely becoming a *Man*; he actually acquires a new male model: rich, powerful, a patriarch, extremely sexual and prolific, Gideon had seventy children from different women (8:30). He replaces the masculinity that God gave him with a different masculinity, better for him, with no wars, and freezes the masculinity of Yhwh the warrior. Gideon shows how ridiculous it is to be proud of war and to build masculinity upon it.

Tomorrow

Out of the massive pile of Israeli army troupes' songs, an extremely popular one contains words about the day Peace will come:

> Tomorrow when the army undresses his uniforms
> Our heart will stand to attention
> And every man will build with his two arms
> All that he ever imagined today.[11]

But what is this tomorrow? Can a tomorrow such as this exist in the state of Israel? As mentioned earlier, the Israeli army is part of the Israeli self and psyche, part of the soul, if you wish, a vital part of the existence of Israel. The Israeli is always in uniform even when he is not wearing one; like Gideon, he cannot see the sword that everybody else sees. Unlike Gideon, though, the Israeli does not understand that a combination of civilian and soldier is impossible. God was the reference point for Gideon's existence; with that point, he could negotiate who he was. But what happens when we do not need God any longer, or do not need the army? The moment we start thinking of it, this reference point starts reproducing itself and by doing so, reproducing you and me. Zionism takes the part of God and of religion; it thrives on its mighty army and does not know how to exist differently, even today.

What I wish to do, immodestly, is to change the myth and produce a new one. If we realize that Gideon was not really a soldier and neither were the other Judges, then perhaps this contributes to thinking about Israel, ancient as well as modern, not as a nation of war but as nation of knowledge and peace. Viewing Gideon in this manner can change the way we look at a central image of *Man* and add more models of manhood and masculinities. These new models will help crack this concrete central image of *Man*, thus allowing more possibilities to males who do not want to be this *Man*, helping us lift the yoke of war and of national responsibility from our shoulders.

Or to put it in Barthes's words:

> It thus appears that it is extremely difficult to vanquish myth from the inside: for the very effort one makes in order to escape its stranglehold becomes in its turn the prey of myth: myth can always, as a last resort, signify the resistance which is brought to bear against it. Truth to tell, the best weapon against myth is perhaps to mystify it in its turn, and to produce an artificial myth: and this reconstituted myth will in fact be a mythology. Since myth robs language of something, why not rob myth? All that is needed is to use it as the departure point for a third semiological chain, to take its signification as the first term of a second myth. (Barthes 1972: 134)

Smells Like Teen Spirit: By Way of Conclusion[12]

At the beginning of the summer of 1996 I went back to the בקו"ם (BAQUM), the Israeli army's initial service base, this time in order to return my uniform and leave the army service prematurely and permanently. It was not an easy task, since one cannot quit the Israeli army without a reason: one needs to show proof of failing health or mental disability in order to be disqualified; in other words: he needs to become less of a *Man*. Since I am a very healthy person physically, I had to claim and demonstrate mental instability. After three months of prolonged psychological evaluations I managed to do so, having repeated the same mantra over and over again: "I am a happy normal boy, but once I wear the uniform I become a different person for whose actions I cannot be responsible, since it is not me." And so, in exchange for the uniform, I got a diagnosis attached to my medical card stating that my personality had difficulties adjusting to the IDF system. And I was discharged.

It was not easy in those days to walk and live among the other Israelis after being discharged. I was called a משתמט (*mishtamet*), a "quitter" that not only quits but also neglects his Israeli calling, which is considered just one level above being a traitor. But I knew then, as I know now, that in order to be a civilian, a person, I had to undress myself from this Israeli myth. I had to break free from the war games that only bring more and more bloodshed and sorrow. Gideon taught me that it is okay to undress yourself if you want to fulfill your life. You do not need to be part of this game if you do not want it. Gideon showed me a different kind of *Man*, one who can create his own self, be successful, and have a good life. He showed me that one does not need to cling to a single male model and that the spectrum of masculinities is broad enough for diverse interpretations. He made me realize that even if your faith and your nation dictate your life and place you in a path of becoming a clear and stable, undisputable male model, there is always a way out and there is always a choice.

In the last verse of the song "The Guard of the Walls," the singer prays for the day when guards over Jerusalem will not be needed anymore. I must stop and ask: How did we even get to this situation, in which we need to employ uniforms and guns to be alive?

When I was discharged I returned to the IDF three sets of uniform, two of which I never wore, and six pairs of socks, none of which I ever wore. "Were you ever a soldier?" asked the girl soldier who took my uniforms and deposited them for future use. "You did not wear any of your uniforms!"

"This is true," I answered. "I never was a soldier, nor will I ever be; I was never that kind of *Man*."

Notes

1. "The Guard of the Walls," lyrics by Dan Almagor, music by Benny Nagari 1977. Sung by Tzevet Havay Piqqud Merkaz (the entertainment troupe that is a section of the army band of the Israeli Army's Central Command, which is in charge of security in Jerusalem as well).

2. Isa. 62:6. This phrase, together with several others from the end of Isaiah, is taught in the state Israeli education system and recited by all. All the verses commemorate Jerusalem as the eternal capital of Israel, and always as a woman: wife (62:3-5), mother (66:7-8, 11), or daughter (62:10). Translations of biblical texts into English in this article follow the JPS throughout.

3. For the full historical review of the science of masculinities, see Connell 2005: 3–81.

4. See also: Bell in Bell and Valentine 1995:1–31; Cornwall and Lindisfarne 1994: 146–71; Whitehead in Whitehead and Franck 2001: 27–56; Whitehead 2005: 411–22; Hoven and Hörschelmann 2005: 1–16, 41–58.

5. "Don't ask, don't tell" (DADT) was the official policy of the United States regarding the military service of those who openly identified as gay, lesbian, or bisexual. From December 21, 1993, to September 20, 2011, the policy barred any person from serving in the U.S. armed forces who disclosed his or her sexual orientation as homosexual or bisexual, while prohibiting

discrimination against persons who kept their sexual orientation private. September 20, 2011, marked the end of DADT.

6. Taken from the official IDF website in Hebrew, my translation. http://www.idf.il/ 1413-10820-he/Dover.aspx.

7. Translated from the Hebrew website of the IDF Golani platoon, of which the Gideon regiment is part: http://www.golani.co.il/show_item.asp?itemId=38&levelId=60747&itemType=0.

8. Though there is much to discuss regarding the leadership of Gideon, such as Gideon's lack of understanding of the differences between his people and the enemy (Klein 1995: 61–63), or the shift in his role and his lack of differentiation between the task of a leader and personal vendetta (Webb 1987: 151–54 and also Butler 2009: 225).

9. The verb משל (*m-sh-l*) Qal with the meaning "to rule" appears eighty-four times in the Hebrew Bible, and its object iseither a man (Gen. 1:18), a nation (Josh. 12:2; Judg. 14:4; Isa. 49:7), an emotion (Gen. 4:7; Prov. 16:32), or natural bodies ruled by God (Gen. 1:18; Ps. 89:10). Its subject in all cases, except for natural bodies, is always a man.

10. For more on the subject of clothing and material culture, see Hansen 2004:369–92. Regarding clothing and the Hebrew Bible, see Galpaz-Feller 2008: 27–94.

11. My translation for the last stanza of the song מחר, "Tomorrow," lyrics and music by Naomi Shemer for the most popular Israeli army choir, the "Nachal choir," in 1962. This last, conclusive stanza ends a song whose theme is the imagining of the day peace will come, "if not tomorrow then the day after."

12. This is the title of a famous song by the Nirvana group. While the lyrics are not easily understood, the song has been recognized as a rebellious youth hymn and a total objection to the conservative Old Order, as here exemplified *inter alia* by the poem I began and will mention again, on guarding the walls of Jerusalem.

12

From the Margins to the Margins
Jephthah's Daughter and Her Father

Pamela J. Milne

Introduction

My full-time teaching career is nearing its conclusion. In the next year or two, I hope to retire. If I had it to do over again, I surely would not choose a career in the same field, nor would I want to work at the same institution. And if I had to find one word to characterize my career, it would be *marginalization.* I cannot think of a time when I have not been on the institutional margins because of my gender, my discipline, and the analytical methods I have used within my discipline. This study of Judges 11 played an unexpected role in moving me from one marginal place to another within my university. The particular focus of the study arose from the context of teaching biblical courses to feminist women's studies students who were completely unaware of the work done by feminist biblical scholars on this or any other biblical text. But the wider context of the study involved the teaching of a core women's studies course on frameworks for feminist research. This was a course I had been asked to develop and teach in the mid-1990s, when the religious studies department closed and I was left without an academic home. As a program rather than a department, women's studies could not provide an institutional home, but it could use my teaching load free of charge to develop a core course it lacked at the time. The course was completely out of my own field of expertise. Its purpose was to explore how feminist research was being done across a wide range of disciplines and to teach undergraduate students how to develop feminist research projects of their own.

The women's studies program has a heavy social science bias, and many of the students taking this course were interested in doing research that involved interviewing people. Any research involving human subjects[1] is tightly monitored on Canadian university campuses by the major government granting agencies.[2] There are very strict ethical protocols to be followed before such research can be undertaken. As someone with no training in qualitative methods and no experience conducting research on human subjects, I could not supervise students in this kind of work. Students learned about qualitative research and examined feminist studies using this approach but could not conduct interview-based research themselves.

When my first opportunity to apply for a sabbatical leave came after I began teaching this course, I decided to propose a retraining project that would allow me to do a small qualitative study and thereby learn the ethics review process firsthand. Completion of that project would make it possible for me to secure the approvals necessary to supervise student work involving human subjects.

This is how I came to undertake a qualitative study based on Judges 11. I consulted widely with feminist social scientists and worked closely with an ethics specialist. Having successfully completed the project, I was then able to acquire ethics approval for a three-year period that allowed me to supervise student research in the frameworks course.

I had anticipated that my efforts to support the women's studies program, itself very marginal within the university, would be regarded in a positive way and that working in a social science area would bring me into closer academic connection with others teaching for women's studies who did not regard feminist biblical studies as particularly relevant to women's studies. I also assumed that since my sabbatical had been approved by a university committee, the institution itself would understand and appreciate the challenges and value of this retraining exercise in a new field.

Neither assumption proved to be the case. When I applied for a subsequent sabbatical, it was denied on the basis that I had not been working in my own field. Because of my homeless status, I had no department head to support my work, nor was any offered by the director of women's studies. Given the negative feedback from the university, I immediately ceased any further qualitative work, including the work required to retain the ethics approval for the frameworks course, and returned to more traditional biblical studies. The response from the director of women's studies was to remove me from the course, claiming that the only valid form of research for women's studies students was qualitative interviewing. She asked the dean to assign me a different course.

I grieved the violation of my academic freedom and the inappropriate change to my teaching load. The university settled the grievance with my union in my favor. I received financial compensation and have resumed teaching the frameworks course as I had originally taught it. But as a consequence for this study of Judges 11, I have moved to a new place on the institutional margins, the margins of the women's studies program, because of my research methods as well as my discipline of biblical studies.

SON OF A PROSTITUTE AND DAUGHTER OF A WARRIOR: WHAT DO YOU THINK THE STORY IN JUDGES 11 MEANS?

1. INTRODUCTION: THE MOTIVATION AND THE ISSUE

How do ordinary readers (i.e., non-biblical scholars) construct meaning when they read the Bible? For many Christians or Jews who attend religious services or activities, meanings may be supplied to them by a religious leader trained in a particular tradition with one or more approaches to interpretation. But what happens when readers have to rely on their own interpretive abilities? How do they make sense of a text that is far removed from them in time, space, and culture?

This is a question that might more typically fall within the interests of psychologists or sociologists but not of biblical scholars. Biblical scholars have focused on constructing their own meanings in an effort to explore literary, historical, and other dimensions of biblical texts. But is the work of academic biblical scholars, and particularly feminist biblical scholars, reaching and influencing nonspecialist, ordinary readers of the Bible?

This question has taken on considerable interest for me since my feminist biblical courses were relocated from a religious studies department to a women's studies program in 1996. I have been struck by the lack of knowledge—indeed, even the lack of awareness—of the work of feminist biblical scholars on the part of the feminist women's studies students in my courses. If feminist students in a university context had not encountered feminist interpretations of the Bible, then what is the likelihood that our work has been reaching a wider general audience? If feminist analysis of the Bible is not reaching beyond the walls of the academy and changing the way ordinary readers read and relate to the biblical text, how can it be relevant?

In my view, the feminist movement is about making the world a better place for women. Feminist biblical criticism is part of that insofar as it challenges traditional interpretations and uses of the Bible that have harmed or impeded women and insofar as it exposes and critiques the patriarchal gender ideologies embedded in the biblical texts. "To be truly academic, and worthy of its place in the Academy," David Clines claims, "biblical studies has to be truly critical . . . critical about the Bible's contents, its theology, its ideology" (Clines 1997: 25). Esther Fuchs has made a similar point with respect to feminist biblical criticism. It should, Fuchs argues, "open up a radical interrogation of biblical theology, biblical literary criticism, biblical religion and biblical historical criticism" (Fuchs 2008: 65) and be *transformational* rather than *inclusional* (Fuchs 2008: 64). I agree wholeheartedly with Fuchs, but I also think that to be transformational, our work must reach beyond the small community of feminist biblical scholars. It must inform the way ordinary readers interpret and relate to biblical texts.

2. FOCUSING ON THE READER

Focus on the reader has become central in academic biblical scholarship. Since the 1980s, the terms *reader-response criticism* and *audience criticism* have been used for the wide range of theories and critical practices examining the reader, the reading process, and the response to reading.[3] Within biblical studies, however, the reader or audience investigated has been the implied original reader (male) or the expert reader/analyst (white, male, and North American) and has generally not acknowledged the ideologies of those readers (Bible and Culture Collective 1995: 57, 67).

David Clines sees this shift to the reader and the reading process as necessary if "we are going to take the presence of the bible in the modern world seriously" (Clines 1997: 11). Meaning does not reside exclusively in the text but is the product of a reader reading a text. But Clines also understands that who is reading the Bible will influence the meaning derived from it. The social location and values of the readers play a role in how they read a text. Such an approach is predicated on one of the key claims of feminist analysis, namely, that bias-free, neutral, or *objective*[4] interpretation does not exit. Moreover, *readers* must not be restricted to imagined ones. As Clines has argued, "We have to concentrate on what people are making of the Bible, what reception it is receiving, how it is being understood, what it is capable of meaning to real live people." But, he concedes, in the academy, "very few people in our field seem to be interested in what is the case" (Clines 1997: 17).

In order to find out what people are "making of the Bible," Clines incorporated several social scientific methods in his course on the Bible and the modern world. Some of his students conducted street surveys about the Bible that were quantitative in nature in Sheffield, England (Clines 1997: 55–68). Others engaged in what might be identified as a combination of participant observer and qualitative studies (Clines 1997: 80–87). Clines himself conducted a content analysis of uses of the Bible in the press (Clines 1997: 68–79). Social scientific studies such as these, carried out with non-scholarly readers or participants, are definitely the exception rather than the rule within the discipline of biblical studies.

3. THE RESEARCH PROJECT

The project I undertook was like those of Clines and his students insofar as it examined how ordinary contemporary readers, not biblical scholars, understand the Bible. But it also had the more specific interest of seeing whether or not, and to what extent, feminist scholarship, biblical and other, is reaching beyond the academic feminist community, beyond the academic community of biblical scholars to the general public. It sought to explore the extent to which feminist biblical criticism is having a transformational effect on the way ordinary readers read the Bible.

I asked a small group of readers to read and interpret a narrative from the Hebrew Bible that had been deemed by Phyllis Trible a "text of terror" because a female character is subject to serious physical violence (Trible 1984: 93–116). I chose the story of Jephthah and his daughter in Judges 11 because this is a text that few of the students who took my course on women and the Bible had been familiar with prior to the course. Even students with strong affiliations to Christianity or Judaism rarely recognized this text as being part of the Hebrew Bible. This fact made Judges 11 a useful text for my study. Unlike Genesis 2–3 (Adam and Eve) or Genesis 19 (Lot, his wife and daughters, and the destruction of Sodom), stories generally known to many people not only by being read or heard in religious contexts but also through other cultural uses of the stories, the story in Judges 11 is not a cultural icon. This made it unlikely that my subjects would have been influenced by cultural interpretations. Nor were they likely to have been influenced by mainstream theological interpretations since it seems this text is rarely used as the basis for sermons or as part of religious liturgies. Judges 11 offered the possibility of presenting my reader subjects with the challenge of depending on their own interpretive strategies rather than drawing on what others had told them about the story.

The research project was a feminist qualitative study of how ordinary readers construct meaning when they read the story in Judges 11. Its particular focus was on how such readers understand and assess the fate of the daughter who is sacrificed by her father, Jephthah, to fulfill his religious vow. To what extent do ordinary readers relate the fate of the daughter to the issue of male violence toward women? To what extent do they notice the daughter's lack of a name and lack of independence? To what extent do they see the daughter as a literary construct that is made to espouse the values of patriarchy by the author/narrator? To what extent do they see her death as the consequence of male power and ego? In other words, do ordinary readers read a story like this with a feminist lens? Do they resist its patriarchal assumptions, or do they give any other evidence of having been influenced by feminist critical approaches to the Bible?

4. THE PROJECT MODEL

The feminist model for my project was Stuart Charmé's study of children's gendered responses to the story of Adam and Eve (Charmé 1997: 27–44). Charmé was interested in examining how girls and boys "without any significant hermeneutic or theological background make sense of this story" (Charmé 1997: 28). Because he was dealing with a story that may well have more theological baggage than any other in the Bible, Charmé sought to minimize the impact of that baggage by choosing research subjects between the ages of four and eleven to see "what children's pre-existing ideas about gender are and how those ideas may influence children's understanding of a well-know biblical story" (Charmé 1997: 29) without complicated theological overlays. Charmé found a strong hermeneutical consistency between the interpretations given by the boys in his study and the traditional interpretations of it through centuries of Western theology (Charmé 1997: 36–37). One of the conclusions from his study is that stories like the Adam and Eve story are likely to elicit and reinforce in many children notions of gender roles and gender identity that presuppose the inferiority and subordination of women (Charmé 1997: 40). He is not at all optimistic that feminist hermeneutic efforts to rehabilitate the story can be successful.

Although my interest was not in children's gender identity, Charmé's study was useful to me in several ways. First, it gave me the model of research on human subjects. Rather than speculating about what a text means to people, we can actually ask them directly. Second, it suggested to me the need to find a way to minimize the impact of traditional interpretations on the interpretations made by the research subjects. Charmé did this by choosing children as subjects. I did this by choosing a relatively obscure text. Third, Charmé's study provided me with a framework that included asking my subjects to explain the story in their own words, to identify with characters and to offer their ideas about what changes they might make in the text if changes were possible.

5. METHOD AND METHODOLOGY

In all of my work, I make a distinction between the terms *method* and *methodology* using the distinction made by Sandra Harding, a feminist philosopher of science. Harding defines *method* as "a technique for gathering evidence," of which there are just three basic categories: listening, observing, and examining historical traces and records (Harding 1987: 2). Such techniques are not feminist. They are merely tools that can be used by feminists and nonfeminists alike to gather data in the research process.

What determines whether research is, or is not, feminist is the way in which the evidence-gathering tools are used. This is methodology. Harding sees *methodology* as "a theory and analysis of how research does or should proceed" (Harding 1987: 3). This is where feminist research distinguishes itself from nonfeminist research. Feminist methodologies begin with women's lived experiences, gather data needed and wanted by women to answer questions of importance to women (Harding 1987: 6–8). They have social change as their overt goal. Feminist research fundamentally challenges and rejects the notion of scientific objectivity. The point of feminist research is to make life better for women and other marginalized groups.

In terms of my study, the method, or research tool, is listening to informants. It is a qualitative method insofar as it seeks an in-depth understanding of how individuals or groups understand the world around them and construct meaning from their experiences. Qualitative research concerns itself with the quality of data rather than the quantity. Whereas quantitative research provides large amounts of data from which generalizations may be made, the results of qualitative research cannot be generalized. Rather, qualitative research allows rich descriptions to be extracted and/or hypotheses to be developed. So the data gathered by listening to my subjects interpret the story in Judges 11 are not generalizable, but they do give me insight into how this small group of readers goes about interpreting an ancient text from the Bible in the context of their contemporary situations. They also allow me to see if any patterns can be discerned in the responses received that might allow me to construct hypotheses to be tested in future studies.

What makes my study feminist is clearly not the fact that I interviewed subjects in a qualitative study, though qualitative research has been a favored method of feminist researchers. My study is feminist because the motivation for it began in the lived experiences of some women, the experiences of subordination in male-dominated cultures, and the experiences of male violence toward women. It starts from the historical evidence that the Bible has played a major role in fostering and sustaining patriarchal attitudes and practices that have had negative consequences in the lives of women in Western cultures over the centuries. Feminist scholarship has identified and challenged problematic patriarchal content in the Bible and offered strategies for minimizing its damaging impact on women today. The purpose of my qualitative study is to explore whether or not the interpretations given by a group of ordinary readers of a biblical text containing violence toward a female character show any evidence of having been influenced by the work of feminist biblical scholars or even feminism in general.

Do such readers read *with* the gender ideology of the text, or do they *resist* it? Do male and female readers interpret the actions of Jephthah and the fate of his daughter in similar or different ways?

6. THE PROJECT DESIGN[5]

The project consisted of interviewing twelve subjects, three women and three men with a strong religious background and three women and three men with little or no religious background.[6] Recruitment was done on the campus of my university so all volunteers were either currently enrolled in a university undergraduate or graduate program or had recently graduated.[7] They ranged in age from nineteen to thirty-six.

When volunteers arrived for the scheduled interview, they were given a description of the research project that told them the purpose of the study was to investigate how modern readers make sense of an ancient text such as the Bible. They were told that there were no correct or incorrect interpretations and that over the centuries readers had given many different interpretations of every biblical text. I emphasized that I would not be assessing whether their interpretations were right or wrong. Rather, I was interested to hear from them what they thought the text meant and what factors led them to their interpretation. Subjects were not deceived about the purpose of the study, but they were not specifically told that I was particularly interested in how readers interpreted the part of the story about the sacrifice of Jephthah's daughter.

Next, subjects were given information about what they would be asked to do, namely, to read the story in Judges 11 and then to answer a set of questions about the story. They were reassured that they did not have to recall the story from memory but could consult the text as much or as little as they deemed necessary in answering the questions.

All of the interviews began with a set of six demographic questions that asked the age, sex, educational background, and religious affiliation of the subject and then asked whether the subject had ever read the Bible. Finally, the subject was asked to indicate her or his level of familiarity with the Bible's content: very familiar, somewhat familiar, somewhat unfamiliar, or very unfamiliar.

Subjects were then asked to read Judges 11. They were provided with a copy of the NRSV translation, from which all textual and other notes had been removed. They were given as much time as they wanted to read the text one or more times. Once they indicated they had finished reading, they were asked a set of twelve questions covering the content and message of the story, characters in the story, their feelings about the story, and changes they would make in the story if they could.[8] Subjects were free to consult the text as much as they needed to answer any of the questions.

The hypothesis for the study was that work of feminist biblical scholars is not making its way into the mainstream and will not have had an impact on the way in which the subjects in this study interpret the text of Judges 11.[9] This hypothesis is based on the lack of knowledge about feminist biblical criticism among the women's studies students I have taught over the last decade.

7. SOME RESULTS[10]

7.1 KNOWLEDGE OF THE STORY

Of those who identified themselves in the demographic survey as having a strong religious affiliation and participation in a church, five rated their familiarity with the Bible as somewhat familiar, and only one claimed to be very familiar. Of those who identified themselves as not having a strong religious background, two said they were somewhat unfamiliar with the Bible and the remaining subjects said they were not very familiar with it or had not read it at all. There was, therefore, a clear difference between the two groups with respect to their perceptions of familiarity with the contents of the Bible. This difference did not carry over to a prior knowledge of the Judges 11 text (Q. 1/1a). Of those with a religious background, only one, a male who identified his religious affiliation as Seventh Day Adventist, said he had read and heard the text many times. He said he had heard it in church and in Sabbath school and had read it when he began reading the Bible for himself at age seven. One of the female subjects, also a Seventh Day Adventist, said she had "probably" read it because she had attended a Roman Catholic school where the book of Judges had been studied, so she felt she had to have read it but could not recall this specific text. All other subjects, with or without a religious background or familiarity with the content of the Bible, said they had neither heard nor read this story before. This was particularly useful information for me because I had wanted to choose a text that was largely unfamiliar to readers so that their interpretations would not merely be restatements of what they had been told by religious leaders or had learned from some other source. Their responses indicated that whatever meanings they drew from the text would likely be of their own construction. The fact that even the majority of those who believed they were familiar or somewhat familiar with the content of the Bible had never heard or read this text underscores the notion of canon-within-the canon. The story of Jephthah and his daughter does not seem to be among the texts that frequently serve as the basis for sermons.

7.2 THE MESSAGE OF THE STORY

With respect to the central or main message the story had for the subjects, there appeared to be a distinct difference between readers with a religious background and those without (Q. 3). All but one of the religious readers mentioned God as part of the central message. They included such ideas as "God will do as he says," "if you stay faithful, the Lord will conquer your enemies," and "God protects his people." One F/R said the central message was that you should be "true to your intentions." One M/R found three central messages, one having to do with the outcast who comes back as head, another that humbleness brings the spirit of the Lord, and the third that when pride replaces humbleness it leads to the loss of what means most.

The nonreligious readers did not see the deity as so centrally connected to the message. Just one M/NR said the central message was that "the will of God cannot be questioned." Despite difficulties, Jephthah's faith in God was "so strong that even when it comes down to sacrificing his own daughter, he does it—he has difficulty doing it but he does it." Other nonreligious readers found messages such as "peace is a better proposition than getting into fights," "conflict of man . . . if you have more than one person you have conflict . . . it was not a good situation—he lost his daughter and a whole bunch of people died most likely," "be careful what promises you make and be careful what you wish for," "betrayal," and "there are always consequences for actions." The nonreligious readers generally focused much more on the human actions and responsibilities.

The answers provided by the subjects to the general questions about the content of the story had some noteworthy features. When asked to tell me in their own words what the story was about, readers offered a wide range of summaries. Some attempted to account for several parts of the text, while others boiled it down to one or two main concepts. In general, the overall grasp of the story did not seem to be strong. Many readers indicated that they found the story confusing, particularly the part about the war.

Of those who retold the story in terms of a major concept, one F/R said it was a story about "a vow to the Lord that had to be kept," while a second said that the basic theme of the story was that of "connections or relations with your family and loyalty." One F/NR said the story "revolved around a man called Jephthah as a person," while a second F/NR said it was essentially a story about conflict, of "our God versus your God." One M/NR saw it as a story of vengeance where Jephthah, betrayed by his family, turned against them to conquer Israel. The remaining subjects attempted to summarize more details of the story such as the war with the Ammonites, the vow made by Jephthah, and the interaction between Jephthah and his daughter. Only half of the readers (two F/R, two M/R, one F/NR, and one M/NR) made any mention of Jephthah's daughter in their summary of the story. This may underscore the contention of many feminist analysts that the narrator has been relatively successful in focusing reader attention on Jephthah and not on the daughter (Fuchs 1993: 116–30).

7.3 WHO IS JEPHTHAH, WHAT DOES HE DO, AND WHY DOES HE DO IT?

Only two readers specifically identified Jephthah as the son of a prostitute (one F/R and one M/NR), and one other (M/R) identified him as an illegitimate child in their retelling of the story (Q. 2). In the follow-up question that asked why Jephthah had fled his home to live in the land of Tob (Q. 2a), six (one F/R, one M/R, one F/NR, and three M/NR) said it was because his mother was a prostitute. Two, one F/R and one M/R, did not use the term *prostitute* but said that Jephthah was the "son of another woman." One F/NR said he was "kicked out because of his brothers' moral problem with his mother not being morally correct." The remaining F/NR said that Jephthah left because he was "not accepted by his own family." Four readers, one F/R and three M/R, linked Jephthah's departure to the issue of inheritance.

When asked why the elders of Gilead invited Jephthah back (Q. 2b), eight explained this by reference to Jephthah's being a good warrior or an experienced fighter. Of these, one M/NR also interpreted this rationale as "opportunistic," while one F/NR said it was "selfish and self-centered" on the part of the elders. Two, one M/R and one M/NR, did not specifically identify Jephthah as a good warrior but said he was invited back because the Ammonites were making war against Israel and the elders "needed" him to command their army. One M/R said he came back as part of an agreement to fight a war.

In contrast, one F/R made no mention of Jephthah's fighting ability per se. Rather, she said that the elders "knew they were in trouble when the war started" and had invited him back because they "knew Jephthah was a man of god, a great man . . . from a great household."

All of the subjects indicated that, in making a bargain with the elders (Q. 2c), Jephthah wanted to become leader or head if he was victorious. Some also saw this as a way for Jephthah to get justice or what was rightfully his. There was a strong consensus among the subjects in their answer to this question.

The question of why Jephthah made a vow to the lord (Q. 2g) received several responses connecting the vow in a causal way to victory. All of the F/R readers made this link. One said that Jephthah "makes the vow so he can win against the Ammonites." A second said "he wanted to win and he knew the only way to win was through the Lord." The third said that it was "important for him to defeat the Ammonites because they were taking away something from his own people" and he was "protecting his own people." Of the M/R subjects, one said he made the vow because he "needed God on his side." A second linked the vow to the spirit coming upon Jephthah. He said that "if the spirit hadn't come, he wouldn't have made any sort of vow" and that the vow was that he would offer whoever came out of his house as a burnt offering if God brought "the Ammonites into his hand." The response of the third M/R, the Seventh Day Adventist, was the most interesting. He was the only respondent who saw the vow as a "mistake." He said that Jephthah "wasn't supposed to make vows" because he "didn't have to, because the spirit of the Lord already came onto him," which was "proof he was chosen of God" and that "he was going to be successful." This reader saw the vow as a huge mistake that resulted from Jephthah's "talking too much" and from "his pride," which led him to ask that the Ammonites be delivered into his hands when he should have asked that they be "delivered to the Lord's hands" because it "wasn't [Jephthah's] battle in the first place."

In answer to another question, this reader went back to the notion of the vow as a mistake. He said that he had been reading this story for years. As a child, he thought Jephthah should keep his vow, although the vow troubled him. Now, however, he said he had realized that when you make a mistake, "you should go back on it." This was as close as any of the subjects came to feminist readings that see the vow as superfluous in light of the reception of the spirit of the Lord (Trible 1984: 96–98)[11] or that see "useless and destructive words" (Exum 1993b: 133) as problematic.

One F/NR and one M/NR also connected the vow to victory. The F/NR explicitly linked winning the war to Jephthah's desire to become head or leader of the Gileadites. The M/NR saw the making of the vow as a way to "secure victory for his people" but the burnt offering itself he saw as a way to "give thanks for the victory." Another F/NR thought there was a causal effect between the vow and what he wanted. She used her own life as a student to illustrate her point. If she wanted an education, she had to work to pay for it. Similarly, if Jephthah wanted victory, he had to offer something he would "miss terribly." Two other M/NR readers were less direct in their linking the vow to victory. One said he was "not sure" why Jephthah made the vow but said that Jephthah *thought* a burnt offering was the "right thing to do," if the Lord gave the Ammonites into his hand. The other saw the vow as a way to "stop the war," by which he meant "giving the Ammonites into [Jephthah's] hands." The third F/NR said it was "because of his faith" that Jephthah made the vow. She said Jephthah "believed the Lord was a fair judge."

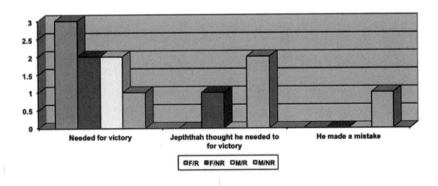

Q 2g. Why did Jephthah make a vow?

7.4 THE FATE OF JEPHTHAH'S DAUGHTER

When asked what happened when Jephthah went home (Q. 2i) and what happened to his daughter (Q. 2j), all respondents said that it was his daughter who came out of his house to meet him. All F/R readers indicated that it was then a *necessity* for Jephthah to kill his daughter. One said "he must kill his daughter because of his deal with God." A second said, "She had to be sacrificed and in the end she was sacrificed." The third agreed that she had to be sacrificed, but said this was "not a good thing." She said that Jephthah was "upset" because his daughter had caused him "great trouble" and put him in a "predicament" because he could not take the vow back. All three M/R readers also indicated the daughter was sacrificed. One nuanced the reason somewhat by saying that Jephthah "*said* he could not take the vow back" and by indicating that the daughter *agreed* that he could not take the vow back. A second made no comment about the role of the vow, but said the daughter made a "covenant with Jephthah" in which he granted her "two months to wander in the mountains to lose her virginity" and "find a husband" before returning to be made a "burnt offering." The third, the Seventh Day Adventist, interpreted Jephthah's tearing of his clothing as a response of mourning because she was his "only daughter and his pride and joy." He thought Jephthah was upset because "he had finally got her the respect that she needed, that the family needed, and now he had to go kill her—what does he have to live for?" This reader knew of interpretations that suggested Jephthah did not kill his daughter, but he rejected them.[12] He said, "I don't care what everyone else says that she was just a virgin the rest of her life! It said 'burnt offering, burnt offering'—he killed her."

Of the F/NR readers, all agreed that the daughter *had to be sacrificed* because of the vow and *was sacrificed*. Two of the three M/NR readers said the daughter had "become a great trouble" for Jephthah. Neither explicitly said she was sacrificed. One only mentioned her bewailing her virginity, while the other said he was "not sure" Jephthah "would have killed her." The third M/NR said Jephthah was upset because he had to sacrifice her because of the vow.

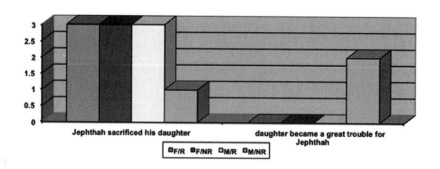

Q. 2j. What happened to Jephthah's daughter?

There was a strong consensus, therefore, that the vow *necessitated* Jephthah's killing his daughter and, except for the one M/R who identified the vow as a "mistake," there was no negative assessment of Jephthah for having made the vow or for having fulfilled it. Most interpreted Jephthah's action in fulfilling his vow, even though it meant killing his only daughter, as an act of faithfulness, not an act of unfaithfulness, as Trible has argued (Trible 1984: 93–102). This consensus lends support to the claim by scholars like Esther Fuchs that "the father's responsibility for his daughter's demise is obscured" by the patriarchal narrative that denies the daughter a name and "creates empathy and admiration for the central male character, God or Yhwh" (Fuchs 2000: 14, 177).

7.5 CENTRAL CHARACTERS IN THE STORY

The responses of the subjects to the questions about characters in the story reinforce this assessment by Fuchs. Eight readers identified Jephthah as the central character (Q. 4). Two identified Jephthah and the deity as the central characters, and two (one F/R and one M/NR) identified the deity alone as the central character. Of those who identified the deity as the central character, both said Jephthah was the second-most-important character. Of those who said Jephthah was the central character, one said the "Lord" was the second most important. The inclusion of the deity as a character is interesting because God is not an active character in the story but is only referenced by some of the characters.[13]

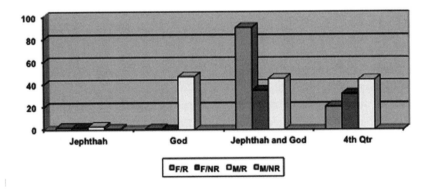

Q 4. Who is the most important or central character in the story?

The inclusion of the deity became more apparent when readers were asked which character they would be, if they could be any of the characters in the story. Four readers, two M/R, one F/NR, and one M/NR chose to be God. Three chose to be Jephthah, one F/R, one F/NR, and one M/MR. Only two respondents, one F/R and one F/NR, chose to be the daughter.

This response was quite different from Charmé's, where over 80 percent of boys identified with Adam, the male character, and less than 10 percent identified with God, while over 60 percent of girls chose to be the female character, Eve, and almost 20 percent chose to be God. In my study, half of the male readers identified with the deity, while only one of six identified with Jephthah, even though five of six saw Jephthah as the central character in the story. None of the male readers chose to be the daughter. Of the remaining two male readers, one chose to be one of Jephthah's men so he could get the "spoils" of the war, while the other chose to identify with none of the characters because he regarded them all as tragic. On the other hand, the female readers were more evenly distributed. Two chose the male character, Jephthah, and two chose the female character, the daughter. One chose another male character, a brother of Jephthah, and the remaining one chose the deity. The F/R reader who chose to be a brother of Jephthah said she did not want to be Jephthah "because he had to kill his daughter." Interestingly, one F/NR reader who chose to be Jephthah said she made this choice because as Jephthah "I wouldn't kill my daughter at the end" but would "deal with any punishment the Lord gave out but I don't think it is right to kill anyone even if you said you would." This explanation was very similar to that of the only male reader, also an NR, who chose Jephthah. He said he saw the story as a "lesson learned" and that, as Jephthah, he would "want to try to do things differently. . . . I would not have acted in the same way in that kind of situation. I would have made a better situation." In contrast, the F/R who chose to be Jephthah did so because "he keeps his vow even though it is hard to do so. It shows his strength and his strong belief in the Lord."

These explanations perhaps hint at differences in ethical priorities between readers with and without religious backgrounds in this study. For the religious readers, fidelity to the deity or to a promise made to a deity is paramount, while for nonreligious readers, human life stands above a promise to a deity.

Four readers, one from each group, identified Jephthah as the character they would least like to be. Two said they chose Jephthah because he "had to kill his daughter"; one said it was because he lost everything, including his daughter; and the fourth spoke of tough decisions Jephthah had to make.

All four had also identified Jephthah as the central character. So, these readers distinguished between a character being central to the plot and being desirable.

Of the two female readers who chose the daughter as the character they would most like to be, the F/R, a Muslim, who had placed the daughter as the second-most-important character in the story after Jephthah, identified with the daughter because she saw her essentially as a martyr. The daughter, she said, was "dedicated to her father's righteousness," so she "doesn't want him to go back on his word to the Lord." For this reader, "death is nothing," and anything is "doable when it is for the Lord." In her view, the daughter was "at a higher level of thinking," so much so that the situation gave the daughter "an opportunity to show her true character." This reader thought the daughter was "doing something good" that would give her "an opportunity to go to heaven." The other reader, an F/NR, who chose to be Jephthah's daughter did so for quite different reasons. She did see the daughter as "courageous" because when she happily danced out to greet her father upon his return from battle, he told her, "You got to die," and "she says OK just give me two months of some fun." The reader thought the daughter wanted to "go and have sex cause she hasn't had sex," but "then she doesn't even do it. She just goes away, has some fun with her friends and then comes back when she's supposed to." Ultimately, however, this reader identified with the daughter because she was the "character I relate to the most as a female." This was the only reader for whom gender identity seemed to be an issue. She saw no other female characters with whom she could identify in this story, so, although the fate of the daughter was troubling to her, the gender of the character was the overriding factor in her identification.

Perhaps even more interesting was the fact that only one reader, the M/NR who resisted being any of the characters because he saw them all as experiencing tragedy, chose the daughter as the character he would least like to be. His reason was precise and concise: he would not want to be the daughter because "she loses her life in a pointless sacrifice." His answer, like that of the readers who chose to be Jephthah in order to change the fate of the daughter, seems to place a high value on the life of the daughter, a value that was of a higher priority than that of keeping a religious vow.

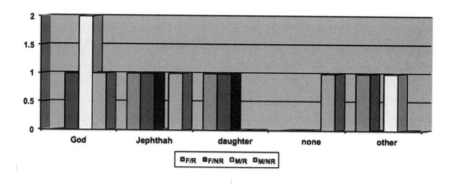

Q. 6 If you could be any of the characters in the story, which would it be?

The other choices for the character a reader would least like to be included three for the Ammonites or the king of the Ammonites. All were male readers. Two M/R readers made this choice because "God is not on their side," "they are not the chosen people," and "they had their land taken away."

Two F/R readers chose the brothers of Jephthah as the character they would least like to be. Their reasons included that the brothers were "hypocrites" and "unjust" and that "they ended up below [Jephthah] and humiliated, when they had to beg him to come back." One F/NR reader chose the elders of Gilead because "I would not be so self-centered." Another F/NR chose the Lord as the character she would least like to be because she felt it would be very "difficult and stressful" "having such a dominance over the lives of people and their happiness."

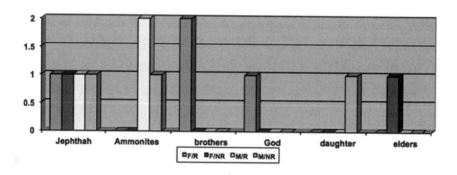

Q. 7 Which character would you least like to be?

All but one reader, an F/NR, saw the deity as the most powerful character in the story (Q. 8). The one exception identified Jephthah as most powerful. The question about the weakest character (Q. 9) drew a range of responses, but only one, an M/R, identified the daughter as the weakest. His reason was that the daughter had no choice but could only ask permission to go to the mountains for two months.

The assessment of characters as good or bad (Q. 10) produced a range of responses. Readers could identify as many characters as they wished in either category. One F/NR and one M/NR did not think any of the characters could be classified as good or bad. Of the other responses, the most popular choice for a good character was the daughter, with eight, followed by Jephthah, chosen by seven, and God, chosen by five. In terms of bad characters, there was less agreement. The Ammonites were seen as bad by six; the half-brothers of Jephthah, by five readers. Two M/NR readers classified Jephthah as bad, while one M/R said the elders were bad.

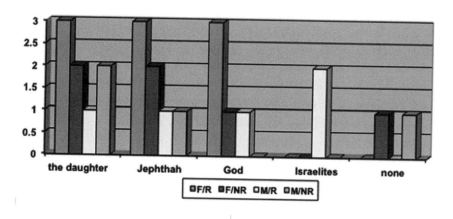

Q. 10 Which characters would you identify as good?

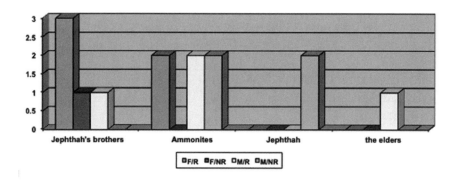

Q. 10 Which characters would you identify as bad?

The most interesting feature of the responses to this question was the ambiguity with respect to Jephthah as a character. Of the seven who classified him as a good character, two, one F/R and one M/NR, made a distinction between how Jephthah was presented in the story and how they evaluated his character. The F/R said that "in the story, Jephthah is made out to be a good character but I'm not convinced he necessarily is." She saw his loyalty to God as good but the fact that he went to war as bad. The M/NR also began his response by saying, "In the context of the story Jephthah is good and the Ammonites are bad." He went on to say, however, that he was not swayed by Jephthah's argument that the lands were given him by God. Rather, he thought Jephthah used God as a "rationale" for conquering land. He regarded this as a negative factor. This reader was also somewhat skeptical about classifying the daughter as good. Because her trust in her father was so great she was willing to sacrifice her life unquestioningly, this reader said: "She is a virtuous character, I suppose." These readers might be said to be resisting readers, insofar as they were intuitively aware of a narrative point of view but were in disagreement with it.

Two other readers, both M/NR, saw Jephthah as bad. One classified him this way because "he probably slept with his daughter." The other reader simply identified Jephthah as bad without offering any explanation.

Interestingly, all of the M/NR readers negatively evaluated Jephthah. Among the M/R readers, only one classified Jephthah as good. The other two did not classify him at all. They chose to mention only other characters. The M readers, therefore, exhibited a strong tendency to see Jephthah negatively or to ignore him. However, four of six female readers, two R and two NR, classified Jephthah as a good character. The female readers were less inclined to be critical of Jephthah. Their responses to this question reinforced the results from the identity question. More female readers than male chose to be Jephthah, and that seems to have been because more female readers saw Jephthah as a good character.

The last question in the interview asked readers what they would change in the story if they could change any part (Q12). The answers to this question revealed a clear difference between R and NR readers. Three R readers, two female and one male, said they would change the part about the sacrifice of the daughter. The first F/R reader said that "instead of making a deal with God that he would sacrifice who he first saw," she would have Jephthah "promise to praise God for the victory." For her, the deal was "pointless" because she could not see how it "glorified God." The second F/R said she would change the story so the daughter "didn't have to die." She said she would make it like the story of Abraham, who "didn't have to sacrifice his son," so she would have Jephthah sacrifice something else instead. This reader would retain the element of sacrifice but would change the outcome for the daughter because the daughter "is an innocent person who dies" and who "doesn't live to her full potential." One M/R, the Seventh Day Adventist who had described Jephthah's vow as a mistake, also said he would "change the part about the sacrifice." He provided the most extensive discussion of this question. He, too, would have Jephthah "sacrifice something else other than his daughter—a goat or something." He also referenced the Abraham/Isaac story. Moreover, he would have Jephthah say he was sorry he had made the vow in the first place because

> you weren't supposed to offer your children as burnt offerings—it specifically said in the law, "do not burn up your children." So offering a daughter as a sacrifice is *definitely* not going to make God happy because it is against his law. You got this conflict that I made vow but it's against God's law—well, God's law gotta supersede over your silly vow. I've heard people say he was expecting a dog or something to come out to greet him but you weren't supposed to offer unclean animals for sacrifice. . . . God doesn't want unclean animals so, he shouldn't have done it. . . . [Jephthah] really did a disservice against God because he put this image in people's mind that if you want something you gotta promise something. That's not why [God] does things. . . . Bad precedent, bad, bad.

One other M/R reader mentioned changing the section involving the daughter. He did not specifically mention changing the sacrifice but rather said that he would give the daughter more of a role and more choice as a female. Implicitly, he might have meant that she would have more of a say about what happened to her, but he did not go into detail. By raising the issue of the femaleness of the character, he did indicate, however, an awareness that connected her lack of choice to her sex in the context of this story.

Four of the NR readers chose a different area of the story to introduce change. Three F and one M readers would have made changes earlier in the story so that the consequences later in the story would be different. All of these NR readers focused on avoiding violence in some way. Three would change the interaction between Jephthah and the Ammonites so that a peaceful resolution to the conflict could occur and bloodshed could be avoided. One F/ NR said, "I would make it so that they could talk about [their difference] and not fight—such a female response." The M/NR who had earlier said that he would choose to be Jephthah so that he could do things differently said that he would change the story so that there was a "reasoned conclusion to the conflict and not a slaughter." When asked why he would make this change, he said, "Maybe it's the optimist in me . . . it doesn't have to resort back to 'I'm going to take this with force' or 'I'm going to slaughter and kill to get what I want.'"

One F/NR chose to make a change right at the beginning of the story. She would not have Jephthah kicked out of his family by the wife's sons. If the whole story started out in a different way, then perhaps "the war wouldn't have happened and there would have been less death and destruction, less unhappiness and suffering overall."

All of these NR change strategies, while not specifically mentioning the vow and subsequent sacrifice of the daughter, were presumably intended to change the whole course of the story, including the fate of the daughter. Whereas the R readers were generally comfortable with the idea of the Israelites fighting the Ammonites in the context of what was given them by their God, the NR readers were less inclined to accept the validity of the claim that the Israelites had any right to the land on this basis. One F/NR said that the two sides were fighting over the land because "they *think* their gods want it." This view echoed that of the M/NR who resisted classifying Jephthah as good because he regarded the appeal to divine approval for the war as a mere "rationale."

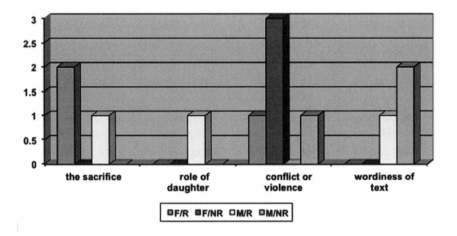

Q. 12 What part of the story would you change?

8. SOME CONCLUDING THOUGHTS

The results of this qualitative study were disappointing but not unexpected. There was no evidence of direct awareness of any feminist studies of this text in the responses of any of the readers. Nor was there any evidence to suggest a conscious application of a feminist critique of patriarchal social structures or gender ideology. None of the readers made gender a central category in their interpretation of the story.

Nevertheless, the results are interesting insofar as they show how ordinary readers deal with various aspects of the text. They did identify as problematic some of the very issues of concern to feminists, including the father's vow and the resulting sacrifice of his daughter. There was clearly a degree of resistance to the death of the daughter, though little analysis of the reasons leading to her sacrifice. The most extensive and critical perspective was supplied by the M/R Seventh Day Adventist, who saw the vow as a mistake and the human sacrifice as wrong. In his analysis, the fault lay completely with Jephthah. It was the individual, not the patriarchal social system or religion, that led to this outcome for the daughter.

Among NR readers, the resistance was focused more broadly on the climate of violence and its multiple manifestations in Jephthah's exclusion from the family, in the war over land claims, and in the sacrifice of the daughter. Although critical of the violence, none of these readers offered an explanation of underlying causes. NR readers were also less likely than R readers to accept the narrative perspective of the text, perhaps because the Bible was not authoritative for them. None, however, made this explicit in their responses.

The resistance of readers, especially male readers, to the character of Jephthah was, for me, one of the most interesting results. While most readers saw his vow as necessary to secure his victory and many saw his fulfillment of the vow as necessary to his commitment, most did not choose Jephthah as the character they would like to be. Four of six M readers judged him to be a "bad" character. Four of six F readers, however, assessed him as a "good" character. The women readers seemed more accepting of Jephthah and his behavior than the men.

While F readers were willing to identify with male characters, no M readers chose to be the daughter. One M reader saw the daughter as the weakest, and one saw her as the character he would least like to be. Only three M readers mentioned her as a "good" character. In contrast, all of the F/R and two of the F/NR readers listed the daughter as a "good" character. Not only does this suggest that the daughter was more marginal to male readers, but it also raises the possibility that female readers are more willing to accept the powerlessness, complicity, and submissiveness of the daughter as positive characteristics.

One final point that was shocking, given that the readers were all university educated, was that when asked what part of the story they would change, half of the M readers said they would shorten or simplify it because it was "too wordy" or the style "too difficult to read." Perhaps the growing irrelevance of the Bible is connected to its incomprehensibility to male readers!

Despite the fact that the results of this small study cannot be generalized, they do not give reason to think that the work of feminist biblical scholars is having much of a widespread impact on society. If our work is to have a transformational effect on the way the biblical tradition influences the lives of women and if it is to play a role in building a truly equitable society, it appears we will have to work harder to take our research out of the academy and into the streets.

Appendix: Interview Questions

Instructions:
Read the story contained in Judges 11, a passage from the Hebrew Bible/Tanak/Old Testament. You can re-read any or all of the text at any time during

this interview. This is not a test. There are no correct or incorrect answers to the questions below. What is important is what you think about the story and its meaning.

Interview questions:
1. Have you ever read or heard this story before?
   a. If so, where and when?
2. Tell me in your own words what this story is about.
   a. Why did Jephthah flee from his home to live in the land of Tob?
   b. Why did the elders of Gilead invite Jephthah to come back?
   c. What was the bargain Jephthah made with the elders of Gilead? What did he want?
   d. Why were the Ammonites making war against Israel?
   e. What was Jephthah's reply to the Ammonites?
   f. How did the Ammonites reply to Jephthah?
   g. Why did Jephthah make a vow to the Lord?
   h. What happened to the Ammonites?
   i. What happened to Jephthah when he went home?
   j. What happened to Jephthah's daughter and why?
3. What is the central, or main, message of the story?
   a. What led you to this conclusion about the meaning of the story?
   b. What are the main factors or clues in the story that point to this meaning for you?
4. Who is the central or most important character in the story?
   a. What makes this character central?
5. Who is the second most important character?
   a. What makes this character second in importance?
6. If you could be any of the characters in the story, which one would it be?
   a. What makes you choose this character?
7. Which character would you least like to be?
   a. What makes you choose this character?
8. Who is the most powerful character in the story?
   a. What makes this character seem powerful?
9. Who is the weakest character in the story?
   a. What makes this character seem weak?
10. If you had to evaluate the characters in terms of good and bad which characters would you identify as good (if any) and which characters would you identify as bad (if any)?

11. What feelings do you have when you read this story?

    a. What factors in the story make you feel this way?

12. If you could change any part of this story, which part would it be?

    a. What change would you make?

    b. Why would you make this change?

Notes

1. When the study was done, the word *subjects* was used in the ethics policies. This has now been changed to *participants* in the revised policies. I will use *subjects* because that was the term used at the time of my study.

2. There are three such granting agencies, the Social Sciences and Humanities Research Council of Canada (SSHRC), the Natural Sciences and Engineering Research Council of Canada (NSERC), and the Medical Research Council (MRC). Together, they have produced the *Tri-Council Policy Statement: Ethical Conduct for Research Involving Humans* (TCPS), http://pre.ethics.gc.ca/eng/policy-politique/initiatives/tcps2-eptc2/Default/.

3. A useful survey of reader-response criticism can be found in the Bible and Culture Collective 1995: 20–69.

4. I put the word in italics because Sandra Harding makes a case for distinguishing between weak objectivity and strong objectivity. It is weak objectivity that is being denied here (Harding 2004: 127–40).

5. All research on human subjects must be approved by the University's Research Ethics Board. The ethical design of the project and the informed consent of all subjects are among the many aspects that are required.

6. In discussing the answers of individual subjects, the group into which they fall will be identified as F/R or M/R for female and male subjects from religious backgrounds and F/NR or M/NR for female and male subjects from nonreligious backgrounds.

7. No one who had taken a course from me at any time was accepted as a volunteer subject.

8. The interview questions are listed in the appendix. A reference to the question numbers will be given in the text as the particular question results are discussed.

9. For a summary of some of the major issues in Judges 11 discussed by feminist biblical scholars, see Miller 2005: 77–93.

10. A full presentation of the responses to all the questions in the interview is not possible here.

11. Trible sees this vow as an "act of unfaithfulness."

12. For a discussion of such interpretations see Marcus 1986: 28-54.

13. It would be interesting to determine if the tendency to read the deity into the story as a character comes about because all readers knew the text was from the Hebrew Bible. A follow-up study could be done in which some readers are told it is a biblical story and others are told it is an ancient Near Eastern story.

13

Delilah—A Forgotten Hero (Judges 16:4-21)

A Cross-Cultural Narrative Reading

Royce M. Victor

INTRODUCTION

The book of Judges presents some of the unforgettable female characters of the Hebrew Bible, and Delilah is one of the most famous figures among them. The history of interpretation has given much attention to this character since ancient days: much ink has been spilled and tons of paper has been used to narrate her story from different perspectives. The Delilah-Samson story is still an attraction for art, music, and literature. For centuries, it has captured readers' imaginations. Interestingly, most writers knowingly or unknowingly approach the story of Delilah from an "Israelite" or from Samson's perspective and depict Delilah as a negative character, a seductive foreign woman who betrays a biblical hero. Some others, however, do acknowledge Delilah's prominence over Samson in the story. A few others look at her as a Philistine hero (Exum 1996; Ackerman 2000). This essay attempts to revisit—from a Philistine perspective—the narrative of Delilah, a Philistine woman who is ready to sacrifice her life for the defense of her land and people. From this perspective, she is a forgotten hero who is on a mission to bring liberation to her people. Her brave attempt to bring peace to the land is simply forgotten not only by Israelites but also by her own people. Forgotten heroes exist in every society.

This paper looks at Delilah's story from a cross-cultural perspective by comparing her story to an unnamed hero, from the great Indian epics of *Ramayana* and *Mahabharata*, who offers her life for the welfare of society. The first part of this essay deals with the story of Delilah and tries to expose how she becomes a forgotten hero in the biblical history. The second section is about the forgotten female hero from the Indian epics. Both of these epics are considered the finest literary works of Indian culture. The *Ramayana* and the *Mahabharata* are not single texts, but instead are composed of many texts, as well as oral renditions. It is generally believed that these texts originated from a period between the fourth century BCE and the second century CE.

As an Indian who grew up in India, I have always been astonished and often challenged by the stories of *Ramayana* and *Mahabharata*. Just as for most Indians, these stories have been part of my life, and the morals behind each of them have become the foundation of my thoughts, worldview, and spirituality. Whenever I read the story of Delilah, my mind immediately goes back to the story of the unknown woman from the *Ramayana* and the *Mahabharata* who was prepared to sacrifice her life for the well-being of her country. This essay is an attempt to see the similarities between the endeavors of these two female heroes from two different cultures.

THE SIGNIFICANCE OF JUDGES 16:4-21

Judges 16:4-23 is part of the larger section about Samson's life, which starts with the announcement of Samson's birth in 13:1 and ends with the narration of his tragic death and burial in 16:31. Several scholars point out the literary artistry of the passage. It exhibits a sophisticated literary patterning, which not only enhances our appreciation of the story but also influences our perception of it (Exum 1981: 3). It is also correct to see the whole section about Samson's activities as a saga.[1] James Crenshaw notes that only on rare occasions did the ancient Hebrews reach such heights in storytelling (Crenshaw 1974: 470).[2]

The story can be divided into two clear-cut parts. Judges 15:20 concludes the first section with the phrase: "he had judged. . . ." Again, in 16:31: "he had judged" is mentioned. It is evident that the redactor divided Samson's story into two segments (13:1—15:20 and 16:1-31): his rise as judge, and his tragic end (Boling 1975: 253). Exum argues that the core of the Samson cycle is composed of two well-balanced sets of stories, chapters 14–15 and chapter 16. Each section begins when Samson sees and desires a Philistine woman. In each, the Philistine leaders persuade a woman to coax Samson to disclose his secret of strength, and the woman does so through pressuring Samson to prove his love for her by revealing a secret. In each case, Samson's disclosure appears to be to his enemys' advantage yet ultimately leads to the destruction of great numbers of Philistines.[3] Furthermore, throughout the cycle, the compilers have woven a rich tapestry of interconnected themes and motifs: knowing and not knowing, telling and keeping secrets, riddles, and the like (Pressler 2002: 209).

Judges 16:4-21 is the penultimate episode of the Samson saga, where Delilah is introduced to the cycle. The previous episode is connected to Delilah's story by the phrase "after this." This reference could be a chronological indicator, noting that Delilah's story occurred after the incident with the prostitute in Gaza (Schneider 2000: 219). When we look from Delilah's perspective, she suddenly appears in v. 4 and gradually acquires dominance over Samson and finally, in v. 21, she disappears immediately after his imprisonment. With v. 22, the story enters into a new phase, the final episode of the saga, which narrates Samson's final slaughter of the Philistines along with his own death, and ends with his burial and a short description of him as a "judge" in v. 31. On the face of it, one can easily detach 16:4-21, as a unit, from the saga itself, because of Delilah's significant presence in it. At the same time, the Delilah unit leads the story to its climax (or anticlimax?), the capturing of Samson by the Philistines. This incident shows that, on the one hand, the Delilah episode is an integral part of the Samson saga and, on the other hand, that it has its own significance within the saga. Crenshaw notes that this story unit is a masterpiece of dialogue, suspense, action, psychological insight, and narration (Crenshaw 1974: 497).

Delilah

Verse 16:4 is important not only because of its connection with the previous episode by means of the phrase "after this" but also because it introduces the main character of the story, Delilah. The verse is about Samson's love for a woman in "the Valley of Sorek," namely, Delilah. One may perceive that many issues vital to this study are implanted in this verse.

Verse 4 expresses the unique display of Samson's feelings for Delilah. However, as Sasson points out, it is interesting to note that when applied to human beings, the biblical root for love—אהב , 'a-h-b Qal and its derivatives—is used very sparingly in biblical Hebrew narratives. Moreover, its designation is not homogeneous. Sasson explains how אהב is being used when speaking of the relationship between married couples, like Isaac and Rebecca and Jacob and Rachel.[4] There are two occasions where the use of the word leads to abuse of women: when Shechem loves Dinah and when Amnon loves his sister Tamar (Sasson 1988: 334–35). The storyteller sets the stage here by using this rare word to show the intensity of Samson's betrayal by his mistress Delilah. As we go through the story, we learn more about why the storyteller needs to explain the profundity of Samson's love. In 14:16, the same word is used in a different way. The Timnite wife accuses Samson of not "loving" her (Sasson 1988: 335). This is the first time the all-knowing author states that Samson "loves." Now that Samson is presented as a subject who "loves," this term clearly has a special purpose to fulfill. It shows Samson's passion toward Delilah and thus also the intensity of her treachery. Interestingly, we do not hear this word anymore in this story, nor do we hear of Delilah's love toward Samson (Schneider 2000: 219–20).[5] The love mentioned here is one-way.

This verse also introduces Delilah, the main character of this story. She is the only named woman in the whole Samson saga. Interestingly, even Samson's mother is unnamed, although she plays a significant role in the birth narrative in chapter 13. However, except for her name and place, nothing is said about Delilah's identity. In the history of interpretation, many scholars have tried their level best to find out the meaning of her name, but none have been able to find out much more than the writer's possible "secret" intention.

Many commentators find the literal meaning of the word דלילה, (letter for letter: d-l-y-l-h) to be "lustrous" or "flirtatious," by comparing it with the Arabic word *dallatuim*, "flirt" (Boling 1975: 248). Some others assign the meaning "affectionate" by comparing it with the Arabic root that permits a pun: "*dalla,* to behave amorously, and Delilah, a guide, here to disaster" (McKenzie 1966: 155). Carolyn Pressler considers that Delilah is derived from לילה (*laylah*), "night." According to this explanation, the name of Samson's lover-betrayer is likely chosen as a play on the meaning of Samson's name, "Sunny": "Night overcomes the 'little sun'" (Pressler 1992: 133). Palmer pointed out as early as in 1913 the possible connection between Delilah and לילה. He argues that *laylah,* לילה, originally means "the all enveloping," or "the veiler," like the Sanskrit *Varuna,* "sky god," from the root *var,* "to cover" (Palmer 1977:129–30). Of course, the name Samson (Hebrew, *Shimshon*) is possibly derived from the word שמש, *shemesh,* "sun." The literary phenomenon of wordplay can be seen throughout the Hebrew Bible, when foreign persons are often pictured negatively through wordplay on their names.[6] It is now an accepted fact that Hebrew proper names in the Bible are more than symbols: they are conferred not merely for purposes of distinction but also because of the idea they express (Gray 1896: 1). Much ink has been spilled on this issue of biblical names, especially in recent times and particularly from the feminist perspective (e.g., Bohmbach 2000: 33–39). Moreover, the primary intention of the wordplay in Delilah's case is to achieve nothing else but to ridicule the bearer of this particular name (Radday 1990: 67). Radday further points out the use of Delilah's name in the Talmud. He quotes, "Rabbi says, were not her name

Delilah, she could be nicknamed thus, because she diminished his [Samson's] strength, his mind and his victories" (Radday 1990: 63–64). For the Hebrews, the night is contrasted to the day as darkness is to light; hence the expression "day and night" (Gen. 8:22; cf. Ps. 1:2 and more). Night is usually a symbol of suffering and sorrow (e.g., Job 7:3), sudden assault (Isa. 15:1), and calamity (Mic. 3:6). According to certain late apocalyptic writings, night is the symbol of evil and sorrow (Zech. 14:7).[7] However, one should note that the pronunciation of the name in Hebrew is *de-lee-lah*, not Delilah, as in English. Hence the phonetic similarity to "night," Hebrew *laylah*, would seem less attractive to Hebrew speakers than to English speakers. It is clear that Delilah might not be her original name but most probably a name distorted so as to ridicule its bearer as well as to picture her as a negative character. It also highlights her possible foreign identity.

Another important clue to Delilah's identity comes from the name of the place she comes from. She is introduced as a woman from "the Valley of Sorek." However, this marker does not provide an adequate solution for revealing her ethnic identity. The location is in the region of Timnah and the northern area of the Philistines, but not far from Zor'ah, Samson's Danite birthplace. However, the book of Judges does not give the precise borders of the Philistine country (Schneider 2000: 220). Since the place had a mixed population, Delilah could be a Canaanite, a Philistine, or even an Israelite. Delilah is not identified by a hometown, but only by the name of a larger region.[8] Klein understands the meaning of this region's name as "torrent bed," a place where water (symbol of fertility) is available in abundance. Furthermore, Delilah is not identified through a male relative. She is an unattached woman, and according to Israelite standards, such women are often depicted as, seductively, leading potentially good men astray (Klein 2003: 24).

Exum argues that one cannot simply assume that the woman is a Philistine. She notes that Delilah bears a Hebrew name and lives on the boundary between Israelite and Philistine territory. Thus the text presents at least the possibility that she is an Israelite (Exum 1993a: 69; Smith 1997: 48; Bronner 1993: 72–95). However, as seen earlier, Delilah's name could possibly be wordplay by the writer, perhaps not original but "changed" in order to serve a specific authorial purpose.

Although the text remains silent about Delilah's ancestry, it does give the impression that she belongs on the other side of the ethnic fence, not Samson's side. Her ability to communicate with Samson hardly requires us to view her as an Israelite. Here language is not an issue at all (although some scholars do think this as an important point). Samson seems to be capable of conversing easily with the Timnites, and the Philistines talk freely with the people of Judah. The story does not record any conversation between the Gaza harlot and Samson. All this shows that the narrator assumes that linguistic differences between Israelites and Philistines pose no serious problem (Crenshaw 1978: 71). In addition, given the parallels between Delilah and the Timnite woman, Delilah's readiness to collaborate with the Philistine lords and Samson's established penchant for Philistine women, Delilah is most probably a Philistine. Moreover, throughout this story, she acts on behalf of the Philistines. One should also note Samson's attraction to Philistine women, mentioned in previous chapters, which provides yet another clue for assuming that this time too he goes to a Philistine woman.

As a Philistine, Delilah's genealogy is inconsequential for an Israelite narrative. None of the names of her relatives is mentioned in the story, and this makes her virtually rootless in time (no genealogical line) and place (no place of origin). As Klein notes, Delilah's "rootlessness" distinguishes the "Children of Israel," the group Samson belongs to, from the rootless "nation," from which Delilah comes (Klein 2003: 24). Therefore, with all this evidence, there is no difficulty in viewing Delilah as a Philistine. Moreover, she is evidently a Philistine because of her frequent contacts with the lords of the Philistines. If she is an Israelite, these regular contacts with the enemies of her community would possibly not be that easy.

SAMSON

As noted earlier, the name Samson (*Shimshon*) derives from the word שמש (*shemesh*, "sun"). The name could mean "little sun." Many scholars are of the opinion that the Samson story is actually a solar myth. According to this line, Samson's seven locks represent the sun's rays, and his blinding recalls the sun as a one-eyed god. Samson's death has similarity with the fate of the sun, which pulls down the western pillars upon which the heavenly vault stands, and brings darkness to all (Crenshaw 1978:15–16).

Others find similarities between Samson's stories and the legends of Heracles. Just as Heracles's wondrous feats were divided into twelve separate incidents, so also Samson's exploits total an even dozen by some reckonings (Crenshaw 1978: 17). However, I conclude with Crenshaw that Samson's story is neither a solar myth nor cosmic legend, but a saga (Crenshaw 1978: 19).

Samson is the last judge in the book of Judges. However, Samson's character as "judge" is radically different from that of other "judges" mentioned in the book.[9] Whereas other judges fight for the well-being of clans, Samson's struggles are more personal in nature. In other words, whereas the other judges' major military forays are to rescue the people from their enemies and to restore their dignity, Samson's fights are to extricate himself from a trap he has inadvertently laid, or to avenge wrongs brought on by his own folly (Crenshaw 1978: 59). Samson is never associated with any group, nor is he ever pictured as leader of a group. He does everything by himself without seeking help from others. His lonesome character distinguishes him from other judges. He neither speaks for God, like Deborah, nor consults with God, like Gideon. Furthermore, he does not ratify his actions before God nor speak of God, like Jephthah. Samson completely ignores the Lord except on two occasions, when he faces extreme distress. Serving God or God's people appears to play no part in his primary motivation. Rather, he does everything for his own contentment.

Samson's portrayal as superhuman (Judg. 16:7, 11, and 13) is another issue of the passage under discussion. He repeatedly says that if he reveals the secret of his strength, then he "will become like any other man" (Margalith 1986b: 229). This superhuman nature makes Samson different from others in his own community. His exceptional strength is integrally connected with his Nazirite vow. Nowhere in the saga does one see Samson taking a vow for himself, although 13:4-5 does inform us of the divine message about his miraculous birth and the Nazirite vow. Samson himself does not make the vow; someone else does this on his behalf. Is he not a victim of the vow? To a certain extent, the vow is imposed on him. He has to follow the rules without being fully convinced. He is a victim similar to Jephthah's daughter (Judges 11). His discontented attitude toward everything around him proves this very fact.

One may also think that the prohibition against haircutting is a duplication of the original message (i.e., the information that Samson is to be a Nazirite in the annunciation to Samson's mother), which in this case (ch. 16) derives from a hand other than that of the saga's author. This impression rests on the fact that Samson's Nazirite status hardly functions in the story (Crenshaw 1978: 73–74).[10] We hear about it only in chapter 13 and once in chapter 16. To this we may retort: on the contrary; the "hair growing" feature of the Nazirite vow is central to the narrative, its plot, its hero's characterization, and its central theme (Niditch 1990: 613).[11] As the narrative stands, the Nazirite vow is important (if not as a main theme) to the character Samson as well as to the whole saga. Even though the very word נזיר (*nazir*) is repeatedly present in the saga, it is carelessly interwoven into the story. The Nazirite vow allows an Israelite writer to employ this folk motif in a special, Israelite way. The narrator is not interested in other aspects of the Nazirite vows as mentioned in Numbers

6 (staying away from alcohol, unclean food, and corpses). Among the rules, only "hair growing" acquires significance in our narrative (Margalith 1985: 225–34).[12] In other words, contours of the plot hinge on Samson's hair and his superhuman strength. Moreover, Delilah's "betrayal" and the "regrowth" of the hair allow for the final and ultimate vindication.

Interestingly, one cannot find any connection between superhuman power and Nazirite vows. That is to say, a Nazirite need not be superhuman. What may be the reason for bringing these two elements together in Samson's story? Could this give the impression that Samson got his incomparable strength through his divine birth? However, throughout the story, one does not find him a blissful character but a violent and brutal character. His arrogant nature toward his parents is evident in his odd demand to make arrangements for his marriage with the woman whom he likes (14:1-3). Usually, the parents find a groom/bride for their child. His unusual attitude is well disclosed in his emphatic reply to his parents' objection in 14:3b: "Get me that one, for she is the one that pleases me." Brutally killing animals (lion and ass) and people reveals his melancholy, deep-rooted in his nature. He seems to have some kind of deep psychological problems in his life. His odd, discontented nature makes him different from others. "He is very much overconfident in his strength, believing that the Lord's spirit will rescue him no matter what he does" (Pressler 2002: 223). He seems to believe in nothing else other than in his own physical strength.

Olson points out that Samson is an embodiment of all that is wrong with the judges who precede him. He is the antithesis of what the good judges were in the early era, a reverse image with a penchant for personal vendettas, selfish rages, reluctance to lead, inability to rally the tribes of Israel into a united community, making covenants with foreigners, and breaking covenant vows. In sum, he represents the implosion of the whole judge system (Olson 1998: 842), the judge who no longer leads Israel nor obeys God. Other scholars, such as Greenstein, argue that Samson is an embodiment of Israel's violent nature (Greenstein 1981: 247–55). His breaking of the Nazirite vow is similar to how Israel repeatedly breaks her covenant obligations with YHWH by worshiping idols. Olson further claims that Samson is the personification of the kind of divine love that cannot let go. Even after his Timnite wife betrays him concerning the answer to his riddle (14:7), he continues to love her (15:1). His love provides a metaphor for God's unfailing love for Israel, in spite of Israel's repeated betrayal of him (Olson 1998: 843); however, one can hardly get this idea from 15:1 because the verb אהב (*'a-h-b*, "love") is not used in 15:1. Moreover, it is not known whether Samson goes to his wife out of love: once again, nowhere in the whole saga, apart from in 16:4-21, does one find that Samson explicitly loves someone. Therefore, it may be more probable that he goes to see his wife to satisfy his sexual needs, much as he goes to another Philistine woman (e.g., 16:1).

In 16:4-21, the verb אהב occurs twice: in v. 4, where the narrator speaks of Samson's love for Delilah, and then again in v. 15, when Delilah accuses him of not loving her. Olson argues that Samson loves Delilah continually, in spite of her frequent betrayals (Olson 1998: 843). However, the narrator never attributes to Samson any knowledge of Delilah's plot to confine him, or of her alleged betrayal. In this scene, Samson is presented as living blindly and foolishly. Olson asserts that God knows of Israel's betrayal but, in spite of that, constantly loves her. Samson, however, is not aware of Delilah's betrayal. Therefore, it is hard to see Samson's figure as an embodiment of God's love, as Olson proposes.

Is Samson Manoah's prodigal son? And what makes Samson an Israelite judge (Boling 1975: 252)? To the first question, we may answer that Samson is a social nuisance. Niditch (1990) and Crenshaw (1978) describe Samson as a social bandit. In fact, he is more than a social bandit; he is a *goonda* (Hindi, meaning "a hired thug"),[13] a serious anti-social nuisance. There are several reasons for this conclusion. Samson is a threat to the Philistines, of course, and we do not know the Israelite attitude toward him. However, the passage 15:10-13 explicitly reveals that he is a problem for Israelites too, a hindrance to peaceful relations with their neighbors, the Philistines. Eradication of an evil character from society is everyone's task. Both Israelites and Philistines want to get rid of him. He becomes a common enemy to both. Everybody knows about his deeds, things he has done to his Timnite wife's relatives and other Philistines. Because of his dreadful nature, it is not easy to love a person like Samson or to have an intimate relationship with him. Only an extraordinary person can deal with an exceptionally brutal person like Samson and win his heart. Delilah undertakes that challenge. Regarding the second question, we have already spent considerable amounts of time and space in dealing with that. Samson is totally different from other judges. Let me add one more question here. Is there any reason to praise Samson as a judge? He is not a conventional Israelite judge, and what makes him a "judge" and brings him to the biblical canon remains an open question. There is nothing to glorify his character except his exceptional superhuman strength. In fact, he is the only such kind of personality mentioned in the whole Hebrew Bible, which is probably balanced by his negative characteristics.

The Issue of Money

After introducing the main characters, Delilah and Samson, and Samson's feelings toward Delilah, the narrator moves on to the issue of money. The topic is introduced in v. 5, when the lords of the Philistines approach Delilah and request her help for finding out the "magic" secret of Samson's strength. Delilah is offered "eleven hundred pieces of silver" from each Philistine lord. We are not informed about the number of the Philistine lords and other details concerning them. Boling revises the amount each lord promises to give to "each man's unit, one hundred." His translation is based on a re-division of the MT (Boling 1975: 248–49). He assumes there were five tyrants (other biblical passages have five lords for five Philistine cities, a Pentapolis; see, for instance, Josh. 13:3; Judg. 3:3; 1 Sam. 6:1-21), and notes that it is too much money to be offered. However, we cannot accept his argument since the text in its present form does not suggest anything to support the number of the lords. Nevertheless, the offer from the lords is a huge sum of money. The lords simply appear in v. 5 without having been invited and again in v. 18, having been called by Delilah into the scene. Even though the word כסף (keseph, "silver") appears only twice in the episode, it seems to change the whole situation.

The present context has many similarities with the story of Samson's wife, in chapter 14. The main difference is that in chapter 14 it is not the leaders who are interested in Samson but those who are defeated in the riddle competition. Instead of offering the wife money, the Philistines threaten the woman's life. In chapter 16, Delilah is offered money by the lords directly (Schneider 2000: 220–23; Ackerman 1998: 233–35). However, we do not know whether she accepts the offer. Many commentators assume that she must have accepted the deal because in the next verse she seeks the source of Samson's strength (Schneider 2000: 221). However, the text does not support this argument unequivocally, and it is evident that there is a gap in the sequence of the story here. Even though the lords reappear in v. 18, Delilah neither demands nor gets money from them. The writer supplies no further information regarding the money. However, many readers believe that Delilah is paid for providing information about Samson's strength. It is true that, as Klein points out, the only way the men can imagine her gleaning that information is through emotional and sexual weakening of the man's resolutions (Klein 2003: 25). Klein further indicates that the primary purpose of the insertion of money into the story is to invite the readers to scorn Delilah for using a hero's love to get what she wants from him (Klein 2003: 25–26). This also seems to imply that women who offer their services for payment are automatically derogated in Israelite culture.

Throughout the Samson saga, one can see the motif of the hero's glorification—from his birth narrative, which states his unusual and divinely ordained birth; and until his extraordinary suicide along with the death of thousands of Philistines, which reminds us of contemporary suicide attacks on innocents. From this perspective, one can see the inclusion of the money motif as a tendentious addition/editorial statement on the part of the story's writer/ editor, intended to glorify Samson, the "great" biblical hero who kills thousands of innocents. We certainly do not know whether Delilah accepts money from the Philistine lords for her services: we simply assume she does. In any case, the money does play a significant part in the history of interpretation for this passage.

One should also remember that the narrative is primarily written for Israelite male audiences/readers, and that the ambiguities of the text stress that the Israelite male cannot comprehend foreign women—their words, their values, and their allegiance (Klein 2003: 25). Delilah is presented as explicitly manipulating Samson, according to the best Israelite standards. Here Klein's question—Should we judge Delilah according to Israelite standards?—is highly valid; she writes: "Delilah is simultaneously protecting her people and is reviled by the reader in sympathy with the Israelites" (Klein 2003: 28). One does not have any evidence to accuse Delilah for her deeds other than the money issue, which in itself is dubious.

ATTEMPTS ON SAMSON'S LIFE

Verses 6-16 narrate Delilah's three fruitless attempts to learn the "magic" of Samson's extraordinary strength, with success in the fourth attempt. Delilah probes Samson for the secret of his strength in all four attempts. She is honest in her words (Schneider 2000: 221). As Fewell points out, Delilah does not—as many commentators are eager to assert—deceive Samson. She asks him directly what she wants to know (Fewell 1998: 79). Throughout all her attempts, Delilah is clear and straightforward in her mission. On the other side, each time Samson comes up with a lie. He, in fact, deceives her throughout this passage.

At this point, Samson is playing a game with Delilah by telling her one story after another. Bal thinks that the use of the third person plural pronoun in 16:7, "If *they* bind me," indicates that Samson has understood the goal of Delilah's questions from the very beginning of her attempts (Bal 1987: 52).[14] However, the text does not support this argument. Rather, one can presume that Samson creates something that sounds magical, which has many similarities with the riddle[15] he has served to a group of people earlier, at his wedding feast.

Samson's image as a Riddler[16] is well exposed here. Apparently, he thinks he is witty, not realizing the ramifications of his actions. Even now, he does not realize that he should question Delilah's intentions (Schneider 2000: 221). It is difficult to understand Samson at this point. He does not show any discomfort with Delilah's approach. Each time she repeats her question about the "source" of his strength, Samson gives her fanciful explanations of his "secret," although with each new version he moves closer to the "secret" itself. On the other side, Delilah fearlessly tries until she achieves her goal.

Many scholars point out the possible similarities between the scene of Samson sleeping and Delilah weaving the hair of his head (16:14), and the story of Jael the Kenite woman in Judges 4–5 (for example, Olson 1998: 858; Schneider 2000: 223–24; and Ackerman 2000: 37–41). In both cases, a woman wins over a man and takes advantage of the situation. Furthermore, in both cases, the women become the liberator of the people. However, there are also notable differences between the two scenes. In Jael's case, Sisera's defeat saves the Israelites, whereas ironically in this case it is Philistines who are saved through the destruction of an Israelite judge. Moreover, in Jael's case, though she is a foreigner (a Kenite), she is glorified because she rescues the Israelites, whereas, in the present case, Delilah's import is overlooked because she saves Israel's enemies. The writer also tries to portray her as a "bad" foreign woman. In the story, Samson is humbled before Delilah and surrenders his life to her. Consequently, she wins the crucial game by defeating her rival and fulfilling her mission.

Bal looks at this issue from a different perspective. She argues that the arbiter of this case is Samson himself because he is the only one who knows the secret, and Delilah's success depends on him (Bal 1987: 56). However, while Samson is indeed the sole holder of his secret, it must be emphasized that it is Delilah's enduring effort that brings the secret out of Samson; he does not reveal it voluntarily. She does everything in order to force it out of him. Therefore, the credit should naturally go to Delilah, not to Samson. She brilliantly makes use of the situation in such a way that he has no other choice. Delilah plans everything quite neatly so that Samson has no clue of what she is aiming at.

The Haircutting

Judges 16:19 speaks of the cutting of the "*seven locks* of his head," which are an integral part of Samson's life. These magical locks endow him with supernatural powers. The power inherent in the locks disappears when they are shorn, and returns with the hair's regrowth. Until now, we do not hear of this particular word, "locks," in the story. Now the locks get more prominence than anything else. With these locks, he has a special relationship with God. Without these locks, there remains nothing of his superhuman strength.

When we trace the *Sitz im Leben* of the story about Samson's locks, we get some interesting information. Margalith concludes that the *Sitz im Leben* of this legend, like the legends of the foxes (Margalith 1985: 224–28)[17] and other legends (Margalith 1986a: 397–405), is not in West-Semitic mythological thought but rather in that of the Minoan-Mycenaean world. These legends were probably adopted from the Philistines by the Danites and absorbed into the corpus of the Danites' tribal lore (Margalith 1986b: 233–34). This would support the notion, presented earlier, that the story of 16:4-21 is originally the story of a female Philistine hero who defeated a dreadful enemy with her extraordinary bravery and brilliance.

Who cut Samson's locks? This is an altogether different question. A variety of translations obtain for v. 19, which contains the reference to the haircutting. The JPS translates, "Then she called in a man, and she had him cut off the seven locks of his head." The NRSV, RSV, and many others opt for a similar translation, according to which the man whom Delilah calls cut the hair. However, I find these translations problematic. All these translations correctly translate the first verb, ותקרא, *wa-tiqra'*, as the third person feminine singular ("and she called"). But it is the second verb, ותגלח, *wa-tegalach*, that is the crux of the matter. It is customarily translated as a third person feminine causative singular form, "and [she, Delilah] *made* [him, the man she called] *cut* . . ." As Sasson notes, as a verb, the root *g-l-ch* occurs in the Hebrew Bible only in the Piel and Hithpael stems, most often controls a direct object, and is only once reflexive (Gen. 41:14). Also the verb never bears a causative or factitive meaning (Sasson 1988: 336).[18] Therefore, if "cutting" is done, it must be by Delilah, and she must be given full responsibility for her act. Such a translation also does justice to the text as it stands, without recourse to an emendation, reading "and he cut," as per most of the modern translations, following the LXX (and cf. BHS).

Another question concerns the identity of the man whom Delilah summons (16:19). Boling suggests that the man is the one who brings a razor, or assists Delilah in cutting the hair (Boling 1975: 250). However, there are good reasons to doubt the presence of an enemy so close to the bedroom Samson is in. Arguably, only after Delilah is convinced of her mastery of the situation, she sends for the Philistines and they show up. Moreover, Delilah has already proven that she is brave enough to handle the situation by herself. Here again one can agree with Sasson, who proposes that Delilah call Samson, not someone else, to make sure how deeply he sleeps (Boling 1975: 337–38),[19] so that she can start her job without his knowledge.

After this scene, the helpless Samson tries hard to get away from the trap. His efforts become fruitless (v. 20), and finally the Philistines enter and arrest him (v. 21). By now he realizes that the Lord has departed from him. Without the divine power he becomes an ordinary human being, exactly as he has already revealed to Delilah. Here ends another phase of the story. Now Samson is in the hands of his enemies. He is given the job of grinding the millstone in prison, usually a job performed by a slave or a woman: he is in fact feminized, becoming like Job's wife (Job 31:10) or the women in Isaiah (Isa. 47:2-3), "grinding" for others (Niditch 1990: 617). He finally occupies a social place that is undoubtedly much lower than that of Delilah.

Delilah—A Forgotten Hero

With verse 21 the story comes to its closure. The penultimate episode of Samson's story ends with his arrest by the Philistines with the help of Delilah. At the same time, one may notice the sudden disappearance of Delilah from the scene. With verse 20 the story of Delilah comes to an end, though Samson's story does continue. We have no information about what happens to her after Samson's imprisonment. No one ever refers to Delilah's life beyond this point. Does she die during the struggle to capture Samson? Is she killed by the Philistine lords in order to avoid giving her money? Does she die during the collapse of the Philistine temple (16:30)? Or, perhaps, does she have a safe and prosperous life thereafter? We have no answers to these questions. She simply disappears from the scene. The biblical narrator shows no more interest in her.

What was the role of Delilah in this story? Delilah's story in Samson's saga has many peculiarities. She is the only named woman in the saga, and has a special place in the history of interpretation. She is often pictured as lacking in ethics and morality. However, a closer look reveals that she is deliberately pictured as a negative figure by being connecting with money. The positive power of woman, which is seen in chapter 13, is completely absent in Delilah's story (Brettler 2002: 56).[20] Her story is deliberately suppressed in order to glorify Samson the Israelite hero. The motif of glorification can be seen throughout the saga: in Samson's birth narrative, his name, the Nazirite vow, his superhuman strength, Delilah's "betrayal," and several other themes. However, as Camp notes, Samson's heroic status is hardly established apart from the foretelling to his mother and his God (Camp 2000: 215). Especially in 16:4-21, Samson is seen as inferior to Delilah. She humbles him by cutting his hair and thus removes his extraordinary strength. Delilah brilliantly strikes Samson at the very spot where he has no strength. The glorification motif ultimately fails to achieve its goal in this passage.

The origin of Delilah, as seen earlier, is not Israelite but probably Philistine. Without proper evidence, she is often pictured in interpretation as a prostitute and a person who has no respect for morality in life. Vickery calls Delilah "a whore at heart" (Vickery 1981; see also Bal 1987b: 50–51). This is because, like a prostitute, she uses her sexuality and a man's desire for her in order to ensure her own well-being (Ackerman 1998: 231). However, it seems to me that it is not for her own welfare that she delivers Samson to the Philistines, but the hope of her community that she bears on her shoulder leads her to perform this mission. As noted, Samson becomes a threat to the whole society, not only to the Philistines but to everyone. Elimination of Samson from society becomes a common necessity for everyone, since he becomes a threat to the peaceful nature of society at large. Members of this society realize that it is simply impossible to "bind" Samson with ordinary human power. At that juncture, Delilah appears and takes up the responsibility. Here, one does not find that her own desires or well-being rule over her; rather, one can very well perceive her as a rescuer of her community, a person who is willing to risk her life for the interests of society. She simultaneously protects her own people and, unfortunately, is hated by the reader in sympathy with the Israelites (Klein 2003: 28). She can appropriately be compared with glorious feminine biblical figures like Esther and Judith, who risk their life for their community. Jeter connects her self-sacrifice with that of Jael (Jeter 2003: 119; also Ackerman 2000). Delilah risks her life by continuously attempting to compromise Samson's life without asking for any help from anyone. She is alone in her mission and handles Samson successfully.

Delilah uses her sexual charm to discover Samson's secret of strength. She inverts the paradigm of male-female relationship: usually woman acts through man, but here man acts through woman, since the Philistine lords work through Delilah. She accepts male authority in order to accomplish what men cannot perform. Thus, even though she accepts male authority, her status remains above the heads of her male counterparts. She brilliantly makes use of Samson's love for her to give support and security to her people. As seen earlier, it is evident that the storyteller uses a story from Philistine circles, sufficiently altering it according to Israelite standards to convince Israelite society (Alter 1990: 48). However, Delilah presents a complex picture of a resourceful woman, a hero to her own people. As a Philistine, she cannot be judged by Israelite standards. In this plot, she is on a mission to bring liberation to her people. That is why her attitude toward Samson is not explicitly revealed in the story. It is irrelevant to her mission.

Delilah is a forgotten hero. Her story does not exist even among the Philistine circles that enjoy the fruits of her heroic acts. If it did exist in some form among them, one could at least make out some trace of it in the story of Samson in Judges or in later interpretation of it. She may not even get a chance to sing, as John Milton in his *Samson Agonistes* makes her do:

> . . . [I]n my country, where I most desire,
> In Ecron, Gaza, Asdod, and in Gath
> I shall be named among the famousest
> Of women, sung at solemn festivals,
> Living and dead recorded, who to save
> Her country from a fierce destroyer, chose
> Above the faith of wedlock-bands, my tomb
> With odours visited and annual flowers.
> Not less renowned than in Mount Ephraim
> Jael, who with inhospitable guile
> Smote Sisera sleeping through the temples nailed
> (Milton 11. 980–90 [p. 466])

She is ignored by her own people, whereas her enemies the Israelites make use of her story for glorifying her prey, Samson, thus degrading her to the level of a whore who sells her body for money. History has forgotten her heroic self-sacrifice, just like that of many others who risk their life for the well-being of the world. She is not the only person who has this kind of fate in human history; there are many to share it with her, especially womenfolk who share everything they have, even to the point of risking their own lives. We can see many similar examples in other cultures. One can see a similar story of an unnamed woman told in the Indian epics *Ramayana* and *Mahabharata*.

A Forgotten Female Hero of Indian Epics

The *Ramayana* (Raa-MAYE-a-na) is a great Indian epic written in the ancient Sanskrit language. It is ascribed to the sage Valmiki and forms an important part of the Hindu canon known as *smriti*.[21] The *Ramayana* consists of twenty-four thousand verses in seven books (some consider it of only six divisions, combining the last two divisions together), known as *kandas*, and five hundred cantos (*sargas*). It tells the story of Rama (an avatar of the Hindu preserver-God

Vishnu) and his wife Sita. Thematically, the *Ramayana* explores human values and the concept of *dharma* (the eternal law of the cosmos, inherent in the very nature of things).

The *Mahabharata* (Ma-haa-BHAAR-a-ta) is another major epic (much larger than the *Ramayana*) written in the ancient Sanskrit language. Traditionally, the authorship of the *Mahabharata* is attributed to Vyasa. The *Mahabharata* in its longest version consists of over one hundred thousand *shloka* or over two hundred thousand individual verse lines (each *shloka* is a couplet), long prose passages, or about 1.8 million words in total. It is one of the longest epic poems in the world. It contains eighteen *parvas* or sections, and each *parva* contains many sub-*parvas* or subsections. The epic tells the story of two sets of paternal first cousins—the five sons of the deceased king Pandu (the Pandavas) and the one hundred sons of blind King Dhritarashtra (the Kauravas)—who become bitter rivals and battle each other in a war at Kurukshetra for the possession of the ancestral Bharata kingdom. Basically, the Mahabharata illustrates the victory of good over evil through the story of the Pandavas, the embodiment of good, who defeats in war the Kauravas, symbolizing all that is evil in human nature.

"Bala Kanda" *Sarga* 8–10,[22] of the *Ramayana*, narrates a story of an unnamed woman who is prepared to sacrifice her life for the welfare of her country. The same story can be found in the *Mahabharata* "Vana Parva."[23]

Although the woman's name is not mentioned in either epic, her story has attracted many writers and artists. Just like the story of Delilah, most of them approach the story from the male hero's point of view. Among these, the Malayalam (the language spoken in the southern state of Kerala, India—my mother tongue) movie *Vaishali*, released in 1988, is significant because the movie narrates the story from the perspective of its female hero. In the film, she also gets an attractive name, "Vaishali," meaning "the prosperous and the rich."

The *Ramayana* and the *Mahabharata* recite the story like this. A long time ago, in the kingdom of Anga, there was a severe drought for several years. Crops withered for want of rain, and animals and humans perished for lack of food and water. All living things were in distress. The king, Romapada, inquired of the local priests the reason and solution for the unprecedented drought. They declared that it occurred because of the disrespect that the king had shown to the *Brahmins* (the priests) earlier in his life. That caused the gods to be angry toward the king and his country. The priests also explained to the king the curse could only be alleviated by a *brahmin* with the powers that come from observance of perfect chastity. They further warned him that until such a person came into the land, there would never be rain in it. The king and his priests found out that only one such person existed in the whole universe. That was the sage Rishyasringa, who lived in a remote forest.

Rishyasringa, who came of divine birth, lived with his father, Vibondaka, who was known for his enormous mental prowess, in a dense forest where there was no other human being. Vibondaka earned immense power through his stringent meditation and severe austerities. If Vibondaka would ever get angry, the whole universe would be burned to ashes. He hardly came out of the forest to mingle with other human beings. Everybody, including the gods in heaven, was afraid of him.

Rishyasringa's father had a specific plan for him. He wanted to raise his son as the most innocent person in the universe and never wanted his son to mingle with any other human being. Rishyasringa had not come across any human being, except his father. Now the problem before the king was to bring Rishyasringa into his country without incurring Vibondaka's wrath. After long discussions with his advisors, he could not come to any solution. Everybody was afraid to take up the mission to bring Rishyasringa to the country because of their fear of Vibondaka. Ultimately, an unnamed courtesan rose to the occasion and said, "If he comes, then the kingdom will be happy. If he doesn't come, only a prostitute will be killed." She declared her willingness to go to the forest to bring him to the country. She was ready to offer herself for the welfare of the country. Everybody was relieved, and she was offered money and property, but she declined payment of any kind.

The unnamed woman went to the forest and spent long days there without Vibondaka's becoming aware of her. Using all her sexual expertise, she played tricks on Rishyasringa, attracted him, and finally brought him to the land of Anga without Vibondaka's knowledge. As the two entered the kingdom, the curse was removed from the country and rain started pouring down. Rishyasringa was given a grand welcome by the king and his people. Everybody rejoiced in the thunder and rain. King Romapada gave his daughter Shanta to Rishyasringa as his wife. They were married and lived long and happily ever after. Rishyasringa later became the ancestor of the dynasty to which the Lord Rama, the great hero of the *Ramayana*, belongs. However, everybody forgot the woman who brought Rishyasringa to the country. The unnamed woman simply disappeared from the scene. The story of Rishyasringa, the dynasty, and the history of the country continued without further mention of the unnamed woman. We do not hear about the bravery and self-sacrifice of this unnamed woman anywhere else in the story.

Just like Delilah the Philistine, the unnamed courtesan of the Indian epics who risked her life for the well-being of her country and people was forgotten for generations. History continues. The self-sacrifice of those mythic female heroes surpasses the cultural barrier. Everywhere, in ancient and modern societies, in Eastern and Western societies, women are treated in a similar way. Society requires the services of such women, but does not want to recognize them and forgets them after they have accomplished their purpose. It is the same in many cultures and in many periods. Delilah, a representative of the numerous forgotten (female) heroes in history, still lives among us. History continues to make heroes and forgotten heroes.

Notes

1. Carol Smith points out that scholars have struggled to categorize the narrative for centuries. For some, it is "legend," for some it is "epic," and for others it is "saga" (Smith 1997: 45). However, it is highly acceptable to see the whole of chapters 13–16 as saga. Since it is beyond the scope of this paper, I am leaving that matter here. Dennis T. Olson points out an interesting discovery: namely, that the writers and editors of the Samson cycle borrowed an extensive number of motifs from earlier Judges narratives and incorporated them into the Samson saga. He lists sixteen significant points of these incidents in the saga. He further points out that these literary echoes suggest that the story's present form was shaped and edited at a late stage of the book's composition, when much of the other material in Judges had already been written and set in place (Olson 1998: 840–42). Olson developed his arguments on the earlier findings by Greenstein (1981: 237–60) and Webb (1987: 162–74).

2. Crenshaw compares this story with the succession narrative of 2 Samuel 9–20 and 1 Kings 1–2, and the Joseph narrative in Genesis 37–50.

3. Exum views ch. 13 as a birth account and does not pay much attention to its place vis-à-vis ch. 16. Her focus is on the thematic symmetry found in chs. 14–15 and ch. 16 (Exum 1981: 3–29).

4. In both cases, the verb's subject is the male figure, and the object is the female character. In both occasions, the hero loves his partner but not vice versa.

5. In the Hebrew Bible, a woman loves a man only in the case of Michal loving David in 1 Samuel 18, and in the Song of Songs. So we must see Delilah's lack of love in context.

6. Yehuda T. Radday provides an interesting article that shows how the ancient Hebrew biblical writers played with the personal and other names of "other" people (Radday 1990: 59–98). According to him, except for the name of Moses' father-in-law, whom the writers of Torah hold in high esteem (Jethro, the name of Moses' father-in-law, is changed to "Reuel" in Exod. 2:18), often the biblical writers change the original name of foreigners to a new and not exactly complimentary one. He concludes that Scripture often uses distorted personal names in order to mock their bearers.

7. S. J. De Vries gives more details on "night" (De Vries 1962: 549). However, there are occasions where one can see that night symbolizes goodness (e.g., night as blessing, Isa. 16:3).

8. Lillian R. Klein gives a detailed study of the region from which Delilah comes (Klein 2003: 24).

9. The scope of this study does not allow me to do a detailed study of the term "judge" as used in the book of Judges.

10. Soggin provides an extensive study of the Nazirite vow (Soggin 1981: 236–37).

11. Niditch brings out the motif of "magic strength resides in hair," found in numerous non-biblical works from all over the world.

12. Margalith compares Judges 13–16 and Numbers 6, where Nazirite vows are set out in detail. He further concludes that it is apparent that the story's narrator did not intend to tell the story of a *nezer* of hair ("crown," "hair," "consecration of hair"), as in Numbers 6.

13. For more details, see http://en.wikipedia.org/wiki/Goonda.

14. Bal finds this incident has similarities with the riddle at Samson's wedding. Her approach to the story is from a perspective of mutual love. However, here love is one-sided, and we do not know what Delilah's attitude toward Samson is. And I could see many other motifs, prominent in the story, other than love. If we tie up the story only with "mutual love," we are consciously diverting its meaning to an entirely different level.

15. Margalith convincingly argues that "riddles" as a literary form are an integral part of the Samson story. The storyteller and his audience, as well as the collector of the biblical stories and the "redactor," must all have been familiar with this literary form (Margalith 1986b: 225–29). It is true that many scholars have struggled to understand the meaning of these riddles, but they all accept that they are primarily riddles (e.g., Bal 1987b: 45 and Soggin 1981b: 243). On the other hand, some scholars claim that these are not riddles at all (e.g., Schneider 2000: 208). Schneider argues that Samson's riddle is not actually a riddle since it is based on his personal experience and cannot be solved by anyone who was not in the vineyard with him when he encountered the lion, since a riddle is a puzzling question stated as a problem to be solved by clever ingenuity. However, it is hard to accept her argument since the form and function are very much similar to that of a riddle. Here I would stand with the majority opinion.

16. Claudia Camp has an extensive study on the subject "Samson as a Riddler" (Camp 2000: 95–143). She interestingly connects the whole issue to the wisdom tradition and tries to offer a "wisdom reading" of the Samson narrative. Finally, she concludes that the narrative is either by a group of scribes outside the temple elite, commenting on their more powerful peers, or by an upstart (younger?) group of temple scribes resisting the politics of their elders.

17. In this short essay, Margalith questions the historicity of Samson's use of foxes, as in Judges 15. He also dismisses the idea that it can be considered a local version of a widely known theme. He points out that the prolonged period of domination by a people of Aegean origin that undoubtedly brought with them not only their pottery but also legends, traditions, and language of their origin in the Mycenaean-Minoan world would result in the fusing of the Canaanite aetiological legends about jackals with legends about foxes.

18. It could most probably mean "cutting" not "shaving" or "snipping," because it is not easy to "shave" or "snip" without the knowledge of the person who is the object of the action.

19. Since the verb קרא, *q-r-ʾ* Qal means "to call, utter a sound"; but some modification is required for determining how the sound produced functions.

20. For Brettler, there is no coherence in the Samson saga. It is a combination of different types of material that come together for a variety of reasons.

21. See http://en.wikipedia.org/wiki/Ramayana.

22. The *Ramayana* is divided into seven *kandas* ("divisions"). The list is: (1) Bala Kanda—Book of the Childhood; (2) Ayodhya Kanda—Book of Ayodhya; (3) Aranya Kanda—Book of the Forest; (4) Kishkindha Kanda—Book of Kishkindha; (5) Sundara Kanda—Book of Auspiciousness; (6) Yuddha Kanda—Book of the War; and (7) Uttara Kanda—Book of the North.

23. The divisions (*parvas*) of the *Mahabharata* are: (1) Adi Parva (The Book of the Beginning); (2) Sabha Parva (The Book of the Assembly Hall); (3) Vana Parva, also Aranyaka-parva, Aranya-parva (The Book of the Forest); (4) Virata Parva (The Book of Virata); (5) Udyoga Parva (The Book of the Effort); (6) Bhishma Parva (The Book of Bhishma); (7) Drona Parva (The Book of Drona); (8) Karna Parva (The Book of Karna); (9) Shalya Parva (The Book of Shalya); (10) Sauptika Parva (The Book of the Sleeping Warriors); (11) Stri Parva (The Book of the Women); (12) Shanti Parva (The Book of Peace); (13) Anushasana Parva (The Book of the Instructions); (14) Ashvamedhika Parva (The Book of the Horse Sacrifice); (15) Ashramavasika Parva (The Book of the Hermitage); (16) Mausala Parva (The Book of the Clubs);

(17) Mahaprasthanika Parva (The Book of the Great Journey); (18) Svargarohana Parva (The Book of the Ascent to Heaven); and an additional section: *Khila-Harivamsa Parva* (The Book of the Genealogy of Krishna, which is not covered in the eighteen *parvas* of the *Mahabharata*).

14

Narrative Loss, the (Important) Role of Women, and Community in Judges 19

Brad Embry

READER-ORIENTED CONTEXT

This essay reflects research that began with a very different end in mind. Initially, I began research on Judges 19 with the intention of sorting out how the story functioned in the subsection of Judges 17–21, how that subsection fit within the wider narrative of the book of Judges, and how the author used the female figure to deliver the story. As the story began to occupy more and more of my thoughts and owing to the difficulty of the story due to its graphic nature and highly problematic characters, I began to reflect on how this story might be received or understood in my specific religious context. As a result, I began to look for the treatment or reference to this story outside my own, academic pursuits.

Currently, I teach at a Christian liberal arts University associated with a Pentecostal-Holiness tradition from North America, the Assemblies of God (AG). My research work unfolds in this context, and so as I was saturating my time with Judges and Judges 19, I was also participating in the religious life of this tradition, the worldview of which is oriented by two primary features. One is the ongoing work of the Holy Spirit in the life of the community. For the AG, the Holy Spirit is an active presence in shaping and guiding a person's life, from aiding in understanding Scripture to helping determine daily, life decisions. The idea is that the community of God (i.e., the AG church community) is led by the Holy Spirit into a deeper relationship with God, and directed in its daily, weekly, and yearly life as to the appropriate actions to undertake to ensure that they are doing God's will. The guidance of the Holy Spirit also extends to an understanding of the biblical narrative and thus to the preaching of the "Word." The second feature of this tradition is that the biblical text (Protestant tradition) is inspired by God, many would say inerrant, and contains the essential "narrative" for how one is to live one's life. Thus it is the "sourcebook" for determining the nature of God, humans, and the interaction between these two characters. Most critically, all of this narrative is true. More specifically, the narrative in its entirety is true. Alongside vocal worship, preaching of that "Word" is the primary expression within a church gathering.

As I continued my research, I was increasingly aware of the importance of Judges 19 for the unfolding narrative of the book of Judges, and that the book of Judges was an important part in the unfolding narrative of the Israelite community. At the same time, as I participated in the life of this faith tradition I was equally impressed by how *unimportant* Judges 19 (and Judges for that matter) was, in practice, to the weekly expression of faith in this community. I realized that, in my five years with this institution and the AG, I had never heard a sermon preached on Judges 19, or a small-group discussion of it, or even had a conversation with a pastor in which this story was part of his thought world.[1] Aside from a few idiomatic comments, the story of Judges 19 simply did not register in the religious conscience of this tradition. Given this tradition's stated understanding of the biblical text as both a central authority and unified whole, this struck me as curious.

As a result, as my research continued to suggest the importance of Judges 19, I began to think about the role played by the story not only in Judges but also in the contemporary community of faith that relied heavily on the biblical narrative to set the parameters for its communal identity. What did a community look like that on the one hand affirmed the canonical authority of Judges as a binding religious document, but on the other hand ceased to integrate this material into its religious consciousness? This dissonance is enhanced by virtue of the fact that the story of Judges 19 is specifically intended for the covenantal community, and so its effacement may be symptomatic of a more deeply seated and communally subconscious impression of the narrative. I realized that I was in a context that was gradually "unreading" the narrative owing to some impulse that finds portions of the narrative either too distasteful, or lacks the wherewithal to integrate these portions into its confessional and practical life. The community creates (is creating) a "canon within a canon," a practical canon set within a theoretical canon.[2]

My research soon became far more interested in the implications behind a potential loss of Judges 19 within my immediate communal framework. What would the narrative of Judges look like without Judges 19? What would a biblical narrative look like without this story? More importantly, what would a community that oriented itself around the biblical narrative (including the Hebrew Bible) look like without Judges 19? I found that I was soon answering the question of my initial research (What does Judges 19 mean for the narrative?) not by simply looking at the biblical text, but by assessing what effect this story could have on a contemporary community. Since one of my interests in Judges 19 had been the role of the female figure in the biblical narrative, I also began to think of the effects of eliding a story such as Judges 19 from the narrative on how modern communities assessed themselves with regard to the female figure. I discovered that an assessment of the part played by Judges 19 within the wider narrative of the book of Judges required an assessment of the role played by the female figure in Judges 19: that is, the role of the female figure in Judges 19 and the role played by Judges 19 in the narrative were interconnected.

Judges 19: Setting Its Context

The books of Joshua and Judges, covering the pre-monarchical period in Israel's investment of the land of Canaan, are shot through with violence. In Joshua there are scenes of conquest and battlefield slaughter; scenes of reflexive violence such as is enacted against Achan; and violent talk and posturing, such as is found in the threats against the Transjordan tribes at the end of the book (Josh. 22:10-34). In Judges the violence is every bit as apparent, but begins to take to itself the idiosyncrasies of the narrative of the book. Initially, violence is directed toward Israel in response to communal sin and idolatry. Thus violence in Judges still manifests itself along the lines of Joshua's internal (Israel) and external (other nations) categories. But Judges reverses the victor/vanquished characters from Joshua; in Judges, other nations conquer and oppress the Israelites. In this way, the violence of Judges represents an inversion of the Joshua narratives, a reversal of that conquest motif.

In narrating the violence-conquest theme from Joshua, Judges introduces a further evolution by shifting the violence from an internal-external (Israel-other nations) to an internal-internal (Israel-Israel) dynamic. Examples of this shift in Judges occur in scenes such as the story of Gideon's son Abimelech. There, the violence and discord is set entirely within the extended family or clan unit; "Remember," Abimelech states in Judg. 9:2, "also that I am your bone and your flesh." The typical source and nature of the struggle in Judges begins to show signs of deterioration, no longer circumscribed by internal (Israel) and external (other nations) categories, but rather by strife and discord that is altogether internal (Israelite). In this way, Abimelech's so-called conspiracy is a departure from the standard cyclical formulation of violence in Judges 3–16; it is no longer simply a question of communal idolatry, sin, and the response to these problems, but now concerns Abimelech's claim to a monarchy and the reaction that this generates. It also foreshadows things to come, laying bare the social fractures that lie close to the surface in Israel and the struggles that the nation might face with the rise of a monarchy. But, in the case of Abimelech, the violence is tightly controlled and restricted to Abimelech and his family unit; Abimelech alone, and his overture to kingship, is the source of the problems in Judges 9.[3]

When this form of inward violence is set alongside the fractious and disintegrated social narrative of the book of Judges, the combination leads inevitably to civil war and the near annihilation of the tribe of Benjamin. Part of the conclusion, therefore, to Joshua, the threat of civil war in Josh. 22:10-34, is actuated in the book of Judges in Judges 20–21 (Niditch 1982: 374–75).[4] Undoubtedly, the clarion call of Joshua—be obedient to the law of Moses—is precisely the problem in the book of Judges. As such, Judges narrates the deterioration of the covenantal society into an individualistic, self-centered community, which is ultimately self-destructive. It is precisely the opposite of Joshua's narrative, in which unity in purpose and covenantal fidelity is maintained and which is given its clearest witness in the fate of Achan for disobeying the commandment prohibiting personal plunder from Jericho. Achan's decision to keep plunder for himself (a personal decision) results in Israel's defeat at Ai (a corporate consequence). The social critique of Joshua is, on one level, an argument against individuality at the expense of the community.

But, this motif of individual-community interaction and tension is expressed in another way in Judges, which is part of the function of Judges 19: when society has fractured along the fault lines of individuality at the expense of the community (e.g., Abimelech's example or the refrain in Judges 17–21 that "everyone did what was right in their own eyes"), the community becomes a place incapable of protecting the individual. The deterioration of society results in the endangerment of the individual. The priest, the concubine, and the old man are endangered not by the actions of one individual but by a mass of "worthless fellows" from Gibeah (Judg. 19:22). So that there is no mistaking the communal problems at this point in Judges, Judg. 20:13-14 points out that the tribe of Benjamin refused to give these worthless fellows over for punishment, which in turn leads to civil war. Thus the failure to create and enforce a society in which the individual is protected (the concubine) results in the near destruction of that society. It is precisely in the protection of proper communal identity and unity that the means for the adequate protection of the individual rests.

Of course, it is the smaller, individual stories that make up this broader narrative. The social deterioration comes at the work or expense of certain characters, such as Abimelech and the Levite. The story of the Levite's concubine is one story. Its graphic nature and difficult subject matter make it standout in the book and difficult to assess. It is not uncommon to read in modern commentaries that the rape and dismemberment of the woman is a *result* of the prevailing social atmosphere of discord in Israel during this period. But the narrative, in my view, does not suggest this. Rather, Judges 19 addresses the deterioration of the Israelite society, the seemingly inexorable movement towards self-annihilation, by *embodying* it. That is, Judges 19 is not simply a result of the social deterioration, but becomes a typology of the society.[5] In a way, the concubine's fate is potentially the fate of the nation; her dismemberment is the community's dismemberment; her rape-murder is their rape-murder; her death at the hands of the wicked is their death at the hands of the wicked. That is, the story of Judges 19 does not *occur* in this context; it defines the context in scope, nature, and detail (Schneider 2000: 245).[6] The story and the concubine are therefore critical to the narrative of Judges.

The Essential Female in the Story:
Both Feet in Sodom? Or, Someone Finally Gets Rape-Murdered

It might seem curious to suggest that the rape and dismemberment of a silent, unnamed concubine is evidence of the *important* role played by women in the biblical story. It seems far more likely that this is yet another case, different in form but similar in kind, of the marginalization of the female figure in the biblical narrative as a commodity to be manipulated.[7] Recent efforts at assessing the role of women in the biblical narratives, including Judges 19, tend to find voice primarily from feminist readings.[8] One of the great values of the feminist critique is that it can make the suggestion that traditional, male-dominated readings of certain portions of the biblical text are not only distasteful from a modern perspective but may actually be a *misreading* of a text.[9]

The story of Judges 19 has been plumbed deeply and widely. Much modern, critically oriented readings have been put to it, all of which have produced interesting and compelling readings of the text.[10] Older commentaries as well as more recent ones have also closely examined the nuances of the Hebrew text.[11]

In the introduction to the book of Judges in the *New Oxford Annotated Bible*, K. Lawson Younger suggests that, in addition to the gradual fracturing of a general Judge-cycle pattern as the narrative unfolds, the "moral decline [of Israel] can also be seen in the characterization of the women of the book" (Younger 2007: 354). This is an important step toward understanding the specific scene of Judges 19, as it marks a departure from the older approaches in which the female figure was either wholly subsumed into the running narrative of the approaching civil war in Judges 20–21, or became a victim once more of a modern effort to moralize the story (i.e., she did something wrong). But Younger's comment also commends a reevaluation of simplistic statements that this was a "man's world" (Steinberg 1984: 185).[12] Furthermore, Younger's comment also argues against the notion that the ancient audience was less scandalized by this story than is a modern audience.[13] In fact, attempts to "explain" the story witness to the scandal it created. Interpretation, because it is by its very nature contextualized to the individual or the individual's particular setting, is not always a matter of simply understanding the text; it is also a case of trying to make sense of something. To be sure, the handling of inter-gender issues is different then and now, but the assumption that this story would have fallen on unperturbed ears due to a less favorable impression of women makes no sense. The Levite's prosaic response to the concubine the morning seems out of sorts as a response because it is out of sorts as a response. The whole idea of Judges 19 is that it is an abomination: the audience, both ancient and modern, would be mortified by what occurred. No reading, ancient or modern, should miss the simple fact that what happens to the concubine is an utter abomination.

One feature that appears in commentaries is the literary connection shared by Judges 19 and Genesis 19, the story of Sodom and Gomorrah. This connection has been thoroughly examined by both ancient and modern commentators. But there is a feature of this comparison that has not, as far as I can tell, been brought to bear on what the author may have been suggesting in Judges 19. It is a connection that makes the communal criticism of Judges 19 all the more potent and its non-reading all the more significant. It is actually a key *difference* between the two stories, and occurs in Gen. 19:9-10 and Judg. 19:25, just at the point in both narratives in which the mob is about to assert itself. In Gen. 19:9-10, Lot has already made the offer of his two daughters to the crowd and has now gone out to confront the crowd with this offer. The crowd is not satisfied, and begins to "press hard" against Lot. This is not with the intention of harming Lot principally, but rather with the intention of breaking down the door to get after their real object—the angelic visitors. But the angels then intervene, and the situation is resolved to no one's harm but the Sodomites.

In Judg. 19:23 we are told that the old man too has gone out to confront the Benjaminites. He too has offered two women, his virgin daughter and the concubine, to the crowd.[14] At this point in both stories, those left behind in the house are the two women and the visitors. And here is the parting of the two narratives: instead of reaching out to rescue the old man and preserve the people in the house, the Levite, in direct opposition to his narrative counterparts in Genesis 19 (the messengers), does not intervene. It has been noted by a number of commentators that there is no angelic figure in Judges 19 to rescue anyone. But this is perhaps not entirely the case. Could not the priest function as a surrogate for the angelic messengers? He is, like the angels from Genesis 19, the target of the mob and is on his way to the "house of God" (Judg. 19:18). Moreover, the priesthood in Israel was to be representative of God's presence on earth, which is a role occupied elsewhere by angelic figures ("angel of the Lord," cf., e.g., Exod. 3:5). It is at this point that the two narratives close, forming a unified reading, and we learn just how precarious the situation was for Lot's daughters. What if they had been sharing living space with a sojourning Levite instead of the angels?

The failure at Sodom, Lot's failure, which is never enacted owing to the intervention of the angelic messengers, is that the females in the story are offered to the licentious mob. But the daughters are rescued by the messengers who, in protecting themselves (and Lot), protect the daughters as well. The angelic intervention allows for a "reasonable" resolution to a precarious and potentially disastrous situation. That is, it takes a miracle to rehabilitate the situation so that no one but those who deserve it is harmed. In Judges 19, there is no such rescue; the female figure is not protected. Instead, in Judges 19, the Levite is "protected" by the concubine's suffering and death. Judges 19 departs from Genesis 19 in this one way. The resultant civil war could be viewed as the destruction sequence of Sodom and Gomorrah.[15]

The attention here to the priesthood only enhances Judges' criticism of Israelite society; the very figures who were charged with the well-being of Israelite society, to educate and lead Israel according to the principles of the Mosaic law (e.g. Lev. 10:11) and fidelity to their worship of Yahweh, have here failed to uphold this society, one in which the concubine should have reasonably expected safety and protection. The author of Judges seems to stop short of making the Levite responsible for pushing his concubine outside, as the antecedent in Judg. 19:25 could be the old man.[16] Regardless, the priest is either guilty of pushing the concubine out or failing to protect her. This is a damning criticism of the priesthood, and we can see in the voiceless and nameless a fate foisted on them by the leadership that has lost its orientation. Given Judges' pronounced slant toward the monarchy and Judean ascendency, this criticism of the Levitical priesthood might have been a way to discredit their leadership and to subordinate them to the Davidides. The Levites' sojourning,[17] their idolatrous activity, and the partial truth told by the Levite in Judges 20 all stand as condemnation of this leadership. Most commentaries do not make much of this criticism of the priesthood, but there is a narrative feature of Joshua–Judges that suggests that the priesthood is a topic of central concern for Judges. This narrative feature occurs in two places, Joshua 24:29 and 33 and then in Judg. 20:28.

Joshua 24:29 records the death of Joshua: "After these things Joshua the son of Nun, the servant of the Lord, died, being 110 years old" (NRSV). Joshua 24 then records the death of Eleazar, the high priest. Joshua has been criticized by certain scholars for not having had the foresight to appoint an heir to take over leadership of the community upon his death, which is cited as one of the key problems in Judges. But notice in the case of Eleazar, Phinehas his son continues in the priesthood. While Joshua's leadership ends with his death, the priesthood continues in verse 33: "And Eleazar the son of Aaron died, and they buried him at Gibeah, the town of Phinehas his son, which had been given him in the hill country of Ephraim" (NRSV) When Joshua's death is reiterated in Judg. 2:8, it ought also to alert us to the continuation of the priesthood in Israel as well, even though the author does not reiterate Phinehas's role. That role is subtly driven home later in Judg. 20:28: "And Phinehas son of Eleazar, son of Aaron, ministered before it in those days, saying, 'Shall we go out once more to battle against our kinsfolk the Benjaminites, or shall we desist?' The Lord answered, 'Go up, for tomorrow I will give them into your hand'" (NRSV). Here again is Phinehas. The book certainly does not expect the reader to believe that this character has lived the entire period of the Judges! Rather, the narrator might here be suggesting to the reader that the priesthood, in view in this last subsection of Judges, was also operative in the body of the book and during the period of the Judges themselves. This provides a priestly "framework" for Judges (which originates at the end of Joshua).

Interest in the priesthood appears to be in view in Judges, so that in viewing the problems in Israel during the period of the Judges, one is viewing the problems of the priesthood. Of course, this is a primary feature of 1 Samuel 1–7 and the context of the last of Judges in the figure of Samuel. There, the main problem in Israel during this period is the house of Eli, the high priest, and in particular his two sons.

Often scholars will suggest that the problem in Israel at this time is with the leadership. But what leadership is being criticized? The book is not solely concerned with the leadership of the Judges, though the progression of the narrative of Judges 3–16 does suggest a slow decline in their relative effectiveness and ability. Rather, the narrative also appears to criticize the priesthood as ineffective in modeling the communal identity installed through the law of Moses. The narrative position of Phinehas in Joshua 24 and Judges 20 reveals one of the important principles of the priesthood, which distinguishes their leadership from that of the Judges, namely, that the priesthood is an inherited office and, as such, transcends generational boundaries. This is not a feature for the judgeship (as Gideon and Abimelech illustrate). Generational instability is a major issue for Judges 3–16, and so the implicit critique is that, when the priesthood has failed, a Judge, who is restricted to his or her generation, must be raised up to re-stabilize the society.

And yet, as fractured as the society might be during the operation of the Judges in chapters 3–16, only the concubine's story illustrates the societal depravity adequately. The cycles of the Judges do not created enough gravity and force to move Israel out of their societal malaise. Even the wandering and idolatrous priests of Judges 17–18 do not. It is only when the concubine suffers as she does that the community is suddenly awakened to the depth of its corruption, something that was introduced to the reader in Judges 1 and 2. In the hands of this author, therefore, the story of the Levite's concubine becomes the means by which the societal decay is revealed most clearly.

What has become more or less clear to the modern critical scholar is that Judges 19 is a finely crafted piece of literature and that it is critical to the ongoing narrative movement from Judges to 1 Samuel, from the period of loosely unified tribal groups to the centralized authority of the monarchy. The story is able to characterize the entire narrative of the book of Judges in a summative way, as well as offer a binding commentary on the status of non-monarchical or pre-monarchical Israelite society, *only* through the inclusion of the female figure in the narrative. This is not to suggest that the female is the original target of the wicked Gibeahites,[18] but rather that, in order for the story to have its intended effect of driving the Israelite narrative toward the monarchy, a rape-murder had to occur.

But Judges 19 must also fulfill certain requirements as demanded by its intertextual coordinate, Genesis 19. One requirement is that there must be a female figure in the story. The narrative connections to Genesis 19 demand it. The person assaulted in Judges 19 *must* be a female and not a male.[19] That is, the female figure is essential to the narrative, as the argumentation relies on precise connections between the two accounts. The point of separation between Genesis 19 and Judges 19 is that in Judges, someone actually gets rape-murdered. Another requirement is location. The priest is clear that he wishes to stay in a town occupied by Israel (Judg. 19:12). This horrific scene occurs in Israel, the community of God. The comment that there is no divine intermediary in Judges 19 to help the concubine is correct, but only in part (e.g., Schneider 2000: 245). There is, ideologically, an intermediary, also sent by God, in place in Judges 19—the priest. But from whom will he protect the concubine (and himself)? His own community is the answer. As an extension of the cultic authority, the ideological undergirding for which is a representation of the place wherein God is "enthroned," the priesthood becomes a tangible reminder of the sovereignty of God (Harris, Brown, and Moore 1998: 270). In this way, the fate of the female figure becomes a way of illustrating the community's rejection of the sovereignty of God.[20]

This reading of the story rehabilitates the role of the female figure narratologically, but also affects how we understand the ideal community as envisioned by the biblical narrative. If the story lays bare the corruption of Israelite society, it does so through the fate of the concubine. This suggests the importance of the female figure as a narrative fixture, but also underscores the societal perspective, which, ideally, accords equal protection to the female figures as to the male figures. Even if gender roles were more defined and static in the ancient world, the ideal vision of Israelite society was one in which the female figure was accorded the same level of protection and inclusion as was the male figure. Far from reflecting a stereotypical commodification of the female figure, Judges 19 suggests that her fate provides the only critique powerful enough to arrest Israel and awaken the community to its state of depravity and disorientation. Israel, in Judges 19, is worse off than Sodom and Gomorrah.

To be clear, this does nothing to rehabilitate the story; the villains are not made less opprobrious, nor the Levite or old man less culpable, nor the concubine less a victim. The specific thrust is to suggest that, at certain, key places in the narrative of the Hebrew Bible, only a female figure works to drive the narrative forward, and, as a result, females are essential to the formation and development of the narrative. A rape-murdered male would not work in Judges 19.[21] Far from making a case for the relegation of women to an inferior status, the narrative dimensions of the story suggest that a high valuation is placed on the female role. It should be stressed that reading something in a literary way does not make it any less real. Narrative often works by virtue of the collection of smaller, individualistic stories and events that are employed as waypoints in a larger developing story. Gender distinctions therefore function as essential characteristics in the narrative formation, which is advanced by virtue of the male/female, and not simply male, figure.[22] Of some note is that the story of Genesis 19, which does not concern the community of God, narrates a destruction of the husband/wife unit as well (Lot's wife turned into a pillar of salt—Gen. 19:26). As the story of Lot and his daughters continues, it adds the element of incest, which may be part of a wider commentary and ongoing engagement with the effects of the Fall (Embry 2011: 417–33).

THE POTENTIAL EFFECTS OF EFFACING THIS STORY FOR A CONTEMPORARY, COVENANTAL COMMUNITY

Given this scene's importance for the book of Judges and the biblical narrative, what are the implications for *not* reading it? There are three implications to the "unreading" of this story, which, from the perspective of this paper, has occurred (is occurring) in a specific religious context (AG). But the implications could apply to any tradition that does not include this story or other segments of the narrative as part of its yearly textual identity.

First, the biblical narrative, which forms an essential foundation on which this tradition is built, is not the narrative of the biblical text; it is the narrative governed by the needs of the community that determines which texts are to be selected. These needs tend to be determined by the social and cultural context of the community. Thus the narrative does not determine the identity of the community; it is mined to supply a religious (divine) character to communal identity. To be sure, this is not altogether a problem; part of being a reader of the narrative is the simple fact that one is a *conditioned* reader. But the narrative also articulates a culture of its own, and is not simply a respondent to one's culture. In this case, the question is no longer, What might the narrative be suggesting to us regarding human behavior or the community of God? But, rather, What is important to this community? The problem is that no one in the tradition would deny the canonical place of Judges 19 within their tradition. Rather, the omission is one of practice, and so the community has ceased to function honestly with regard to its ideological orientation to the narrative. Another way of putting this is that there is no longer a biblical narrative; it has been replaced by a communally derived biblical narrative.

This is axiomatic of a postmodern (largely Western) religious context. In this context, the struggle is to find a point of orientation for each individual rather than to suggest that nothing is oriented but the individual.[23] And so, many modern readings are oriented around a group dynamic—liberation, feminist, homosexual, Marxist, environmental, and so on. This is different from the traditional reading of Scripture in, for instance, the historical-grammatical method, which exerted a communal power over the text, but not through preexisting communal structures. It was an artificial community; humans are not "historical-grammatical." Humans are poor or sympathetic to the poor (liberation), female or sympathetic to the female (feminist), politically motivated (Marxist, free market), and so on, who might read "historical-grammatically." Communal concerns are much more dominant in hermeneutical orientation than are methodological procedures and approaches to the text. Part of the problem of the past was to place a priority on the method and relegate the practitioner to a secondary status. The modern reaction is to prioritize the situation of the practitioner in interpretation.

But, a disabled narrative—that is, one in which the entire narrative is no longer functioning—does no one any good. Neither a dominant reading (e.g., historical-critical) nor an alternative reading (e.g., feminist) can engage with something that no longer exists for the community. Incidentally, it is often the case that the problematic portions of the narrative that fall into stasis for dominant readings or mainline communities are often the first texts reengaged by the alternative readings. This is natural because it seeks to "reawaken" the dominant tradition, which for alternative readers has lost its orientation. But selectivity of this variety runs the risk itself of alienating the practitioner of its reading, or the committed person of faith, from the narrative; it might elide other elements for the sake of its own ideological orientation and thus does not guarantee the reader a more central status in its interpretation. It rather makes the text "secondary" and disposable, which ironically can weaken oriented readings. Worse rather, it risks making the text a tool of propaganda, sloganeering, and abuse.[24]

This debilitation can lead to a second, and I think potentially more catastrophic, result. By disabling the narrative and disengaging from it, the community of faith eliminates an important method of reflection on its own potential and capacity for evil. In Judges, individuality is consistently defined in relationship to the community. The Judges respond to communal needs and then pass away with their generation. So, even while the individual characters are idiosyncratic, there is a certain sense of interchangeability to them. The interplay between the communal concerns and the individual characters in Judges (the individual-community dynamic) is one of the brilliant literary mechanisms on display in Judges, and is the backbone for the frustrating, cyclical spiral and gradual deterioration in the book. It has long been noted that the Judge cycle is not operative in Judges 17–21, which illustrates a breakdown of this dynamic. Judges 19 is the climax to this breakdown, but furthers the deterioration by narrating the death of the individual at the hands of the community; it is an anti-Judge narrative. Societal decay as illustrated in Judges leads to the eradication of the individual. Thus Judges 19 is a story of the possibility that the community of God could deteriorate, largely unbeknownst to itself, to the point that the individual is no longer safe in its borders (cf. Judg. 19:30). The story is an essential reminder to the community of its capacity for evil. Can a contemporary community understand its potential adequately without this story?

Finally, by omitting this text routinely, systematically, and categorically, a community of faith, while in principle recognizing this text as part of a canon to which they ascribe, is in fact creating a de facto canon that is shaped by their own sociocultural (religious?) needs and dimensions, a "canon within a canon." It is here that the disenfranchised voices of interpretation stand to teach mainline readings a thing or two about the narrative by emphasizing places in the narrative that provoke tension. In doing this, they are often reminding the wider community of other portions of the biblical narrative that are difficult, problematic, and often liturgically forgotten.

It is alarming that the elided story narrates the abuse of the female figure, and argues clearly that this is a problem. It should be added that many modern Christian traditions do incorporate women into the active ministry (AG included). But I fear that this is in response to modern notions of the rights of women rather than reliance on the biblical text. This may reflect the struggle that some contemporary Christian communities have with what has historically been taught to them regarding women in the narrative (unimportant, subservient, problem causers) and contemporary sentiments regarding the role of women in society (as equals to men). The idea sometimes communicated is that the modern, secular world has "corrected" the archaic backwardness and misogyny of the biblical narrative and, by default, the traditions that rely almost exclusively on it for their communal identity. This creates tension for many communities of faith by ostensibly introducing a choice between their loyalties to the biblical narrative or association with secularism, which can often convey criticism of the faith traditions as small-minded. This does not help faith communities to engage with the narrative in honest ways, insofar as finding themselves in agreement with the secular community oftentimes is tantamount to being on the wrong hermeneutical track. The suggestion here is not only that one should take a more positive view of the role of women in the biblical narrative as of central and irreducible importance, but also that this is the correct view. That is, the positive valuation of the female figure occurs at the level of the biblical narrative, at the level of the stories themselves. The narrative supports the modern evaluation of the female figure not merely as an equal to the male figure in the ongoing narrative of the community of faith, but as essential and irreducible to the community's functions and identity.[25] Put another way, sometimes only a female figure will do in the narrative. Women should not be marginalized, but rather be accorded the same protection provided to the male figures. In fact, when they are abused, this abuse becomes a signal of the abominable state of affairs of society. This is part of the lesson of Judges 19, and its elision from a contemporary community's ideological orientation is worrisome.

Judges 19 therefore functions as a warning that this type of behavior is possible within the covenantal community. Notably, it is one of only two stories that illustrate this potential in such a graphic, direct, and concrete way. The other is the rape of Tamar, which is more isolated in its application to the house of David (2 Samuel 13).[26] While the prophets often mention sociological problems such as bloodshed and injustice, these become categories rather than concrete examples. The danger is that they are abstractions, and Judges 19 allows for no abstraction.

Judges 19, contrary to the opinion of a number of commentators, is not the result of a lack of leadership, adjudicators, and stabilizing forces in the community. To be sure, the judges address corrupt and failed leadership, but this is an abdication of the role of leadership, rather than a wholesale loss of it. What the nameless concubine continues to commend to us is the possibility that a seemingly stable community might become inured to the decay of its society—its just laws and moral parameters must extend to all members of the community. This social reality is governed by the presence of Yahweh in the midst of the community, not only binding together the community but also prescribing the just society and the application of care and concern for everyone in its borders. The irony, and I believe gravity, of this commentary in Judges 19 is that the story occurs precisely in the midst of the conquest and occupation narratives, wherein we have already had stories of the acceptance and provision for non-Israelite characters (such as Rahab and the Gibeonites).

The fact that Yahweh does not speak in Judges 19, or otherwise intervene, and that addresses from Yahweh are relatively rare in the book by comparison to the Pentateuch, is of no real surprise. In Judges, the reality on the ground is that Israel, as the community of God, is now to be governed by the cult, wherein the sovereignty of God is manifest by virtue of the ark of the covenant and, ideally, through the work of the priests. Moreover, as Leviticus 10 makes clear, it is the duty of the priests to educate and guide the people (Lev. 10:11). The question of sovereignty in the book of Judges, with the phrase "no king in Israel" appearing at the end of the book, is not simply a positive nod to the monarchy to come; it is also a criticism of Israelite society that should have been operating under the notion of a king as indicated by the symbolism of the tabernacle. The fact that the story in Judges 19 is enacted by a Levite only enhances this feature.

When a contemporary community of faith effaces memories such as these from its yearly lectionary, it loses a narrative dialogue partner that reminds it of its potential. A covenantal community is only as strong as its ability to reflect on its potential, and Judges 19 makes it clear that one potential for the community of God (= Israel) is the perpetration of a horrific crime. The story of Judges 19 is not exclusively about hospitality or social categories for women, but rather about the potential for the community of God to foster and perpetrate this type of abomination. But this commentary on the community is made possible through the individuation of the narrative, by the typology of individual experience as a reflection on the community, the rape-murder of the concubine. When a community loses, or forces out, this possibility through effacing this story in practice, either intentionally or unintentionally, does it run the risk of finding itself in Gibeah of Benjamin, hearing knocking on the door or, worse yet, knocking on the door itself?

Notes

1. The Assemblies of God is predominately male at the ministerial level and all of my exposure to sermons, small groups, or discussions were with male pastors.

2. Notice that the new "canon" is smaller than the real canon; it is more restrictive. It could be that traditions that become more restrictive of their canonical narratives do so by replacing some of the narrative pieces with other regulations that develop out of a cultural or social milieu of the tradition. For instance, AG forbids the consumption of alcohol, which has historically been related to issues of holiness. In this way, holiness and alcohol consumption are mutually exclusive. Of course, there is no biblical regulation prohibiting the consumption of alcohol, much less a tradition that brings the two together. But the tradition has developed a strong sense of this prohibition as being divinely mandated.

3. His father, Gideon, does not share his interest in the monarchy (cf. Judg. 8:22-23).

4. Niditch notes this connection, but does not emphasis the effect that it might have on the unfolding narrative in Judges.

5. Both Niditch (1982: 371) and Lasine (1984: 37–38) suggest as much, though this does not form the central thrust of their work. For Schneider (2000: 245), this event is central to the whole of the book, explaining what has happened previously and what will happen subsequently.

6. This does not make of the story an analogue. But in the hands of its author, the story is something of a parable, the literary form of which is not uncommon to Judges; e.g., Judges 9 and the parable of the trees in the story of Abimelech.

7. Perhaps along the lines enumerated by Exum (1989: 19–39).

8. Though not always; cf. Levenson 1978: 230–34. Unfortunately, feminist readings of the biblical texts face potential marginalization themselves on two fronts. On the one hand, the reaction against feminism tends to critique the approach as a symptom of postmodernity and therefore lacking a sense of objectivity allegedly intrinsic in the older approaches. On the other hand, feminism can sometimes become mired in its own dogmatism. Its reaction to an androcentric or male-dominated reading of the text occasionally begins as a reaction to the

impalpability of the traditional readings in a modern age, rather than with the possibility that traditional readings are *misreadings*. Put another way, the approach assumes that the text has *legitimately* engendered a male-dominated reading because this has been the state of affairs in scholarship and society.

9. Jewett (1975: 15, 179–85) makes the important observation that some conclusions reached in regard to the male/female thread in the biblical narrative have wrongly placed emphasis on the female aspect of reality. So, Mary is the perfect personification of obedience. The *imago Dei* is a combination, only, of the male/female. Where Jewett overdoes his retraction is in failing to emphasize the narrative role played by female characters in places where a certain mode or type of behavior is modeled. For instance, could Mary's role of modeling perfect obedience have been fulfilled by a *male* character? The birth narrative, by necessity, must focus on the female to some degree. The same principle, with different criteria, may be found in the role played by two of the wives of the patriarchs: Sarah and Rebekah. Without these female figures, the narrative simply does not work, as Isaac is specifically from the Abraham-Sarah, and not just Abraham (or Ishmael would suffice), and the revelation of who will serve whom between Jacob-Esau is given to Rebekah and not Isaac, whom we are told unequivocally is satisfied with Esau. Put another way, there are places in the narrative where only a woman's presence will suffice.

10. A few examples of the range of applied, modern, critical theories, apart from commentaries, are as follows: feminist, e.g., Trible 1984; Keefe 1993: 79–97; Reis 2006:125–46, Bach 1998: 1–19; Bohmbach 1999: 83–98; queer/homosexual, either in orientation, e.g., Cheng 2002: 119–33 or examination, e.g., Stone 1995: 87–107; literary-critical, Hudson 1994: 49–66; structural or form analysis, Chisholm 2009: 171–82; Gillmayr-Bucher 2009: 687–702; Frolov 2009: 24–41; or other alternative lifestyle orientations, e.g., Ng 2007: 199–215. It should also be noted that most of the feminist readings also strongly emphasize a literary-critical method, which Frolov (2009: 24–27) rightly notes is the dominant contemporary approach to the book. This represents a departure from Noth's original (1943) and received (60s, 70s, early 80s) evaluation of the literary quality of Judges within the D-history—namely, that it had little if any independent literary value.

11. For example, Burney 1970; Boling 1975; or Schneider 2000.

12. This stems from both non-feminist and feminist sources. So, e.g., Robert G. Boling states: "It was a man's world" (1975: 274); or Steinberg (1984: 185), who states, "The public domain is not intended for women." In my view, Reis (2006: 126) is correct when she notes, "Men are not privileged but exposed to scorn; the author's attitude toward the concubine is empathic."

13. Harris, Brown, and Moore (1998: 273) seem to suggest this. Boling (1975: 277) suggests that Israel as a nation "will overreact" to the rape-murder of the concubine so as to "compound the tragedy a thousand times over, and permit the situation to develop into a full-scale civil war." Civil war is not an escalation of the problem at the end of Judges; the rape-murder of the Levite's concubine is the climax; civil war is the outcome that follows this outrage. To put a finer point on it, Israel acted *appropriately* from a covenantal standpoint in nearly wiping out Benjamin.

14. This is a difference as well between the two stories. In Genesis, it is two virgins, whereas in Judges it is only one virgin. In both cases, the virgins are not harmed.

15. In this reading, the civil war is contextualized by the rape-murder and dismemberment of the concubine. That is, the civil war is contextualized by Judges 19 and not the other way round.

16. The verse might be intentionally ambiguous so as to implicate both the old man and the Levite. It reads: "But the men [worthless fellows] were unwilling to listen to him [old man—cf. v. 24]. And so the man [old man/Levite?] pushed his [Levite's] concubine outside to them."

17. The Hebrew term *ger* is never used for a permanent residence in the Pentateuch. LXX and LXX A both use the verb *paroikeō* ("to live away from your home") to translate this term. See Schneider 2000: 247.

18. So the ancient reading of Josephus and some of the church fathers; see Feldman about Josephus's portrayal of the Benjaminites (2000: 255–92). Josephus also rearranges the stories in Judges, likely for apologetic and narratological reasons, and places the story of the concubine just

after Judges 2 and so prior the work of the Judges in 3–16: Feldman 2000: 258–59. See also Gunn's summary of other ancient readings of this passage (2005: 244–46).

19. Unfortunately, Christians have not always been aided in their valuation of the roles occupied by women by their interpretation of Paul. On the one hand, Paul is constrained in his understanding of social categories by the prevailing cultural climate to which his letter is addressed. On the other hand, he is also articulating the gospel message, which is quite progressive in its explication of sociocultural categories. The problem is that the interface of the sociocultural context and the underlying message of the gospel do not always fold together seamlessly, and so Paul must articulate this message with some effort and, as 1 Pet. 3:15 notes, results in something that is "difficult to understand." Such constraints are not part of the Hebrew Bible, which speaks to a context, Israel-as-the-community-of-God, that is not foreign to its message. Put another way, the sociocultural context of ancient Israel is the narrative of the Hebrew Bible. So Hudson (1994: 49) has it backward when he states, "Narrative does as society does." Society, and particularly in the case of the traditions of the Hebrew Scriptures—Jewish, Christian, and Muslim—do as the narrative does. The question is, What does the narrative mean?

20. This explains two things in the D-history. The first is found in Judg. 8:22-23, where Gideon, having delivered the Israelites from the Midianites, rejects the Israelite offer of the monarchy to him and his family. He explains his refusal on the grounds that God was already king in Israel. The second is the problem with the priesthood in 1 Samuel 1–7 and the house of Eli. For Samuel, the primary problem in Israelite society, and which forms the immediate background for the rise of the monarchy, is leadership in the priesthood.

21. In fact, raped males appear nowhere in the biblical narratives, including Noah's experiences in the tent in Genesis 9, as I have argued elsewhere (2011: 417–33). One need also not assume that this is a case of homosexual desire unleashed in Gibeah and Benjamin. As Reis notes (2006: 138–39), it may be that this type of activity results from xenophobia, rather than homosexual urges, as a way of dominating a foreigner. In this way, the behavior is positively animalistic.

22. Part of the effort of the feminist critique has been to assess the merits of a "patriarchal" narrative. See Trible 1973: 30–48; Evans 1983: 11–31; and also Collins 1978: 358–69.

23. Sartre's existentialism or Kant's metaphysics, while guiding lights for the modern and postmodern movements, are not in principle what people gravitate toward. All interpretations are conditioned by an orientation to something more general than the individual. Even personalized, seemingly individualistic interpretations are governed by a historical setting that is specific to the communal context out of which that individual operates.

24. A reader-primary hermeneutical approach is the other side of the coin to a dominant reading. It simply makes the "dominant reader" the readers themselves, which may prove a Trojan horse to group specific and exclusivistic readings.

25. That is, one could say that the male figure is equal to the female figure to the degree that each are essential elements of the human, which is part of what drives the narrative forward. Incidentally, if Barth is correct in asserting that the image of God is a *means* by which the human being is capable of engaging in a relationship with God, then the role of the female figure in the unfolding, contemporary narrative of communities of faith becomes all the more pronounced. Even if Barth's understanding of the "image of God" is that it is a quality of the human condition that enables each individual to interact with God, it is only the human, qua male/female, that is able to engage in a relationship with God.

26. Notably, Tamar was a virgin, which seems to have made her untouchable to Amnon (cf. 2 Sam. 13:2).

15

Judges 19: Text of Trauma

Janelle Stanley

INTRODUCTION

Judges 19 tells the story of an unnamed woman who is gang raped, murdered, and dismembered. Though there has been significant scholarship on this passage from a variety of perspectives, there has been little or no scholarship that focuses on reading the text through a psychological lens. This essay aims to fill this gap. I argue that there are a number of aspects of Judges 19 that carry markers of trauma, and that by reading the text as a text of trauma, one gains new insights.

In writing this essay I am informed by my backgrounds in both clinical social work and biblical scholarship. Studying trauma, and working with those who have survived trauma, has heightened my awareness of the multitude of ways trauma is expressed, both individually and culturally. Trauma is communicated and processed through movies, art, music, poetry, and stories; so it is no surprise to me that trauma can also be found in sacred texts. Reading a traumatic text with an awareness of how trauma influences and infiltrates narrative structures has informed how I read the text.

Before this rereading of Judges 19 can be accomplished, I will first explore elements of traumatology that apply to the discussion at hand; namely, three classical symptoms of trauma: dissociation, repetition compulsion, and fragmentation. I will also examine the structure of trauma narrative as a distinct type of narrative that carries within it the markers of trauma.

In the second and third sections, I will address the text of Judges 19 itself. I will look at scholarship, including feminist biblical scholarship, beginning with Trible's (1984: 65–91) landmark work in *Texts of Terror*, Lasine's (1984: 37–59) examination of Judges 19 within the anthropological framework of hospitality, and Lapsley's (2005: 35–68) analysis of the narrative structure, which brings to life the authorial condemnation of the events. I will reference signatures of trauma that appear in the text to focus on what the presence of these symptoms can tell us about both the text as well as trauma itself. Understanding this story through a traumalogical lens gives voice to many silenced issues that arise out of the experience of trauma.

I will conclude by applying the modern lessons gleaned from traumatology and narrative psychology towards a reading of Judges 19 as a potentially healing text. There is therapeutic value in breaking the silence, in hearing and telling traumatic narratives. Looking across a wide range of clinical examples—from Holocaust victims to survivors of 9/11 to survivors of rape and incest—this essay will look at the ways in which a victim's exposure to stories of trauma functions to reground trauma experiences within a broader picture of reality and to reduce the experience of unique aloneness characteristic of trauma.

Trauma

The nature of trauma is that it overwhelms our coping mechanisms. Trauma is experienced as life-threatening: it threatens our psychological and/or physical existence. The terror that arises from such threats elicits a physiological response. Judith Herman (1996: 6) describes this body response:

> Attention is narrowed and perceptions are altered. Peripheral detail, context, and time sense fall away, while attention is strongly focused on central details in the immediate present. When the focus of attention is extremely narrow, people may experience profound perceptual distortions, including insensitivity to pain, depersonalization, derealization, time slowing and amnesia.

Modern neuroscience has noted structural changes in the brains of children exposed to extreme or chronic trauma. Cohen et al. (2006: 14) note that traumatized children "have higher resting pulse rates and blood pressure, greater physical tension . . . smaller intracranial volume, [and] smaller corpus collosi." Trauma has been shown to influence neurotransmitter pathways in the brain as well, increasing the size and tenacity of neural connections formed during the trauma, and pruning away synapses that contradict the new trauma-formed paths (National Scientific Council on the Developing Child 2005).

Long before this biophysical evidence was discovered, Freud (1966: 283) noticed traumatic memories presented as amnesia, which were actually "no true amnesia, no missing memory; just a connection that had been broken." This "broken connection" changes the way the trauma is remembered, and it changes the way we store memories going forward. These changes become manifest in traumatic symptoms.

The primary response to trauma—both individually and culturally—is denial and dissociation from the trauma (Herman 1997: 1). Trauma is simply too scary to think about, and the threat of annihilation triggers our fight-or-flight response: we try to psychologically flee from or eliminate the trauma. Returning soldiers and rape victims have long called attention to the social pressure to ignore, minimize, or "move on from" traumatic experiences. This is denial on a large scale, a social pressure to preserve the greater culture from the threat of an individual's trauma. We cannot bear to think about it, so we cannot bear to hear about it. This also happens on an individual level when we experience trauma.

I remember this clearly in my own response to 9/11. When colleagues called me into a conference room to watch as the first of the twin towers collapsed, I initially thought they were pulling a bizarre prank. "What's going on?" I asked repeatedly, unable to comprehend the enormity of what was actually happening. My reaction was not atypical (Cohen 2002: 114–17). Many people could literally not understand what was happening, even as they watched it unfold. Our psyches fled from the possibility that what we were experiencing could be real. This is dissociation—it is the first thing we do when we experience trauma.

The inability to comprehend trauma as it is happening, and to not understand it even in the aftermath, is a hallmark of traumatic experience (Caruth 1995: 6–8). Dissociation is the first and most common response to trauma, but its effects are not limited to the moment of traumatic experience. Dissociation continues on, influencing personality development in younger individuals and radically changing the way the personality is structured in mature personalities. The ability to bear any level of self-reflection—whether related to the trauma or not—becomes impaired (Lemma and Levy 2004: 112–13). Elements of the personality that became dissociated in the traumatic moment may continue to be dissociated long after the fact. Victims of sexual assault who felt disconnected from their body during their assault report continuing difficulties experiencing sensation—both good and bad—long after the assault is over (Herman 1997: 53).

In addition to continuing body effects, traumatic memories often become difficult to integrate with other memories. Trauma severs "these normally integrated functions from one another. The traumatized person may experience intense emotion but without clear memory of the event, or may remember everything in detail but without emotion" (Herman 1997: 34). What begins as dissociation becomes fragmentation. Fragmentation allows life to go on by dividing up unbearable experience and distributing it to different parts of our selves. Donald Kalsched (1996: 12–13) states, "This means that the normally unified elements of consciousness (i.e., cognitive awareness, affect, sensation, imagery) are not allowed to integrate."

Ongoing memory is affected. It is not just painful memories that become split off from conscious thought, but often experiences after the event as well, such that a physical sensation can be felt without connecting it to the triggering event—a sudden feeling of pain will, for example, not be connected in the mind of a PTSD (post-traumatic stress disorder) sufferer with the hammer that just hit their thumb.

Faced with this new and frightening existence, the psyche tries to adapt. Repetition compulsion is a third common symptom of trauma. Freud referred to this as the inevitable symptom of trauma (Freud 1948: 41–43). The repetition compulsion is, at its most basic, an attempt by the psyche to experience a different outcome of the traumatic event. This can happen either by the intrusion of the unconscious mind into the victim's conscious mind, or through partially conscious actions taken by the victim. Sufferers of PTSD report dreams, waking hallucinations, and flashbacks that intrude on their life. Ironically, those who are least able to consciously recall the details of a trauma event are most susceptible to the uncontrolled intrusions of repetition compulsion: "The excess that defines trauma is an inability to say what is happening at the time, and later to say what has happened in any fully accurate or complete way. In other words, the excess of trauma is given a wordless burial . . . trauma repeats, almost inevitably" (Rogers 2006: 262).

In flashbacks or dreams, the repetition is "an attempt to relive and master the overwhelming feelings of the traumatic moment" (Herman 1997: 34). Repetition can also be carried out in waking life. Children who have been traumatized will re-create the trauma in their play, and the very nature of their repetitive play is telling: there is little improvisation, the sequence and events of their play do not morph over time, it is difficult for them to stop midgame, and it is exactly repeated. "Post-traumatic play is so literal that if you spot it, you may be able to guess the trauma with few other clues" (Terr 1990: 247).

Adults will also repeat experienced trauma. Rape victims sometimes seek out dangerous sexual situations—dangerous because of the partners they select, the locations in which they have sexual intercourse, or because of the violent nature of the sexual behaviors (Herman 1997: 41–42). Culturally, we tell and retell stories, or show the same news footage over and over, trying to find a way to comprehend the incomprehensible, desperately seeking a different ending (Denham 2008: 408).

Judges 19:1-15: Early Indicators of Trauma

The story contained within Judges 19 is undeniably one of the most disturbing stories in the Hebrew Bible. I will argue here that it is also a traumatic text. By that I mean the text itself shows distinct signs that it is recounting a trauma event. The arc of a trauma narrative shares symptoms with the trauma itself: dissociation, fragmentation, repetition compulsion. These will be evident not only in the subject of the story but also in the manner the story is told. The cues at the story's beginning are subtle; as the narrative progresses, the symptoms become more obvious. One of the most fascinating aspects of reading Judges 19 this way is that signatures of trauma that were not understood until the twentieth and twenty-first centuries now seem present in the text.

From the very first verse, the story warns the reader that it will be a difficult text: "In those days, when there was no king in Israel" (Judg. 19:1 NRSV). The book of Judges uses that exact phrase several times (17:6; 18:1; 19:1; 21:24). In all cases, it presages increasingly dire circumstances: theft, idolatry, desecration, and a massacre. By Judges 19, one expects that when this phrase is used, we will not find a happy ending.

Indeed, we soon discover that a Levite priest takes a wife who, either out of anger or out of unfaithfulness, leaves her husband and travels (alone?) to her father's house. This is unusual behavior for a woman in the Hebrew Bible. The text gives no further details on her departure, nor does it speculate as to why it takes him four months to look after her. Cheryl Exum (1993a: 179) proposes that no matter what the initial cause, the woman asserted "her sexual autonomy by leaving her husband . . . [and therefore] is guilty of sexual misconduct. By daring to act autonomously in the first place, [she] puts herself beyond male protection, and for this she must be punished." Lapsley (2005: 38) speculates the exact opposite, musing that "the Levite's ignominious behavior later in the story casts a deep shadow over this first scene: he abuses her explicitly later in the story, so we may well suspect him of it here." Regardless of the motivations of the Levite or the *pilegesh*,[1] she leaves of her own volition, and resides in her father's house for four months before her husband sets out after her.

The next eight verses (19:3-10) are odd. They recount, in some detail, the husband's journey, arrival, and stay at the house of the *pilegesh*'s father. Scholarship has often skimmed over this section of the text, paying little attention to what reads as excessive detail with little contribution to the narrative.[2] Lapsley (2005: 39) notes that these verses "have long puzzled commentators." These verses are, however, another clue that Judges 19 is a text of trauma.

Narrative psychology looks at how humans deal with experiences through the construction and telling of stories. Narrative psychology states that the chronological linearity of a traumatic story will be broken whenever the subject comes close to the moment of trauma (Laszlo 2008: 147). As with the way we experience a trauma event, time in the story may radically slow down, speed up, or rapidly pendulate when approaching the point of trauma. The focus can also become extremely narrow, with some details falling away and others leaping to the fore. These profound perceptual distortions are a hallmark of trauma and of trauma narratives, and we begin to see evidence of them here: no details are given surrounding the story's motivating event, but then whole conversations with details ancillary to the plot are recounted. Similarly, time is not moving consistently through this narrative.

The distorted perception that characterizes trauma is evident also in the textual shift: the person who is the initial focus of the story—the Levite's *pilegesh*—seems to have disappeared entirely. Though she begins the story with an unusual amount of agency—leaving her husband, journeying some distance to the house of her father—by this point in the story she is unaccountably absent. Additionally, though the Levite's stated purpose of the journey was to "speak to the heart of his wife" (v. 3), the text makes no mention of any such attempt. These narrative contradictions are strange in a normal narrative arc, but are normative within traumatic narratives. As Herman (1997: 1) has noted, people often tell traumatic narratives "in a highly emotional, contradictory, and fragmented manner."

There are more conflicts within the text. Even as the narrative seems to forget the *pilegesh*, it also attempts to remind us of her. Lapsley (2005: 40–41) points out that

> reference to her appears repeatedly in the language used to designate her father: "the father of the young woman." This epithet, more cumbersome than the succinct *hoten* "father-in-law," appears six times in vv. 3–8, sometimes in opposition to "father-in-law." Through the repetition of "young woman" the readers and hearers of this story are constantly reminded of her, and of her absence from the story.

Another level of dissociation can already be discerned by this point: none of the characters in this story has been named. It is not unusual for women in the Hebrew Bible to have a major role in a narrative without being named, but it is strikingly unusual for male characters to remain nameless. Ilse Mullner (1999: 137) states that this contributes to "the confusing situation the narrative relates" and makes "it virtually impossible for the reader to identify with one of the characters; and the fact the characters described in the narrative are not given names has a distancing effect." The narrative is pushing us away from the characters even as it moves forward. This "conflict between the will to deny horrible events and the will to proclaim them aloud is the central dialectic of psychological trauma" (Herman 1997: 1). As Athalya Brenner (1993: 12) points out,

> Male figures in Judges are usually designated by a name at the very least. . . . The Judges' exceptions to the male-naming rule are the male quartet of ch. 19: the Levite, his servant, the woman's father and the 'old man' (the host). There can be no doubt that the namelessness of *all* male figures within a single story constitutes a narrative device.

Interestingly, it is not naming in general that the narrator in Judges opposes. In the text up to this point, places are distinctly named—v. 1 describes the Levite as "residing in the remote parts of the hill-country of Ephraim," and his *pilegesh* is twice described as being from "Bethlehem in Judah." It is only with regard to the identity of the *people* that the narrative remains vague. This type of fragmented recall is also typical of traumatic memory. It has been most thoroughly documented with regard to PTSD symptoms in soldiers (though it is certainly not limited to that subgroup), wherein the aftereffects of trauma "kept traumatic memories out of normal consciousness, allowing only a fragment of the memory to emerge" (Herman 1997: 45). Recalling a place but not peoples' names, or the time of day but not what day of the week or even time of year, is typical.

What of other traumatic clues? The signature of trauma, repetition, makes an early appearance as well. I have already pointed out Lapsley's identification of the phrase "the father of the young woman," repeated six times. There is also a repetition of events: four times the Levite gets up to leave, and the father of the young woman makes another offer for him to stay (19:5, 7, 8, 9). In vv. 5, 7, 8, and 9, the text repeats and repeats again, almost as if it is compulsively searching for a different end. Two days pass in these four verses, but the situation and location remain the same. Each day, the man arises early in the morning, he gets up to go, and he stays (Yamada 2008: 75–76). While the Hebrew Bible often repeats words or phrases, it is worth noting the scale of repetition here.

Lapsley (2005: 39) notes also that the word "heart" (*leb*) has been repeated several times, often awkwardly.

> This phrase, "strengthen your heart" (v. 5) here as elsewhere means essentially to eat something in order to regain strength. The woodenness of this translation of the Hebrew has the virtue, however, of disclosing that the father's entreaty has reintroduced the word "heart" into the story. . . . [This] would not in and of itself be especially noteworthy, indeed, it would appear to be mere coincidence, if it were not for the fact that the father-in-law repeats this word in each of his three further efforts to detain the Levite. . . . The fourfold repetition of "heart" cannot be dismissed as mere coincidence.

As Lapsley notes, repetition of some words may be coincidence. But repetition on this scale is not.

In v. 10, the narrative changes. Verse 10 states that "the man would not spend the night; he got up and departed, and arrived opposite Jebus (that is, Jerusalem). He had with him a couple of saddled donkeys, and his concubine was with him." Through some means, then, the Levite has secured the *pilegesh*, who makes her first explicit appearance in the narrative since she has left the Levite in v. 2. Having just reappeared, however, she is again dissociated from the narrative. The man and his servant have an extensive conversation (vv. 11-13) regarding where they should stay, and again, the attention to detail here is notable.

In the course of their conversation, attention is drawn to the danger of staying in a town where "the people are not Israelites" (v. 12). The Levite's description of the foreign *other* as dangerous is part of the consciousness of the narrative, and "emphasizes the hostility towards the unfamiliar that underlies this image of a town full of non-Israelites" (Mullner 1999: 136). This is a dark foreshadowing of events to come; as Trible (1984: 70) points out, "Though his reasoning makes sense, he knows not the violent irony of his decision."

By the time the travelers choose and enter a city (Gibeah in Benjamin, v. 15), we reach the halfway point in the story. Up to this point, the narrative focus has been almost entirely on the Levite's travels. The dialogue has been dominated by the unnamed men, and all the speech reports have focused on the Levite's decisions regarding lodging (vv. 5, 6, 8, 9, 11-13). At this point it might be useful to contrast Judges 19 with Genesis 19, a text recognized to share a striking similarity (Lasine 1984: 38; Yamada 2008: 85–90). I mention it because at this point in the narrative, Genesis 19 and Judges 19 share almost *no* characteristics. It took the narrator in Judges fully half the narrative to get to the same story-point that the narrator in Genesis reached halfway through the first verse of his story (cf. Gen. 19:1 and Judg. 19:15).

What are we to make of this? The parallels between Genesis 19 and Judges 19 become quickly obvious—Lasine (1984: 39) points out that the speech used by the old man in Judges 19 "follows Lot's example [in Genesis 19] so precisely that it is almost as though he were following a 'script.'" But here, the first half of Judges departs from that script (cf. Gen. 19:2 with Judg. 19:20).

It has been persuasively argued that the narrator of this text is extraordinarily subtle,[3] and that the narration style is such a departure from other Hebrew Bible narrators' that it may be reasonable to consider the possibility that the author of Judges was a woman (Bledstein 1993: 34). Whether the author was male or female, there is wide agreement that the style of narration is a departure from similar narratives in the Hebrew Bible. Biblical scholars have unwittingly noted what traumatologists have noticed elsewhere: trauma narratives are told differently from other narratives. Even when the author of Judges relies on the template of Genesis 19, to the extent that some parts read almost as word-for-word copies, half of what we read in Judges 19 is different (Lasine 1984: 38–39). The recounting of events has been distorted: The way the story is put together, the fragmented nature of some details peeking through and others becoming obscured, the extreme focus on some details at the expense of others, the repetition of words and phrases—all of these are characteristic of traumatic narratives and texts of trauma.

Judges 19:16-30

If the first half of Judges 19 gives hints and clues that it is a traumatic narrative, the events in the last half of the chapter leave no doubt. The first six verses (vv. 16-21) introduce a new character, an old man who—the narrator tells us—is, like the Levite, "from the hill country of Ephraim" (v. 16). The old man, who also remains unnamed throughout the text, converses with the Levite who reveals that "nobody has offered to take me in" (v. 18), though the Levite is hasty to add that it is only shelter they require, having brought with him "straw and fodder for our donkeys, with bread and wine for me and the woman and the young man along with us" (v. 19). The old man offers hospitality, cares for their donkeys, and takes them into his home.

Lapsley (2005: 45) points out that "to this point the narrator has presented the old man in quite a favorable light: not only did he take in the Levite's group, but he also personally cared for the donkeys (v. 21)." The old man also shares a number of traits with the Levite, which the narrator calls attention to, not only using the same language to describe their origins but also describing them both as sojourners (Yamada 2008: 82).

It would again prove useful to contrast Judges 19 against Genesis 19, as this is when the two begin to show the striking resemblance that many readers have already noted. In four verses, both narrators describe the same series of events: a resident of a doomed city happens upon travelers, sees them, invites them in to eat and drink, washes their feet, and puts them up for the night (Gen. 19:1-4; Judg. 19:17-21). In Genesis, however, Lot all but begs the visitors to come stay with him; in Judges, it is the travelers who all but beg for lodging. In Genesis, the visitors claim they will spend the night out in the open (v. 2); in Judges, those same words are said, but by the resident, who urges the visitors not to spend the night out in the open (v. 20). Throughout these speech reports, "the behavior of the host intentionally copies *and* 'inverts' Lot's hospitality" (Lasine 1984: 39).

Trible (1984: 21) calls attention to an increasing amount of repetition in the narrative at this point: "The dialogue repeats the pattern: two speeches by the old man (19:17b and 19:20) surround the words of the master (19:18-19). Crucial to the symmetry of the unit is the word *house*. It appears once at the beginning (19:15b), once at the end (19:21), and twice in the middle (19:18)." There is yet another repetition: "In this same speech to the old man, a curious repetition appears. The Levite repeats nearly word for word to the old man something that the narrator had stated back in verse 15" (Lapsley 2005: 43). By this point in the story, the author is repeating words and phrases not only from the Genesis 19 script but also from within his own text—despite, in some cases, the wooden feel this creates.

Then the narrative takes a sharp turn for the worse. As in Genesis 19, men from the town surround the house, calling inside for the male guest to be sent outside in order to be raped. The old man references hospitality codes, offering, as Lot did, his own virgin daughter and the Levite's concubine to the mob instead. Here, Yamada (2008: 87) points out two differences between Genesis 19 and Judges 19 that are chilling: first, "while both hosts offer up women to the mobs outside their doors, it is only the men of Gibeah who act out their lustful violence. . . . Second, the old man's words are more explicit than the words of Lot in that he implores the men to 'rape' his daughter and the Levite's concubine." Then, in the first explicitly narrated interaction between the Levite and the woman, he seizes the *pilegesh* and "put her out to them. They wantonly raped her, and abused her all through the night until the morning. And as the dawn began to break, they let her go" (v. 25).

In one verse the narrator has described the forcible eviction, gang rape, brutal abuse, and abandonment of the *pilegesh*. Whereas the text spent twenty-four verses describing the travels of the Levite, here the scarcity of text calls attention to itself: "Raped, tortured, and released: brevity of speech discloses the extravagance of violence" (Trible 1984: 75).

The truncated description of the trauma itself is another hallmark of trauma narratives. It is "something that seems oddly to inhabit all traumatic experience: the inability fully to witness the event as it occurs. . . . Central to the very immediacy of this experience . . . is a gap that carries the force of the event and does so precisely at the expense of simple knowledge and memory" (Caruth 1995: 7). Trauma narratives that recount extraordinary detail leading up to the traumatic event suddenly find that words cannot encompass the enormity of what happened at the actual event.

Next, daybreak comes. "As morning appeared, the woman came and fell down at the door of the man's house where her master was, until it was light" (v. 26). There are several things to note in this verse. First, the *pilegesh* is described for the first time not in relation to anyone, but simply as "the woman." The *pilegesh* is described out of relation to any character. She is no one's wife, no one's daughter. She is, like so many victims of trauma are, isolated by her trauma, out of relationality, alone. One of the "most insidious features of PTSD" is "a sense of *isolation* from others and from their primary communities of affection and care. Because they have difficulty in speaking and remembering, trauma survivors find it hard to communicate with loved ones and friends. Because they lack energy or optimism, they find it tough to sustain relationships . . . because a hostile external force has violated them, they find it hard to trust people. . . . Further, others often find it uncomfortable to be around trauma survivors" (Jones 2009: 18). The actions of her husband only serve to emphasize her aloneness, and the ambiguity of the text as we move forward will complicate this out-of-relationality even more:

> In the morning her master got up, opened the doors of the house, and when he went out to go on his way, there was his concubine lying at the door of the house with her hands on the threshold. "Get up," he said to her, "we are going." But there was no answer. Then he put her on his donkey; and the man set out for his home (vv. 27–28).

Many scholars have had a great deal of criticism for the Levite throughout the story, but such commentary hardly compares to the unified censure of his actions here.[4] Yamada (2008: 90) states that "his initial response, consistent with his neglect of his concubine in the first scene, is calloused and indifferent." Bal (1993b: 229) points out that "he stands over her, fails to see her, ineffectively and abusively speaks to her, and steps over her." The Levite's actions and words are bizarre and shocking, and the text describes them in efficient, but brutal, detail.

Trible states that the Greek and Hebrew Bibles offer ambiguous translations. "The Greek Bible says, 'for she was dead,' and hence makes the men of Benjamin murderers as well as rapists and torturers. The Hebrew text, on the other hand, is silent, allowing the interpretation that this abused woman is yet alive. Oppressed and tortured, she opens not her mouth" (Trible 1984: 79). Trible's attention to detail highlights an important part of this narrative: the *pilegesh*'s silence. In fact, she is silent throughout the entire narrative. She never once has a speaking role in the text, and by this point in the narrative her silence is deafening. If Trible's interpretation is correct, and the Hebrew text leaves open the possibility that at this point the *pilegesh is* still alive, her silence speaks to the fact of the trauma. Narrative psychologists have noted that traumatic narratives must be wrested out of silence.

> Prolonged silence is constructed on the ashes of betrayal, fear or shame, hatred and hopelessness. It rests on the assumption that telling is dangerous and that the possible story will be unacceptable to a more powerful other. The unwillingness or the inability to tell generates a structure of muteness which, if it persists, ultimately leads to a contraction of humanity (Gersie 1997: 32).

Indeed, the role of the *pilegesh in* the narrative is not yet complete, and her "contraction of humanity" not yet finished. Her muteness will ominously persist. As Bal (1993b: 222) points out, the *pilegesh* "dies several times, or rather, she never stops dying." That the time of her death is left open to interpretation allows her death itself to become part of the repetition compulsion characteristic of trauma. It happens once when she is thrown out to the mob, again when her husband finds her, and again in the next verse.

"When he had entered his house, he took a knife, and grasping his concubine he cut her into twelve pieces, limb from limb, and sent her throughout all of Israel" (v. 29). This verse, more than any other, brings all the signs of trauma to the fore. It holds within it all three markers of trauma: dissociation, repetition compulsion, and grotesque fragmentation. The Levite is himself dissociated, no longer described as her husband, "the Levite," or even "the man." Like the *pilegesh*, he is outside of relationality. He is further dissociated both from his own grief as well as from the body of the *pilegesh*—he does not seek to have her buried, does not even mourn. Instead, he attempts to communicate with his nation, but even in that he falls into traumatic patterns. As Kamuf (1993: 201) points out:

> The Levite's publication of the crime is, if not its representation, then in some way its repetition. Clearly, the mutilation he performs repeats in a calculated fashion the brutal, frenzied mutilation of the same body by the Benjaminites. But is there not as well a suggestion of another repetition in the very gesture of sending the body as one would send a delegate or envoy or representative? In this sense, the gesture repeats or recalls not the Benjaminites' crime—rape—but the Levite's delegation of his concubine in his stead, the crime, if you will, of representation. The Levite's publication thus takes the form of his crime and sends a self-accusatory message.

Verse 29 also contains within it fragmentation so common to trauma. Here it is rendered explicitly, with the physical body of the *pilegesh* fragmented into twelve pieces, and then fragmented further when those pieces are scattered to the twelve corners of Israel. Herman (1997: 34) points out, "Traumatic symptoms have a tendency to become disconnected from their source and to take on a life of their own. This kind of fragmentation, whereby trauma tears apart a complex system of self-protection that normally functions in an integrated fashion, is central to the historic observations on post-traumatic stress disorder."

Though a thorough examination of the aftermath of Judges 19 is outside the scope of this essay, it bears mentioning that traumatic symptomologies that began with the rape of the *pilegesh* continue through the end of the book of Judges. Israel is incited further to civil war, nearly exterminating the tribe of Benjamin, and then "the men of Israel sanction the abduction of two hundred young women as they come out to dance in the yearly festival of Yahweh (21:23). In total, the rape of one has become the rape of six hundred" (Trible 1984: 83). As Peter Levine points out, "Trauma begets trauma and will continue to do so, eventually crossing generations in families, communities and countries" (Levine 1997: 9).

Conclusion

This essay has argued that there are many clues within the text of Judges 19 that indicate it is a traumatic narrative—but why is this important? How does reading it as a text of trauma add to our understanding of the text? How does reading this as a text of trauma help *us* deal with trauma?

First, this story models what modern clinicians have only recently recognized as critical in trauma therapy: constructing the narrative. In nearly all forms of trauma therapy, it is crucial that the trauma memory be recovered, told, and retold (Cohen 2002: 118–19). This recovery and telling is an extremely difficult task. Because of the effect that trauma has on memory, reassembling the story of a trauma is difficult. The "broken connection" represents the challenge of any trauma therapy, and its repair is the marker of therapeutic success. In writing about the role of narrative in the work with Holocaust survivors, Dori Laub (1995: 63–64) writes: "The survivors did not only need to survive so that they could tell their stories; they also needed to tell their stories in order to survive."

When traumatic stories cannot be told, when they are silenced and repressed, healing is aborted. Impairment results. Annie Rogers writes that when a trauma is silenced, symptoms of trauma will break through because "the unconscious insists, repeats, and practically breaks down the door to be heard. [This occurs] everywhere, in speech, in enactments, in dreams, and in the body" (Rogers 2006: 298). When traumatic stories *are* recovered, however, when they are told and retold, healing can occur. Judith Herman (1997: 175) writes that "this work of reconstruction actually transforms the traumatic memory, so that it can be integrated into the survivor's life story."

In order to heal from the trauma, in other words, it must be integrated into our own canons. Telling the story stops the fragmentation process. It allows a victim of trauma to begin re-associating events and emotions, sensation and memory. No matter how traumatic the story is, the ability to tell it heals.

In telling this story, the text also starts to heal relationality. Sandra Butler (1978: 8) writes that "victims thought that what had happened to them had never happened to anyone else and felt alone in their loss of faith . . . and [alone] in their rage at a world." The text here works against that feature, assuring others who have experienced trauma that they are *not* alone. It provides a story with common traumatic symptomology contained within it, providing a locus of identification for other victims.

I have not yet referenced the last words in Judges 19. The chapter opened with a warning, and closes by saying: "Consider it, take counsel, and speak out." Contained in the text, we find instructions to not forget this story. We are not just to read this account but also to let the account enter into our heart and be considered. Then it instructs that we "take counsel" or "discuss it" (NJB). The text calls here for a communal response to trauma. It raises awareness about how trauma affects victims and their families. Finally, it says to "speak out." This breaking of silence is widely recognized to be the first step in healing from trauma (Alcoff and Gray 1993: 261). The last words of this chapter instruct us to speak out, to fight against our own innate instincts to silence the trauma, and, instead, give it voice.

Judges 19 is a horrible story. All trauma narratives are. We want to deny them, to forget them, to move past them. But they persist. Just as this text persists. And somehow, without access to decades of clinical research, this text recognizes the power of constructing a traumatic narrative. It first warns us it will be a hard story, and then goes on to tell it.

Our understanding of trauma does not begin in the modern age—it began when the first traumatic story was told, when the first text of trauma was written down. In Judges 19, we find such a text. I have looked at Judges 19 through a traumatological lens, identifying markers of trauma and pathways toward healing that modern psychology has already discovered. I wonder, though, what markers I have missed.

Is there wisdom in this text of trauma that modern psychology has not yet found? Are there other traumatic narratives in the Bible that might tell us more? At its best, psychology is more than a lens through which we read the Bible. At its best, psychology can be a way to *dialogue* with the Bible: to both speak and listen. To learn. Such a dialogue is outside the scope of this essay, but I hope that future work might begin to look at both sides of this rich conversation.

Notes

1. I am persuaded by Exum's argument that neither "concubine" nor "wife" serves as an adequate translation, and will therefore use the original referent *pilegesh* when referring to the unnamed woman in Judges 19. See Exum 1993a: 176.

2. A notable exception to this is scholarship that focuses on the hospitality culture evident in Judges 19. See, e.g., Matthews 1992: 3–11 and also, to a lesser extent, Stone 1995: 87–107.

3. Lapsley argues that "the narrative also offers subtle but profound critical commentary on dominant cultural attitudes" (Lapsley 2005: 36). Yee argues for a subtle rendering of propaganda against the Levites (Yee 2007a: 153–54).

4. An argument can be made that the Levite himself has experienced trauma, and his actions and speech—here and elsewhere in the story—are consistent with many PTSD symptoms. That analysis is outside the scope of this paper.

Bibliography

Abbott, John S. C. 1875. *A History of the State of Ohio*. Detroit: Northwestern.

Ackerman, Susan. 1991. "The Deception of Isaac, Jacob's Dream at Bethel, and Incubation on an Animal Skin." In *Priesthood and Cult in Ancient Israel*, eds. Gary. A. Anderson and Saul M. Olyan. 92–120. Sheffield: JSOT Press

———.1998. *Warrior, Dancer, Seductress, Queen: Women in Judges and Biblical Israel*. New York: Doubleday.

———. 2000. "What if Judges Had Been Written by a Philistine?" *BibInt* 8/1–2: 33–41.

Aharoni, Yohanan. 1968. "Arad: Its Inscriptions and Temple." *BA* 31: 2–32.

Ahituv, S. 1995. *Joshua, with an Introduction and Commentary (Mikra le-Yisrael)*. Tel Aviv and Jerusalem: Am Oved and the Magnes Press (Hebrew).

Albright, William F. 1963. "Jethro, Hobab and Reuel in Early Hebrew Tradition." *CBQ* 25: 1–11.

Alcoff, Linda, and Laura Gray. 1993. "Survivor Discourse: Transgression or Recuperation." *Signs* 18/2: 260–90.

Allen, James, et al. 2000. *Without Sanctuary: Lynching Photography in America*. Santa Fe, N.M.: Twin Palms.

Alpert, B. 2002. "Introduction: Concepts and Ideas in Curricula as Leading Texts." In *Values and Goals in Curricula in Israel*, ed. A. Hoffman and Y. Shanel, 9–32. Even-Yehuda: Beit Berl and Rekhes (Hebrew).

Alter, Robert. 1981. *The Art of Biblical Narrative*. New York: Basic.

———. 1983. "From Line to Story in Biblical Verse." *Poetics Today* 4: 615–37.

———. 1985. *The Art of Biblical Poetry*. New York: Basic.

———. 1990. "Samson Without Folklore." In *Text and Tradition: The Hebrew Bible and Folklore*, ed. Susan Niditch, 48–56. Atlanta: Scholars.

———. 1992. *The World of Biblical Literature*. New York: Basic.

Amihai, Y. 1971. *Poems 1948–1962*. Jerusalem and Tel Aviv: Schocken (Hebrew).

Amit, Yairah. 1986. "Teaching the Book of Joshua and the Associated Problems." *Al ha-Pereq* 2: 16–22 (Hebrew).

———. 1987. "Judges 4: Its Contents and Form." *JSOT* 39: 89–111.

———. 1997. *History and Ideology in the Bible*. Tel-Aviv. Ministry of Defence publishing (Hebrew).

———. 1999. *Judges*. Tel Aviv: Am Oved (in Hebrew).

———. 1999a, 1999b. *The Book of Judges: The Art of Editing*. Trans. Jonathan Chipman. Biblical Interpretation 38. Leiden: Brill (in Hebrew 1992).

———. 1999c. *History and Ideology: Introduction to Historiography in the Hebrew Bible*. Rev. and annotated from the Hebrew version, 1997. Sheffield: Sheffield Academic.

———. 2000. *Hidden Polemics in Biblical Narrative*. Trans. Jonathan Chipman. Biblical Interpretation 25. Leiden: Brill.

———. 2001. *Reading Biblical Narratives: Literary Criticism and the Hebrew Bible*. Trans. Yael Lotan. Minneapolis: Fortress Press.

———. 2009. "The Book of Judges: Dating and Meaning." In *Homeland and Exile: Biblical and Ancient Near Eastern Studies in Homeland in Honour of Bustenay Oded*, ed. G. Galil, M. Geller, and A. Millard, 297–322. Leiden: Brill.

Assis, Elie. 2005. "'The Hand of a Woman': Deborah and Yael (Judges 4)." *JHS* 5: 1–12.

Aviner, S. 1982. "The Gate of the Land." *Artzi* 1: 7–34 (Hebrew).

Avishur, Yitzhak. 1981. "The Ghost Expelling Incantation from Ugarit." *UF* 13: 13–25.

Ayers, Brenda, ed. 2003. *The Emperor's Old Groove: Decolonizing Disney's Magic Kingdom*. New York: Peter Lang.

Bach, Alice. 1998. "Rereading the Body Politic: Women and Violence in Judges 21." *BibInt* 6/1: 1–19.

Bal, Mieke. 1987a. *Murder and Difference: Gender, Genre, and Scholarship on Sisera's Death*. Bloomington: Indiana University Press.

———. 1987b. *Lethal Love: Feminist Literary Readings of Biblical Love Stories*. Indianapolis: Indiana University Press.

———. 1988a, 1988b. *Death and Dissymmetry: The Politics of Coherence in the Book of Judges*. Chicago: University of Chicago Press.

———. 1988c. "Tricky Thematics." *Semeia* 42: 133–55.

———. 1993a. "Myth à la Lettre: Freud, Mann, Genesis and Rembrandt, and the Story of the Son." Repr. in *A Feminist Companion to Genesis*, ed. A. Brenner, 343–78. Sheffield: Sheffield Academic. (Orig. pub. in *Discourse in Psychoanalysis and Literature*, ed. S. Rimon-Kenan, 57–89. London: Methuen, 1987.)

———. 1993b. "A Body of Writing: Judges 19." In *A Feminist Companion to Judges*, ed. A. Brenner, 208–30. Sheffield: JSOT Press.

Barrett, J. Franck. 1996. "The Organizational Construction of Hegemonic Masculinity: The Case of the US Navy." *Gender, Work & Organization* 3/3: 129–42.

Barthes, Roland. 1972. *Mythologies*. New York: Hill and Wang.

Bates, Katherine Lee. "America the Beautiful." In *Fellowship Hymns*, ed. C. A. Barbour. New York: YMCA Press, 1910.

Bell, Elizabeth, Lynda Haas, and Laura Sells, eds. 1995. *From Mouse to Mermaid: The Politics of Film, Gender, and Culture*. Bloomington: Indiana University Press.

Bell, D., and G. Valentine. 1995. Mapping Desire: Geographies of Sexualities. London: Burns & Oates.

Bellah, Robert. 1984. *The Broken Covenant: American Civil Religion in Time of Trial*. San Francisco: HarperSanFrancisco.

Bellinger, Charles K. n.d. "Religion and Violence: A Bibliography." Wabash Center for Teaching and Learning in Theology and Religion. http://www.wabashcenter.wabash.edu/resources/article2.aspx?id=10516. Revised and expanded from a bibliography published in *The Hedgehog Review* 6/1 (2004): 111–19.

———. n.d. "Religion and Violence." Internet Guide to Religion, Wabash Center for Teaching and Learning in Theology and Religion. http://www.wabashcenter.wabash.edu/resources/result-browse.aspx?topic=549&pid=427.

Ben-Artzi, H. 1986. "Thoughts about the Place of the Talmudic Literature in the Secular School System." *Dappim* 4: 19–30 (Hebrew).

Bergman, Samuel Hugo. 1970. *The Quality of Faith; Essays on Judaism and Morality*. Trans. Yehuda Hanegbi. Jerusalem: Youth and Hechalutz Department of the World Zionist Organization.

Berkhofer, Robert L., Jr. 1978. *The White Man's Indian: Images of the American Indian from Columbus to the Present*. New York: Vintage.

Bible and Culture Collective. 1995. *The Postmodern Bible*. New Haven: Yale University Press.

Bible Curriculum. 2003. *Curriculum: The Bible for the State School System, from Kindergarten through Grade 12*. Jerusalem: Ma'alot (Hebrew).

Bin-Nun, Y. 2001. "The Bible in a Historical Perspective and the Israeli Settlement in the Land of Canaan." In *The Controversy over the Historicity of the Bible*, ed. L. I. Levine and A. Mazar, 3–16. Jerusalem: Yad Izhak Ben-Zvi and Merkaz Dinur (Hebrew).

Bird, Phyllis A. 1989. "'To Play the Harlot': An Inquiry into an old Testament Metaphor." In *Gender and Difference in Ancient Israel*, ed. Peggy L. Day, 75–94. Minneapolis: Fortress Press.

———. 1997. *Missing Persons and Mistaken Identities: Women and Gender in Ancient Israel*. Minneapolis: Fortress Press.

Black, Jeremy, Graham Cunningham, Eleanor Robson, and Gábor Zólymoi. 2004. *The Literature of Ancient Sumer*. Oxford: Oxford University Press.

Bledstein, Adrien Janis. 1993. "Is Judges a Woman's Satire of Men Who Play God?" In *A Feminist Companion to Judges*, ed. A. Brenner, 34–54. Sheffield: JSOT Press.

Bohmbach, Karla G. 1999. "Conventions/Contraventions: The Meanings of Public and Private for the Judges 19 Concubine." *JSOT* 83: 83–98.

———. 2000. "Names and Naming in the Biblical World." In *Women in Scripture: A Dictionary of Named and Unnamed Women in the Hebrew Bible, The Apocryphal/Deuterocanonical Books, and the New Testament*, ed. Carol Meyers, Toni Craven, and Ross S. Kraemer, 33–39. Grand Rapids: Eerdmans.

Bohn, Babette. 2006. "Death, Dispassion, and the Female Hero: Artemisia Gentileschi's *Jael and Sisera*." In *The Artemisia Files: Artemisia Gentileschi for Feminists and Other Thinking People*, ed. Mieke Bal, 107–27. Chicago: University of Chicago Press.

Boling, Robert G. 1975. *Judges: A New Translation with Introduction and Commentary*. AB 6A. Garden City, N.Y.: Doubleday.

Bonechi, Marko, and Marie Durand. 1992. "Oniromancie et magie á Mari á l'époque d'Ébla." In *Literature and Literary Language at Ebla*, ed. Pelio Fronzaroli, 151–59. Quaderni di Semitistica 18. Florence: Dipartimento de Linguistica, Università de Firenze.

Bottéro, Jean. 1992. *Mesopotamia: Writing, Reasoning, and the Gods*. Chicago: University of Chicago Press.

Bottigheimer, Ruth B. 1996. "Philogyny, Misogyny, and Erasure: Jael and Sisera." In *The Bible for Children, From the Age of Gutenberg to the Present*, 142–51. New Haven: Yale University Press.

Boyarin, Daniel. 1995. *Carnal Israel: Reading Sex in Talmudic Culture*. Berkeley: University of California Press.

Braverman, Mark. 2010. *Fatal Embrace: Christians, Jews, and the Search for Peace in the Holy Land*. Austin: Synergy.

Brenner, Athalya. 1985. *The Israelite Woman: Social Role and Literary Type in Biblical Narrative.* Sheffield: JSOT Press.

———. 1990. "A Triangle and a Rhombus in Narrative Structure: A Proposed Integrative Reading of Judges 4 and 5." *VT* 40/2: 129–38. See also 1993a,in *A Feminist Companion to Judges*, ed. Athalya Brenner, 98–109. Sheffield: Sheffield Academic.

———. 1993b. Introduction to *A Feminist Companion to Judges*, ed. Athalya Brenner, 9–22. Sheffield: JSOT Press.

———. 1994. "Who's Afraid of Feminist Criticism? Who's Afraid of Biblical Humour? The Case of the Obtuse Foreign Ruler in the Hebrew Bible." *JSOT* 63: 38–55.

Brettler, Marc Zvi. 1989. "The Book of Judges: Literature as Politics." *JBL* 108/3: 395–418.

———. 2002. *The Book of Judges.* New York: Routledge.

Brison, Ora. 2007. "Aggressive Goddesses, Abusive Men: Gender Role Change in Near Eastern Mythology." In *VI Congresso Internazionale di Ittitologia Roma, 5-9 settembre 2005*, ed. Archi Alonso and Francia Rita, part 1, 67–74. Studi Micenei ed Egeo-Anatoloci 49. Rome: Cnr, Istituto per Gli Studi Micenei Ed Egeo-Anatolici.

Brode, Douglas. 2005. *Multiculturalism and the Mouse: Race and Sex in Disney Entertainment.* Austin: University of Texas Press.

Bronner, L. L. 1993. "Valorized or Vilified? The Women of Judges in Midrashic Sources." In *A Feminist Companion to Judges*, ed. Athalya Brenner, 79–95. Sheffield: Sheffield Academic.

Brueggemann, Walter. 2002. *The Land: Place as Gift, Promise, and Challenge in Biblical Faith.* 2nd ed. Minneapolis: Fortress Press.

———. 2009. *Divine Presence amid Violence: Contextualizing the Book of Joshua.* Eugene, Ore.: Cascade.

Buber, Martin. 2002. *Meetings: Autobiographical Fragments.* Ed. Maurice Friedman. 3rd ed. New York: Routledge.

Burney, C. F. 1970. *The Book of Judges.* New York: KTAV.

Butler, C. Trent. 2009. *Judges.* WBC 8. Nashville: Thomas Nelson.

Butler, Judith. 1999. *Gender Trouble: Feminism and the Subversion of Identity.* 2nd ed. New York: Routledge.

Butler, Sandra. 1978. *Conspiracy of Silence: The Trauma of Incest.* San Francisco: New Glide.

Camp, Claudia V. 2000. *Wise, Strange and Holy: The Strange Woman and the Making of the Bible.* JSOTSup 320. Sheffield: Sheffield Academic.

Campbell, Hugh, and M. Micheal Bell. 2000. "The Question of Rural Masculinities." *Rural Sociology* 65/4: 532–46.

Carus, Paul. 1907. *The Story of Samson and Its Place in the Religious Development of Mankind*. Chicago: Open Court.

Caruth, Cathy. 1995. *Introduction to Trauma: Explorations in Memory*, ed. C. Caruth, 3–12. Baltimore: Johns Hopkins University Press.

Cassuto, Moshe D. 1952. *The Goddess Anat*. Jerusalem: Mosad Bialik (Hebrew).

Cayton, Andrew R. L. 2005. "The Significance of Ohio in the Early American Republic." In *The Center of a Great Empire: The Ohio Country in the Early Republic*, ed. Andrew R. L. Cayton and Stuart D. Hobbs, 2–9. Athens, Ohio: Ohio University Press.

Chan, Joseph M. 2002. "Disneyfying and Globalizing the Chinese Legend Mulan: A Study of Transculturation." In *In Search of Boundaries: Communication, Nation-States and Cultural Identities*, ed. Joseph M. Chan and Bryce T. McIntyre, 225–48. Westport, Conn.: Ablex Publishing.

Charmé, Stuart. 1997. "Children's Gendered Responses to the Story of Adam and Eve." *JFSR* 13/2: 27–44.

Cheng, Patrick S. 2002. "Multiplicity and Judges 19: Constructing a Queer Asian Pacific American Biblical Hermeneutic." *Semeia* 90–91: 119–33.

Cherry, Conrad, ed. 1998. *God's New Israel: Religious Interpretations of American Destiny*. Rev. and updated ed. Chapel Hill: University of North Carolina Press.

Chin, Frank, ed. 1991. *Aiiieeeee! An Anthology of Asian American Writers*. 1974. Repr. New York: Mentor.

Chisholm, Robert B. 2009. "What's Wrong with This Picture? Stylistic Variation as a Rhetorical Technique in Judges." *JSOT* 34/2: 171–82.

Chow, Rey. 2002. *The Protestant Ethnic and the Spirit of Capitalism*. New York: Columbia University Press.

Christiansen, Keith, and Judith Mann. 2001. "Jael and Sisera." In *Orazio and Artemisia Gentileschi*, 344–47. New York and New Haven: Metropolitan Museum of Art and Yale University Press.

Christianson, Eric. 2007. "The Big Sleep: Strategic Ambiguity in Judges 4–5 and in Classic Film Noir." *BibInt* 15/4–5: 519–48. See also 2008, in *Images of the Word: Hollywood's Bible and Beyond*, ed. David Shepherd, 39–60. Atlanta: Society of Biblical Literature.

Clines, D. J. A. 1997. *The Bible and the Modern World*. Sheffield: Sheffield Academic.

Cohen, Judith A., Anthony P. Mannarino, and Esther Deblinger. 2006. *Treating Trauma and Traumatic Grief in Children and Adolescents*. New York: Guilford.

Cohen, Phyllis F. 2002. "The New York Inferno: Taking Solace from the Stories." *Journal of Religion and Health* 41/2: 113–20.

Cohen, Y. 1999. "Everything Is Coming." *Beth Mikra* 44: 45–70 (Hebrew).

Collins, Adela Yarbro. 1978. "Inclusive Biblical Anthropology." *ThTo* 34/4: 358–69.

Collins, John J. 2005. *The Bible after Babel: Historical Criticism in a Postmodern Age*. Grand Rapids: Eerdmans.

Connell, W. Raewyn. 2005. *Masculinities*. 2nd ed. Berkeley: University of California Press.

Cornwall, Andrea, and Nancy Lindisfarne. 1994. *Dislocating Masculinity: Comparative Ethnographies*. Male Orders. New York: Routledge.

Creach, Jerome F. D. 2003. *Joshua*. IBC. Louisville: Westminster John Knox.

Crenshaw, James L. 1974. "The Samson Saga: Filial Devotion or Erotic Attachment?" *ZAW* 86: 470–504.

———. 1978. *Samson: A Secret Betrayed, a Vow Ignored*. Atlanta: John Knox.

Cross, Frank M. 1997 (1973). *Canaanite Myth and Hebrew Epic: Essays in the History of the Religion of Israel*. Cambridge, Mass.: Harvard University Press.

Crossfield, Bernard. 1997. "A Critical Note on Judges 4, 21." *ZAW* 85: 348–51.

Cutler, Manasseh. 1787. *An Explanation of the Map Which Delineates that Part of the Federal Lands*. Salem: Dabney and Cushing. Repr. in Cayton 2005: 1, 2.

Denham, Aaron. 2008. "Rethinking Historical Trauma: Narratives of Resilience." *Transcultural Psychiatry* 45: 391–414.

Dippie, Brian W. 1982. *The Vanishing American: White Attitudes and U.S. Indian Policy*. Lawrence: University of Kansas Press.

Donaldson, Laura E. 1999. "The Sign of Orpah: Reading Ruth through Native Eyes." In *Ruth and Esther: A Feminist Companion to the Bible*, ed. Athalya Brenner, 130–44. Sheffield: Sheffield Academic.

———. 2006. "Red Woman, White Dreams: Searching for Sacagawea." *Feminist Studies* 32: 523–33.

Dong, Lan. 2011. *Mulan's Legend and Legacy in China and the United States*. Philadelphia: Temple University Press.

Dor, Y. 2006. *Have the "Foreign Women" Really Been Expelled? Separation and Exclusion in the Restoration Period*. Jerusalem: Magnes Press (Hebrew).

Dor, Y., and I. Yaniv. 2004. "Training Bible Teachers for the State Secondary System: Research Report (internal)." Oranim College and Mofet Institute (Hebrew).

Du Bois, W. E. B. 1994 (1903). *The Soul of Black Folks.* Chicago: Dover.

Dube, Musa. 2000. "Gender, Method, and Empire-Building in Exodus." In *Postcolonial Feminist Interpretation of the Bible*, 70–83. St. Louis: Chalice.

———. 2001. "Divining Ruth for International Relations." In *Other Ways of Reading: African Women and the Bible*, ed. Musa W. Dube, 179–95. Atlanta: Society of Biblical Literature.

———. 2004. "Postcolonialism and Liberation." In *Handbook of U.S. Theologies of Liberation*, ed. M. De La Torre, 288–94. St. Louis: Chalice.

———. 2006. "Rahab Says Hello to Judith: A Decolonizing Feminist Reading." In *The Postcolonial Biblical Reader*, ed. R. S. Sugirtharajah, 142–58. Oxford: Blackwell.

Dweeb. 2010. "Disney Princesses—Role Models for Young Girls?" *Fanpop.* http://www.fanpop.com/spots/disney-princess/articles/45394/title/disney-princesses-role-models-young-girls.

Earl, Douglas S. 2010. *The Joshua Delusion? Rethinking Genocide in the Bible.* Eugene, Ore.: Cascade.

Eldad, I. 1972. *Thoughts about the Bible.* Jerusalem: Carta (Hebrew).

Elitzur, A. 2004. "The Memory of Amalek and the Taste of Pork: The Anatomy of Metaphysical Hatred." In *The Crucible of Creativity: Fifty Years of Work by Shlomo Giora Shoham*, ed. H. Bin-Nun, A. Elitzur, et al. 118–82. Hod Hasharon: Sha'arei Mishpat College (Hebrew).

Embry, Brad. 2011. "The 'Naked Narrative' from Noah to Leviticus: Reassessing Voyeurism in the Account of Noah's Nakedness in Genesis 9.22-24." *JSOT* 35/4: 417–33.

Eshed, E. 2000. "Joshua." http://www.haayal.co.il/story_368 (accessed December 23, 2012) . (Hebrew).

Evans, Mary J. 1983. *Woman in the Bible: An Overview of All the Crucial Passages on Women's Roles.* Downers Grove, Ill.: InterVarsity.

Exum, Cheryl J. 1980. "Promise and Fulfillment: Narrative Art in Judges 13." *JBL* 99/1: 43–59.

———. 1981. "Aspects of Symmetry and Balance in the Samson Saga." *JSOT* 19: 3–29.

———. 1983. "The Theological Dimension of the Samson Saga." *VT* 33/1: 30–45.

———. 1989. "Murder They Wrote: Ideology and the Manipulation of Female Presence in Biblical Narrative." *Union Seminary Quarterly Review* 43/1-4:19-39.

———. 1992. "Delilah." In *ABD* 2:133.

———. 1993a. *Fragmented Women: Feminist (Sub)versions of Biblical Narrative.* Valley Forge, Pa.: Trinity Press International.

———. 1993b. "On Judges 11." In *A Feminist Companion to Judges*, ed. A. Brenner, 131–44. Sheffield: Sheffield Academic.

———. 1996. "Why, Why, Why, Delilah?" In *Plotted, Shot, and Painted: Cultural Representations of Biblical Women*, 175–237. Sheffield: Sheffield Academic.

———. 2007. "Feminist Criticism: Whose Interests Are Being Served?" In *Judges and Method: New Approaches in Biblical Studies*, ed. Gale A. Yee, 65–89. Minneapolis: Fortress Press.

Faber, Walter. 1995. "Witchcraft, Magic, and Divination in Ancient Mesopotamia." In *Civilizations of the Ancient Near East*, ed. Jack Sasson, 3:1895–909. New York: Scribner.

Feldman, Louis. 2000. "Josephus' Portrayal (*Antiquities* 5.136-174) of the Benjaminite Affair of the Concubine and Its Repercussions (Judges 19-21)." *JQR* 90/3–4: 255–92.

Fetterley, J. 1978. *The Resisting Reader: A Feminist Approach to American Fiction.* Bloomington: Indiana University Press.

Fewell, Danna Nolan. 1998a. "Joshua." In *Women's Bible Commentary*, ed. Carol A. Newsom and Sharon H. Ringe, 69–72. Expanded ed. Louisville: Westminster John Knox.

———. 1998b. "Judges." In *The Women's Bible Commentary*, ed. Carol A. Newsom and Sharon H. Ringe, 73–83. Expanded ed. Louisville: Westminster John Knox.

Fewell, Danna Nolan, and David M. Gunn. 1990. "Controlling Perspectives: Women, Men, and the Authority of Violence in Judges 4 & 5." *JAAR* 58: 389–411.

Fierke, K. M. 2004. "Whereof We Can Speak, Thereof We Must Not Be Silent: Trauma, Political Solipsism and War." *Review of International Studies* 30/4: 471–91.

Finkelstein, Israel, and Neil Asher Silberman. 2001. *The Bible Unearthed: Archaeology's New Vision of Ancient Israel and the Origin of Its Sacred Texts.* New York: Simon and Schuster.

Finkelstein, Jacob J. 1956. "Hebrew ḫbr and Semitic ḫbr." *JBL* 75: 328–31.

Fitzgerald, James L., ed. 2009. *The Mahābhārata: The Great Epic of India.* http://www.brown.edu/Departments/Sanskrit_in_Classics_at_Brown/ Mahabharata/.

Fleming, Daniel E. 2000. "Mari's Large Public Tent and the Priestly Tent Sanctuary." *VT* 50: 484–98.

Fleming, Robyn C. 2005. "Jael's Gender: A Story of Appropriation." http://revena.dreamwidth.org/128023.html?#cutid1.

Fontaine, Carole. 1988. "The Deceptive Goddesses." *Semeia* 42: 84–102.

Freud, Sigmund. 1948 (1922). *Beyond the Pleasure Principle.* Trans. C. J. M. Hubback. London: Hogarth.

———. 1966 (1920). *Introductory Lectures on Psychoanalysis.* Trans. James Strachey. New York: W. W. Norton.

Frick, Frank. 2002. *Journey through the Hebrew Scriptures.* 2nd ed. Belmont, Calif.: Wadsworth.

Frolov, Serge. 2009. "Rethinking Judges." *CBQ* 71: 24–41.

Frymer-Kensky, Tikva. 1992. *In the Wake of the Goddesses: Women, Culture and Biblical Transformation of Pagan Myth.* New York: Fawcett Columbine.

Fuchs, Esther. 1982. "Female Heroines in the Biblical Narrative." *Mankind Quarterly* 23: 149–60.

———. 1985. "Who Is Hiding the Truth? Deceptive Women and Biblical Androcentrism." In *Feminist Perspectives on Biblical Scholarship*, ed. Adela Yarbro Collins, 137–44. Chico, Calif.: Scholars Press.

———. 1993. "Marginalization, Ambiguity, Silencing: The Story of Jephthah's Daughter." In *A Feminist Companion to Judges*, ed. Athalya Brenner, 116–30. Sheffield: Sheffield Academic.

———. 1999. "Status and Role of Female Heroines in the Biblical Narrative." In *Women in the Hebrew Bible: A Reader*, ed. Alice Bach, 77–84. New York: Routledge.

———. 2000. *Sexual Politics in the Biblical Narrative: Reading the Hebrew Bible as a Woman.* Sheffield: Sheffield Academic.

———. 2008. "Reclaiming the Hebrew Bible for Women: The Neo-Liberal Turn in Contemporary Feminist Scholarship." *JFSR* 24/2: 45–65.

Gafney, Wilda. 2008. *Daughters of Miriam: Women Prophets in Ancient Israel.* Minneapolis: Fortress Press.

Galil, G., and Y. Zakovitch. 1994. *Joshua.* Olam ha-Tanakh. Tel Aviv: Dodson-Itti (Hebrew).

Galpaz-Feller, Pnina. 2008. *The Sound of Garments: Garments in the Bible: Do the Clothes Make the Man?* Jerusalem: Carmel Publishing (in Hebrew).

Gersie, Alida. 1997. *Reflections on Therapeutic Storymaking: the Use of Stories in Groups*. London: Jessica Kingsley Publishers.

Gillmayr-Bucher, Susanne. 2009. "Framework and Discourse in the Book of Judges." *JBL* 128/4: 687–702.

Gitlin, Todd, and Liel Leibovitz. 2010. *The Chosen Peoples: America, Israel, and the Ordeals of Divine Election*. New York: Simon and Schuster.

Glender, S., and H. Friedman (forthcoming). "Genocide in the Bible: A Curriculum" (Hebrew).

Goldreich, A. 2006. "Hizbollah's Strategic Weapon." http://www.nfc.co.il/Archive/003-D-17086-00.html?tag=15-06-48 (Hebrew).

Gore, Charles, Henry Leighton Goudge, and Alfred Guillaume, eds. 1928. *A New Commentary on Holy Scripture*. London: SPCK.

Graff, Gerald. 1992. *Beyond the Culture Wars: How Teaching the Conflicts Can Revitalize American Education*. New York: W. W. Norton.

———. 1994. "Taking Cover in Coverage." In *Teaching the Conflicts: Gerald Graff, Curricular Reform, and the Culture Wars*, ed. W. E. Cain, 3–15. New York: Garland.

Gray, John. 1967. *Judges*. London: Thomas Nelson.

Gray, G. Buchanan. 1896. *Studies in Hebrew Proper Names*. London: Adam and Charles Black.

———. 1986. *Joshua, Judges, Ruth*. NCB. Rev. ed. Grand Rapids: Eerdmans; Basingstoke, U.K.: Marshall Morgan & Scott.

Greenberg, Moshe. 1986. "The Use of Talmudic Midrashim as an Educational Resource in the Study of the Book of Joshua." In *The Treasure and the Power*, ed. M. Greenberg, 11–27. Haifa: Oranim, Hakibbutz Hameuchad, and Sifriyat Poalim (Hebrew).

Greenspahn, Fredrick E. 1986. "The Theology of the Framework of Judges." *VT*. 36/4: 385–96.

Greenstein, Edward. 1981. "The Riddle of Samson." *Prooftexts* 1/3: 237–60.

———. 1997. "Kirta." In *Ugaritic Narrative Poetry*, ed. Simon B. Parker, 9–48. Atlanta: Scholars Press.

Griffin, Patrick. 2005. "Reconsidering the Ideological Origins of Indian Removal: The Case of the Big Bottom Massacre." In *The Center of a Great Empire: The Ohio Country In The Early American Republic*, 11-35. Athens: Ohio University Press.

Gross, V. 1978. "The Book of Joshua as a Topical Example of Multidirectional Thinking." *Hahinnukh* 50/3–4: 176–80 (Hebrew).

Grossfeld, Bernard. 1997. "A Critical Note on Judges 4, 21." *ZAW* 85: 348–51.

Guest, Deryn. 2005. *When Deborah Met Jael: Lesbian Biblical Hermeneutics*. London: SCM.

———. 2008. "Looking Lesbian at the Bathing Bathsheba." *BibInt* 16: 227–62.

———. 2011. "From Gender Reversal to Genderfuck: Reading Jael Through a Lesbian Lens." In *Bible Trouble: Queer Reading At the Boundaries of Biblical Scholarship*, ed. Teresa Hornsby and Ken Stone, 9–43. Atlanta: Society of Biblical Literature.

Gulin, E. G. 1922. *Maanpakoa varhaisempien profeettojen käsitys siveellisyydestä*. Helsinki: Helsingin Yliopiston.

Gunn, David M. 2005. *Judges*. Blackwell Bible Commentaries. Oxford: Blackwell.

Gvaryahu, H. M. 1989. "Memories of the Bible Study Group." In *Ben-Gurion and the Bible: A People and its Land*, ed. H. Kogan, 70–74. Beer Sheba: Ben-Gurion University of the Negev (Hebrew).

Habel, Norman C. 2005. *The Land Is Mine: Six Biblical Land Ideologies*. Minneapolis: Fortress Press.

Haber, Beth K. 1995. *Drawing on the Bible: Biblical Women in Art*. New York: Biblio.

Hackett, Jo Ann. 1985. "In the Days of Jael: Reclaiming the History of Women in Ancient Israel." In *Gender and Difference in Ancient Israel*, ed. Peggy L. Day, 15–38. Minneapolis: Fortress Press.

Hagag, R. 2004. "Introduction to the Book of Joshua." In *Israelite Society in Formation: From the Bondage in Egypt to the Judges: Teachers' Guide*, 92–105. Even-Yehuda: Rekhes (Hebrew).

Halpern, Baruch. 1983. "The Resourceful Israelite Historian: The Song of Deborah and Israelite Historiography." *HTR* 76/4: 379–401.

———. 1992. "Kenites." In *ABD* 4:17–22.

Hansen, T. Karen. 2004. "The World in Dress: Anthropological Perspectives on Clothing, Fashion, and Culture." *Annual Review of Anthropology* 33: 369–92.

Harding, Sandra. 1987. Introduction to *Feminism and Methodology*, ed. Sandra Harding, 1–14. Bloomington: Indiana University Press.

———. 2004. "Rethinking Standpoint Epistemology: What Is 'Strong Objectivity?'" In *The Feminist Standpoint Theory Reader: Intellectual and Political Controversies*, ed. Sandra Harding, 127–40. New York: Routledge.

Harpaz, Y. 2005. *The Hook, Bait, and Fish: Approaches to Education in Thinking*. Jerusalem: Branco Weiss Institute (Hebrew).

Harrington, Daniel J. 1985. "Pseudo-Philo: A New Translation and Introduction." In *The Old Testament Pseudepigrapha*, ed. James H. Charlesworth, 2:296–377. Garden City, N.Y.: Doubleday.

Harris, J., C. Brown, and M. Moore. 1998. *Judges*. Nashville: Abingdon.

Hawk, L. Daniel. 2000. *Joshua*. Berit Olam. Collegeville, Minn.: Liturgical.

———. 2010. *Joshua in 3-D: A Commentary on Biblical Conquest and Manifest Destiny*. Eugene, Ore.: Cascade.

Hays, J. Daniel, and Donald A. Carson. 2003. *From Every People and Nation: A Biblical Theology of Race*. New Studies in Biblical Theology. Downers Grove, Ill.: InterVarsity Press.

Helin, Janne. 2006. *Maa vahva, Jumala väkevä*. Master's thesis, University of Helsinki.

Herman, Judith. 1996. "Crime and Memory." In *Trauma and Self*, ed. C. B. Strozier and M. Flynn, 3–17. Lanham, Md.: Rowman and Littlefield.

———. 1997. *Trauma and Recovery: The Aftermath of Violence—From Domestic Abuse to Political Terror*. New York: Basic.

Herzog, Z. 2001. "The Scientific Revolution in Land of Israel Archaeology." In *The Controversy over the Historicity of the Bible*, ed. L. I. Levine and A. Mazar, 52–65. Jerusalem: Yad Izhak Ben-Zvi and Merkaz Dinur (Hebrew).

Hoffner, Harry A., Jr. 1967. "Second Millennium Antecedents to the Hebrew 'OB." *JBL* 86: 385–401.

———. 1974a. "*ôbh*." *TDOT* 1:130–34.

———. 1974b. *Alimenta Hethaerum: Food Production in Hittite Asia Minor*. New Haven: American Oriental Society.

———. 1998. *Hittite Myths*. Atlanta: Scholars Press.

Houston, Tom. 2004. "Biblical Models of Leadership." *Transformation* 21/4: 227–33.

Hoven, Bettina van, and Kathrin Hörschelmann. 2005. *Spaces of Masculinities*, Critical Geographies. New York: Routledge.

Hudson, Don Michael. 1994. "Living in a Land of Epithets: Anonymity in Judges 19-21." *JSOT* 62: 49–66.

Hughes, Richard T. 2003. *Myths America Lives By*. Urbana: University of Illinois Press.

Huntington, Samuel P. 1996. *The Clash of Civilizations and the Remaking of World Order*. New York: Simon and Schuster.

Huttunen, Niko. 2011. "The Bible, Finland, and the Civil War 1918. Reception History and Effective History of the Bible as Contextualized Biblical Studies." *Studia Theologica. Nordic Journal of Theology* 65: 146–71.

Jackson, Beverley. 1997. *Splendid Slippers: A Thousand Years of an Erotic Tradition.* Berkeley: Ten Speed Press.

Jackson, Melissa. 2002. "Lot's Daughters and Tamar as Tricksters and the Patriarchal Narratives as Feminist Theology." *JSOT* 26/4: 29–46.

Jackson, Melissa. 2012. *Comedy and Feminist Interpretation of the Hebrew Bible: A Subversive Collaboration.* Oxford Theological Monographs. New York: Oxford University.

Janzen, J. Gerald. 1982. "Metaphor and Reality in Hosea 11." *Semeia* 24: 7–44.

Jeffers, Ann. 1996. *Magic and Divination in Ancient Palestine and Syria.* Leiden: Brill.

Jeter, Joseph R., Jr. 2003. *Preaching Judges.* St. Louis: Chalice.

Jewett, Paul K. 1975. *Man as Male and Female.* Grand Rapids: Eerdmans.

Jokipii, A. E. 1941. "Sota-ajan asettamia vaatimuksia kristilliselle julistukselle." *TAik* 46: 1–15.

Jones, G. L. 1999. "Sacred Violence: The Dark Side of God." *Journal of Beliefs and Values* 20/2: 184–99.

Jones, Serene. 2009. *Trauma and Grace: Theology in a Ruptured World.* Louisville: Westminster John Knox.

Jones-Warsaw, Koala. 1998. "Toward a Womanist Hermeneutic: A Reading of Judges 19–21." In *A Feminist Companion to Judges*, ed. Athalya Brenner, 172–86. Sheffield: Sheffield Academic.

Kafkafi, A. 1988. "Like Olive Saplings—The Process Method: The Educational Philosophy of Mordecai Segal and Its Implementation in the Schools of the United Kibbutz Movement." *Dor le-Dor* 12: 171–208 (Hebrew).

Kalkin-Fishman, D. 2002. "Biographies of Teachers and the Biography of the State." In *Teachers in Israel: A Feminist Perspective*, ed. M. Zellermaier and P. Peri, 89–114. Tel Aviv: Hakibbutz Hemeuchad (Hebrew).

Kalsched, Donald. 1996. *The Inner World of Trauma: Archetypal Defenses of the Personal Spirit.* New York: Routledge.

Kaminsky, Joel. 2000. "Humor and the Theology of Hope: Isaac as a Humorous Figure." *Int* 54/4: 363–75.

Kamionkowski, S. Tamar. 2011. "Queer Theory and Historical-Critical Exegesis: Queering Biblicists—A Response." In *Bible Trouble: Queer Reading At the Boundaries of Biblical Scholarship*, ed. Teresa Hornsby and Ken Stone, 131–36 Atlanta: Society of Biblical Literature.

Kamuf, Peggy. 1993. "Author of a Crime." In *A Feminist Companion to Judges*, ed. Athalya Brenner, 187–207. Sheffield: JSOT Press.

Kasher, R. 2006. "Bible and Morality and in Modern Bible Scholarship." *Beth Mikra* 51/1: 1–42 (Hebrew).

Kaufmann, Y. 1970. *The Book of Joshua.* Jerusalem: Kiryath Sepher (Hebrew).

Keefe, Alice A. 1993. "Rapes of Women/Wars of Men." *Semeia* 61: 79–97.

Keil, Carl Friedrich, and Franz Delitzsch. 1996. *Joshua, Ruth, 1 & II Samuel.* Trans. James Martin. Commentary on the Old Testament. Peabody, Mass.: Hendrickson.

Kelle, Brad E., and Frank R. Ames, eds. 2008. *Writing and Reading War: Rhetoric, Gender and Ethics in Biblical and Modern Contexts.* Leiden: Brill/Society of Biblical Literature.

Keren R. 2002. *The Book of Joshua.* Netanya: Amihai (Hebrew).

Keren, M. 1983. *Ben-Gurion and the Intellectuals: Power, Knowledge, and Charisma.* DeKalb: Northern Illinois University Press.

Killebrew, Ann E. 2004. *Biblical Peoples and Ethnicity: An Archaeological Study of Egyptians, Canaanites, Philistines, and Early Israel 1300–1100 B.C.C.* SBLABS. Atlanta: Society of Biblical Literature.

Kim, Uriah Y. 2007. "Postcolonial Criticism: Who Is the Other in the Book of Judges?" In *Judges and Method: New Approaches in Biblical Studies*, ed. Gale A. Yee, 161–82. 2nd ed. Minneapolis: Fortress Press.

Kingston, Maxine Hong. 1977. *The Woman Warrior: Memoirs of a Girlhood Among Ghosts.* 1976; repr., New York: Vintage.

Kirk-Duggan, Cheryl. 2012. "How Liberating is Exodus, and for Whom?: Deconstructing Exodus Motifs in Scripture, Literature, and Life," in *Exodus and Deuteronomy*, Texts @ Contexts, eds. Athayla Brenner and Gale Yee, 3–28. Minneapolis: Fortress Press.

Kitamori, Kazoh. 2005. *Theology of the Pain of God.* Eugene, Ore.: Wipf and Stock.

Klein Abensohn, Lillian. 2012. "The Art of Irony: The Book of Judges." In *Words, Ideas, Worlds: Biblical and Other Essays in Honour of Yairah Amit*, ed. A. Brenner and F. H. Polak, 133–44. Sheffield: Sheffield Phoenix.

Klein, Lillian R. 1988. *The Triumph of Irony in the Book of Judges.* Bible and Literature. Sheffield: Almond.

———. 1993. "The Book of Judges: Paradigm and Deviation in Images of Women." In *A Feminist Companion to Judges*, ed. Athalya Brenner, 55–71. Sheffield: JSOT Press.

———. 2003. *From Deborah to Esther: Sexual Political in the Hebrew Bible.* Minneapolis: Fortress Press.

Knapp, H. S. 1863. *A History of the Pioneer and Modern Times of Ashland County.* Philadelphia: J. B. Lippincott.

Koehler, Ludwig. 1919. "Die Offenbarungsformel 'Fürchte dich nicht!' im Alten Testament." *SThZ* 36: 33–39.

Kook, Z. Y. 1982. "A People and Its Land," *Artzi* 2: 15–23 (Hebrew).

Korach-Segev, D., and Y. Silberman. 1994. *The Book of Joshua.* Tel Aviv: Modan (Hebrew).

Laffey, Alice L. 1988. *An Introduction to the Old Testament: A Feminist Perspective.* Philadelphia: Fortress.

Laine, Esko M. 1997. "Kulttuuri, politiikka ja yhteiskunta Teologisen aikakauskirjan lehdillä sotavuosina 1939–1944." *TAik* 102: 504–25.

Lan, Feng. 2003. "The Female Individual and the Empire: A Historicist Approach to Mulan and Kingston's Woman Warrior." *Comparative Literature* 55/3: 229–45.

Landay, Lori. 1998. *Madcaps, Screwballs and Con Women: The Female Trickster in American Culture.* Philadelphia: University of Pennsylvania Press.

Lapsley, Jacqueline E. 2005. *Whispering the Word: Hearing Women's Stories in the Old Testament.* Louisville: Westminster John Knox.

Lasine, Stuart. 1984. "Guest and Host in Judges 19: Lot's Hospitality in an Inverted World." *JSOT* 29: 37–59.

Laszlo, Janos. 2008. *The Science of Stories: An Introduction to Narrative Psychology.* New York: Routledge.

Laub, Dori. 1995. "Truth and Testimony: The Process and the Struggle." In *Trauma: Explorations in Memory*, ed. C. Caruth, 61–75. Baltimore: Johns Hopkins University Press.

Latvus, Kari. 1993. *Jumalan viha. Redaktiokriittinen tutkimus Joosuan ja Tuomarienkirjojen jumalakuvasta.* [*The Anger of God. A Redaction Critical View of the Concept of God in the Books of Joshua and Judges*] Helsinki: Finnish Exegetical Society.

Latvus, Kari. 1998. *God, Anger and Ideology: The Anger of God in Joshua and Judges in Relation to Deuteronomy and the Priestly Writings.* JSOTSup 279. Sheffield: Sheffield Academic.

Lavery, Jason Edward. 2006. *The History of Finland.* London: Greenwood.

Leach, E. 1967. "Magical Hair." In *Myth and Cosmos*, ed. John Middleton, 77–108. Garden City: Natural History.

Lee, Robert G. 1999. *Orientals: Asian Americans in Popular Culture.* Philadelphia: Temple University Press.

Lemma, Alessandra, and Susan Levy. 2004. "The Impact of Trauma on the Psyche: Internal and External Processes." In *The Perversion of Loss: Psychoanalytic Perspectives on Trauma*, ed. A. Lemma and Susan Levy, 108–26. Philadelphia: Whurr.

Leneman, Helen. 2007. "Re-Visioning a Biblical Story Through Libretto and Music: Debora E Jaele by Ildebrando Pizzetti." *BibInt* 15/4–5: 428–63.

Lernoux, Penny, et al. 1995. *Hearts on Fire: The Story of the Maryknoll Sisters*. Maryknoll, N.Y.: Orbis.

Levenson, Jon D. 1978. "1 Samuel 25 as Literature and History." *CBQ* 40/1: 11–28.

———. 1985. "Is There a Counterpart in the Hebrew Bible to New Testament Antisemitism?" *JES* 22/2: 242–60.

Levine, Peter A. 1997. *Waking the Tiger—Healing Trauma: The Innate Capacity to Transform Overwhelming Experiences*. Berkeley: North Atlantic Books.

Levinson, Bernard. 2008. *Legal Revision and Religious Renewal in Ancient Israel*. Cambridge: Cambridge University Press.

Lewis, Theodore J. 1989. *The Cult of the Dead in Ancient Israel and Ugarit*. Atlanta: Scholars Press.

———. 1997. "The Birth of the Gracious Gods (23. CAT 1.23)." In *Ugaritic Narrative Poetry*, ed. Simon B. Parker, 205–14. Atlanta: Scholars Press.

Li, Siu Leung. 2003. *Cross-Dressing in Chinese Opera*. Hong Kong: Hong Kong University Press.

Licht, Yaakov, S. 1962. "ה מלאך, מלאכים" ("Angel of God, Angels"). In *Encyclopedia Biblica*, 4:975–90. Jerusalem: Mosad Bialik (Hebrew).

Lipschits, Y., and O. Lipschits. 2000. *History, Bible, and What Happened: The Book of Joshua for the Upper Elementary Grades in the State Schools* (with teacher's manual). Jerusalem: Yad Ben-Zvi (Hebrew).

Loewenstamm, S. A. 1965. "Herem." In *Encyclopedia Biblica*, 3:290–92. Jerusalem: Mosad Bialik (Hebrew).

Lohfink, N. 1986. "חרם." In *TDOT* 5:180–99.

Löwisch, Ingeborg. 2009. "Genealogies, Gender, and the Politics of Memory: 1 Chronicles 1–9 and the Documentary Film *Mein Leben Teil 2*." In *Performing Memory in Biblical Narrative and Beyond*, ed. Athalya Brenner and Frank H. Polak, 228–56. Sheffield: Sheffield Phoenix.

Lukács, G. 1938/1969. *The Historical Novel*. Trans. H. and S. Mitchell. Harmondsworth, U.K.: Penguin.

Luz, Ulrich. 1989. *Matthew 1–7: A Continental Commentary*. Trans. Wilhelm C. Linss. Minneapolis: Fortress Press.

———. 2007. *Matthew in History: Interpretation, Influence, and Effects.* Minneapolis: Fortress Press.

Ma, Sheng-Mei. 2000. *The Deathly Embrace: Orientalism and Asian American Identity.* Minneapolis: University of Minnesota Press.

———. 2003. "Mulan Disney, It's Like, Re-Orients: Consuming China and Animating Teen Dreams." In *The Emperor's Old Groove: Deconomizing Disney's Magic Kingdom,* ed. Brenda Ayres, 149–64 New York: Peter Lang.

Madacy Entertainment Group. 1999. *Mulan.* Troy, Mich.: Anchor Bay Entertainment.

Malamat, Abraham. 1962. "Mari and the Bible: Some Patterns of Tribal Organizations and Institutions." *JAOS* 82: 143–50.

———. 1998. *Mari and the Bible.* Leiden: Brill.

Malamet, Abraham, 1969. "The Conquest of the Land and the Settlement on it." In H. H. Ben Sasson, ed., *The History of the People of Israel,* 1:57–70. Tel Aviv: Dvir (Hebrew).

Mann, Susan. 2000. "Myths of Asian Womanhood." *Journal of Asian Studies* 59/4: 835–62.

Marcus, David. 1986. *Jephthah and His Vow.* Lubbock: Texas Tech Press.

Margalith, Othaniel. 1985. "Samson's Foxes." *VT* 35/2: 224–29.

———. 1986a. "More Samson Legends." *VT* 36/4: 397–405.

———. 1986b. "Samson's Riddle and Samson's Magic Locks." *VT* 36/2: 225–34.

———. 1987. "The Legends of Samson/Heracles." *VT* 37/1: 63–70.

Martin, D. James. 1975. *The Book of Judges.* Cambridge: Cambridge University Press.

Matthews, Victor H. 1991. "Hospitality and Hostility in Judges 4." *BTB* 21: 13–21.

———. 1992. "Hospitality and Hostility in Genesis 19 and Judges 19." *BTB* 2/1: 3–11.

Mayfield, Tyler D. 2009. "The Accounts of Deborah (Judges 4–5) in Recent Research." *Currents in Biblical Research* 7: 306–35.

Mazar, Benjamin. 1965. "The Sanctuary of Arad and the Family of Hobab the Kenite." *JNES* 24: 297–303.

Mazor, L. 2003. "The Rise and Fall of the Book of Joshua in the State School System in Light of Ideological Changes in Israeli Society." *Iyyunim ba-Hinnukh ha-Yehudi* 9: 21–46 (Hebrew).

McCann, J. Clinton. 2002. *Judges.* IBC. Louisville: Westminster John Knox.

McKenzie, John L. 1966. *The World of the Judges.* Englewood Cliffs, N.J.: Prentice Hall.

Medan, Y. 2000. "The Conquest of the Land and Moral Values: A Look at the Book of Joshua." In *The Morality of War and Conquest: Proceedings of a Symposium at Herzog College,* 2–34. Alon Shevut: Tevunot–Herzog College (Hebrew).

Meisler, B. 1950. "The Sixth National Conference for Knowledge of the Land, Ha-gelilah." *Bulletin of the Hebrew Society for the Study of the Land of Israel and Its Antiquities* 15/3–4: 116–31 (Hebrew).

Meyers, Carol. 2005. *Exodus.* Cambridge: Cambridge University Press.

Miller, Barbara. 2005. *Tell It on the Mountain: The Daughter of Jephthah in Judges 11.* Collegeville, Minn.: Liturgical.

Miller, Patrick D. 2000. "God's Other Stories: On the Margins of Deuteronomic Theology." In *Israelite Religion and Biblical Theology: Collected Essays.* JSOTSup 267. Sheffield: Sheffield Academic.

Milton, John. 2010. *The Poetic Works of John Milton.* Fairford: Echo Library.

Moor, Johannes C. de, and Wilfred G. E. Watson, eds. 1993. "General Introduction." In *Verse in Ancient Near Eastern Poetry.* AOAT 42. Kevelaer: Butzon & Bercker.

Moore, Stephen D. 2006. *Empire and Apocalypse: Postcolonialism and the New Testament.* Sheffield: Sheffield Phoenix.

Moran, William L. 1969. "New Evidence from Mari on the History of Prophecy." *Bib* 50: 15–56.

Mossinson, B. 2005. "The Bible in the Schools." In *The Bible and Israeli Identity,* ed. Anita Shapira, 39–40. Jerusalem: Magnes Press (Hebrew).

Mullner, Ilse. 1999. "Lethal Differences: Sexual Violence as Violence Against Others in Judges 19." In *Judges: A Feminist Companion to the Bible,* ed. Athalya Brenner, 126–42. Sheffield: Sheffield Academic.

Murray, Donald F. 1979. "Narrative Structure and Technique in Deborah-Barak Story (Judges 4. 4-22)." In *Studies in the Historical Books of the Old Testament,* ed. John Emerton, 155–89. Leiden: Brill.

Murthy, K. M. K., and Desiraju Hanumanta Rao. *Valmiki Ramayana.* http://valmikiramayan.net/.

Murtorinne, Eino. 1975. *Veljeyttä viimeiseen asti. Suomen ja Saksan kirkkojen suhteet toisen maailmansodan aikana 1940–44.* Helsinki: Suomen kirkkohistoriallinen seura.

Murtorinne, Eino, and Markku Heikkilä. 1980. *Kotimaa 1905–1980. Routavuosien kristillis-yhteiskunnallisesta lehtiyrityksestä monipuoliseksi kristilliseksi kustannusyhtiöksi.* Helsinki: Kirjapaja.

Mustonen, Matti A. 1941. "Bolsevistinen moraali ja puoluekuri." *TAik* 46: 471–89.

Na'aman, Nadav. 2006. "Towards the Reconstruction of the Ancient History of the People of Israel: Bible, Archaeology, and Historiography." *Zemanim* 94: 8–19 (Hebrew).

National Scientific Council on the Developing Child. 2005. "Excessive Stress Disrupts the Architecture of the Developing Brain: Working Paper #3." Cambridge, Mass.: The Center on the Developing Child at Harvard University.

Nelson, R. D. 1981. "Josiah in the Book of Joshua." *JBL* 100: 531–40.

———. 1997. *Joshua: A Commentary.* Louisville: Westminster John Knox.

Newsom, Carol A., and Sharon H. Ringe, eds. 1992, 1998, 2012. *The Women's Bible Commentary.* Louisville: Westminster John Knox.

Ng, Andrew Hock-Soon. 2007. "Revisiting Judges 19: A Gothic Perspective." *JSOT* 32/2: 199–215.

Nguyen, Mimi. 1998. "Role Models: Mulan." *Theory.org.uk.* http://www.theory.org.uk/ctr-rol2.htm.

Niditch, Susan. 1982. "The 'Sodomite' Theme in Judges 19–20: Family, Community, and Social Disintegration." *CBQ* 44/3: 365–78.

———. 1989. "Eroticism and Death in the Tale of Jael." In *Gender and Difference in Ancient Israel*, ed. Peggy L. Day, 43–57. Minneapolis: Fortress Press.

———. 1990. "Samson as Cultural Hero, Trickster, and Bandit: The Empowerment of the Weak." *CBQ* 52/4: 608–24.

———. 1993. *War in the Hebrew Bible: A Study in the Ethics of Violence.* Oxford: Oxford University Press.

Niemelä, Pauli M. K. 1999. *Antti Filemon Puukko. Suomalainen Vanhan testamentin tutkija ja tulkitsija.* SES 74. Helsinki: Suomen eksegeettisen seuran julkaisuja.

Nilsson, Marco. 2010. *War and Unreason: Bounded Learning Theory and War Duration.* Gothenburg Studies in Politics. Gothenburg: University of Gothenburg Press.

Nissinen, Martti. 2008. "From Holy War to Holy Peace: Biblical Alternatives to Belligerent Rhetoric." In *Isaiah's Vision of Peace in Biblical and Modern International Relations: Swords into Plowshares*, ed. R. Cohen and R. Westbrook, 181–97. New York: Palgrave Macmillan.

Noegel, Scott B. 2007. *Nocturnal Ciphers: The Allusive Language of Dreams in the Ancient Near East.* New Haven: American Oriental Society.

Nussbaum, Martha. 2007. *The Clash Within: Democracy, Religious Violence, and India's Future.* Cambridge, Mass.: Harvard University Press.

O'Connor, M. 1986. "Northwest Semitic Designations for Elective Social Affinities." *JANES* 18: 67–80.

Okihiro, Gary Y. 1994. *Margins and Mainstreams: Asians in American History and Culture.* Seattle: University of Washington Press.

Olson, Dennis T. 1998. "Judges." In *NIB* 2:723–888. Nashville: Abingdon.

Oppenheim, Leo A. 1956. *The Interpretation of Dreams in the Ancient Near East.* Philadelphia: Lancaster Press.

———. 1960. "The City of Aššur in 714 BC." *JNES* 19: 133–47.

Orbach, D. 2007. "There is No Fanatic to Compare with an Apostate Fanatic." http://www.hofesh.org.il/ (Hebrew).

Oron, Y. 2006. *Thoughts about the Inconceivable: Theoretical Aspects in the Study of Genocide.* Ra'anana: The Open University of Israel (Hebrew).

Otto, Rudolf. 1936. *Das Heilige: Über das Irrationale in der Idee des Göttlichen und sein Verhältnis zum Rationalen.* München: C.H. Beck'sche Reihe Verlagsbuchhandlung.

Palmer, A. Smythe. 1977. *The Samson-Saga and Its Place in Comparative Religion.* London: Sir Isaac Pitman & Sons.

Parida, A., and R. Sela. 2004. *The Bible with Friends.* Holon: Yesod (Hebrew).

Parker, Simon B. 1997. "Aqhat." In *Ugaritic Narrative Poetry*, ed. Simon B. Parker, 49–80. Atlanta: Scholars Press.

Parpola, Simo. 1997. *Assyrian Prophecies.* State Archives of Assyria 9. Helsinki: Helsinki University Press.

Parpola, Simo, and Kazuko Wattanabe, eds. 1988. *Neo-Assyrian Treaties and Loyalty Oaths.* State Archives of Assyria 2. Helsinki: Helsinki University Press.

Patte, Daniel, et al., eds. 2004. *The Global Bible Commentary.* Nashville: Abingdon.

Penner, Todd, and Caroline Vander Stichele, eds. 2005. *Her Master's Tools? Feminist And Postcolonial Engagements of Historical-Critical Discourse.* Global Perspectives on Biblical Scholarship. Atlanta: Society of Biblical Literature.

Peri, M. 2005. "A Helpmate: Rebecca, Her Slave Groom, and God's Coalition with Women in the Biblical Tale." *Alpayim* 29: 193–271 (Hebrew).

Petersen, William. 1966. "Success Story, Japanese American Style." *New York Times.* January 9.

————. 1971. *Japanese Americans: Oppression and Success.* New York: Random House.

Polak, Frank. 1994. *Biblical Narrative: Aspects of Art and Design.* Jerusalem: Mosad Bialik (Hebrew).

Polzin, Robert. 1980. *Moses and the Deuteronomist: A Literary Study of the Deuteronomic History.* New York: Seabury.

————. 1989. *Samuel and the Deuteronomist: A Literary Study of the Deuteronomic History: 1 Samuel.* San Francisco: Harper & Row.

————. 1993. *David and the Deuteronomist: A Literary Study of the Deuteronomic History: 2 Samuel.* Bloomington: Indiana University Press.

Pressler, Carolyn. 2002. *Joshua, Judges, and Ruth.* Westminster Bible Companion. Louisville: Westminster John Knox.

Prior, John Mansford. 2006. "Power and 'the Other' in Joshua: The Brutal Birthing of a Group Identity." *Mission Studies* 23: 27–43.

Prior, M. C. M. 1997. *The Bible and Colonialism: A Moral Critique.* Sheffield: Sheffield Academic.

Prucha, Francis Paul, ed. 2000. *Documents of United States Indian Policy.* 3rd ed. Lincoln: University of Nebraska Press.

Puukko, A. F. 1941. "Jumalan hallitus ja maailmanhistoria." *TAik* 46: 349–66.

Rabin, H. 1970. "The Moabite Stone." In *Encyclopedia Biblica*, 925–29. Jerusalem: Mosad Bialik (Hebrew).

Rad, Gerhard von. 1991. *Holy War in Ancient Israel.* Trans. and ed. Marva J. Dawn. Bibliography by Judith E. Sanderson. Grand Rapids: Eerdmans.

Radday, Yahuda T. 1990. "Humour in Names." In *On Humour and the Comic in the Hebrew Bible*, ed. Yehuda T. Radday and Athalya Brenner, 59–98. Sheffield: Almond.

Ravitzky, A. 1999. *Freedom on the Tablets: Other Voices of Religious Thought.* Tel Aviv: Am Oved (Hebrew).

Reis, Pamela Tamarkin. 2005. "Uncovering Jael and Sisera: A New Reading." *SJOT* 19/1: 24–47.

————. 2006. "The Levite's Concubine: New Light on a Dark Story." *SJOT* 20/1: 125–46.

Rhoads, David M., ed. 2005. *From Every People and Nation: The Book of Revelation in Intercultural Perspective.* Minneapolis: Fortress Press.

Robnolt, I'Laine. 1995 "Jael's Husband Returns from War after the Death of Sisera." *Daughters of Sarah* 21/3: 1.

Rogers, Annie G. 2006. *The Unsayable: The Hidden Language of Trauma.* New York: Random House.

Rosenberg, S. 2000. "War and Peace: Joshua and Isaiah." In *The Morality of War and Conquest: Proceedings of a Symposium at Herzog College*, 47–60. Alon Shevut: Tevunot–Herzog College (Hebrew).

———. 2003. "The Bible and Values." *Iyyunim ba-Hinnukh ha-Yehudi* 9: 293–302 (Hebrew).

Rowlett, Lori. 2000. "Disney's Pocahontas and Joshua's Rahab in Postcolonial Perspective." In Culture, Entertainment and the Bible, ed. George Aichele, 66–75. Sheffield: Sheffield Academic.

Ryan, M. 1989. "Political Criticism." In *Contemporary Literary Theory*, ed. G. D. Atkins and L. Morrow, 200–213. Amherst: University of Massachusetts Press.

Said, Edward W. 1978. *Orientalism*. New York: Pantheon.

Sakenfeld, Katharine Doob. 1997. "Deborah, Jael, and Sisera's Mother: Reading the Scriptures in Cross-Cultural Context." In *Women, Gender, and Christian Community*, ed. Jane Dempsey Douglass and James F. Kay, 13-22. Louisville: Westminster John Knox.

———. 2008. "Whose Text Is It?" *JBL* 127/1: 5–18.

Sasson, J. M. 1988. "Who Cut Samson's hair? (And other Trifling Issues Raised by Judges 16)." *Prooftexts* 8: 333–39.

Scheffler, Eben. 2009. "War and Violence in the Old Testament World: Various Views." In *Animosity, the Bible, and Us: Some European, North American, and South African Perspectives*, ed. J. T. Fitgerald, F. J. van Rensburg, and H. F. van Rooy, 1–17. Atlanta: Society of Biblical Literature.

Schneider, Tammi J. 2000. *Judges.* Berit Olam. Collegeville, Minn.: Liturgical.

Schwartz, Regina M. 1997. *The Curse of Cain: The Violent Legacy of Monotheism.* Chicago: University of Chicago Press.

Segovia, Fernando F., and Mary Ann Tolbert, eds. 1995. *Reading from This Place.* Vol. 1, *Social Location and Biblical Interpretation in the United States.* Minneapolis: Augsburg Fortress Press.

———. 1995. *Reading from This Place.* Vol. 2, *Social Location and Biblical Interpretation in Global Perspective.* Minneapolis: Augsburg Fortress.

———. 2004. *Teaching the Bible: The Discourses and Politics of Biblical Pedagogy* (repr., Eugene, Ore.: Wipf and Stock [originally 1997]).

Seppo, Juha. 1997. "Teologinen aikakauskirja sodan ja Lundin teologian varjossa 1940–1953." *TAik* 102: 526–55.

Shahor, A. 1996. *Joshua.* Tel Aviv: Or Am (Hebrew).

Shapira, Anita. 2005. *The Bible and Israeli Identity*. Jerusalem: Magnes Press (Hebrew).

Sharon, Diane M. 2007. "Choreography of an Intertextual Allusion to Rape in Judges 5: 24-27." In *Bringing the Hidden to Light: Studies in Honor of Stephen A. Geller*, ed. Kathryn F. Kravitz and Diane M. Sharon, 249–69. Winona Lake, Ind.: Eisenbrauns.

Sharp, Carolyn. 2011. *Wrestling the Word: The Hebrew Scriptures and the Christian Believer*. Louisville: Westminster John Knox.

Showalter, Elaine. 1986. "Feminist Criticism in the Wilderness." In *The New Feminist Criticism*, ed. Elaine Showalter, 243–70. London: Virago.

Simon, U. 1991. *Man in the Image: Humanistic Education and Study of the Bible*. Tel Aviv: Am Oved (Hebrew).

———. 2001. "Post-Biblical Archaeology and Post-Zionism." In *The Controversy Over the Historicity of the Bible*, ed. L. I. Levine and A. Mazar, 3–40. Jerusalem: Yad Izhak Ben-Zvi and Merkaz Dinur (Hebrew).

———. 2002. *Seek Peace and Pursue It: Topical Issues in the Light of the Bible, the Bible in the Light of Topical Issues*. Tel Aviv: Yedioth Ahronoth (Hebrew).

Singer, Itamar. 2002. *Hittite Prayers*. Atlanta: Society of Biblical Literature.

Sister, M. 1955. *Some Problems of Biblical Literature*. Tel Aviv: Hakibbutz Hameuchad (Hebrew).

Slotkin, Richard. 1973. *Regeneration through Violence: The Mythology of the American Frontier, 1600–1860*. Norman: University of Oklahoma Press.

Smith, Anthony D. 1986. *The Ethnic Origins of Nations*. Oxford: Blackwell.

———. 2003. *Chosen Peoples: Sacred Sources of National Identity*. Oxford: Oxford University Press.

Smith, Carol. 1997. "Samson and Delilah: A Parable of Power?" *JSOT* 76: 45–57.

———. 1999. "Delilah: A Suitable Case for (Feminist) Treatment?" In *Judges: A Feminist Companion to the Bible*, ed. Athalya Brenner, 93–116. 2nd series. Sheffield: Sheffield Academic.

Smith, Mark S. 1997. "The Baal Cycle." In *Ugaritic Narrative Poetry*, ed. Simon, B. Parker, 81–176. Atlanta: Scholars Press.

Smitherman, Geneva. 1997. "Black English/*Ebonics*: What It Be Like?" *Rethinking Schools: An Urban Educational Journal* 12: 8–9.

Soggin, Alberto J. 1981a. "Heber der Qenit. Das Ende eines biblischen Personnennamens?" *VT* 31: 89–92.

———. 1981b. *Judges: A Commentary*. Trans. J. S. Bowden. Philadelphia: Westminster.

———. 1987. *Judges*. OTL. London: SCM.

Solá-Solé, Josep María. 1966. "Nueva inscripción fenicia de España (Hispania 14)." *RSO* 41: 97–108, tavv. I–II.

Stannard, David E. 1992. *American Holocaust*. Oxford: Oxford University Press.

Steinberg, Naomi. 1984. "Gender Roles in the Rebekah Cycle." *Union Seminary Quarterly Review* 39/3: 175–88.

Stephanson, Anders. 1995. *Manifest Destiny: American Expansion and the Empire of Right*. New York: Hill and Wang.

Sternberg, Meir. 1985. *The Poetics of Biblical Narrative: Ideological Literature and Drama of Reading*. Bloomington: Indiana University Press.

Stone, Ken. 1995. "Gender and Homosexuality in Judges 19: Subject-Honor, Object-Shame?" *JSOT* 67: 87–107.

Ta-Shma, M. 2006. "Parallels that Never Meet: The Tosafists' Yeshivot and the Academic Environment in France in the Twelfth and Thirteenth Centuries." In *Yeshivot and Batei Midrash*, ed. E. Etkes, 75–84. Jerusalem: Shazar Center (Hebrew).

Tamarin, R. G. 1973. "The Influence of Ethnic and Religious Prejudice on Moral Judgment." In *The Israeli Dilemma: Essays on a Warfare State*, 243–70. Rotterdam: Rotterdam University Press.

Tang, Jun. 2008. "A Cross-Cultural Perspective on Production and Reception of Disney's *Mulan* Through Its Chinese Subtitles." *European Journal of English Studies* 12/2: 149–62.

Tannen, R. S. 2007. *The Female Trickster: Post Modern and Post-Jungian Perspectives on Women in Contemporary Culture.* London: Routledge.

Tarragon, Jean-Michel de. 1995. "Witchcraft, Magic, and Divination in Canaan and Ancient Israel." In *Civilizations of the Ancient Near East*, ed. Jack Sasson, 3:2071–81. New York: Scribner.

Tchernichowsky, S. 1937. *Complete Poetry of Saul Tchernichowsky.* Jerusalem: Schocken (Hebrew).

Terr, L. 1990. *Too Scared to Cry*. New York: HarperCollins.

Tibbon, A. 2006. "Dangerous Ideological Education." http://hagada.org.il/ 2006/03/04/%D7%97%D7%99%D7%A0%D7%95%D7%9A- %D7%90%D7%99%D7%93%D7%99%D7%90%D7%95%D7%9C%D7%95 %D7%92%D7%99-%D7%9E%D7%A1%D7%95%D7%9B%D7%9F/ (Hebrew).

Tirosh, A., and B. Geller-Talitman. 2000. *With Joshua* (including teacher's manual). Even-Yehuda: Reches (Hebrew).

Toorn, Karel van der. 1994. *From Her Cradle to Her Grave: The Role of Religion in the Life of the Israelite and Babylonian Woman*. Trans. Sarah J. Denning-Bolle. Sheffield: JSOT Press.

Tri-Council Policy Statement: Ethical Conduct for Research Involving Humans (TCPS). 2010. Government of Canada Panel on Research Ethics. http://pre.ethics.gc.ca/eng/policy-politique/initiatives/tcps2-eptc2/Default/.

Trible, Phyllis. 1973. "Depatriarchalizing in Biblical Interpretation." *JAAR* 41: 30–48.

———. 1984. *Texts of Terror: Literary-Feminist Readings of Biblical Narratives*. OBT. Minneapolis: Fortress Press.

Valler, S. 2012. "Strong Women Confront Helpless Men: Deborah and Jephthah's Daughter in the Midrash." In *Words, Ideas, Worlds: Biblical and Other Essays in Honour of Yairah Amit*, ed. Athalya Brenner and Frank H. Polak, 236–54. Sheffield: Sheffield Phoenix.

Varnum, James Mitchell. 1788. *An Oration Delivered at Marietta, July 4, 1788*. Newport, R.I.: Peter Edes.

Vattioni, Francesco. 1967. "Deuteronomio 18,11 e un'inscrizione spagnola." *Orientalia* 36: 178–80.

Vickery, J. B. 1981. "In Strange Ways: The Story of Samson." In *Images of God and Man: Old Testament Short Stories in Literary Focus*, ed. B. O. Long. Sheffield: Almond.

Vries, S. J., De. 1962. "Night." In *Interpreter's Dictionary of the Bible*, ed. George Arthur Buttrick and Keith R. Crim, 3:549. Nashville: Abingdon.

Vuori, Timo Tapani. 2011. "Paimen vailla hiippakuntaa. Kenttäpiispan viran synty ja vaikutus sotilaspapiston asemaan Suomen puolustusvoimissa ja kirkossa vuosina 1939–1944". (Ph.D. Dissertation: Helsinki.)

Wang, Georgette, and Emilie Yueh-yu Yeh. 2005. "Globalization and Hybridization in Cultural Products: The Cases of *Mulan* and *Crouching Tiger, Hidden Dragon*." *International Journal of Cultural Studies* 8: 175–93.

Wansbrough, Ann. 1992. "Blessed Be Jael Among Women: For She Challenged Rape." In *Women of Courage: Asian Women Reading the Bible*, ed. Lee Oo Chung et al., 101–22. Seoul: Asian Women's Resource Centre for Culture and Theology.

Warrior, Robert Allen. 1991. "A Native American Perspective: Canaanites, Cowboys, and Indians." In *Voices from the Margin: Interpreting the Bible in the Third World*, ed. R. S. Sugirtharajah, 287–95. Maryknoll, N.Y.: Orbis.

———. 2005. "Canaanites, Cowboys, and Indians." *Union Seminary Quarterly Review* 59/1–2: 1–8.

Washington, George. 1779. "Instructions to Major General John Sullivan." In *The Writings of George Washington from the Original Manuscript Sources.* Electronic Text Center, University of Virginia Library. http://etext.virginia.edu/etcbin/toccer-new2?id=WasFi15.xml&images=images/modeng&data=/texts/english/modeng/parsed&tag=public&part=165&division=div1.

Webb, G. Barry. 1987. *The Book of the Judges: an Integrated Reading.* JSOTSup 46. Sheffield: Sheffield Academic.

Weems, Renita. 1995. *Battered Love: Marriage, Sex, and Violence in the Hebrew Prophets.* Minneapolis: Fortress Press.

Weinfeld, Moshe. 1977. "Ancient Near Eastern Patterns in Prophetic Literature." *VT* 27/2: 178–95.

———. 1984. "The Inheritance of the Land—Right and Obligation: The Conception of the Promise in Texts of the First and Second Temple Periods." *Ziyyon* 49: 115–36 (Hebrew).

———. 1988. "Expulsion, Dispossession, and Proscription of the Pre-Israelite Population in Biblical Law," *Ziyyon* 53(2): 135–147 (Hebrew).

Whitehead, Anthony. 2005. "Man to Man Violence: How Masculinity May Work as a Dynamic Risk Factor." The Howard Journal 44, 4: 411–22.

Whitehead, Stephen, and Barrett. J. Franck. 2001. *The Masculinities Reader.* Cambridge: Polity.

Whitelam, Keith W. 1996. *The Invention of Ancient Israel: The Silencing of Palestinian History.* New York: Routledge.

Wiggleworth, Michael. 1871. "God's Controversy with New-England." *Proceedings of the Massachusetts Historical Society* 12 (May): 83–93.

Williams, Robert. 1975. *Ebonics: The True Language of Black Folks.* St. Louis: Institute of Black Studies.

Wilson, Karina. 2011. "Animated Children's Films: Mulan: The Twinkie Defense." *Bitch Flicks* weblog. November 28. http://www.btchflcks.com/2011/11/mulan-twinkie-defense.html.

Winnicott, D. W. 1965. *The Maturational Processes and the Facilitating Environment: Studies in the Theory of Emotional Development.* Madison: International Universities Press.

Wright, George Ernest. 1957. "The Deuteronomistic History of Israel in Her Land." In *The Book of the Acts of God: Christian Scholarship Interprets the Bible,* ed. E. G. Wright and R. H. Fuller. Garden City, N.Y.: Doubleday.

Wu, Frank H. 2002. *Yellow: Race in America Beyond Black and White.* New York: Basic.

Yamada, Frank M. 2008. *Configurations of Rape in the Hebrew Bible.* Studies in Biblical Literature 109. New York: Peter Lang.

Yamashita, Karen Tei. 1997. *The Tropic of Orange.* Minneapolis: Coffee House Press.

Yarkoni, Rivka. 2004. *Chapters in the History of the Hebrew Language.* Unit 1. Tel Aviv: The Open University Press (Hebrew).

Yee, Gale A. 1993 "'By the Hand of a Woman': The Biblical Metaphor of the Woman Warrior." *Semeia* 61: 99–132.

———. 1997. "Inculturation and Diversity in the Politics of National Identity." *Journal of Asian and Asian American Theology* 2: 108–12.

———. 2006. "Yin/Yang Is Not Me: An Exploration into an Asian American Biblical Hermeneutics." In *Ways of Being, Ways of Reading: Asian-American Biblical Interpretation*, ed. Mary F. Foskett and Jeffrey K. Kuan, 152–63. St. Louis: Chalice.

———. 2007a. "Ideological Criticism: Judges 17–21 and the Dismembered Body." In *Judges and Method: New Approaches in Biblical Studies*, ed. Gale A. Yee, 138–60. Minneapolis: Fortress Press.

———, ed. 2007b. *Judges and Method: New Approaches in Biblical Studies.* 2nd ed. Minneapolis: Fortress Press.

Yizhar, S. 1993. "Current Dialogue—Against Joshua, S. Yizhar Now." *Sevivot* 31: 139–56 (Hebrew).

Yonai, Y. 1997. *The Bible in the State Education System.* Jerusalem: Publications Department, Ministry of Education, Culture, and Sport (Hebrew).

Younger, K. Lawson, Jr. 2002. *Judges, Ruth.* NIV Application Commentary. Grand Rapids: Zondervan.

———. 2007. "Judges." In *New Oxford Annotated Bible with Apocrypha*, ed. Michael D. Coogan with Marc Z. Brettler, Carol A. Newsom, and Pheme Perkins. Oxford: Oxford University Press.

Zakovitch, Yair. 1981. "Sisseras Tod." *ZAW* 93: 364–74.

———. 2003. "On the Problem of Teaching the Book of Joshua Today." *Iyyunim ba-Hinnukh ha-Yehudi* 9: 11–20 (Hebrew).

Zalmanson-Levy, G. 2005. "Teaching the Book of Joshua and the Conquest." In *Militarism in Education*, ed. H. Gur, 131–45. Tel Aviv: Babel (Hebrew).

Zohar, E. 1996. *Learning, Thinking, and Learning to Think.* Jerusalem: Israel Ministry of Education, Culture, and Sport; the Branco Weiss Institute (Hebrew).

Author Index

Scripture Index